RAPE OF THE INNOCENT

RAPE OF THE INNOCENT

Understanding and Preventing
Child Sexual Abuse

Juliann Whetsell-Mitchell, Ph.D.

ACCELERATED DEVELOPMENT
A member of the Taylor & Francis Group

USA	Publishing Office:	ACCELERATED DEVELOPMENT
		A member of the Taylor & Francis Group
		1101 Vermont Avenue, N.W., Suite 200
		Washington, DC 20005-3521
		Tel: (202) 289-2174
		Fax: (202) 289-3665
	Distribution Center:	ACCELERATED DEVELOPMENT
		A member of the Taylor & Francis Group
		1900 Frost Road, Suite 101
		Bristol, PA 19007-1598
		Tel: (215) 785-5800
		Fax: (215) 785-5515
UK		Taylor & Francis Ltd.
		4 John Street
		London WC1N 2ET
		Tel: 071 405 2237
		Fax: 071 831 2035

RAPE OF THE INNOCENT: Understanding and Preventing Child Sexual Abuse

1 2 3 4 5 6 7 8 9 0   B R B R   9 8 7 6 5

This book was set in Times Roman by Sandra F. Watts. Technical development by Cynthia Long; additional editing by Lisa Speckhardt. Cover design by Michelle Fleitz. Author photograph by Terry Snee. Printing and binding by Braun-Brumfield, Inc.

A CIP catalog record for this book is available from the British Library.
∞ The paper in this publication meets the requirements of the ANSI Standard Z39.48-1984 (Permanence of Paper)

Library of Congress Cataloging-in-Publication Data

Whetsell-Mitchell, Juliann.
    Rape of the innocent: understanding and preventing child sexual abuse / Juliann Whetsell-Mitchell.
        p. cm.
    Includes bibliographical references.
    1. Child sexual abuse—United States—Prevention.   2. Child molesters—United States—Psychology.   3. Child development—United States.   4. Child psychology—United States.   I. Title.
    HV6570.2.W45   1995
    362.7'67'0973—dc20   95-15255
                                                                                                    CIP

ISBN 1-56032-408-2 (cloth)
ISBN 1-56032-394-9 (paper)

This book is dedicated to the Intensive Family Service Team—
Susan Leyman, Mary Smith, and Robert Swan
for all they taught me in our work together;
and to all the survivors over the years who have courageously
shared their childhood experiences with me.

TABLE OF CONTENTS

LIST OF FIGURES

LIST OF TABLES

PREFACE

This book is a direct result of my work with one of the Intensive Family Service Teams of Children and Youth Services in Maryland. It is because of the them that I felt compelled to write this book. Nothing I have done professionally in the last fourteen years has made such an impact on me as my work with Children and Youth Services. What I have learned in writing this book is how much there is yet to be understood. There are no quick and easy solutions to the problems inherent in child sexual abuse treatment and prevention.

Rape of the Innocent was written to meet several needs. Parents, educators, mental health professionals, clergy, and anyone who works with children need to have an understanding of what constitutes child sexual abuse; what can be done to protect children, clients, congregation members, or pupils; what to do if a child discloses abuse to them; how pornography fits into abuse; what causes someone to abuse a child (which is speculative at best); what to do if abuse is suspected; how to talk to children about protecting themselves; why minority and special needs children have an increased risk of being abused; how child development theory can be helpful in designing and implementing child prevention programs; and a comprehensive glossary that incorporates the most common as well as uncommon terms involving the sexual abuse of children. A resource section is also included.

ACKNOWLEDGMENTS

First I would like to thank my editor and publisher, Dr. Joe Hollis of Accelerated Development. None of this would have been possible without him and his belief in this project. I also want to thank my parents, Jim and Mary Whetsell, for their love and belief in my abilities. I must thank my mother and my dear Aunt Jean Morse, for all their prayers for these many years. Their prayers have certainly made a difference in my life. A special thanks to my mother for all her help in caring for Mirabella during the writing of this book. Her dedication to this project enabled me to make many trips to the library, go to my office to write and see clients, and do my workshops. Cecile Hecker, Marlene Lowrey, and Karen Nagem are three friends whom I must thank for their support and gentle encouragement throughout this arduous process. All three listened with their hearts as I needed to talk about the enormity of the task. I have had the honor of knowing and being friends with Cecile for the last decade, and her friendship has been one of the very best parts of my life. Almost 15 years ago, I had the privilege of having three people come into my life within a six-month period: Dr. Jack G. Zealand, Anna Neilson-Taylor, and Rick Davidson. All three have remained a significant and special part of my life. A special thanks to Rick Davidson with whom I have had many conversations about making dreams a reality. At "The Studio" (Rick and Michelle's salon) I have found nurturance for my physical as well as emotional self. Certainly a deep heartfelt thanks to Anna and her family who welcomed me into their hearts and lives. I also want to say a most heartfelt thank you to my husband David, who has been supportive and has encouraged me and my work, whose sense of humor has been invaluable during this process, and on whose computer this book was typed and retyped. He laughs and says, "To think this started out as just a pamphlet." David also deserves the credit for the title.

Special thanks to my precious child, Mirabella; had she not been born, this book would not have been written at this time in my life. Because of her I have grown and been creative in ways I never dreamed possible. Sweet child, what a blessing you are in my life. Special thanks to my cousin, Jill Morse for all her help in many different ways, from caring for Mirabella to reading the manuscript.

I would also like to mention some special professors at the University of Pittsburgh, Dr. Nancy Elman, Dr. Judith Scott, and Dr. Carol Baker, all three of whom are some of the finest and most skilled professionals in their respective fields in this country. I was fortunate enough to be able to be exposed to their high academic standards and professionalism. I have been extremely fortunate to have the privilege of knowing and being friends with Dr. Jasem Hasan; his friendship, warmth, and caring are beyond compare and I always go away from our interactions with a better understanding of the word "compassionate" and a sense of lightness in my life. In coming to know him I learned to know myself better. Last, but certainly not least of all, my humblest thanks to God for healing the Churg-Strauss vasculitis, allowing me a second chance at life and for being an ever-constant presence in my life.

Chapter 1

THE MANY FACES OF CHILD SEXUAL ABUSE

Most likely someone you know is a survivor of child sexual abuse. In this country at least one in three females and one in five males will be sexually abused before the age of eighteen (Bagley & Ramsey, 1986; Herman, Russell & Trocki, 1986; Kilpatrick, Saunders, Veronen, Best & Von, 1987). Peters, Wyatt, and Finkelhor (1986) reported sexual abuse prevalence rates from 6% to 62% for females and 3% to 31% for males. Children as young as two months have been victimized. There are several studies that indicate that younger children are more at risk for sexual abuse. Summit (1983) reported that 25% of children treated for sexual abuse at a Seattle sexual assault center were five years of age or younger. Another study (Gomes-Schwartz, Horowitz, & Sauzier, 1985) found that 29% of the participants in a treatment program for sexually abused children had been victimized by the age of six. This information strongly suggests that one-fourth of the reported sexual abuse is occurring in children under the age of six. Another reported factor is that children are frequently victimized by more than one offender. In a study conducted by Conte, Wolf, and Smith (1989) of 420 adult survivors of childhood sexual abuse, 30% reported being abused by two offenders, 24% by three offenders, 11% by four offenders, and 5% by five or more offenders. Burgess (1984) also substantiated that children are frequently victimized by multiple offenders.

Too often parents and other professionals believe that sexual abuse of children is committed by strangers. This is true in only about 10% to 15% of the cases. Parents will warn their children about strangers by saying, "Don't talk to strangers," or "Don't take candy from strangers." Warning children to avoid unknown

1

persons may be an unclear message for children. First, who is a stranger? Is he or she a person who says, "Hi, aren't you Tom's son? I work with your dad." A child might reply, "No, my dad's name is Jack." "I always get his name mixed up," says the man. "Your dad and I eat lunch together all the time. He sure has told me about you. He says you really like gum. I was just on my way to the store and I'd be glad to buy you some. Why don't you come with me? It would sure please your dad to know I saw you." A manipulative person can easily win over a child, and before too long the new person is not a stranger but a new friend.

The younger the child the more challenging it becomes to teach the child to differentiate between a stranger and a friend. By age six, according to developmental theory, a child can be taught the difference between the two terms. Children need to know some of the following concepts. A stranger can be a man or a woman. A stranger can be any age: young, middle-aged, or elderly. A stranger can wear nice clothes; drive a new car, van, pick-up truck, ice cream truck, motorcycle; ride a bicycle; or walk. Children should always avoid all strangers and never accept rides from strangers. If an adult asks a child to help him or her the child should ask another adult to help the adult. Adults help adults. All strangers are not harmful or hurtful but none of us, even adults, can tell the difference.

Yet even if the word *stranger* has been clearly explained, the child might not know *why* strangers should be sidestepped. The child might not understand what he or she should do if someone approaches him or her. This can create and generate feelings of anxiety for children. The irony of it is that in at least 85% of the cases of child sexual abuse the offender is known to the child. In at least 25% of the cases the offenders live in the child's home (Sasalwsky & Wurtele, 1986).

Currently prevention programs are based on some generalized beliefs, such as the belief that all children need to know how to deal with strangers who might try to engage them in conversation. Children also need the skills necessary to handle situations that could be abusive when it involves people known and trusted by the child. These people include both adults and adolescents. Secrets are not okay to keep but surprises as secrets are fine. They need to know that their bodies belong to them and only them and that no one has the right to touch their body unless they give the person permission to do so. (This does not include coerced permission.) Prevention theory has suggested if a child knows how to handle himself or herself in potentially abusive situations, then he or she may be less likely to become a victim of sexual abuse. Children need to be reassured that most adults and adolescents do not want to molest them. Later in the book these concepts will be addressed on a more in-depth level.

A DEFINITION OF TERMS

The phrase *child sexual abuse* is used frequently by professionals and lay people with the idea that this term has the same meaning for both groups. A partial list of the phrases used to describe child sexual abuse is: sexual victimization, sexual exploitation, sexual assault, sexual misuse, child molestation, sexual maltreatment, and child rape (Haugaard & Reppucci, 1988; Russell, 1983). (See Figure 1.)

Atteberry-Bennett and Reppucci (1986) stated, "A review of the literature suggests that total agreement of the definition of child sexual abuse, even in cases where sexual intercourse has taken place between an adult and child, does not exist" (p. 1). Mental health, legal, and social service personnel also differ in their definition of child sexual abuse (Violato & Genuis, 1993).

Because of so much discrepancy in the mental health and legal field the following three terms will be defined as this author plans to use them in the context of this book.

Child sexual abuse—a child is used for the sexual gratification of an adult (National Committee for the Prevention of Child Abuse, 1988, p. 5).

Incest—the imposition of sexually inappropriate acts or acts with sexual overtones by, or any use of a minor child to meet the sexual or sexual/ emotional needs of, one or more persons who derive authority through ongoing emotional bonding with that child. If children are sexually abused by a caretaker with which there was an emotional bond, then what transpired was incest (Blume, 1989, p. 4). Therefore, incest could include anyone with whom the child has established an emotional relationship. This is a much broader definition of incest than has been given in the past.

Sexual exploitation—an act that usually involves a commercial element:

TERMS TO DESCRIBE CHILD SEXUAL ABUSE

Sexual Victimization
Sexual Exploitation
Sexual Assault
Sexual Misuse
Child Molestation
Sexual Maltreatment
Child Rape

Figure 1.　Terms to describe child sexual abuse.

children selling themselves or being sold as prostitutes or models (National Legal Resource Center for Child Advocacy and Protection, 1984, p. 1).

Just as a variety of terms connotate child sexual abuse, even more terms are used for those individuals who sexually abuse children. These names can include *offender, abuser, molester, perpetrator, rapist, child assaulter, intrafamilial abuser, extrafamilial abuser,* or *pedophile.* (See Figure 2.) The terms molester, offender, abuser, perpetrator, rapist, and child assaulter can apply to both members of a family and nonmembers. When the term *extrafamilial abuser* is used it is to denote abuse perpetrated by persons outside the family system. These offenders could be neighbors, friends of the family, day-care personnel, clergy, teachers, coaches, camp counselors, mental health professionals, pediatricians, or Scout leaders (Faller, 1990). (See Figure 3.) An *intrafamilial abuser* is a name for someone who commits child sexual abuse within the family system. Intrafamilial abuse is another name for incest. Intrafamilial abusers can be fathers, stepfathers, grandfathers, uncles, mothers, grandmothers, aunts, siblings, or cousins (Faller, 1990). Regardless of what word is used to describe child sexual abuse, it is about sexual violence, power, control, and dominance. It is also about rape. A rape of the body, the soul, and the spirit of the child.

HISTORY OF CHILD SEXUAL ABUSE

Freud originally theorized that children are indeed sexually abused by their parents. In a letter to Wilheim Fleiss (Bonaparte, Freud, & Kris, 1954) Freud wrote, "I have come to the opinion that anxiety is to be connected, not with a

TERMS FOR SEXUAL ABUSERS

Offender
Abuser
Molester
Perpetrator
Child Assaulter
Intrafamilial Abuser
(abuses children in his/her own family)
Extrafamilial Abuser
(abuses children outside his/her family)
Pedophile

Figure 2.   Terms for sexual abusers.

A SEXUAL ABUSER OF CHILDREN CAN BE . . .

Male
Female
Family Members:
Mother
Father
Sister(s)/Brother(s)
Aunts/Uncles/Cousins
Grandmother/Grandfather
Stepmother/Stepfather
Stepsisters/Stepbrothers
Friends
Parents of Friends
Brother(s)/Sister(s) of Friends
Neighbors
Babysitters
Child Care Workers
Clergy Members
Scout Leaders
Sunday School Teachers
Health Professionals
Mental Health Professionals
Anyone—Known or unknown

Figure 3.   A sexual abuser of children can be . . . .

mental, but with a physical consequence of sexual abuse" (p. 28). In 1896 Freud went public with his theory that hysteria was caused by childhood sexual abuse. He presented 18 separate cases of patients diagnosed with a condition of hysteria, all of whom were individuals with a history of sexual abuse in their childhood (Freud, 1905/1963). Unfortunately, by 1905 Freud had recanted his original theory on the causes of hysteria (Freud, 1905/1963). He postulated that most adult's memories of being sexually abused were projections against their own childhood sexual desires for the parent of the opposite sex (the Oedipal theory). The reports of sexual abuse were labeled as fantasies on the part of the child (Freud, 1966; Masson, 1984; Miller, 1984). Freud's renunciation of his seduction theory was harmful to the study of the effects of child sexual abuse on children. This renunciation caused others to question the existence of child sexual abuse and deny its existence. Another group of individuals had an additional impact on professionals and the general population's views on incest. Havelock Ellis, Iwan Block, and August Fogel, noted sexologists of the 1920s, proposed that sometimes family members do become sexually involved with children in the family, but that this sexual contact has a positive or neutral effect on the children. Any negative feelings that were reported were labeled as originating from the persons who found out about the sexual activity rather than from the children who were abused. Later, when it was determined that sexual abuse was indeed a reality, the child was frequently blamed for the abuse, and the existence of negative effects was denied (Bender & Blau, 1937; Lukianowicz, 1972; Sloane & Karpinski, 1942; Weiss, Rogers, Darwin & Dutton, 1955). In the 1950s Kinsey, Pomeroy, Martin, and Gebhard (1953) published the results of their study of 4,441 Caucasian women. These data were collected from women 16 to 50 years of age. The women were most often from the middle to upper socioeconomic classes. When the results were tabulated to include physical contact and noncontact incidents, 25% of the women indicated that they had been victimized before the age of 18. When only sexual activity was included the response rate was 9.2%. So even though Kinsey et al.'s (1953) study indicated that almost one in every four women had been victimized either in a contact or noncontact situation before the age of eighteen, little was made of the study's results. During the 1960s and 1970s some clinicians began to blame the mother for any incestuous abuse that occurred. The mother was labeled "collusive." The thought was that in most incest cases she was aware of the abuse that was occurring between the father and the child (Lustig, Dresser, Spellman, & Murray, 1966; Machotka, Pittman, & Flomenhaft, 1967; Sarles, 1975; Walters, 1975). Some theorists over the years have even gone so far as to suggest that the offender is the real victim. He or she is considered to be the victim because he or she is seduced by the child and urged on by the mother (Lustig et al., 1966; Mayer, 1983; Weiner, 1964). The issue of child sexual abuse began to be quite seriously addressed in 1971 when Dr. Henry Giarretto began the first child sexual abuse program in San Jose, California. The professionals were genuinely beginning to address the issue of sexual abuse. From his work came the organizations Parents Anonymous, Parents United, and Adults Molested As Children. Just as the professionals were addressing the issue of sexual abuse, the public was slowly beginning to face the reality that sexual abuse does indeed exist.

What brought abuse to the forefront in the United States were four books and a movie. Interestingly it has been the survivors who were the first persons to publicly address this issue. During the late 1970s, two first-person account books were written by adult female survivors of incest: *Kiss Daddy Goodnight: A Speak-Out on Incest* (1978) by Louise Armstrong, and *Conspiracy of Silence: The Trauma of Incest* (1978) by Sandra Butler. Two professional books were published at this point in time as well: Susan Forward and Craig Buck (1978) wrote *Betrayal of Innocence*, and Karen Meiselman (1978) published *Incest*. By this time the issue of incest was no longer sparsely written about in professional journals or just fictionalized by well-known American authors, such as in Tennessee William's *Cat on a Hot Tin Roof.* The issue of child sexual abuse was addressed in books available in mainstream bookstores around the country. Subsequently (in 1983) the movie *Something about Amelia* was aired on national television. By now the public and professional community had been exposed through books and television to the issue of child sexual abuse, and no longer could it be denied, ignored, or blamed on children's fantasies. The harsh reality of just how pervasive it is was beginning to become apparent. Child sexual abuse could no longer be as easily swept under the rug by professionals. The 1970s and early 1980s heralded a new way of thinking regarding sexual abusers. Blame was put on the offender rather than on the child. The emphasis is currently on the offender's abuse and exploitation of power and the child's powerlessness (Groth, 1982; Sgroi, Blick, & Porter, 1982). The child is known to be the true victim (Haugaard & Reppucci, 1988; Miller, 1984, 1990, 1991).

While it is true that a very rapid increase has occurred in the numbers of reported cases of child sexual abuse in the last decade, it is not clearly indicative that this is reflective of any real rise in the incidence of sexual abuse (Feldman, Feldman, & Goodman, 1991). Much of the increase is most likely accounted for by the incest survivor's recovery movement, stories presented in the media (such as *Something about Amelia*), professional education about the detection of abuse, and popular figures in the media revealing their abuse. Persons such as Oprah Winfrey, Roseanne, and so on have come forth and courageously admitted that they are survivors of childhood sexual abusive experiences. When a subject such as child sexual abuse is written about, had movies made about it, and had superstars reveal it as part of their past, it gives other members of our society permission to admit that it happened to them.

SEXUALLY ABUSIVE BEHAVIORS

A wide variety of persons are victimized by abuse, and a variety of behaviors are encapsulated in the definition of child sexual abuse, or what is commonly referred to as molestation. These behaviors can include any or all of the following but are divided into two groups of behavior: noncontact sexual abuse and contact sexual abuse. (See Figure 4.)

Noncontact Sexual Abuse

Noncontact sexual abuse includes sexual comments, exhibitionism, and voyeurism (Courtois, 1988; Sgroi et al., 1982). Pornography that involves taking pictures of the child naked or having the child view sexually explicit magazines, films, or videos can be included in this section.

FORMS OF NONCONTACT SEXUAL ABUSE OF CHILDREN

Sexual Comments
Exhibitionism
Voyeurism
Watching Pornographic Films/Videos

FORMS OF CONTACT SEXUAL ABUSE OF CHILDREN

Open-mouth Kissing
Handling or Fondling
Oral Sex
Frottage
Pornography
(child participates in making of sexually explicit videos or pictures)
Intercourse
Bondage
Anal Sex
Bestiality
(sexual acts with animals)

Figure 4.   Forms of noncontact and contact sexual abuse of children.

1. *Sexual Comments.* These can include any statements made to a child that are of a sexual nature, including obscene phone calls.

   Eight-year-old Bonnie's next door neighbor invited her into his house to look at his new kittens. While she was there, he started telling her how sexy she looked in her tight jeans. So sexy that he was getting turned on and was going to have to go satisfy himself in the bathroom. He tells her that men really like little girls like her.

2. *Exhibitionism.* This is the act of an adult exposing their genitals to a child. It could be within the context of taking a bath or shower or undressing. It could also refer to an adult opening their pants to expose their genitals to a child. Within the confines of a family situation it becomes more difficult to decide whether or not a situation is abusive, because families have different levels of how much nudity is acceptable.

   Bart, age 9, visits his aunt and uncle. While his aunt goes to the grocery store, Bart's uncle (age 26) flips an X-rated movie in the video recorder, unzips his pants, and begins to manipulate his penis. He asks Bart if he knows how to make a man get a "hard-on" and begins stroking his own penis.

   Betty, age 10, visits her cousin who is 8 years older than she.

While visiting, the male cousin makes it a point to use the bathroom and expose his genitals while Betty is watching.

3. *Voyeurism.* An act in which an adult observes a child as they undress, take a bath, or use the bathroom is termed voyeurism. This is an act that is difficult to label abusive within the context of the family or even day care, where it might be appropriate to observe children going to the bathroom or dressing.

Veronica, age 14, lives with her mother and her mother's boyfriend, Tom. The boyfriend decides to take the bathroom door off its hinges and places the door in the basement. He convinces Veronica's mother that this is a good way to prevent Veronica from smoking pot in the bathroom. Tom's favorite chair in the living room is positioned so that he can see directly into the bathroom.

4. *Pornography.* Using pictures, videotapes, or films that reveal specific sexual acts between adults, adults and children, or children and children is termed pornography. Children may be exposed to this as a part of a desensitization process. The child sees other children participating in these films and feels that it must be okay.

Darlene, age 12, and a friend play at a neighbor's house. Lately, Henry, the neighbor, has been taking lots of pictures of the girls. When it started they would wear bathing suits and pretend to be making suntan lotion commercials. Last week Henry asked them to take off their bathing suit tops and pretend they were posing for a national magazine.

Bill, age 7, likes to visit his aunt and uncle. They are very good to him, always buy his favorite treats, and pay lots of attention to him. Lately, though, when he goes over to their house they have all been watching some X-rated videos his aunt has picked up at the local video store.

Contact Sexual Abuse

Contact sexual abuse includes those behaviors of frottage, handling, kissing, oral sex, penetration, intercourse, or pornography. The pornography can include bestiality, which is sexual acts with animals (Courtois, 1988; Sgroi et al., 1982).

5. *Kissing.* Sexual abuse may occur when an adult gives the child intimate kisses on the mouth or when the adult sticks his or her tongue in the child's mouth. It is important to find out how long the kiss lasts and how the child feels. The kissing may involve other parts of the child's body, such as breasts, vagina, penis, and so on.

Six-year-old Freddie went to visit his grandparents. When it came time to go to bed, he French-kissed his grandmother. When asked where he learned to do this, he told his grandmother that those kinds of kisses were the way his mother and her friends always said goodnight or good-bye to him.

6. *Handling or Fondling.* The sexual abuse of handling or fondling is when an adults touches, caresses, or rubs a child's genitals or breasts or has the child touch the adult's body in the same way. Handling may occur within the context of some other activity such as bathing or reading to the child. Rubbing a child's back, head, or other nonsexual parts of their body may be determined as abusive if the idea is to engage the child in a situation in which the ultimate goal is to be sexual with the child. Again, if the goal is sexual gratification or sexual stimulation of the adult then the behavior is abusive.

Eleven-year-old Denise's mother asks her daughter to give her a massage, including massaging her vagina and anus.

7. *Fellatio or Cunnilingus.* When a child is forced to have oral–genital contact with an adult or when an adult has oral–genital contact with the child, the act is termed fellatio or cunnilingus.

Five-year-old Wally tells his mother that at day care they play a game called Pee Wee. The game involves the teacher sucking his penis and then having the children to do the same thing to the teacher.

8. *Vaginal or Anal Intercourse.* This occurs when an adult penetrates the child's vagina or anus with a penis, finger, or object or when an adult requires the child to penetrate him or her with fingers, objects, or a penis. This includes parents giving their children such things as Lysol douches.

Three-year-old Shawn's mother put her finger in his anus each week to make sure that he was not constipated.

9. *Frottage.* This occurs when an adults rubs himself or herself against a child in a sexual manner. The adult is usually clothed; however, the act has definite sexual overtones.

Sheila's father likes to wrestle with her. When they wrestle, it feels more like he is rubbing up against her than wrestling with her, and he always gets an erection during these "play" sessions.

10. *Pornography.* This involves pictures, films, or videos of children per-forming sexual acts with one another, with adults, or with animals.

Debbie, age 11, began posing for her mother's boyfriend in the nude. He offered her twenty dollars each time she would pose. Just recently he forced her to have oral sex with one of his male friends while he videotaped the act.

CHARACTERISTICS OF SEXUALLY ABUSIVE SITUATIONS

In addition to certain sexual behaviors, child sexual abuse has a number of characteristics. These include lack of consent, ambivalence, exploitation, secrecy, force, and intent (Conte, 1986b). Knowing more about these characteristics is helpful in deciding if sexual victimization has occurred. (See Figure 5.)

First and foremost, the child is never the one at fault if sexual abuse occurs. A noted researcher, David Finkelhor (1979) has purported that children are incapable of giving their consent to sexual behavior with adults because a child does not completely understand to what he or she is giving consent. Secondly, the child does not have the power or control to refuse to participate. Children cannot give consent to engage in sexual contact with adults. That a child is a victim of sexual abuse is never an indicator that they have consented to being victimized. Children never have had a choice about the matter (Miller, 1984).

Some sexual abuse may begin at an age when the child has no comprehension of what sexuality means (Conte, 1986b). The abuse may occur after a long process in which the child has been "groomed." During this "grooming process" the adult discovers what the child likes, dislikes, or fears, and then uses this knowledge to coerce or force the child into a sexual relationship. This "grooming process" may take months. Once the sexual relationship has started the adult may use this knowledge about the child to force the child into continuing in the sexual encounters.

The second characteristic of sexual abuse is ambivalence (Conte, 1986b). Even though most children do not want to continue to be sexually abused, some positive characteristics may develop as a result of the abusive situation.

CHARACTERISTICS OF SEXUALLY ABUSIVE SITUATIONS
(Conte, 1986b)

Lack of Consent
Ambivalence
Exploitation
Secrecy
Force
Intent

Figure 5.   Characteristics of sexually abusive situations.

These may be the extra attention or special rewards the child receives. Sometimes children may enjoy certain aspects of the relationship because it feels good to be touched in certain places and in certain ways. On the other hand, some children may hate everything that is being done to them but are too afraid to tell anyone.

Third, sexual abuse always means that some form of exploitation has occurred (Conte, 1986b). An older individual is more knowledgeable, skillful, or resourceful than a child. The abuser uses this to manipulate or force the child into sexual activities. Sometimes adults lie by saying things like, "This is okay to do, everyone learns about sex at home." Frequently adults will give children presents, money, or special privileges if the child will promise not to tell anyone about the sexual activities that are transpiring between them.

The fourth component of sexual abuse always involves some level of force (Conte, 1986b). Force can be used in a variety of ways, both physically and psychologically. Sometimes animals are killed in front of the children, and the children are told that if they tell anyone about the abuse that the same thing will happen to them, their siblings, or their parents. Often the abuser will tell the child that he or she will not bother their siblings if they continue to participate in the abusive situation. If the abuser is a family member, he or she may tell the child that the family will be torn apart or that he or she will have to go to jail if the child tells anyone what is happening. The one consistent factor about child sexual abusers is their manipulativeness.

The fifth characteristic is the intent of sexual gratification of an adult. Intent is a factor to consider when deciding if a behavior or behaviors are abusive (Conte, 1986b). If the end goal is the sexual gratification of an adult, then the behavior is indeed sexually abusive. For instance if an adult had oral sex with a child, this is definitely abusive. An adult watching pornographic films with a child is also abusive. This is true even when no sexual relationship exists between the child and the adult. The act is abusive because the purpose is the adult's sexual gratification or the intent may be to desensitize the child as part of the grooming process.

Secrecy is the final characteristic of child sexual abuse (Conte, 1986b). Most adults who sexually abuse children will want to keep their activities a secret. Having the child keep the secret may involve threats, bribery, rewards, or force (physical or psychological). Remember that most sexual abuse occurs in an established relationship between the molester and the child. The child experiences great stressors and pressures, including dealing with the abuse itself, the manipulations, and maintaining the secret itself. Frequently children feel that they are at fault or that they are "bad" for allowing it to happen. So they keep the secret.

REVIEW OF THE RESEARCH LITERATURE

Research on the incidence of child abuse actually started in 1929 with the publication of a book by Hamilton, entitled *A Research in Marriage*. Kinsey, Pomeroy, Martin, and Gebhard (1953) published the first national study on the prevalence of child sexual abuse. Little was made of the information revealed about females who had been victims of child sexual abuse. Since Kinsey et al., the research has continued but within the last fifteen years it has substantially increased. Various methods have been used to gather data. Many of the early studies used very small samples or certain segments of the population, such as small numbers of college students or married persons (Hamilton, 1929; Landis, Landis, & Bolles, 1940). More recently a concerted effort has been made to determine the incidence of child sexual abuse in the general population (Finkelhor, 1984, Finkelhor, Hotaling, Lewis, & Smith, 1990; Russell, 1983; Sigel, Sorenson, Golding, Burnam, & Stein, 1987; Wyatt, 1985). To determine the incidence of sexual abuse for the general population studies have been made where adults were asked whether or not they had been sexually abused during childhood. Such studies are called retrospective studies.

RETROSPECTIVE STUDIES

Adult retrospective studies are probably the most accurate with regards to the frequency that child sexual abuse has occurred in the general population. This simply means that in retrospective studies, adults reveal information about events (in this case, child sexual victimization experiences) that occurred in their childhoods. Retrospective studies are sometimes called community surveys.

In this section some of the most recent large-scale retrospective studies that have been completed on the incidence of child sexual abuse are reviewed. These studies have been conducted by noted researchers, including Diana Russell, Gail Wyatt, and David Finkelhor in his collaboration with Hotaling, Lewis, and Smith (see Table 1). This last study by Finkelhor et al. is the only national study that has been done on the incidence of child sexual abuse in the general population. An additional study was completed in the Los Angeles Epidemiological Catchment Area (LAECA) by Sigel, Sorenson, Golding, Burnam, and Stein (1987).

TABLE 1
Retrospective Studies

Researcher	Number of Participants	% Reporting Abuse	Format
Russell (1983)	930 women in San Francisco area	54% including contact and noncontact before age 18 38% just contact abuse before age 18 28% contact abuse before age 14	Face-to-face interviews
Finkelhor (1984)	521 parents of children ages 6–14, Boston, MA area Number of men = 187 Number of women = 334	6% before age 18 (men) 15% before age 18 (women)	Face-to-face interview and self-administered questionnaire about childhood sexual abuse
Finkelhor, Hotaling, Lewis & Smith (1990)	2626 total participants, national study Number of men = 1145 Number of women = 1481	16% before age 19 (men) 27% before age 19 (women)	Telephone interview
Siegel, Sorenson, Golding, Burnam, & Stein (1987)	Los Angeles area Number of men = 1480 Number of women = 1645	4% before age 15 (men) 7% before age 15 (women)	Face-to-face interview
Wyatt (1985)	Los Angeles area 248 women	62% contact and non-contact before age 18 45% contact	Face-to-face interview

Russell, Wyatt, and the LAECA researched their studies on the West Coast, and Finkelhor (1984) researched his on the East Coast. Finkelhor et al. (1990) gathered data on a national level, including both the East and the West Coasts.

Russell (1983) conducted a study regarding the incidence of sexual abuse in the childhood of adult females. She and her team of intensively trained female interviewers randomly surveyed 930 women (over the age of 18) in San Francisco and found 38% had "at least one experience of intrafamilial or extrafamilial sexual abuse before the age of 18 years," and 28% reported "at least one such experience before 14 years of age" (p. 137). Of the 38%, 16% had seen abused by a family member. When Russell included nonphysical contact (exhibitionism, verbal propositions) she found the incidence of abuse went to 54% (504 women).

Gail Wyatt (1985) and her team of researchers interviewed two groups of females over the age of 18. The women were from two ethnic groups, African American ($N = 126$) and Caucasian American ($N = 122$). A total of 248 women were interviewed, all between the ages of 18 and 36. The women were randomly chosen by telephone numbers generated in Los Angeles County and then were invited to participate in a face-to-face interview. Wyatt found that 62% of the women interviewed admitted to being sexually abused before the age of 18. This figure, 62%, includes unwanted sexual experiences with peers less than five years older. There were no significant differences found between the two ethnic groups. Both the Wyatt and Russell studies involved asking a number of different questions concerning child sexual abuse experiences, and both used face-to-face structured interviews. This usage of face-to-face interviews is associated with higher percentage rates.

The LAECA study had a sample size of 3,125 persons; the number of men participants was 1,480 (47%) and the number of women participants was 1645 (53%). All were at least 18 years of age and from two separate areas of Los Angeles. East Los Angeles was the first catchment area, and 83% of this population was Hispanic American. Venice/Culver City was the second area, with 63% of the population being non-Hispanic Caucasians. Participants were obtained through stratified sampling procedures based on census blocks. Interviews were conducted in either English or Spanish (interviewees and interviewers were not matched for gender). Estimating the prevalence and incidence of eight psychiatric disorders was the major goal of the study. (The LAECA was only one of five areas designated for the research study.) However, added to the Los Angeles survey were two questions involving sexual assault and sexual abuse: "In your lifetime has anyone ever tried to pressure or force you to have sexual contact?" and a clarification, "By sexual contact, I mean their touching your sexual parts, your touching their sexual parts, or sexual intercourse." The abuse needed to have happened before or at 16 years of age.

Forty percent of the sample population identified their ethnicity as Mexican American, 42% were non-Hispanic Whites, and the other 18% were of other ethnic backgrounds. Sigel, Sorenson, Golding, Burnam, and Stein (1987) found the rate of child sexual abuse to be 7% for females and 4% for males. Female participants reported sexual abuse in childhood at a frequency of almost 2 times greater than male participants. Non-Hispanic Whites reported a prevalence rate of child sexual abuse almost 3 times higher than the Hispanic American participants ($N = 45$). These prevalence rates are the lowest of any of the retrospective studies in the United States. It has been suggested that the low prevalence rate may be a result of the narrow definition of child sexual abuse that was used and the wording of the questions (pressured or forced) sexual contact. Respondents were not questioned about noncontact sexual abuse.

One of the most comprehensive national studies was reviewed by Finkelhor, Hotaling, Lewis, and Smith (1990). This study involved a national random sample of 2,626 American women ($N = 1481$) and men ($N = 1145$), all over the age of 18. The interview was conducted over the telephone. Phone numbers were randomly picked by a computer for all fifty states. It was discovered that of the adults polled, 27% of the women admitted to being sexually abused before the age of 18. Sixteen percent of the men reported being a victim of sexual abuse before the age of 18. Twenty-two percent of the men and 23% of the women who reported being abused stated the abuse occurred before the age of 8.

Finkelhor (1984) completed a study in Boston where 521 parents were randomly selected and interviewed face-to-face and then asked to complete a self-administered questionnaire. Fifteen percent of the women reported having been sexually abused before the age of 16 and 6% of the men reported being sexually abused.

These results may be lower than either the Wyatt (1985) or the Russell (1983) study because the Finkelhor study was designed to explore other issues, for example, the parent's opinions of child sexual abuse. Finkelhor limited his interviews to parents with children age 6 to 14 years, thus excluding all childless and elderly persons.

The use of face-to-face interviews is associated with a higher percentage rate than the usage of self-administered questionnaires or telephone interviews. Secondly, higher percentage rates are reported in research studies that use multiple questions to ask about specific types of abusive sexual behavior. In both the Russell and Wyatt studies more than one question was asked pertaining to child sexual abuse. Both researchers used female interviewers whose ethnicity matched that of the research participant. Russell's interviewers spent 65 hours in specialized training. Wyatt's research team underwent three months of training. Thus in both the Russell and Wyatt studies the interviewers were adequately trained to deal with the subject matter of abuse in a face-to-face interview situation.

These studies have been informative about the rate of sexual abuse within a variety of sociodemographic subdivisions in the communities that were studied. What is apparent from the studies cited is that regional differences, educational level, socioeconomic status, and ethnic background does not appear to have an effect on prevalence rates of sexual abuse experiences as a child.

It is noteworthy that there is great variance in the prevalence rates of child sexual abuse reported in the studies, with the range at one end being 4% and escalating to a figure of 62% prevalence rate among the general population. The use of different information gathering techniques and different definitions makes for difficulty in comparing one study's results with another's, but may account for the discrepancy rate in percentages of abuse in the general population. This is true except in the case of the Russell (1983) and the Wyatt (1985) studies.

Retrospective studies also provide information about the abuser. Abuse by family members has been identified as constituting anywhere from 24% (Russell, 1983) to 30% (Finkelhor, 1979), to 47% (Conte & Berliner, 1981) of all abuse. Other persons known to the child such as neighbors, family friends, child care personnel, and other persons in positions of authority are responsible for anywhere from 42% (Conte & Berliner, 1981) to 43% (Finkelhor, 1979) to 60% (Russell, 1983) of the abuse. Strangers, those persons not known to the child, are responsible for only about 15% of the abuse (Bagley & Ramsey, 1986; Finkelhor , 1984; Keckley Market Research 1983; Russell, 1983; Wyatt, 1985). Conte and Berliner (1981) put the incidence of stranger abuse even lower, at 8%. Thus, about 85% to 92% of the time the child knows the person or persons who are sexually abusing him or her.

The prevalence studies have revealed that males are victims of child sexual abuse, though not as frequently as females. Being male does not ensure that victimization will not take place. Another factor not to be ignored is that some of the females and some of the males in the prevalence studies were victimized by females. Until quite recently female perpetrators were considered a rarity

(Mathis, 1972; Wahl, 1960). The number of female child molesters is suggested to be grossly underestimated (Allen, 1991; Lawson, 1991; Mathews, Matthews, & Speltz, 1989; Plummer, 1981). However some recent studies refute this "rarity" phenomenon. The following is a partial list of recent studies that deal with the topic of female perpetrators. The number in parentheses indicates the percentage of abuse cases in that particular study in which children were victimized by female perpetrators. This list is as follows: American Humane Association Study, 1981 (6%-14%); Finkelhor, Williams, Burns, and Kalinowski, 1988 (40%); Kendall-Tackett and Simon, 1987 (3%); and McCarthy, 1986 (4%). (For more on female perpetrators, see Chapter 3.)

In conclusion, just defining the term *child sexual abuse* and labeling those individuals who victimize children is a multifaceted, complex issue. It becomes more and more a reality that child sexual abuse is a pervasive societal problem, affecting all of us on some level. This is true especially when it is estimated that one in three females (Bagley & Ramsey, 1986; Kilpatrick, Saunders, Veronen, Best, & Von, 1987) and one in five males will experience some form of sexual abuse before they reach 18 years of age. Lack of clarity in definitions causes confusion for professionals, but can cause even more confusion for the survivors.

Chapter 2

INDICATORS OF CHILD SEXUAL ABUSE: CHILDREN AT RISK

The variety of responses that a child or an adolescent makes to being sexually abused are limitless. The premise is not to attach a symptom or symptoms to the individual, but to see him or her as a whole person. Finkelhor (1979) proposed that by focusing only on the signs and symptoms of the sexual abuse, the individual is victimized even further. The following chapter does discuss some indicators of child abuse. Every person who is a survivor is not going to exhibit all of the symptoms listed in this chapter. A few persons may not exhibit any of the signs.

Every child has the potential to become a victim of child sexual abuse. However, persons who molest children have a tendency to look for children who can be easily controlled. Most molesters seek out children who they think will keep a secret. Those children who would be at risk for being abused outside the home are those who (Budin & Johnson, 1989; Gilgun & Connor, 1989)

- don't believe and know that it is okay to say "no" to adults,
- have a fear of being punished,
- have needs for love and belonging that are not being met,
- are physically or mentally challenged, or
- have very little supervision from a parent.

Based on this information, the deduction can be made that children who are very respectful may be an easy target for a molester. Frequently children are taught that it is disrespectful to say "no" to an adult, and inappropriate to make a fuss or create a scene. Children also learn that if someone asks them to keep a secret that they should respect their wishes. These kinds of rules help molesters prey on children. Children need to be taught that adults are not always "in the right" because children do not automatically know what is and is not harmful.

Finkelhor (1979, 1982) identified eight factors that increase a female's chance for victimization before the age of eighteen. Those factors are

- if the child has a stepfather,
- if the child lives apart from the mother,
- if the child is not close to the mother,
- if the child's mother didn't finish high school,
- if the child's mother displays sexually punitive behavior,
- if the child's mother fails to give physical affection to the child,
- if the family's income is less than ten thousand dollars per year, and
- if the child has two or fewer friends.

Finkelhor (1979, 1982) reported that having a stepfather doubled the child's chances for sexual abuse. A stepfather may be more likely to become sexually involved with a child because he may not be bonded to the child in the same manner as a natural father, and the child is not his "flesh and blood." Therefore there are less social and anthropological constraints for becoming involved with a stepchild. Children who lived in families where the fathers believed that children should be obedient and women need to be subservient to men had a greater chance of being abused. If a child lived without her mother, it increased her chances for sexual abuse threefold. A child was also at an increased risk for abuse if her mother was emotionally distant and if the mother had less of an education than the father.

INDICATORS OF CHILD SEXUAL ABUSE

Children often will not talk directly about sexual abuse. But just because a child does not talk about an event does not mean that it is not occurring. Children rarely straightforwardly tell if they have been abused. Frequently, they do not tell because they were threatened or made to feel as if the abuse was their fault. Sometimes children will subtly reveal that they have been abused. The child might make such statements as "I don't want to spend time with Mr.

Jones," or "Miss Smith has funny underwear," or "Mr. Jones acts different with me." Determining if a child has been sexually abused is a complicated procedure (Heiman, 1992; Weissman, 1991). Indicators of child sexual abuse may be considered under four headings: physical signs, behavioral signs, familial indicators, and psychological issues.

Physical Signs

The following may, but will not necessarily always, be present:

- difficulties in walking and sitting;
- trauma to the genitals and rectum that could include bruises, bleeding, lacerations, pain and itching, or inflammation;
- pregnancy; and
- the presence of sperm in or on the body.

Venereal diseases that include gonorrhea (Bays & Chadwick, 1993; DeJong & Finkel, 1990; Ingram, White, Durfee, & Pearson, 1982; Paradise, 1990), chlamydial infections (DeJong & Finkel, 1990; Hammerschlag, Doraiswamy, Alexander, Cox, Price, & Gleyzer, 1984; Paradise, 1990), herpes simplex type 2 (Gardner & Jones, 1984), venereal warts (DeJong, Weiss, & Brent, 1982), and syphilis (Bays & Chadwick, 1993; DeJong & Finkel, 1990; Neinstein, Goldenring, & Carpenter, 1984; Paradise, 1990) can also be indicative of sexual abuse. These diseases are often found in the rectum, throat, and genitals of children that have been abused. Bays and Chadwick (1993) had this to say about sexually transmitted diseases: "When perinatal transmission has been ruled out, gonorrhea or syphilis infections are diagnostic of sexual abuse. Herpes type 2, chlamydia, trichomoniasis, and condyloma infections are extremely likely to be due to abuse, particularly in children out of infancy" (p. 99).

These signs are definite indicators, especially if no history exists of socialization with one's peers (Orr, 1980). Finkel (1991), a professor of pediatrics, stated, "sexual injuries can heal with little or no scarring, or with unanticipated residual" (p. 56). The implications of this statement are that a child can be sexually abused and there will be no physical evidence to reinforce what the child might be revealing. Jason, Williams, Burton, and Rochat (1982) report that 91% of their nonhospitalized sexually abused participants revealed no physical evidence of abuse.

One group on which little information has been documented is male children who may have been sexually abused. Bays and Chadwick (1993) present a comprehensive overview of this phenomenon in their article, "Medical Diagnosis of the Sexually Abused Child." This article discusses the signs to help identify if sexual abuse has occurred and includes a review of the literature on certain physical conditions that may be quite similar to those found in children who have been sexually abused.

These authors discussed the factors that contribute to sexual abuse not being identified in more children who are indeed being abused. The first contributing factor is if the child is not taken for a medical exam immediately when abuse is suspected. Second, if more than three days have passed since the child was assaulted, semen will not likely be present, especially if the child has bathed or washed in that time period. Third, healing may occur quickly if a child has been cut during the abuse. Scars may not be present even though abuse has occurred. Fourth, certain kinds of sexual offenses are not physically discernible (for example, if a child has been forced to perform fellatio or cunnilingus). Fifth, sometimes a child may be penetrated but the offender does not ejaculate or the child may be penetrated with fingers or other objects. Sixth, the child may be assaulted in the anal area and there may be no sign of penetration, especially if the offender did not ejaculate. Lastly, sometimes in female children the hymen is enlarged because of sexual molestation, but the hymen is not broken. This type of situation may happen if the child has been penetrated with only a finger and nothing else.

The research data available supports the concept that "sexualized" behavior is the most consistent indicator of sexual abuse, and that is so in all of the age groups (Friedrich, 1993). It seems appropriate to say that victims of child sexual abuse are much more likely to exhibit some type of age-inappropriate sexual behavior. In children this becomes apparent in several ways, all of which can include developmentally inappropriate sexual play, excessive masturbation, sexually aggressive behavior, and age-inappropriate knowledge of sexual behaviors (Alter-Reid, Gibbs, Lachenmeyer, Sigal, & Massoth, 1986; Deblinger, McLeer, Atkins, Ralphe, & Foa, 1989; Einbender & Friedrich, 1989; Finkelhor, Araji, Baron, Browne, Peters, & Wyatt, 1986; Friedrich & Luecke, 1988, Gale, Thompson, Moran, & Sack, 1988; Goldston, Turnquist, & Knuston, 1989; Kendall-Tackett, Williams, & Finkelhor, 1993; Kolko, Moser, & Weldy, 1988; Livingston, 1987). Yet all children who have been abused do not act out sexually, and all children who exhibit sexualized behaviors or act out sexually have not been abused.

Conte, Sorenson, Fogarty and Rosa (1991) asked 212 professionals to determine identifying markers of child sexual abuse by rank ordering 41 indicators that are often used in assessments of sexual abuse. The following eight items were identified by the professionals as being the most important indicators of sexual abuse: presence of physical findings (e.g., sexually transmitted diseases); the child possesses information about sexual acts that are not appropriate for his or her age group; the child does not change information he or she gave about abuse occurring over time; the child's report of sexually abusive incidents includes small details (e.g., "He would always open my bedroom door, step inside and then scratch his face once before he shut the door"); the child's account demonstrates or explains how sexual activities took place over time (e.g., the grooming process involved); the child engages in sexualized behaviors during the consultation evaluation; the child's report has identifiable traits of coercion; or the child acts in a seductive manner during the evaluation. These eight clinical markers were rated by 85% to 99% of the professionals as the most important indicators in identifying an abused child.

Certain assessment tools have been used to support the notion that children who have been sexually abused exhibit inappropriate sexual behaviors. These have included parent ratings of the Child Behavior Checklist (Achenbach & Edelbrock, 1983), a 113-item scale that the parent or caregiver completes that assesses how often certain behaviors exhibited by the child have occurred in the last six months (Friedrich, 1987, 1989; Friedrich, Beilke, & Urquiza, 1987; Friedrich, Grambsch, Broughton, & Beilke, 1988; Friedrich & Reams, 1987). Another utilized behavior rating scale is the Louisville Behavior Checklist (Miller, 1981). Gomes-Schwartz, Horowitz, and Cardarelli (1990) found differences on the Louisville Behavior Checklist when preschool and school-age children who had been identified as being sexually abused were compared with a group of children who had not been abused. Briere (1989; Lanktree & Briere, 1991, 1992) has developed a Trauma Symptom Checklist for children (TSC-C).

More recently Friedrich (1990) developed the Child Sexual Behavior Inventory, comprised of 36 items, designed to identify certain sexual behaviors in children who have been or are suspected of being sexually abused. Eight hundred eighty nonabused children were compared to 276 children who had been sexually abused. Children in both groups ranged from 2 to 12 years of age. Twenty-five of the 36 behaviors were found to be statistically significant in identifying sexual behaviors in children who had been abused when compared to the control group (Friedrich, Grambsch, Broughton, Kuiper, & Beilke, 1991; Friedrich, Grambsch, Damon, Hewitt, Koverola, Lang, & Wolfe, 1992).

Other assessment methods have been utilized to determine if children have been sexually abused. One method is by observing children playing with anatomically correct dolls (Boat & Everson, 1988; Britton & O'Keefe, 1991; Glaser & Collins, 1989; Jampole & Weber, 1987; Sivan, Schor, Koeppl, & Noble,

1988; White, Strom, Santilli, & Halpin, 1986). Another is to examine children's artwork that involves drawing human figures (Cohen & Phelps, 1985; Hibbard & Hartman, 1990; Hibbard, Roghmann, & Hoekelman, 1987). No empirical proof has been obtained that all children who have been sexually abused will display inappropriate sexual behavior. Some children may be asymptomatic (Caffaro-Rouget, Lang, & vanSanten, 1989; Mannarino & Cohen, 1986; Tong, Oates, & McDowell, 1987). The range of children displaying inappropriate sexual behavior has been estimated from 10% (Hibbard et al., 1987) to 90% (Jampole & Weber, 1987), depending on the assessment technique utilized.

Finkelhor (1993) had this to say about the clinical identification of sexual abuse:

> One important conclusion about clinical identification stands out from this epidemiologic literature: There are no identifiable epidemiological markers that could lead someone to readily exclude the possibility of sexual abuse. The prevalence of sexual abuse is widespread enough, and in no subgroup is it clearly absent or rare. This is significant because there are obsolete social prejudices that presume the problem is rare in children of certain ages, gender, or social backgrounds. (p. 67)

An important note to remember is that some of these behavioral indicators of sexual abuse can be exhibited by children experiencing other types of stressful situations besides sexual abuse. These situations could include divorce, conflict between parents, war, absence of the father, and almost any stressful situation a child might encounter (Berliner & Conte, 1993; Emery, 1982; Hughes & Barad, 1983; Jaffe, Wolfe, Wilson, & Zak, 1986; Mannarino, Cohen & Gregor, 1989; Porter & O'Leary, 1989; Wallerstein & Kelly, 1980).

Behavioral Signs

The following can be behavioral signs of child sexual abuse. The symptoms are presented according to age groups.

3- to 5-year-old (Gale, Thompson, Moran, & Sack, 1988; Goldston, Turnquist, & Knuston, 1989; Kempe, 1978; Mian, Wehrspan, Klajner-Diamond, LeBaron, & Winder, 1986; Kendall-Tackett, Williams, & Finkelhor, 1993; Ryan, 1984).

- Exhibits fears about sleeping in the dark
- Has nightmares
- Cries out at night for no apparent reason

- Experiences developmentally regressive behaviors—thumb-sucking or enuresis (bed-wetting)
- Exhibits seductive behavior
- Exhibits age-inappropriate sexual knowledge
- Places objects into the vagina or anus
- Engages in excessive masturbation
- Has sudden change in behavior, e.g., becoming shy and clinging or brazen and aggressive
- Exhibits phobias
- Participates in obsessive cleanliness
- Neglects self

6- to 12-year-old (Deblinger, McLeer, Atkins, Ralphe & Foa, 1989; Friedrich & Luecke, 1988; Goldston et al., 1989; Kendall-Tackett, Williams, & Finkelhor, 1993; Livingston, 1987, Rosenfeld, 1979).

- Experiences anxiety, depression
- Has sleep difficulties
- Changes eating habits—dislikes eggs or milky liquids (reminds them of semen)
- Runs away from home
- Becomes truant from school
- Obtains failing grades in school
- Displays abrupt changes in behavior
- Engages in self-mutilating behavior—picking or scraping the skin, cutting self
- Neglects self
- Exhibits sexually inappropriate behaviors, e.g., excessive masturbation, sexual preoccupation, and sexual aggression

13- to 18-year-old (Burgess, Hartman, McCausland, & Powers, 1984; Gomes-Schwartz, Horowitz, & Sauzier, 1985; Kendall-Tackett, Williams, & Finkelhor, 1993; Lindberg & Distad, 1985b; Runtz & Briere, 1986; Sansonnet-Hayden, Haley, Marriage, & Fine, 1987).

- Becomes anxious and depressed
- Withdraws from social activities
- Acts out
- Engages in delinquent acts
- Runs away from home
- Becomes pregnant or is sexually promiscuous
- Abuses drugs
- Attempts suicide

Familial Indicators (Conte et al., 1986)

- Mother or father displays extreme dominance, restrictiveness, or protectiveness
- Family lacks connections to the community or support groups outside the family
- History of sexual abuse exists for either parent
- Parents or children abuse alcohol or other substances
- Violence is present in the home
- Parental absence exists caused either by chronic illness, divorce, or separation
- Parents label a child as "seductive."

Psychological Issues

The psychological issues need to be considered. These include the child's ability to trust others, guilt, grief, and psychic pain, which may result in dissociation, anger, rage, helplessness, powerlessness, and hopelessness. The child's trust has been violated, especially if he or she has been abused by a family member. Family members are supposed to protect one another and be there for each other. In a sexually abusive home this is not the case. A child who is a victim of sexual abusiveness in the home learns that he or she cannot trust his or her family, thus he or she cannot really trust anyone else. What the child does learn is that adults send conflicting messages about love. Love gets confused with sexual acts. To an abused child, I love you means "I will not respect the fact that your body is your own, it belongs to me [the adult] to do with what I will."

Children frequently experience guilt about the sexual pleasure dimension of the abuse. Courtois (1988) calls this the "secret within the incest secret " (p. 221). A child who is sexually violated is often told, "If you didn't like this, your body wouldn't respond," or "Because you had an orgasm, that means you really enjoyed what happened." Bass and Thornton (1983) discussed the sexual pleasure aspect of child sexual abuse by stating the following:

> In some instances the abused child's body may respond to the sexual stimulation even as her consciousness is horrified. . . . Because she does not know that her body can respond without her consent, or even that it can respond in such a way at all, the abused child feels that she must have wanted the abuse, must have asked for it in some way. It is this betrayal of herself by her body that she sometimes finds the hardest to forgive. And again, she does not tell; she fears that anyone she tells would surely blame her as much as she blames herself. (pp. 18–19)

Children also experience the emotions of grief and of pain. There may be the physical pain of the sexual abuse (e.g., being sodomized, having intercourse long before the body is ready to accommodate adult sexual organs, having objects inserted into the rectum or vagina, being given Lysol or chlorine douches, and so on). Psychological pain results from being victimized and feeling as if there is no one to whom to they can turn, as well as being afraid because of the threats that have been made to keep them silent. Then the feeling of grief is associated with losses. When a child is sexually abused many losses occur. Secondary losses include the loss of innocence, the loss of an unencumbered and carefree childhood, the loss of trust and the belief that adults only want what is best for you, and the loss of the ability to trust one's feelings of what is right. Keeping secrets is psychologically taxing work.

Anger is another feeling expressed by abused children. Don't expect children to say, "I'm angry." The angry feelings might be expressed in their behavior—temper tantrums, rebelliousness, or outbursts of rage. Anger is a normal and justified feeling when the child experiences powerlessness, helplessness, and a belief that their body does not belong to them.

Indicators for Teachers to Observe (Broadhurst, 1986)

Consider that a child in your classroom may be a victim of sexual abuse if the child:

- Is uncomfortable walking or sitting
- Is very reluctant or refuses to participate in physical activities
- Appears to be knowledgeable about sexual matters or exhibits sexual behavior
- Becomes pregnant or contracts a venereal disease
- Runs away
- States that he or she is being sexually abused by an adult
- Demonstrates sudden changes in behavior or inability to do school-work
- Appears to be waiting for something bad to happen
- Does not want to go home from school and stays at school as long as possible

Consider sexual abuse as a possibility if the parent or caretaker:

- Limits the child's contact with other children
- Is secretive

- Openly admits marital difficulties that involve the issues of power or sex
- Is not responsive where the child is concerned, in such matters as parent–teacher conferences or home visits
- Denies that problems exist
- Blames the child for any of the problems
- Expects the child to meet the adult's needs for emotional satisfaction

Indicators for Children at Highest Risk for Being Abused

According to recent community studies (Finkelhor & Baron, 1986) the following, if present, would mean that the child is at risk for being sexually abused: (1) a child who lives with only one biological parent; (2) a child whose mother is unavailable because she works outside the home, is disabled, or has a chronic illness; (3) a child who reveals that the parents' marriage is full of conflict the marriage is unhappy; (4) a child who has a poor relationship with the parents or a child who is a victim of extreme punishments; and (5) a child who has a stepfather.

ABUSE-SPECIFIC VARIABLES

Abuse specific variables have been defined as those entities that may impact on the child and his or her development and long-term and short-term symp-tomatology with regards to sexual abuse. The abuse-specific variables are as follows: age at which the first abusive incident took place; use of force by the perpetrator; severity of symptoms thought to be a result of the abuse; duration or length of time the abuse continued; recurrence of sexual abuse; the severity of the abuse (e.g., contact versus noncontact abuse); intrusive versus nonintrusive acts; gender of the child; and relationship of the perpetrator to the child.

To date the research literature is a mixed bag on the relationship between age of onset (age at which the abuse first happened) and severity of symptoms developed as a result of the abuse. Some studies have found greater impact on a child when sexual abuse occurred in preadolescence and adolescence rather than in the early years of life (Adams-Tucker, 1982; Peters, 1976; Sedney & Brooks, 1984; Sirles, Smith, & Kusama, 1989). Others have reported the opposite to be true; abuse that occurs at a younger age results in greater trauma to the child (Courtois, 1979; Meiselman, 1978; Russell, 1986). These discrepancies may exist because, when young children are assessed, the complete range of symptoms and behaviors that are a result of the abuse may not be obvious at the time of the assessment, but as children grow and develop new symptoms may become apparent. Secondly, when sexual abuse is recognized and addressed in younger children, it may be related to the length of time the child was abused; younger children could be abused for a shorter period of time than older children. Thus the impact of the abuse may not be as significant on the younger child because the abuse was identified sooner. All of this is speculative at best.

Force is another key factor to consider. The less control the child or adolescent believed he or she had and the amount of force used during the victimization seems to be related to the degree of trauma he or she experiences (Abel, Becker, & Cunningham-Rathner, 1984; Burgess, Groth, Holstrom, & Sgroi, 1978; Condy, Templer, Brown, & Veaco, 1987; Constantine, 1980; Finch, 1973; Finkelhor, 1979, 1984; Finkelhor, Araji, Baron, Browne, Peters, & Wyatt, 1986; Friedrich & Luecke, 1988; Rogers & Terry, 1984). The greater the force the greater the trauma. Intrusive sexual acts (e.g., anal, oral, or vaginal penetration) and the use of force have been reported to produce higher levels of trauma in the survivor (Browne & Finkelhor, 1986; Courtois, 1988; Elwell & Ephross, 1987; Herman, Russell, & Trocki, 1986; Mullen, Romans-Clarkson, Walton, & Herbison, 1988; Russell, 1986; Sedney & Brooks, 1984).

Recurrence of sexual abusive incidents and length of time (e.g., weeks, months, years) the abuse took place are additional abuse-specific variables. Certain researchers have determined that the longer a child was abused the greater the degree of psychological trauma (Bagley & Ramsay, 1986; Herman, Russell, & Trocki,1986; Morrow & Sorrell, 1989; Russell, 1986; Sirles, Smith, & Kusama, 1989; Tsai, Feldman-Summers, & Edgar, 1979).

Gender is another factor to be considered in abuse-specific variables. Most of the retrospective research data has centered on female children abused by adult males. But males also are victimized by both male and female adults. If professionals do not believe males are victimized then they might not explore if the symptoms presented are related to a sexually abusive childhood.

Relationship to the perpetrator is another abuse-specific variable. Sexual abuse by an intrafamilial abuser (natural father or stepfather) is reported to produce more significant and long-lasting effects than sexual abuse by an extrafamilial abuser (someone outside the family system) (Adams-Tucker, 1982; Courtois, 1979; Feinauer, 1989; Finkelhor, 1979; Friedrich, Urquiza, & Beilke, 1986; Gomes-Schwartz, Horowitz, & Cardarelli, 1990; Herman, Russell, & Trocki, 1986; McLeer, Deblinger, Atkins, Foa, & Ralphe, 1988; Meiselman, 1978; Peters, 1976; Sirles, Smith, & Kusama, 1989). Living in a home environment where one cannot feel safe and free but must remain constantly alert and vigilant, an environment from which there is no escape, traumatizes the child.

Two variables that contribute to the child or adolescent's adjustment to how he or she behaves after the sexual abuse has been terminated is based on (1) what happens to the offender, and (2) how others respond once the disclosure of the victimization has been made, especially family members (Alter-Reid, Gibbs, Lachenmeyer, Sigal, & Massoth, 1966; Finkelhor, Araji, Baron, Browne, Peters, & Wyatt, 1986; Yates, 1982). Two researchers (Rogers & Terry, 1984) found that adolescent males behaved sexually aggressively more frequently if the perpetrator was not made to be legally accountable for his or her abusiveness and was not incarcerated for his or her inappropriate sexual acts. Obviously, if a perpetrator is not even brought to trial the message is clear: "Children have no rights; adults can do as they please with no fear of involvement of the legal system."

Lastly, if parents negate, minimize, or blame the child or adolescent for the victimization, he or she may be more traumatized (Abel, Becker, & Cunningham-Rathner, 1984; Rogers & Terry, 1984). At a deeper level, when parents and other family members respond negatively, it feeds into the whole cycle of the child or adolescent beginning to believe what the molester said about him or her really "asking for it."

Sexually abused children are more likely to live in single parent or blended families (Gruber & Jones, 1983), the parents are often depressed or addicted to alcohol or other substances (Adams-Tucker, 1981; Bliss, 1984; Burgess, Hartman, & McCormack, 1987; Coons & Milstein, 1986; Friedrich & Luecke, 1988; Russell, 1986; Silbert & Pines, 1981; Smith & Israel, 1987), and the mothers may have been sexually abused during childhood (Friedrich & Reams, 1987; Sansonnet-Hayden, Haley, Marriage, & Fine, 1987; Smith & Israel, 1987).

All of this suggests that children experience more trauma (1) if the sexual abuse involved intrusive acts; (2) if force was used by the perpetrator; (3) if the perpetrator was a biological father, stepfather, or caregiver within the family system; (4) if multiple perpetrators were involved; (5) if the offender was not punished; and (6) if parents denied or minimized the abuse. The data are inconsistent between age of onset and outcome. Periods of long victimization and more frequent abuse results in a greater incidence of the child viewing it traumatically. Also, the greater the difference in age between the child or adolescent and the offender, the greater the trauma (Abel, Becker, & Cunningham-Rathner, 1984; Constantine, 1980; Finkelhor, 1979, 1984; Finkelhor, Araji, Baron, Browne, Peters, & Wyatt, 1986; Landis, 1956; Rogers & Terry, 1984).

RESEARCH ON THE DIFFERENCES
IN SYMPTOMATOLOGY BETWEEN
MALE AND FEMALE CHILDREN

The research literature often has lacked data regarding the effects of sexual abuse on males. The few studies that have been completed have determined that males have the same patterns of symptoms as females: fears, sleep difficulties, and distractedness. The researchers (Conte, Berliner, & Schuerman, 1986) in a study of 37 different symptoms found no differences between male children and female children in 33 of the symptoms. A study done at Tuft's New England Medical Center (1984) found no differences between male and female children in 31 of 33 items.

When differences exist between male children and female children these problem behaviors are exhibited either by "externalizing" or "internalizing" behaviors (Friedrich, Beilke, & Urquiza, 1987; Friedrich, Urquiza, & Beilke 1986). Children who display internalized behaviors are usually isolated and withdrawn (Fagot, Hagan, Youngblade, & Potter, 1989) Often these children will be withdrawn and will not seek out interactions with others, will demonstrate signs of clinical depression, be deficient in spontaneity, be overcompliant, develop phobias, be anxious, have sleep disorders, act regressively (may wet the bed or suck their thumb), complain of headaches and stomachaches, develop eating disorders, use and abuse drugs, attempt suicide, mutilate the body, and dissociate (Gil, 1988). Externalizing behavior is when the child's aggressive behaviors are directed toward others. Male children who have been abused have been found to exhibit more externalizing behaviors than females. These behaviors include acting aggressively, such as fighting with siblings (Gomes-Schwartz, Horowitz, & Cardarelli, 1990; Tufts, 1984), killing or torturing animals, and acting in a "sexualized" manner (Gil, 1988). One researcher believes that the lack of differences in the symptoms of males and females is because of the types of reactions the researchers have attempted to measure. Most of the research thus far has focused on stress-related symptoms such as anxiety, depression, aggression, and sleep disturbances. These problems are the usual response to stress. Some studies have found survivors that display few to no symptoms (Caffaro-Rouget, Lang, & vanSanten, 1989; Conte & Schuerman, 1987; Kendall-Tackett, Williams & Finkelhor, 1993; Mannarino & Cohen, 1986; Sirles, Smith, & Kusama, 1989; Tong, Oates, & McDowell, 1987). This does not mean that children who are sexually abused are unscathed by the experience. What it may mean is that the current research instruments used are not sophisticated enough, that the studies did not ask the right questions or that the right symptoms to measure have not been identified. If parents are uncertain about the child's accusations or are in a state of denial then the tendency is to minimize the child's trauma (Abel, Becker, & Cunningham-Rathner, 1984; Everson, Hunter, Runyan, Edelsohn, & Coulter, 1989; Rogers & Terry, 1984). It also might mean that when the children are evaluated, they are in a state of denial about what has occurred, but at a follow-up interview the symptoms have begun to appear (Gomes-Schwartz, Horowitz, Cardarelli, & Sauzier, 1990; Tufts, 1984). Finally, it is possible that these children who appear asymptomatic have suffered less serious abuse (Finkel-hor, 1990a; Kendall-Tackett, Williams, & Finkelhor, 1993). The research available shows that children with no identifiable symptoms have been abused for a shorter period of time, usually have had no evidence of violence or penetration, have not been victimized by a father or father-figure, and have been supported by the family when the abuse was discovered (Browne & Finkelhor, 1986).

DEMOGRAPHICS ON MALE AND FEMALE CHILDREN WHO WERE SEXUALLY ABUSED

Finkelhor (1984) reviewed data from the American Humane Association (total $N = 6,096$, male $N = 803$) and found the following: males were generally younger than females when sexually molested; males were more frequently molested by someone outside the family system; males came from families with a lower socioeconomic status than females; males more often resided in single-parent families. Physical abuse occurred more often in male survivors when compared with female survivors (also confirmed by Sansonnet-Hayden, Haley, Marriage, & Fine, 1987); female perpetrators were less financially stable than male perpetrators; and the abusive mothers in the study were more likely to use a combination of physical and sexual abuse.

Pierce and Pierce (1985) compared male ($N = 25$) and female ($N = 180$) survivors of sexual abuse. Males and females were compared by family size, offender gender, and factors contributing to continuity of abuse. These authors found male child survivors had more siblings than female child survivors; more males than females lived with their biological mothers; males were more often molested by their stepfathers than the females; the females were abused more frequently by biological fathers; males frequently lived in homes where a sibling also was being sexually abused; the males were more often coerced into sexual activities such as masturbation or oral sex; and males were more inclined to be threatened by the offender. In terms of actions taken by child protective services, fewer males were removed from the home than females, and male child survivors received less therapy than female child survivors. A study by Burgess, Groth, Holstrom, & Sgroi (1978b) found male children more likely to be involved in pornography and sex rings than female children.

More recently, Kendall-Tackett and Simon (1992) compared male ($N = 40$) and female ($N = 325$) adults molested as children. Those authors found that biological fathers sexually offended males and females in about the same numbers—33% of the males and 39% of the females were molested by their fathers; stepfathers were more likely to molest females than males—8% of the males and 22% of the females reported their stepfathers had been sexually abusive; and family friends sexually offended more males than females—38% of the males and 10% of the females. No significant age differences were found relating to when the first sexually abusive incident occurred (7.65 years for males, 7.60 years for the females). These authors proposed the following:

> One possible explanation for this similarity may have been of the physical resemblance between boys and girls before the development of secondary sex characteristics. Some perpetrators have been attracted to the relative androgyny of young children—seeing their childishness, rather than their gender, as attractive. (p. 60)

The average onset at which the molestation began for both males and females may be similar because it might have been the earliest the child, regardless of gender, could remember the abuse. Actually the sexual abuse may have begun much earlier but these memories have been repressed from the child's conscious awareness in the form of dissociation.

The average time period the molestation continued was 3.91 years for males and 5.6 years for females. Kendall-Tackett and Simon (1992) posit this explanation for these particular statistics:

> Molestation may have ended sooner for boys because the perpetrators were likely to be from outside the family and did not have continuous access to the child. There may have been a greater amount of physical trauma for male victims because of either force or type of sexual acts, which required medical intervention. Or, male victims may have been physically strong enough to ward off future advance, thus ending the molestation at an earlier age. (p. 60)

ADULT DISORDERS THAT CAN BE RELATED TO CHILD SEXUAL ABUSE

Do not be deceived into thinking that the effects of incest are cured by time. Sometimes other problems become symptomatic for the abuse experienced as a child. These can include: ***substance abuse*** (Courtois, 1979; deYoung,

1982; Herman, 1981); *borderline personality disorder* (Barnard & Hirsch, 1985; Bryer, Nelson, Miller, & Krol, 1987; Herman & Schatzow, 1987; Ogata, Silk, Goodrich, Lohr, Westen, & Hill, 1990; Shearer, Peters, Quaytman, & Ogden, 1990; Zanarini, Gunderson, Marino, Schwartz, & Frankenburg, 1989); *eating disorders* (Courtois, 1988; Root & Fallon, 1988); *dissociation* (Chu & Dill, 1990; Gelinas, 1983; Goodwin, 1982; Herman, Russell, & Trocki, 1986; Reiker & Carmen, 1986; van der Kolk & Kadish, 1987); *multiple personality disorders* (Baldwin, 1984; Bliss, 1984; Braun, 1984; Coons & Milstein, 1986; Kluft, 1985; Putnam, 1984); *depression* (Briere & Runtz, 1986; Browne & Finkelhor, 1986; Gorcey, Santiago, & McCall-Perez, 1986; Mullen, Romans-Clarkson, Walton, & Herbison, 1988; Peters, 1988; Sedney & Brooks, 1984; Wozencraft, Wagner, & Pellegrin, 1991); *skin-carving* (deYoung, 1982; Lindberg & Distad, 1985a); *suicide attempts* (Bagley & Ramsey, 1986; Briere & Runtz, 1986; Browne & Finkelhor, 1986; Bryer et al., 1987; Fromuth, 1986; Wozencraft et al., 1991); *low self-esteem* (Courtois, 1979, 1988; Herman, 1981); *revictimization experiences* (Alexander & Lupfer, 1987; Briere, 1984; Fromuth, 1986; Gorcey et al., 1986; Runtz, 1987; Russell, 1986); and *feeling crazy* or *different*.

Chapter 3

SEXUAL ABUSER PROFILES

A plethora of information has been written in both books and professional journals on individuals who sexually abuse children. The intention of this book is not to provide an in-depth analysis on the subject of sexual offenders but rather to supply an overview of the definitions, issues, current research studies, theoretical approaches, and problems inherent in defining and treating individuals who sexually abuse children. Abusers of children have been for the most part divided into two separate and distinct categories, intrafamilial and extrafamilial abusers (Pawlak, Boulet, & Bradford, 1991). The first category has focused mostly on father–daughter or stepfather–daughter sexual abuse. Pedophiles, or extrafamilial abusers, are usually considered to be a separate and distinct group from intrafamilial abusers. These individuals were originally purported to be quite different from intrafamilial abusers. Traditionally, pedophiles have been defined as individuals who sexually abuse children outside the family system. A pedophile can be homosexual (abuses a child of the same gender), heterosexual (abuses a child of the opposite gender), or bisexual (abuses children of both genders). Certain studies have questioned the validity of definable differences between extrafamilial and intrafamilial abusers. Abel, Becker, Cunningham-Rathner, Mittleman, and Rouleau (1988) found that 49% of the fathers and stepfathers in their study who were sexually abusing a child within their own families had abused children outside the family system, and 18% of these males were raping adult women simultaneously with molesting children. Presented in this chapter are data regarding both intrafamilial and extrafamilial abusers, male and female offenders in both groups, and adolescent sexual abusers. The reader is cautioned against accepting the validity that two separate, distinct groups of adult offenders exist: intrafamilial and extrafamilial (Abel et al., 1988; Pawlak et al., 1991). A more appropriate way to categorize offenders may be by gender or distinctions between adolescent and adult offenders. Data on female offenders are too scarce to make any generalizations at this time. This chapter has been divided into three separate groups of sexual offenders: extrafamilial adult, intrafamilial adult, and adolescent offenders. Based on the most recent studies of adolescent offenders, researchers are suggesting that adolescents are indeed a separate and distinct group from adult offenders.

HISTORICAL PERSPECTIVE

History reveals that the sexual abuse of children has a long and sordid past. The ancient Greeks and Romans used children for sexual gratification (Brown, 1985; Jones, 1982). In Greece, prepubescent males were often forced into a sexual relationship with an older male. It was common practice in Greece for men to debauch and sodomize male children (Dover, 1978). This was considered normal behavior by the child's parents and the Greek government (Ellis, 1933). The homosexual relationship ended when the male child began to develop secondary sexual characteristics.

The Romans also supported homosexual behavior between older men and young boys. Young boys, girls, and women were sold into prostitution and slavery on a regular basis. In fact, young prostitutes celebrated a special public holiday (Kahr, 1991).

During the Renaissance period females did not fare any better than the young males of Ancient Greece and Rome. Medieval canon law forbade females less than 12 years of age to marry. However, it was not unusual to find children 10 years of age married to old men (Noble, 1976).

During the 1600s and 1700s many female children were "imprisoned, tortured and burnt at the stake because their tormentors insisted that they had fornicated with the Devil and had attempted to seduce innocent and unsuspecting men" (Kahr, 1991, p. 202). Other historical accounts from the 1700s showed that same sex adult/child sexual relationships were not at all unusual in China, Japan, Africa, Turkey, Arabia, and Egypt (Trumbach, 1977). Even as late as 1800 the selling price of a twelve-year-old virgin in London was 400 pounds (Bullough, 1964).

In the 20th century, sex with children is not only still available but certain publishers have produced books that make the information public knowledge: *The Discreet Gentleman's Guide to the Pleasures of Europe* (1975) and *Man-*

koff's Lusty Europe (1973). Both detail where child prostitutes are available in Europe. As can be seen from this brief sojourn through the history of child sexual abuse, it has been with us for centuries. Lloyd de Mause (1974) put it all in perspective with his statement, "the history of childhood is a nightmare from which we have only recently begun to awaken" (p. 1).

PEDOPHILIA

Definitions

In the late 1800s, a German psychiatrist by the name of Krafft-Ebing (1886/ 1965) coined the term *pedophilia*. The term was used to characterize someone who had a psychosexual perversion. The perversion was identified as an adult individual who was sexually attracted to children and had no sexual attraction toward adults. According to Krafft-Ebing the pedophile could be male, female, homosexual, heterosexual, or bisexual. He believed that the "true" pedophile could not be rehabilitated because the acts of sexual offending were an inherent part of the person's personality structure. He believed that two types of offenders existed: (1) "individuals who use the child as a substitute for a physically mature partner" (p. 5), and (2) true pedophiles whose "condition is a disorder" (p. 5).

Since Krafft-Ebing, the word pedophile has been defined as "inclusive," which includes children and adolescents, or "exclusive," which only includes children under the age of 11 or 12. Certain researchers (Mohr, Turner, & Jerry, 1964) have used the term pedophilia to describe any sexual contact or interest in children, regardless of whether the interest is short-term or lifelong. Other researchers have restricted the word pedophile for individuals who have a long-lasting and preclusive interest in children (Groth, 1979b; Howells, 1981). Some researchers have made a distinction between pedophiles and pederasts. Pedophiles are those persons, either male or female, who have sexual contact with and are attracted to children to whom they are not related. The children are usually age 12 or under (Cohen, Seghorn, & Calmas, 1969; Gebhard, Gagnon, Pomeroy, & Christenson, 1965; Mohr, 1964). Other studies have included children and adolescents in the definition of pedophilia (Fitch, 1962; Langevin, 1983).

Pederasts are those individuals who are attracted to adolescents or children over the age of 12. A pederast has been described as a person who is an "eternal adolescent in his erotic life. He becomes fixated upon the youth and sexual vitality of the adolescent boy. . . . Pederasts love the boy in themselves and themselves in the boy" (Geiser, 1979, p. 83).

Pedophilic Individuality

Probably as much diversity exists in personality composition of child sexual abusers as in those individuals having addictions, asthma, or arthritis. Their most common characteristic is their individuality. Most likely at least one person you know sexually abuses children, either his or her own or someone else's.

To have a better understanding of child sexual abusers a real need exists for controlled studies comparing the general population with child sexual abusers who are not incarcerated. Such studies are needed before any concrete assertions can be made that correctly illuminate the "average child sexual abuser," although it is doubtful such a person exists.

Rothblum, Solomon, and Albee (1986) caution one to remember that categorizing and treating mental disorders is reflective of the cultural biases of the time. Thus simply categorizing pedophiles is not enough to help understand the roots of this deviant behavior. These authors challenge us to look more deeply for reasons rooted in society. They state,

> . . . We may find specific personality disorders that identify men who have been guilty of rape or the sexual abuse of children. But we neglect to look for the larger cause in the sexist nature of our society with it's emphasis on male domination of females, with the focus in mass media of male violence and female passivity, and with a pervasive and subtle sexism that is everywhere present. What is the cause of the cause? What causes sexism and what can we do about sexism as a cause of psychopathology? (p. 169)

Prevalence of Pedophiles

No measure is available to obtain an accurate estimate of the number of child sexual abusers in the general population. If the statistics indicate that one in every three females and one in every five males will be sexually abused (includes noncontact and contact forms of sexual abuse) before the age of 18 it would appear that a substantial number of sexual offenders live in our society.

Pedophile Organizations

A number of organizations are devoted exclusively to pedophiles in the United States and Great Britain. All of these societies promote pedophilic sexual behavior. Some of these organizations are the Howard Nichols Society, which publishes a pamphlet entitled, "How To Have Sex with Kids"; the Rene Guyon Society, whose reported slogan is "Sex by Year Eight Or Else It's Too Late"; the North American Man-Boy Love Association (NAMBLA); and the Pedophile Information Exchange (called PIE) in Great Britain. These groups purport themselves to be "prochild," claiming that children can and should make decisions in all areas of their lives, including the decision to have sex with adults (deYoung, 1982).

Classification of Pedophiles

Classification of pedophiles is as diverse and varied as types of diseases. Karpman (1954) published the first book in the 20th century that focused exclusively on the subject of sexual offenders. Karpman classified pedophiles into two groups: (1) those who committed sexual offenses because the weaning process was traumatic, and (2) those who acted deviantly because of unresolved Oedipal issues.

Fifteen years later, Cohen, Seghorn and Calmas (1969) proposed the existence of three specific subtypes of pedophiles: (1) immature, (2) regressed, and (3) aggressive. Tollison and Adams (1979) defined the three types based on the work of Cohen et al. (1969) as

> 1. The personally immature offender has never been able to establish or maintain satisfactory interpersonal relationships with male or female peers during his adolescence, young adult or adult life. . . 2. The regressed offender, who during adolescence shows apparently normal development with good peer relationships and adequate social and heterosexual skills as well as heterosexual experience. . . 3. The aggressive offender whose motivation for pedophilic behavior is both aggressive and sexual. Such offenders have a history of antisocial behavior and frequently are characterized as hostile, aggressive, psychopaths. . . . (pp. 328–329)

At the present time, data from empirical research do not support these three categorizations of pedophiles.

The DSM-IV (American Psychiatric Association, 1994) places pedophilia (302.2) in a category called paraphilias. These authors stated,

> The paraphiliac focus of Pedophilia involves sexual activity with a prepubescent child (generally age 13 years or younger). The individual with pedophilia must be age 16 years or older and at least 5

years older than the child. . . . Some individuals prefer males, others females, and some are aroused by both males and females. . . . Some individuals with Pedophilia are sexually attracted only to children (Exclusive Type), whereas others are sometimes attracted to adults (Nonexclusive Type). . . . The disorder usually begins in adolescence, although some individuals with Pedophilia report that they did not become aroused by children until middle age. The frequency of pedophiliac behavior often fluctuates with psychosocial stress. The course is usually chronic, especially in those attracted to males . . . do not include an individual in late adolescence involved in an ongoing sexual relationship with a 12- or 13-year-old. (pp. 527–528)

Groth and Birnbaum (1978) used two terms to describe child sexual abusers: fixated or regressed. They described a fixated child molester as ". . . a person who has from adolescence, been sexually attracted primarily or exclusively to significantly younger people" (p. 176). This attraction has persisted throughout his or her life, regardless of what other sexual experiences he or she has had. A fixated child molester fits the criteria for exclusive pedophilia in the DSM-III R (1987). Other researchers have concurred with this categorization of some pedophiles having a lifelong preference for sexual relations with children (Cohen, Seghorn, & Calmas, 1969; Gebhard & Gagnon, 1964; Groth & Birnbaum, 1978; Groth, Hobson, & Gary, 1982; Howells, 1981; Karpman, 1954; McCaghy, 1971; Seghorn, 1981; Summit & Kryso, 1978; Swanson, 1971).

Groth and Birnbaum (1978) described the regressed offender as someone who "has not exhibited any predominant sexual attraction to significantly younger persons during his sexual development—if any such involvement did occur during adolescence it was situational or experimental in nature" (p. 178). For the "regressed" child molester the sexual interaction with a child or children is usually only a one-time occurrence or episodic. The theory that is espoused is that a stressor or stressors such as marital difficulties, unemployment, and so on causes the individual to seek out a child who is supposedly a surrogate for the preferred but unavailable adult (Cohen, Seghorn, & Calmas, 1969; Gebhard & Gagnon, 1964; Groth & Birnbaum, 1978; Groth, Hobson, & Gary, 1982; Howells, 1981; Karpman, 1954; McCaghy, 1971; Swanson, 1971).

Another way in which research studies label pedophiles is in the differentiation that is made between pedophilic sex object choice. Certain studies have categorized pedophiles according to their child preference—male object (pedophiles preferring males) or female object (pedophiles preferring females) (Fitch, 1962; Gebhard & Gagnon, 1964; Goldstein, Kant & Hartman, 1973; Mohr, Turner, & Jerry, 1964).

One of the most recent explanations of pedophilia to emerge is that of Knight and Prentky (1990). Their typology is identified as MTC: CM3, which has two "axes." Axis I requires rating in two areas: degree of fixation and social competence of the pedophile. Fixation (Decision 1 on Axis 1) "assesses the strength of an individual's pedophilic interest, that is, the extent to which children are a major focus of the individual's cognition and fantasies" (Knight & Prentky, 1990, p. 32). Social competence (Decision 2 on Axis 1) "assesses the offenders' success in employment and adult relationships and social responsibilities" (Knight & Prentky, 1990, p. 32). Axis 2 decisions are made based on the amount of contact the pedophile has with children and then involves sequential decision-making regarding the degree of fixation (high or low); types of sexual relationships (nonorgasmic aim or phallic, orgasmic aim); amount of physical injury to the child involved (low injury, e.g., threats, or high injury, signs of victimization apparent); and involvement of sadistic fantasies or behaviors (Knight & Prentky, 1990).

More recently, MacHovec (1992) and MacHovec and Wieckowski (1992) have developed the 10-factor contiunua/treatment model as a way to classify and categorize sex offenders. MacHovec stated, "MacHovec and Wieckowski (1992) developed a 10-factor system to classify male and female sex offenders by type, victim and underlying dynamics. Each of the ten factors are rated on a 5-point scale from 1 (no clinical significance) to 5 (extreme severity)" (p. 18). The 10 factors in this classification system are: "physical aggression (aggression specific to sex offending . . .), asocialization (ability to conform to sociosexual norms . . .), fantasy (fantasy about deviant sexual behavior . . .), sexual arousal (deviation in what is sexually arousing . . .), offense cycle (awareness and ability to interrupt the cycle and pattern of sex offending . . .), cognitive distortions (recognizing cognitive distortions or unrealistic expectations . . .), denial-minimization (offender's use of denial and minimization and conversely self-disclosure . . .), remorse-empathy (social sensitivity, adaptive and coping skills . . .), [and] prognosis (readiness and potential for therapy . . .)" (p. 18). Also included in this assessment is victim gender, victim age, specific sex offenses by type, kind of contact (e.g., vaginal, anal), other deviant behaviors (e.g., bestiality, exhibitionism), and other treatment issues (e.g., DSM disorders, family dysfunction, etc.) (pp. 18–19).

ETIOLOGIES OF PEDOPHILIA

The following are some of the most common etiologies that are proposed to explain pedophilia.

Physiological

Miller, Cummings, McIntyre, Ebers, & Goode (1986) described eight cases of either hypersexuality or altered sexual preference after injury to the brain. Lilly, Cummings, Benson, & Frankel (1983) reported that bilateral temporal lobe dysfunction (called the human Kluver-Bucy syndrome) results in altered sexual orientation. This theory was supported by the Miller et al. (1986) study. Miller et al. deduced that certain sexual changes are a result of lesions in the limbic system—particularly the temporal lobe. Henn, Herjanic, and Vanderpearl's (1976) statements are in agreement with Miller et al. (1986) and Lilly et al. (1983), that child sexual abuse could be a result of brain dysfunction.

Other researchers (Bradford, 1985) have theorized that changes in neurotransmitters might have an impact on sexual behavior. Gaffney and Berlin (1984) studied 3 different groups of males: pedophiles, nonpedophiles (with some form of paraphilia other than pedophilia), and a control group with no diagnosed paraphilia. Their study found that pedophiles had greater levels of luteinizing hormones than either the nonpedophile or the control group. The authors suggested their results may indicate a hypothalamic–pituitary gonadal disorder to explain pedophilic behavior. Recently LeVay (1991) demonstrated differences in the hypothalamic structure of homosexual and heterosexual males. If this finding can be substantiated, some researchers might begin to study the hypothalamus of pedophilic individuals. However, the presentation of a few studies concerning neuroanatomy and neurochemistry is hardly enough to make any kind of concrete statement about their relationship to pedophilic behavior. Other researchers have theorized that child sexual offenders have genetic abnormalities, causing them to give credence to the supposition that there may be an inherited tendency toward pedophilia (Bradford, 1985; Gaffney, Shelly, & Berlin, 1984).

Psychodynamic

Two prevailing schools of analytic thought have emerged with regards to pedophilia. The first is Freudian and the second is Kohutian, or self-psychology (Juda, 1986). Freud's views have strongly influenced the psychodynamic viewpoint. He postulated that, "in the course of development all people find children sexually attractive and need to be weaned away from such 'perverse' attractions by social conditioning and repression" (Freud, 1948, p. 28). Opposition to this theoretical assumption is based on certain researchers' findings that many individuals do not become sexually aroused when shown pictures or slides of naked children (Freund, McKnight, Langevin, & Cibiri, 1972; Glueck, 1965; Henson & Rubin, 1971; Laws & Rubin, 1969).

Freud (1905/1963) defined a pedophile as "someone who is cowardly or has become impotent and adopts children as a substitute, or when an urgent instinct (one which will not allow postponement) cannot at the moment get possession of any more appropriate object" (p. 23). As can be seen from the two quotes, Freud believed pedophilia was a form of neurosis, a regression to infantile sexuality or a regression to the phallic stage of development, which results in unresolved Oedipal conflicts (Howells, 1981). Freud was convinced that one of a pedophile's greatest unconscious fears was being castrated (Rada, 1978). He purported that adult women who reported being sexually abused in childhood by their fathers were actually repressing fantasies from childhood and manifesting unresolved Oedipal issues and penis envy (Freud, 1905/1963).

Originally Freud was convinced that the adults he saw who presented with symptoms of hysteria had been sexually abused in childhood. In his study of 18 individuals, 6 males and 12 females who had hysteria, all 18 individuals had been sexually abused in childhood. From these cases he delineated 3 specific kinds of sexual abuse in childhood: assault, which he defined as the actual sexual attacking of the child; sex between a child and an adult known to the child; and sexual contact between children, where one or both had been sexually abused by an adult. Tragically, Freud's presentation of the "Aetiology of Hysteria" to the Society of Psychiatry and Neurology in Vienna was poorly received (Masson, 1984). In an attempt to save his career he renounced his original theory on sexual abuse and stated the notions of sexual abuse in childhood were just fantasies (Freud, 1905/1963).

Kohutian psychologists believe pedophilia is an aberrant male defense mechanism that does not permit or allow the ego to be overwhelmed. Self-psychology views the kind of mothering received during infancy as crucial in defining personality development and developing psychopathology. Pedophiles have never developed a well-defined sense of self (Juda, 1986). Some ego-psychologists (Stoller, 1979) highlight the role of aggression in pedophilia. In a figurative manner the pedophile is attempting to protect himself from trauma experienced as a child. According to this viewpoint the pedophile himself, as a child, wanted to be sexual with his mother but feared castration from his father if he acted on his desires. Therefore when he chooses children for sexual gratification, he is unconsciously saving his genitals from castration. According to this viewpoint, pedophiles are portrayed as males who are dependent on their mothers and are socially immature and narcissistic. It is their symbiotic relationship with their mothers that prevents them from establishing satisfactory sexual relationships with women their own age.

Howells (1981) theorized that having sexual contacts with children enables the pedophile (again with the assumption that the pedophile is male) to surmount the sense of shame, humiliation, or powerlessness that had been experienced during victimization experiences as a child. Other theorists have called this identification with the aggressor (Stoller, 1985; Freeman-Longo, 1986; Groth, 1979b). The sexual abuse of a child is a repeated and unproductive attempt to master his own sexually abusive experiences as a child through reenactment of his own trauma. The trauma is reenacted every time he abuses a child, but in these cases the offender is now the aggressor rather than the victim. The purpose of the identification with the aggressor is purported to be the suppression of feelings of helplessness, control of anxiety, and the renewal of masculinity (Burgess, Hartman, McCausland, & Powers, 1984; Burgess, Hartman, & McCormack, 1987; Rogers & Terry, 1984). Please note that most individuals who were sexually abused as children do not grow up to molest children. Wurtele and Miller-Perrin (1992) stated, "There is no simple causal relationship between early sexual victimization and subsequent status as an adult molester; previous victimization must interact with other personal, situational, or sociocultural factors to increase the risk of abusing" (p. 31).

Family Theories

Family systems theorists report that family systems in which incest thrives are usually enmeshed, rigid, and lacking well-defined boundaries within the family unit (Alexander, 1985; Gutheil & Avery, 1977; Will, 1983). Families in which incest occurs are suggested to be socially and physically isolated from other members of society. Family members are described as enmeshed (depending only on one another to fulfill individual needs) and there is a lack of proper boundaries or no existent boundaries between family members and across generations. Frequently the child becomes "parentified," in that he or she assumes the caretaking role for the entire family. The child often engages in caretaking roles involving care of both the physical and the emotional needs of the parents. This is carried to the extreme when the child becomes sexually involved with one or the other parent, or both parents. The needs of the children are given very little, if any recognition by the parents. The child gives up "the self" to meet the needs of the parents.

Kempe and Kempe (1984) have identified two different types of families in which incest occurs more frequently: the "chaotic family" and the "normal-appearing" family. The chaotic family is typically of low socioeconomic status; is dysfunctional in its patterns of functioning in society (e.g., family members have generational histories of substance abuse, delinquency, and incarcerations); and most members of the family fail to graduate from high school, are chronic welfare recipients, and have unstable intimate relationships. Children reared in these families are frequently targets of intrafamilial and extrafamilial abuse. If the abuse is reported to the authorities and a trial ensues often the perpetrator is imprisoned, especially since the family lacks sufficient monetary resources to hire adequate legal counsel.

The "normal-appearing" family, as the phrase suggests, is exactly that—an illusion that the family members present to the community (Kempe & Kempe, 1984). Frequently the parents have been married for years, are financially secure, and have established roles in the community. Parents in this type of family structure are often unable to nurture themselves or their children. They are usually quite needy and turn to their children to meet their needs, sexually as well as emotionally. Addictions are rampant in these "normal-appearing" families. Often the mother expects the daughter to assist in daily maintenance of the household and the father uses the child to meet his sexual and emotional needs. It is also not uncommon for the children to become sexual with one another. A brother may sexually abuse his sister in patterning after the father's incestuous acts. Abuse that is discovered and reported in the "normal-appearing" family rarely results in a conviction of the offender and most likely he or she will continue to reside in the home and further abuse the child.

In both the "chaotic" and the "normal-appearing" families incest is often transmitted from one generation to the following generation. This has been called the intergenerational transmission of incest. A number of researchers have found similarities in families in which the intergenerational transmission of incest occurs (Cooper & Cormier, 1982; Goodwin & Di Vasto, 1979; Margolin 1992; Pelto, 1981). Frequently both the mother and father were emotionally, physically, and sexually abused themselves in childhood.

Calof (1987), as discussed in Courtois (1988), presented a summary of characteristics frequently utilized by families in which incest occurs. The incest is an attempt to preserve family functioning and balance in the family unit. The characteristics are as follows: (1) pervasive denial by all family members about incest or addiction; (2) the situation is not how the individual family member perceives it but how the family defines the situation or says that it is; (3) isolation from the community; (4) all problems are denied; (5) lack of clear boundaries and roles; (6) triangulation between mother, father, and child—it becomes the child's responsibility to maintain the family, and frequently the parents have a dysfunctional sexual relationship; (7) little acceptance of anger, conflict, and deviations from what is considered the norm in the family; (8) rigidity in religious beliefs (e.g., the child is taught that it is a sin to engage in premarital sexual activities, meanwhile the father sexually abuses him or her); (9) touching that is nonsexual and genuinely loving and nurturing is nonexistent; (10) children's emotional and often physical needs are ignored; (11) emotional abuse is rampant, and children are often excoriated and shamed; (12) parents are withdrawn and emotionally and physically unavailable; one or both parents may be addicted to work or alcohol; (13) children are not wanted and are treated as such; (14) rampant inconsistencies in treatment of the child—behavior that is acceptable one day may be unacceptable the following day; (15) threats of violence which sometimes erupt; and (16) the child is isolated and there is no one he or she can tell, so the child deals with the situation the best he or she knows how. This may be through disassociation, or, in cases where the abuse is extreme, he or she may develop multiple personality disorder as a survival mechanism (pp. 42–44).

Steele and Pollock (1968) suggested from a psychodynamic perspective that incest occurs in families where parents have an unhappy marriage but are quite dependent on each other. The parent (father) who molests believes himself to be devalued and not well understood by his partner, the child supposedly has the same experiences with the nonoffending parent (the mother), and this results in the father and female child meeting one another's needs for love and affection in a sexualized manner.

Low Self-esteem

Pedophilic behavior is thought to be a result of emotional, physical, or sexual trauma. The trauma is so painful that it results in emotional underdevelopment or retardation in development (Groth, 1982; Tollison & Adams, 1979). As a result of this retardation in development the individual may age in years but not emotionally. The pedophile begins to depend on children and view them as sex objects. The children are then used to relieve feelings of anxiety and low self-esteem (Groth, 1979a; Langevin, 1983). Using children in a sexual manner to deal with uncomfortable feelings is reinforced and becomes an ingrained behavior pattern.

A male pedophile who views himself as a child can develop a desire to connect to other children (Bell & Hall, 1971). Some researchers have concluded that male pedophiles are sexually immature and have low self-esteem, based on test scores of the Blacky picture test (Hammer & Glueck, 1957; Stricker, 1967). The MMPI has been used frequently in studies of male pedophiles (Cavallin, 1966; Levin & Stava, 1987; Panton, 1978). Levin and Stava reviewed 36 studies that utilized the MMPI in pedophilic populations. Results were mixed and no clear pattern emerged from all of the studies they examined. Some researchers have found the MMPI profiles to be normal for male sexual abusers (Chaffin, 1992; Hall, 1989; Hall, Maiuro, Vitaliano & Proctor, 1986; Scott & Stone, 1986). The problem with many of these studies is that researchers frequently make inferences about the test scores that are too broad based on small sample sizes.

Social Skills Theories

Dysfunctional or underdeveloped social skills has been suggested as another explanation for molesting behaviors, especially in relating to persons of the opposite sex (Anderson & Mayes, 1982; Bell & Hall, 1971; Cohen, Seghorn, & Calmas, 1969; Fisher & Howell, 1970; Gebhard, Gagnon, Pomeroy, & Christenson, 1965; Groth, Hobson, & Gary, 1982; Hammer & Glueck, 1957; Hayes, Brownell, & Barlow, 1983; Howells, 1981; Langevin, 1983; Mohr, Turner, & Jerry, 1964; Overholser & Beck, 1986; Pacht & Cowden, 1974; Panton, 1978; Virkkunen, 1976; West, 1977). Certain studies have assessed the social skills of convicted sexual offenders. Segal and Marshall (1985, 1986) compared rapists, child molesters, nonsexual offenders, and two control groups on social skill ability based on videotaped conversations with females. The researchers found that the rapists, child molesters, and nonsexual offenders were less socially competent than the control groups. The child molesters were less skilled socially than the rapist group. The child molesters were also less skilled at predicting and evaluating their own performance in heterosexual situations. Interacting with children may give the pedophile a feeling of power and control and reduce feelings of anxiety experienced in peer relationships (Hammer & Glueck, 1957).

Recently a study was done that examined the social problem-solving skills of sex offenders by presenting case vignettes to the research participants (Barbaree, Marshall, & Connor, 1988). Both sex offenders and nonoffenders were presented with the vignettes, which were of situations involving sexual abuse. Research participants were asked to determine the appropriate course of action to be taken by people in the case studies. Situations involving both children and adults were presented in the vignettes. The child molesters were as skilled as the nonoffenders in realizing that a problem existed. However, the child sexual abusers more frequently than the nonoffenders chose socially unacceptable solutions to scenarios presented and were unable to see negative outcomes as a result of the solutions they chose. Cognitive distortions and denial appeared to be quite ingrained in this population (Abel, Gore, Holland, Camp, Becker, & Rathner, 1989).

From the studies just mentioned some support is given for the theoretical assumption that pedophiles who have been incarcerated are lacking interpersonal skills for relating to members of the opposite sex. However, this may be a function of their incarceration rather than the direct result of being a child sexual abuser.

Pedophilia as a Learned Behavior

Some social learning theorists (McGuire, Carlisle, & Young, 1965) believe the pedophile becomes conditioned to responding to young, sexually underdeveloped bodies. It has been suggested that boys begin masturbating to fantasies that involve sexually immature bodies, and then become conditioned to these images and need them to create sexual satisfaction. It is then taken a step further when the pedophile actually plays out the fantasy in real-life situations. Garland and Dougher (1990) theorized two reasons for this behavior leading to the development of pedophilic behavior: (1) an adolescent's sexual activity with persons his or her own age could condition sexual arousal to pubescent children, and (2) through memory distortions that have occurred with the passage of time, the child or adolescent who was sexually victimized by an adult developed a fantasy that places him or her in the role of the aggressor rather than in the role of the victim. As a result of this recurrent fantasy, he or she then becomes sexually conditioned to respond to children.

Other professionals believe that pedophilia is caused by sexual abuse in childhood. In other words, the pedophile was abused as a child and learns to "model" this behavior. This information is based on pedophiles self-reporting what happened to them as children (Groth & Burgess, 1977). Groth (1979a) explored the sexual abuse history of three groups: sex offenders of children, rapists, and police officers. Less than 3% of the police officers reported a history of sexual abuse. This was in marked contrast to 13% of the rapists and 25% of the child molesters.

Feminist Theory

According to feminist theory, children are objects of choice because of the value that a patriarchal society puts on the male being the dominant, powerful, and controlling member in initiating sexual relationships (Hite, 1981; Rush, 1980; Russell, 1986). So males connect with "partners who are younger, smaller, and weaker than themselves" (Finkelhor & Araji, 1985, p. 149). Children fulfill all of these criteria, sometimes even better than adult partners.

Some feminists (Densen-Gerber, 1983; Dworkin, 1983; McCaghy, 1979; Rush, 1980) assert that child pornography and advertising have a role in the development of pedophilia. The theoretical tenets of this are based in the belief that viewing pornography eroticizes children, and teaches adolescents to become aroused by children. Hence, in masturbating to the pornographic images, the individuals then become conditioned to finding children sexually arousing.

Much of the feminist writings in incest are grounded in the writing and research on rape. Two classic examples are Brownmiller's (1975) book, *Against Our Will: Men, Women and Rape* and Russell's (1975) book, *The Politics of Rape*. These works did much to denounce the theories of women wanting to be raped, "asking for it," and being responsible for the rape. Both Rush (1980) and Brownmiller (1975) believe incest has its roots in and continues to exist because society is patriarchal. Women and children in a patriarchal system are nothing more than the personal property of men . Rush (1980) posits that beginning in early childhood, female children are "eroticized" in a variety of ways (e.g., men exposing their genitals to female children, girls being fondled, the manner in which females are depicted in the media, and so on), all in an attempt to socialize the female child to adopt an inferior position in society and view the sexual abuse of females as "normal."

Herman and Hirschman (1977) maintained that as long as rigid sex-role stereotyping exists in which mothers are relegated to being the nurturers and fathers the monetary providers, father–daughter incest will continue. Rape and incest meet the male need for power. Herman (1990) stated, "Sexual assault asserts male dominance and intimidates women; it also provides the aggressor with sexual pleasure" (p. 182). For more information on the feminist theory of pedophilia, read Barrett (1993), Barrett, Trepper, & Stone Fish (1990), Fish and Faynik (1989), Trepper and Barrett (1989), and Wheeler (1989).

Pedophilia as a Form of Addiction

Patrick Carnes (1983) was one of the first authors of the 1980s to develop a model of sexual addiction to explain the behaviors of sexual abusers. Carnes contended that molestation of children is a sexual addiction. He explained that the addict cycles through a four-stage process, with the process becoming more addictive each time the cycle is repeated.

Preoccupation is the first stage. The addict is unable to think about anything else except sex. At this point he then begins to seek sexually titillating experiences. Ritualization is the second stage, and during this time addicts will engage in specific behaviors that culminate in sexually acting out behaviors. Compulsive sexual behavior is the third stage, which encompasses the sexual act itself. Despair, is the fourth stage; this is what the addict experiences regarding his "sexually acting out" behaviors. He realizes there is a lack of control over the compulsive behavior.

Carnes (1983) suggested three different levels of addiction. Level one behaviors are identified as usage of pornography, compulsive masturbation, engaging repeatedly in sexual relationships that have little or no meaning, and prostitution. Level two behaviors involve illegal actions and another person being sexually victimized (e.g., exhibitionism, voyeurism, obscene phone calls, or lewd verbal suggestions). Level three includes rape, incest, and pedophilic behaviors. Blanchard (1985) suggested a progressiveness to the addiction and purported that an adolescent may begin at level one and a few years later find himself or herself at level three. Herman (1990) stated that once an addiction is ensconced a cure is nonexistent, only control and abstinence are possible, and abstinence is not equated with cure.

Other Theories about the Etiology of Pedophilia

Some studies have demonstrated that consuming alcohol frequently is a precursor to committing sexual acts with children (Aarens, Cameron, & Roizen., 1978; Gebhard, Gagnon, Pomeroy, & Christenson, 1965; Morgan, 1972; Rada, 1976; Stokes, 1964). This has been called the alcohol disinhibition theory.

In addition, Finkelhor and Araji (1985) have presented a four-factor model to explain why adults are sexually attracted to children. Their model is based on much of the existing research rather than theoretical tenets and is quite encompassing. The four reasons are: emotional congruence, sexual arousal, blockage, and disinhibition.

1. *Emotional congruence*—"Adults find it emotionally satisfying to relate sexually to a child" (p. 140). Certain emotional needs are met in sexual abusers who choose children as sexual partners. Some of these needs might be to reenact the abuser's sexual molestation, to express an immature sexuality, to maintain power and control, and to satisfy and gratify sexual needs with someone who is younger and more immature.

2. *Sexual arousal*—Suggests some adults are more sexually aroused by children than by other adults. This is based on a behavioral model in which the molester has been conditioned (through repetition and masturbation) to fanta-

size about sexual acts with children. Other theories suggest biological or hormonal factors are involved.

3. *Blockage*—Explains why some persons are unable to get their sexual and emotional needs met in adult relationships. There appears to be two categories of blockages: developmental (e.g., castration anxiety, dysfunctional social skills, or marital discord); and situational, which includes strict beliefs about masturbation and extramarital sex.

4. *Disinhibition*—explains why pedophiles do not have inhibitions or are able to overcome the moral and legal sanctions against performing sexual acts with children. Lowering inhibitions can be a result of alcohol usage, social isolation, or senility.

Another part of the disinhibition theory is what these two researchers have labeled as failure of the incest avoidance mechanism. They have theorized "that because of different norms or different exposure to the child at an early age, stepfathers are less inhibited from sexual feelings toward a child than are natural fathers" (Finkelhor & Araji, 1985, p. 31).

Society as a Contributing Factor in Pedophilic Behavior

Groth, Hobson, and Gary (1982) discovered that race, religion, intelligence, education, occupation, and socioeconomic status are not different in pedophiles when compared with the general population. Finkelhor (1984) determined that frequently the pedophile's victims are children who are in some way related to the pedophile, thus giving him easy access to the children.

Socialization theory posits that an adult's reactions to others has its roots in the manner in which he or she learned to respond to adults during childhood (Gelles, 1973). Butler (1985) believed both men and women are victimized by society. She wrote,

> These men are victims, not only of their particular parents, school systems and economic circumstances, but of something more pervasive than the sum of all these things. They are victims of male-defined standards of appropriate behavior that leave little room for the acknowledgment of deeply felt and repressed needs for love, acceptance, nurturing and warmth. Victims of not being permitted to feel and express the full range of human feelings and of not being taught to understand the strength in admitting weakness; victims of not being able to open their arms or hearts to others, never having

experienced arms in which they were encircled and made to feel
safe. (pp. 76–77)

Finkelhor (1979, 1984) contended that certain forms of socialization contribute to and maintain sexual abuse. Eight forms of socialization were listed:

1. Men are not taught to express intimacy in any other way except through
   sexual interactions.
2. Women are oppressed members of society with little status or power.
3. Parents who are rigid, authoritarian and punitive and do not ever discuss
   sexual matters with their children place them at increased risk for being
   sexually abused.
4. Blended families place females at greater risk for abuse by a stepfather
   or mother's boyfriend.
5. Traditional values that sanction against incest are less important than in
   the past.
6. A sharp increase has occurred in the availability of child pornography.
7. Adults may turn to children for sex because their peers are not really
   sexually available.
8. Children have been eroticized by the media.

SEXUAL BEHAVIORS OF ABUSERS

Howells (1981) is convinced that pedophiles fall on a continuum. He stated,
"Adults sexually involved with children vary from technically pedophilic persons to those of normal orientation" (p. 77).

Abel, Becker, Mittleman, Cunningham-Rathner, Rouleau, and Murphy (1987)
have provided us with an assessment of the number of "sexual acts" committed
by a study of sexual offenders who were treated on an outpatient basis. Five
hundred sixty-one offenders committed 291,737 acts of abuse. The 224 extrafamilial heterosexual pedophiles victimized 4,435 females; 155 extrafamilial homosexual pedophiles sexually victimized 29,981 male children; 158 intrafamilial
heterosexual pedophiles victimized 286 female children; and 44 intrafamilial
homosexual pedophiles abused 75 male children. The study suggested that pedophiles who abuse children related to them commit more sexual acts per child,
while extrafamilial pedophiles sexually abuse more victims, with less sexual
acts per child. Other researchers (Conte, 1986a, 1989; Tufts, 1984) have found
that frequently children are victimized by more that one abuser. Abuse continues to be underreported (only 2% of intrafamilial and 6% of extrafamilial cases
were reported to authorities in Russell's [1984a] study).

The presentation of three separate studies follow; each reports the sexually abusive behaviors of pedophiles with a different population. The first study is based on self-reporting by pedophiles, the second is an adult survivors retrospective study reporting on occurrences of molestation in childhood, and the third is the reports of children who were identified as being sexually abused.

Erickson, Walbek, and Seely (1988) reported different types of sexual victimization. Two hundred twenty-nine offenders were asked to report what types of contact they had with their male and female victims: vaginal contact (with 42% of the female victims); anal contact (with 33% of the males victimized and 10% of the females victimized); oral sex on children (with 41% of the males victimized and 19% of the females victimized); and fondling of children (43% of the male victims and 54% of the female victims).

Kendall-Tackett and Simon (1987) reported on the sexual victimization experiences of 365 adult survivors. The information revealed that 64% were fondled from the waist up; 92% were fondled from the waist down; 48% had oral sex performed on them; 19% had intercourse attempted on them; 44% had intercourse; and 9% had anal intercourse performed on them.

Kercher and McShane (1984) described the sexual molesting behaviors to which 619 children were exposed: 42% were fondled by offender; 39% had heterosexual intercourse experiences; 6% had homosexual intercourse; 2% had experienced photographing of the child in the nude or engaged in sexual acts; and 2% were victims of prostitution.

Fondling seemed to be the behavior that occurred most frequently in the three studies discussed; the incidence of intercourse was high also. It has been suggested that the high percentage rates of fondling may occur as part of the "grooming process," in which child sexual abusers desensitize children to touch by progressively moving from nonsexual to sexual touch (Hollin & Howells, 1991). Singer, Hussey, and Strom (1992) provide an enlightening and thought-provoking account of a letter that chronicles a 38-year-old male's efforts to engage a 16-year-old adolescent male to participate in sexual acts. The letter serves to exemplify how knowledgeable the adult sexual offender is in his attempts to "initiate exploitative sexual relationships with teenage victims" (p. 878).

Baby-sitting as a Situational Factor in Pedophilia

Adult offenders also have been found to sexually abuse children entrusted to their care in baby-sitting situations. Margolin (1991) studied a situation in which female and male child care workers were abusive to children placed in their care. She examined the case records of 325 families in which abuse by an extrafamilial caregiver was documented. There were seven major types of situations in which the extrafamilial sexual abuse occurred. First the sexually abusive acts perpetrated by extrafamilial caregivers were found to be done in a situation in which the caregiver was consistently employed by the family. The largest number of female abusers (24 out of 27) were less than 20 years of age. A much greater diversity was found in the male extrafamilial caregivers with the average age of the males 25.4 years (for females it had been 17.7 years)

She found that in 31% of the cases (101 families) the child was sexually abused by an extrafamilial caregiver who was chosen by the parent, compensated monetarily for their caretaking activities, and used by the family on a regular basis (45 male abusers and 27 female abusers). The 27 female molesters sexually abused male children in 55% of the cases. Male perpetrators sexually abused females 69% of the time. A second caretaking situation in which a child ($N = 27$ children) was molested was a result of a one-time baby-sitting arrangement (e.g., parent need to attend a funeral, child had to be taken to emergency room and parent needed a sitter for sibling, etc.) Third, 52 children were sexually abused by a friend or relative of the baby-sitter. These perpetrators were males in all but one instance. Average age of the child in these instances was 5.7 years. The fourth situation involved 19 children who were molested during a sleep-over at a friend's house. Again, the overwhelming majority of molesters were male (18 of the 19 perpetrators). Thirty-seven percent of these children were vaginally or anally penetrated by the perpetrator. A fifth situation identified by Margolin (1991) involved sexual molestation by a live-in caregiver (2 were male perpetrators and 2 were female perpetrators). In the sixth identified situation, 21 children were molested by an adult friend of the child (17 of the 21 children molested were males). The seventh situation was a family friend sexually molested a child in 29 cases. All of the perpetrators in this situation were males, and the children were all female ($N = 27$) except in two instances.

Information garnered from the study suggests more than one kind of baby-sitting arrangement places a child at risk to be sexually abused. Parents need to take into account not only the caregiver who is responsible for the child but who the child may come into contact with because of the baby-sitting arrangement.

Parents needing a baby-sitter for whatever reason should first select a trusted family member. For instance, if the parent had a brother, sister, mother, or father who sexually abused him or her during childhood, it would not be a safe assumption that the sibling or parent's abusive behavior had improved over time and that a child would be safe in this household. If using a trusted family member is not possible, learn to know a male or female baby-sitter's family. Pay attention to how the potential baby-sitter is treated by other family members. If the baby-sitter is humiliated, denigrated, or put down in any way, rethink using that individual to care for a child. Determine if the potential baby-sitter has friends his or her own age. If the baby-sitter does not, think again about choosing him or her to provide child care. The research literature has indicated that in many cases sex offenders are socially isolated and have few to no friends. Do not assume that a female sitter would not sexually abuse a child; the research literature indicates otherwise.

If a child is placed in a baby-sitter's care, reassure the child that he or she will be called frequently. Speak directly to the child on the telephone when calling. Develop a special code word for the child to use if he or she is frightened or fears being harmed. Do not accept any reason that the child might not be able to come to the phone. If unable to speak to the child, return home immediately.

If a baby-sitter is already established in the home and the child's relationship with the baby-sitter becomes intense or the two become inseparable, pay attention to what might be occurring. Exclusivity between an adult caretaker and a child can be an indicator of child sexual abuse. Parents also need to know the child's friends. If the friends are always older, determine if the older child has friends his or her own age. If the baby-sitter is an individual who the parent does not know, ask for at least five references who can be contacted. Call the local police department or Children and Youth Services to determine if the potential baby-sitter has ever been reported for any improprieties. Parents have a responsibility to keep their child safe.

Measuring Pedophiles' Responses in a Laboratory Setting

Some research studies have demonstrated through phallometric assessment that pedophiles are more sexually aroused to children than the general population (Freund, 1967; Freund & Blanchard, 1989; Freund, Langevin, & Cibiri, 1973; Murphy, Haynes, Stalgaitis, & Flanagan, 1986). These researchers in a variety of studies explored penile responses of offenders and nonoffenders to slides of children (male and female) and mature adults. Phallometric assessment measures changes in penile tumescence in a laboratory setting. During the assessment the individual is shown different sexual and nonsexual pictures or slides and then his response is assessed using a penile plethysmograph. In the studies just mentioned, substantially more arousal occurred to the slides of children in the pedophile groups than in the homosexual and heterosexual male groups. However, even though it has been demonstrated that some pedophiles do show more arousal to children sex objects of their choice (male or female), it is unclear whether this is true for all child molesters, including intrafamilial abusers. In addition, certain pedophiles can purposefully inhibit their responses. Using phallometry as an assessment technique does require certain specific equipment (Laws & Osborn, 1983; Quinsey & Laws, 1990). Data garnered from phallometric assessments appear to have its greatest usefulness in deciding if a sexual offender has a preference for children or if children are victimized because they are more readily available than adults.

MALES AS EXTRAFAMILIAL ABUSERS

Research Studies on Males Who Abuse Males

Marshall, Barbaree, and Butt (1988) studied erectile responses of men who were referred to outpatient treatment for sexually molesting male children ($N = 21$). The offenders responses were contrasted to the reports of a matched group of males who were not child molesters. Offenders were divided into two groups: those demonstrating a homosexual preference ($N = 7$), and those demonstrating a heterosexual preference ($N = 14$). When shown slides of both naked males and females ranging in age from 3 to 24 years, and hearing verbal stimuli consisting of sexual activities involving force and contact sexual abuse between adult males and male children, all male child sexual abusers demonstrated sexual arousal (20% to 40% experienced full erections as measured by penile plethysmography) to nude males of all ages. Nonoffenders demonstrated no response to the nude male slides and audiotapes. The two groups did not differ in their response to the naked female slides.

The molesters were subdivided into homosexual ($N = 7$) and heterosexual ($N = 14$) based on their erection reactions measured by penile plethysmography, with the homosexual group demonstrating the strongest erectile response to 15-year-olds, with a small decrease in response to adult males and a sharper decline in penile tumescence to males younger than 15. In the group designated heterosexual the offenders had the highest arousal rates to 11-year-old males and a great decrease in response to males older than 11. Secondly, in response to the audiotapes the homosexual molesters demonstrated higher levels of response to the noncoercive situations than the heterosexual molesters. These researchers wrote

Our results reveal two important features of men who molest boys. First, their sexual response to males in general (the slide set) were greater than those displayed by controls, and their arousal to sex with boys (the audio-tape set) was also greater than that of the controls. . . . The second, and perhaps the most important observation we made is that a homosexual and a heterosexual subgroup can be delineated among these offenders . . . it is clear that men who molest boys are not a homogeneous population. . . . The homosexually-oriented offenders showed greater arousal to the males than did the heterosexually-oriented offenders, particularly once the males depicted attained the age of 13 years and over. Perhaps, most importantly, the homosexuals were far more aroused by sexual interactions with boys even when those interactions required the man be forceful. . . . The homosexuals were equally aroused at least by the consenting and mildly forceful intercourse than they were by the less intrusive sexual acts. . . . With respect to these differences amongst our offenders, we also observed that the heterosexually-oriented men characteristically chose victims who were clearly prepubescent, whereas the homosexually-oriented offenders chose pubescent boys. (Marshall, Barbaree, & Butt, 1988, pp. 389–390)

Obviously, there are some real limitations to this study, including the very small sample size and how the research data were gathered (e.g., use of penile tumescence as arousal indicators is controversial at best because some offenders are able to control their penile response in a laboratory setting). However, the most important finding is demonstrating that just as males who sexually abuse female children do not have one simple typology, the same can be said for male adults who molest male children.

Statistics on Male Survivors of Abuse

Survey research studies on male survivors present a mixed bag of results. A number of researchers believe the abuse of male children is underreported (Hunter, 1990; Peake, 1989; Rew & Esparza, 1990). A Finkelhor (1979) study of 796 college students revealed 9% of the males reported being sexually abused as children. DeJong, Weiss, and Brent (1982) reviewed published clinical studies and found male sexual abuse percentages ranging between 11% and 17%. Farber, Showers, Johnson, Joseph, and Oshins (1984) and Showers, Farber, Joseph, Oshins, and Johnson (1983) reported a figure of 15% of the male participants in their studies had been sexually abused as children.

Studies of incarcerated male sex offenders have reported male children to be sexually victimized in at least one third of the sexual offenses the male inmates have admitted to occurring (Groth, 1979a; Groth, Hobson, & Gary, 1982). Groth's (1979a) study of males found guilty of sexual offenses determined that 25% of the offenders in his study exclusively chose male children to victimize.

Homosexuality as a Learned Response to Sexual Abuse

Certain studies have suggested that young males who have been sexually victimized by older men have a four times greater chance of practicing homosexual activity when compared to males who have not been sexually abused (Finkelhor, 1984). Finkelhor posited the male survivor may believe himself to be a homosexual because the male sexual perpetrator found him (meaning the child or adolescent) to be so attractive. This view that he must be homosexual will increase if the survivor sustained any physical pleasure during the aggressive sexual incidents.

Johnson and Shrier (1985) reported the male survivors in their study who were sexually abused by a male to be seven times more likely to engage in homosexual activities and were six times more likely to label themselves bisexual when compared with a group of males who had no history of sexual abuse. In contrast, Woods and Dean (1984) only found 12% of their study of nonclinical males (who had a history of sexual abuse) to have engaged in homosexual activities the preceding year. However, the clinician at this point in time cannot assume that every homosexual client was sexually abused in childhood or adolescence.

Pescosolido (1992) stated,

> The idea that same sex abuse of boys is homosexually motivated reinforces victim's notions that they are involved in homosexual behavior. Essentially the victim may believe that there is something within himself that almost magically communicated a homosexual invitation prompting the molestation. Thus, he can be left with a distorted sense of sexual identity, even though homosexual desire was not a motivating factor in the perpetrator's choice of a victim or decision to commit the offense.
>
> The male victim's anatomy and physiology provide further complicating responses which add to his confusion. Penile erection and ejaculation are a normal physiological response when the male genitals are orally and/or manually stimulated. It becomes difficult and almost impossible for the victim to deny the physical reactions which

are usually associated with voluntary sexual pleasure and arousal. Accordingly, the victim is left to question his sexual orientation, asking himself, "Why else do these physical responses occur?"

These reactions provide seemingly irrefutable evidence to the victim he was sexually aroused by another male during molestation. The physical response can be psychologically distorted by the victim to validate a homosexual identity, i.e., "I must be homosexual because why else would I have an erection?"

The equating of involuntary sexual arousal or erections with the victim "liking" and/or "enjoying" the molestation represents an insidious, powerful effort by the perpetrator (and society) to blame the victim as well as to rationalize the often continued pattern of abuse. (p. 11)

Coping Styles of Male Sexual Abuse Survivors

Summit (1983) has suggested that when a male child is sexually abused there is a loss of power and control—two core elements in the socialization process of males in this society. He posited that aggression and antisocial behaviors are ways a male child regains control over his life. He suggested that the assaultive relationship (for survivors who become abusers) is affirming to the male perpetrator who was abused because it allows him to regain the power and control lost during his own sexually abusive experience. Summit believed the survivor will continue to reaffirm the abusive experiences in adulthood by reenacting the experiences with male children or male adolescents.

Finkelhor and Browne (1986) contended that children, both male and female, do adapt to being sexually abused. However, these authors believed that the child's thoughts and feelings about the world are affected by the abusive experiences. Self-esteem is affected as is the child's affective abilities. Finkelhor and Browne proposed four areas that explain the symptoms connected to child sexual abuse: traumatic sexualization, betrayal, powerlessness, and stigmatization.

Traumatic sexualization is ". . . the conditions in sexual abuse under which a child's sexuality is shaped in developmentally inappropriate and interpersonally dysfunctional ways (Finkelhor, 1988, p. 69). With traumatic sexualization sex and love are confused.

Betrayal occurs when "children discover that someone on whom they were vitally dependent has caused them or wishes to cause them harm" (Finkelhor,

1988, p. 70). A child or adult survivor may react in any of the following ways: become depressed, angry, overly dependent, or act in antisocial ways. Stigmatization occurs as a result of the negative messages the child receives from society and family members about being a survivor of abuse, that he or she is "less than" because of the abuse. Children may also experience feelings of isolation or of "being different" as a result of the abuse.

Powerlessness occurs when "children feel that they are not in control of their bodies and lives. Their will, wishes, and sense of self-efficacy are repeatedly overruled and frustrated" (Finkelhor, 1988, p. 71).

Finkelhor and Browne (1986) provided some examples of how this prototype of traumagenic dynamics relates to males who have been sexually abused. Traumatic sexualization may cause a young male who has been sexually abused by a male to fear he is now a homosexual. These feelings of powerlessness could then result in the male acting aggressively and engaging in illegal sexual activities (molesting a child) and other kinds of behaviors.

FEMALES AS EXTRAFAMILIAL ABUSERS

Mic Hunter (1990) has had this to say about societal views of males being victimized by females:

> Films often portray women being sexual with boys as harmless and glamorous. "Private Lessons" and "Homework" are two examples of this glamorization. These films are rated R and are widely available on videotape, in the comedy section of video rental stores. The cover of "Private Lessons" shows an illustration of a boy standing on three schoolbooks in order to become tall enough to reach the lips of the adult maid who is entrusted with his care. Even more graphic is the cover for "Homework," which reads, "Every young man needs a teacher." In "Homework," Joan Collins proves the perfect teacher for young Tommy, but her classes are conducted after school and definitely do not include the three R's. But who's complaining? Not Tommy. Meanwhile, back in the school yard, Tommy's buddy Ralph has his own private tutor, Ms. Jackson, who teaches him those tricky French conjugations. (p. 36)

Finkelhor (1984) interviewed parents on their views regarding different forms of sexual abuse. Both male and female parents regarded sexual abuse by females with either male or female children less harmful than abuse by adult males who either abused males or females. This position is reflective then of who will be identified as a survivor and who will receive treatment. Finkelhor (1984) stated,

> What people think is abusive may also affect how they react toward the participants. If people think having an encounter with an exhibitionist is extremely abusive they will react with more alarm when a child reports such an encounter, even if the child is not upset. If they think that a sexual encounter between a 12-year-old boy and a 27-year-old woman is not very abusive they may laugh about it even if the child feels exploited. (pp. 107–108)

Research Studies on Female Perpetrators

Presented in the following section is research on females who were found to be sexual offenders. In presenting these data the reader will discover there is some overlap in studies that present and include both intrafamilial and extrafamilial female abusers. A more complete discussion of intrafamilial female abusers can be found in the intrafamilial abuse section of this chapter under "Mothers as Intrafamilial Abusers."

In 1982, Sarrel and Masters categorized three types of females who sexually abused male children. The authors distinguished among (1) forced assault, in which the female physically confined or used threats of violence to force the male child to participate in sexually abusive acts; (2) baby-sitter, which was categorized as the older unrelated female who was left in charge of caring for a male child; and (3) incestuous abuse, which occurred when a female who was related to the male child or adolescent sexually abused the child.

Mathews, Matthews, and Speltz (1989) studied 16 adult female sexual offenders. Victims were 44 children and one adult. Sixty-four percent were female ($N = 28$) and 36% ($N = 16$) were male. She divided the perpetrators into 3 groups: (1) Teacher/lover—An older female engaged in sexual relationships with adolescents. All the perpetrators in this category were victimized in their families of origin by harsh and punitive verbal and emotional abuse. (2) Intergenerationally predisposed—Female perpetrators belonging to this group had a history of sexual abuse in childhood, and other family members frequently also had a history of abuse. It was not uncommon for the abuse to begin early in the life of this offender and continue until puberty. Sometimes there were multiple perpetrators of the abuse when she was a child. (3) Male-coerced—Women in this category were co-offenders with males. Women in this category felt their husbands "forced" them to participate in sexually abusive acts with children.

Every woman in this group had been sexually abused in childhood by at least one male. The male co-offender also physically, psychologically, and sexually abused the women in this group. Some common denominators were apparent in this group of molesters studied: all had a history of sexual abuse in childhood either by an intrafamilial or extrafamilial abuser, were socially isolated as adults, all suffered from feelings of low self-worth, and all reported being dependent on males in adulthood.

Faller's (1987) study involved 40 female perpetrators who sexually abused 63 children. Eighty-five percent of the sexual offenders ($N = 34$) were mothers to at least one of the children abused. Fifty-five percent ($N = 22$) were exclusively sexual with their own children. Thirty percent ($N = 12$) of the remaining women perpetrators molested their own children and those outside the family system. Six women were not sexually abusive toward their own children but abused other children who were accessible to them. These six women perpetrators had the following relationships to the children: girlfriend of the father of the child ($N = 2$), grandmother ($N = 1$), sister ($N = 1$), baby-sitter ($N = 1$), sister and neighbor ($N = 1$). Faller noted that the overrepresentation of intrafamilial offenders was because the majority of the molesters were referred from child protective service agencies. Faller (1988) categorized sexual offenders into 11 different types; female offenders meet the criteria for 5 of the categories. The categories are as follows:

1. *Polyincestuous abuse*—72.5% ($N = 29$) of the females met Faller's criteria for sexually molesting children in a polyincestuous family constellation, in which there were a minimum of two abusers and at least two or more children are sexually abused. Intergenerational transmission of sexual abuse is a commonality in this type of family group. Faller stated:

   > In 24 of the polyincestuous cases in our sample, the child's description of the sexual abuse suggested that men, rather than women, played a leadership role in the abuse. . . . The kind of account given by the children that suggested the secondary role of women was as follows: The children would typically begin with revelations about a male offender and would attribute extensive sexual abuse to him. Usually, in response to later questions about where their mother was or whether she knew about the sexual abuse, they would reveal her role. (p. 266)

2. *Single-parent abuse*—15% ($N = 6$) of the female molesters were categorized in this group. These women were not involved in sexual relationships with men. Some other researchers also have found women perpetrators who were not involved with members of the opposite sex at

the time the women began molesting the children (Justice & Justice, 1979; McCarty, 1986). The oldest child in the family in Faller's study of this group (single parent) was always molested, and frequently functioned in a role of surrogate partner.

3. *Psychotic abusers*—Constituted 7.5% ($N = 3$) of the female offenders in this study. Faller (1987) stated, "Thus our findings do not support earlier clinical assertions that most female perpetrators are highly disturbed and often psychotic at the time of their sexual abuse" (p. 267).

4. *Adolescent perpetrators*—Comprised 7.5% ($N = 3$) of the female offenders in this study, and got close to their victims via baby-sitting or befriending younger children. This is similar to Margolin's (1991) findings of adolescents being able to access children through baby-sitting situations.

5. *Non-custodial abusers*—One mother sexually abused her children during their visits with her. Faller (1987) stated,

> The children become both the source for emotional gratification and an outlet for the expression of anger. The lack of structure and unsupervised access to the child afforded by visitation play a precipitating role in the sexual abuse. (p. 268)

Categories of sexual abusiveness by the female perpetrators in Faller's study were divided into the following groupings: fondling, 38.1% ($N = 24$); oral sex, 31.7% ($N = 20$); digital penetration, 25.4% ($N = 16$); intercourse, 14.3% ($N = 9$); group sex, 44.4% ($N = 28$); exploitation (women permitting other individuals to molest the child), 15.9% ($N = 10$); pornographic photos taken, 9.5% ($N = 6$); child forced to watch sexual acts of female perpetrator and a partner, 23.8% ($N = 15$); forced child to engage in sexual acts with other children, 14.3% ($N = 9$); and other not specified sexual activities, 27% ($N = 17$).

Ninety-five percent ($N = 38$) of the female offenders were Caucasian, 5% ($N = 2$) were African American. The average age was 26.1 years (youngest offender was 13; the oldest, 47). Over 75% of the study population of women were between the ages of 20 and 30. Socioeconomic status of 82.5% ($N = 33$) was lower class and 17.5% ($N = 7$) were middle class. However, there is a great overrepresentation of persons from a lower socioeconomic background who are involved with child protective services, so this is in no way indicative that women who are sexual abusers are primarily from a lower socioeconomic status.

Of the children who were molested, 94% ($N = 59$) were Caucasian; 6.3% ($N = 4$) were African American; 36.5% ($N = 23$) of the children molested were male; and 63.5% ($N = 40$) were female. The average age of a child at the time he or she was interviewed was 7 years for males and 6.1 years for females. This is a much younger age than reported by the American Humane Association's (1981) study, which reported 9 as the average age at which molesting began.

Psychological impairment of the abusers also was assessed with the following results: 47.5% ($N = 19$) were mentally impaired; 32.5% ($N = 13$) were mentally retarded or had an organic brain syndrome disorder; 55% ($N = 22$) of the female perpetrators were substance abusers; 72.5% ($N = 29$) had been either physically neglected, physically abused, or emotionally abused as children; and 47.5% ($N = 19$) had been sexually abused as children.

Although the existence of female offenders is now beginning to be recognized, it is still met with great skepticism in certain groups. Accepting the harsh reality that females can and do abuse (sometimes quite violently) children and adolescents in both gender groups perhaps attacks one of the last remaining vestiges of cultural myth: the myth that mothers or females are always protective toward children and could not be abusive, violent, or sadistic, sexual offenders.

INTRAFAMILIAL ABUSERS

The empirical research literature has been unable to determine a set of psychological characteristics that delineate between child sexual abusers and the general population (Armentrout & Hauer, 1978; Langevin, Hucker, Ben-Avon, Purins, and Hook, 1985; Quinsey, 1977). In addition, for some years the assumption has been that the father who molests his daughter or son is somehow quite different in character than the pedophile who molests children to whom he is not related. Conte (1985) and Lanyon (1985) contend that all of the sexual abuse committed against children are still sexual acts, regardless of whether it is intrafamilial or extrafamilial abuse. There is clinical evidence to suggest that single sexual molesters (operating individually) can and do sexually abuse many children both inside and outside the family system (Abel, Becker, Murphy, & Flanagan, 1981; Bolton, Morris, & MacEachron, 1989; Burgess, Groth, & McCausland, 1981).

Father–Daughter Intrafamilial Abuse

Father–daughter incest has been the most studied of all types of sexual abuse. Cormier, Kennedy, and Sancowicz (1972/1973) described fathers molesting a daughter as the behavior of an immature adult, who acts in an adolescent manner yet uses his power and position in the family. Incest is viewed as a result of internal and external forces in the family in which the father is seen as pathological and the mother as unassertive and clinging.

Justice and Justice (1979) suggested four categories of fathers who sexually abused their daughters: symbiotic, psychopathic–sociopathic, pedophiliac, and other.

1. *Symbiotic type* included the largest number of abusers, 80 to 85%. The symbiotic father is characterized by having a family of origin that was non-nurturing. He has a real neediness for affection and love which is always expressed or established through sexual relationships. Symbiotic fathers have been categorized into four subgroups depending on how sex is utilized to be close to the daughter: (a) introverted, (b) rationalizing, (c) tyrannical, (d) alcoholic.
   a. *Symbiotic introverts* appear to the world as "good husbands and fathers." They are quite family-oriented and have few other relationships outside their nuclear families. The symbiotic introvert may appear to be an extrovert but this is just an illusory image he presents to society. He often feels stressed by his work and retreats to the home environment to escape the job stressors. Depression that is untreated or masked is common. Often he is sexually dysfunctional with his wife and begins to substitute the daughter for the wife.
   b. *Symbiotic rationalizers* are fathers who rationalize their incestuous acts as a form of sex education, a loving game, a way of preventing the daughter from engaging in sexual acts with other males, or a right since the daughter is seen as his property. These sexual acts are not seen as at all hurtful or harmful.
   c. *Symbiotic tyrants* are characterized by having control issues and feeling entitled to complete obedience from family members. The father tyrant has difficulties when the daughter begins to date (he believes his daughter having boyfriends is a form of betrayal toward him). He may physically abuse the males in the family.
   d. *Alcoholic incestors* are characterized by using alcohol as a means to lower inhibitions about having sex with their daughters. Later, when sober, the alcohol provides a reason for the incestuous acts. Often the mother has emotionally if not physically abandoned her husband and as a result the daughter assumes the mother's role. The alcoholic perpetrator engages in a cyclical pattern of drinking alcohol, molesting the daughter, feeling guilty, and then drinking more to "numb" the guilt feelings. Frequently the alcoholic perpetrator is dually

addicted to something besides the alcohol, for example, compulsive gambling (Carnes, 1983).

2. *Psychopathic-sociopathic fathers* are characterized by using sex with the daughter as a "thrill-seeking" type of behavior. These fathers are unable to love or form lasting relationships with anyone. Sex is never a way to "get close" to the daughter, it is only used for physical stimulation and physical release.

3. *Pedophilic incestuous fathers* are characterized by a sexual attraction to a prepubescent daughter. This offender loses interest once the daughter reaches puberty and may begin to sexually abuse other younger females in the family. These incestors are immature in thought and actions.

4. Other types include the *psychotic* or *culturally-permissive* fathers. The culturally-permissive father was reared in a family in which sexualized behaviors with children were normalized and encouraged.

Justice and Justice (1979) stated some overlap may be present between the categories and a father may fit into more than one of the groups described.

Meiselman (1978) had two other categories of incestuous offenders—*mental defectives* and *situational abusers*. Mental defectives are those men who have borderline intelligence, may be retarded, and have poor impulse control. Situational incest is a one-time incestuous act or incest that occurs for a short period of time and is a result of a life stressor that causes a crisis in the incestuous offender's life.

Williams and Finkelhor (1990) studied 118 incestuous fathers. Their sample population was composed of males in the Navy ($N = 55$) and civilians receiving treatment for incest ($N = 63$). A matched control group of nonincestuous fathers was utilized. Every male participant was interviewed for a minimum of 6 hours. The research team identified five types of fathers who are perpetrators.

Type 1—Sexually Preoccupied.   Twenty-six percent ($N = 29$) of the fathers fit the profile for this typology. These males were obsessed with sexual thoughts about their daughters. This category was further subdivided into early sexualizers in which the female child had been objectified since her birth. Often these males themselves had a childhood history of sexual abuse.

Type 2—Adolescent Regressives.   Thirty-three percent of the fathers in the study began to sexually abuse their daughters when the females entered puberty. Sometimes the fathers in this group would fantasize for years before the abuse began.

Type 3—Instrumental Self-gratifiers.   Twenty percent of the participants belonged to this category. These men fantasized about someone else while sexually abusing the child. These men expressed concern about their actions and experienced guilt feelings.

Type 4—Emotionally Dependent.   This type of offender comprised 10% of the males in the study. These fathers could be described as needy, lonely, and depressed.

Type 5—Angry Retaliators.   Ten percent of the fathers belonged in this group. Most of these men had criminal records for assault and rape. The sexual abuse of the daughter was frequently a retaliatory move against the mother.

Seventy percent of the males in these 5 different groups had been sexually abused themselves as children, 44% had been physically abused by the mother, and 50% physically abused by the father.

Father–Son Intrafamilial Abuse

Much of the emphasis in the research literature has been on females who were molested as children by adult males. Justice and Justice (1979) reported on 110 children who were survivors of incest; 103 were parent–child, 5 father–son and 2 mother-son cases. With regards to the father–son incest the authors stated, ". . . father–son incest is rarely reported, perhaps because it violates two moral codes: the one against incest and the one that has previously existed against homosexuality" (p. 196). Orr and Prietto (1979) found 12 of the 14 male individuals in their study had been sexually abused by their fathers. Kempe and Kempe (1984) reported that "incest between father and son is not rare" (p. 73). Bolton, Morris, and MacEachron (1989) concur with this. They stated,

> In one sense, the reluctance to report frequently found in the male victim creates a "self-victimization" in which others minimize the impact the event may have recorded upon the child. The male victim, when faced with an inescapable need to disclose the event, may overtly minimize the impact himself. Fearing allegations of homosexuality or working from male socialization messages demanding "macho," this young male reports, "I'm fine." (pp. 42–43)

Male children are culturally indoctrinated at a young age to be "strong," not to cry or express feelings that could in any way be misconstrued as tenderness. They are told they can and should be able to look after themselves.

It appears from the cases and literature presented that male children and adolescents are indeed sexually abused, although the males may have increased difficulties in admitting that sexual transgressions occurred against them.

Effects of Intrafamilial Abuse

There are those minimization theorists who claim the negative effects of child sexual abuse are overestimated. Herman (1981) called these investigators "pro-incest" (Bender & Blau, 1937; Kinsey, Pomeroy, Martin, & Gebhard, 1953; Lukianowicz, 1972; Sloane & Karpinski, 1942). Conte (1985) has contended there is a "political" stance to the supposition of few ill-lasting effects of sexual abuse on children. He contended, " . . . there often appears to be an unspoken assumption that if sexual abuse turns out rfot to produce significant long-term trauma then there is nothing wrong with it" (p. 117). Kempe and Kempe (1984) stated,

> Boys do worse than girls as victims of sexual abuse. Both mother–son and father–son incest leave a boy with such severe emotional insult that emotional growth is often blocked. Some of the boys tend to be severely restricted and may be unable to handle stress without becoming psychotic, while others may have symptoms but never be recognized as incest victims. Incest, then, can be ruinous for the male. . . . (p. 190)

Mothers as Intrafamilial Abusers

Reports of female sexual abusers, even mothers as sexual abusers, are becoming more frequent. Hopefully this is beginning to dispute the myth that females, especially mothers, do not sexually abuse children. New research has begun to suggest that mothers may be singular molesters or that they may molest in conjunction with fathers or with other males (Borden & LaTerz, 1991, 1993; Faller, 1988; Matthews, Matthews, & Speltz, 1989; McCarty, 1986). An accurate percentage of mothers who abuse their children is unknown at this time. McCarty (1986) reported 4% ($N = 26$) of the participants in the Dallas Incest Program as being female intrafamilial abusers. Kendall-Tackett and Simon's (1987) retrospective study of adults identified 3% of their study participants (total $N = 365$) as being sexually abused by females. The American Humane Association study (1981) identified 6% of females were molested by women and 14% of the males had been sexually abused by females. Faller's (1987) study found 13.8% ($N = 40$) of her study population ($N = 289$) of perpetrators were female. Finkelhor, Williams, Burns, and Kalinowski (1988), in a three-year study of sexual abuse in day-care centers across the country determined that of the abusers reported, 40% of the perpetrators were female. This may appear to be an inflated figure, but only 5% of the day-care employees were males.

Alice Miller (1990) had this to say about mothers who are perpetrators:

> Mothers also abuse their children. Only the truth, even the most uncomfortable, endows a movement with the strength to change society, not the denial of truth. . . . Hence young children, male as well as female, can become victims of adults of either sex. . . . Psychoanalysts protect the father and embroider the sexual abuse of the child with the Oedipus, or Electra, complex, while some feminist therapists idealize the mother, thus hindering access to the child's first traumatic experiences with the mother. Both approaches can lead to a dead end, since the dissolving of pain and fear is not possible, until the full truth or the facts can be seen and accepted. (pp. 78–79)

In continuance, Welldon (1988) had this to say about mothers as perpetrators, "Are we blocked from perceiving this by our own idealization of motherhood? Surely we are, and this is why even in the original Oedipal situation we fail to notice Jocasta's responsibility. Hers is the most important case of incest" (p. 85).

Lastly, Borden and LaTerz (1993) had this to say about mother–daughter incest: "Not only may the incidence be higher, but the aftereffects may be stronger. Many maternal incest survivors report an added feeling of shame about their abuse. They describe feeling an added stigma and isolation because others perceive their abuse to be out of the ordinary" (p. 6).

Earlier research suggested that female perpetrators are severely psychologically disturbed or are psychotic. Groth (1982) disputed the theory of the "severely mentally ill" incestuous mother. He has suggested that certain females who did not fit the criteria of "severely mentally ill" were still quite capable of being sexual abusers of children.

A study published 4 years later by McCarty (1986) reviewed 26 case records of mothers who were perpetrators. She classified the female molesters into three different categories: independent, co-offender, and accomplice. Independent offenders themselves had been sexually abused in over 75% of the cases, most often by a brother. All of the women in this group were of average intelligence, over 65% had a steady job, over 80% married as a teenager, but over 65% were single at the time of the study. Over 45% used and abused drugs and at least one-half of the women had serious emotional problems. Sixty percent of these women sexually abused a daughter. Co-offenders had been sexually abused in every case, most often by an adult. Almost 60% of the women were less than average intelligence, and almost 80% were homemakers. Every woman in this group married as an adolescent and almost one-half (44%) were in their second or third (44%) marriage. Women in this co-offender group most often abused a son.

Accomplice is the third group of identified offenders in McCarty's study. All of the women in this group had a job, over 75% had average intellectual abilities, 60% married as an adolescent, and 75% of the mothers abused a daughter.

Sexual abuse with the mother as the perpetrator may be even more difficult for an individual survivor to share because of the additional stigma attached to this type of abuse (Borden & LaTerz, 1993). Until quite recently the sexually abusive mother in the research literature had been described as very emotionally disturbed, psychotic, or sociopathic. As is evident from the studies just discussed, all female perpetrators are not psychotic. However, the sociopathic, psychotic mother may be quite violent and sadistic in her sexual abuse.

Many of the females who have been identified as perpetrators are extremely demanding and dependent. A dependent mother who is a perpetrator often sees the female child as a continuance of herself. Courtois (1988) says, "The sexual activity is best described as highly intrusive, narcissistic, and almost masturbatory in nature" (p. 67).

Mother–Son Intrafamilial Abuse

Literature references regarding mother–child incest have been scant (Mathis, 1972; Wahl, 1960). Banning (1989) has stated, "until recently mother–child incest was considered to be virtually nonexistent" (p. 563). Krug (1989) suggested the following as a way of explaining why males rarely report sexual abuse by their mothers: (1) men cannot become impregnated; (2) mothers are viewed as "all good"; (3) males have been too ashamed to disclose anything regarding maternal incest; (4) the myth has been perpetrated in society that males are not affected by molestations from females; (5) both clients and professionals have been oblivious to the correlation between mother–son incest and adult male interpersonal relationship difficulties. Often when sex occurs between a mother and a son, the male may view himself as being responsible. Nasjleti (1980) responded to this notion by having written, "Boys often fear that having sex with the mother is indicative of their having a mental illness. Because mothers are viewed as nonsexual beings in this culture, incapable of sexually abusing their own child, boys molested by their mothers often assume responsibility for their own molestation" (p. 269).

Lawson (1991) cited a common cultural myth that mothers are seen as "asexual" beings and men as always being the sexually dominant and aggressive partner. Thus maternal incest is seen as a form of affection rather than molestation with the male child. Male survivors of maternal incest might not even view the sexual molestation as abusive if force and violence were not used.

A few cases have been reported in the literature on maternal incest that included masturbation or genital fondling of the son (Chasnoff, Burns, Schnoll, Burns, Chisum, & Kyle Spore, 1986; Margolin & Craft, 1989; Wahl, 1960). Other researchers have presented seductive actions on the part of the mother toward the son as a form of exhibitionism and other forms of noncontact abuse (Krug, 1989).

Bolton, Morris, and MacEachron (1989) described the different categories of mother–son sexual abuse. Their "abuse of sexuality model" included homes that were (1) sexually free to a detrimental degree, (2) negatively as well as covertly seductive, and (3) an openly sexual environment. Lawson has characterized these types of mother–son incest as being "subtle, seductive, or overt." What follows are case examples of each type.

Case 1.   The first case is an example of what Bolton, Morris, and Mac Eachron (1989) would label sexually free to a detrimental degree, and Lawson would term "subtle."

> A 33-year-old woman, Mrs. A, called for an appointment and stated she was very depressed and unhappy in her relationship with her husband. She discussed her husband's jealousy regarding her relationship with their sons, ages 11, 12, and 14. She said her husband complained all the time about her helping the boys bathe, preparing their favorite treats if they rubbed her back and legs, and generally ignoring his needs. She described her husband as very rough in his treatment of her and felt isolated and alone most of the time. Her only source of pleasure she described was her interactions with her sons.

Case 2.   Bolton would identify this next example as negative as well as covertly seductive abuse and Lawson would identify it as seductive abuse.

> Child Protective Services became involved with T. (an 11-year-old male) and his family after coming to school with severe bruises on his neck. The teacher referred him to the school counselor. T. revealed that his father would drink and then hit T., his brother, and his mother. Investigation revealed T's mother to be afraid of the father and she sought comfort in her two sons. She would often bathe and use the bathroom with the door open (always when T's father was not home). T. and his 10-year-old brother were always home and close by when she would undress for her bath. If she observed them looking in the bathroom she would cover herself with a towel but did not make any efforts to close the bathroom door. In the summertime, T. stated his mother would go topless when sunbathing in the backyard. He and his brother had to kiss their mother on the mouth every night before they went to bed (although there was never any genital contact). T.'s mother was quite interested in their physical development, especially as T. was approaching puberty. At least once a month, sometimes more often, she would ask him to let her examine him in his underwear, just to make certain "everything was as it should be." T. and his brother described feelings of confusion, anger, and sometimes excitement about his mother's behavior.

Case 3.   A case example of an openly sexual environment (Bolton, Morris, & MacEachron, 1989) or a situation Lawson (1991) would identify as "overtly" incestuous.

> Bill, a 40-year-old male, was referred as a result of his recent arrest for DUI. He was married for the third time and had three children, one child with each of his wives. He had a history of extramarital affairs with women throughout his marriages. His parents were married and had been for nearly fifty years at the interview but he described his father as having had many other sexual relationships outside the marriage. Bill described his mother as controlling and clinging. At age five Bill contracted pneumonia and following that time had to sleep in the same bed with his mother until he was 16. Both parents were alcoholic, and when Bill reached puberty his mother seduced him repeatedly until he left home at 22. Her sexual abuse continued throughout his college days, as he lived at home and commuted to school. Bill has had no contact with his parents since he was 25 years of age.

Factors Placing Females at Risk to Become Abusers

Four factors have been identified which seem to increase the likelihood sexual offenses being committed by females (Courtois, 1988; Groth, 1982; Lawson, 1991):

1. *Absent fathers*—This can include fathers who are physically not present or the father may live at home but because of work or addictions is away from the house much of the time.
2. *Mother is socially isolated*—She may have few to no friends and feels very lonely.
3. *Mother has a history of substance abuse*—Two of the eight mothers in Krug's study (1989) were alcoholic; one of the two mothers in Wahl's (1960) study was an addict; five of fifteen mother's in Margolin's (1987) study were addicted to substances; and all three mothers in Chasnoff, Burns, Schnoll, Burns, Chisum, & Kyle-Spore's (1986) study were addicts.
4. *Mother has a history of childhood sexual abuse*—McCarty (1986) reported 17 of the 26 female perpetrators in her study had been sexually abused as children. Faller (1987) reported that 19 women or 47.5% of her participants had a history of sexual abuse in their childhoods.

Lawson (1991) suggested the following may be helpful for the clinician in recognizing that maternal molestation may be occurring. Clinicians need to gather information about the following from mother of child:

- intergenerational information regarding sexual or physical abuse or neglect
- intergenerational history of alcohol or drug use or abuse
- marital quality
- degree of sexual satisfaction in the parental marital relationship
- degree of mother's social isolation
- current use or abuse of alcohol or drugs
- how affection is physically expressed within the family
- mother's involvement in bedtime, bathroom, and bathing rituals
- family sleeping arrangements
- history of sexual experiencess
- how sexuality was expressed within family of origin
- child's confusion or discomfort with mother's expression of affection (pp. 491–492)

uld add to these questions some others regarding early
He also urged clinicians to inquire about enema ex-

evaluations I've discovered a number of patients who
..e early experience of enema as having been forceful, ag-
.ssive, intrusive and in violation of their boundaries. Often these
same patients also report other types of abuse during childhood after
their earliest enema abuse experiences. . . . I urge all mental health
professionals to inquire about enema experiences as a part of routine
history taking and data gathering during evaluation . . . enema abuse
appears to have similar consequences on emotional, social, and the
cognitive development and adult functioning as child sexual abuse.
As clinicians, we cannot afford to overlook, neglect, or deny enema
abuse as a potential primary source of early childhood trauma with
resulting long term negative consequences. (p. 13)

Male Versus Female Offenders

A number of different reasons appear to explain why females have a much
lower rate of abusing children than do males. Banning (1989) stated,

The incidence of female sexual offenders will probably remain much
lower than that of males. However it is highly likely that we have
underestimated the true incidence due to our disbelief that this can
occur. In Freud's time father–daughter incest could not be accepted.
Child physical abuse was not recognized or acknowledged until the
1960s and child sexual abuse in the mid 1970s. Not until the 1980s
were male victims recognized and studied and their victimization
found to be more frequent than previously recognized. Mother–son
and mother–daughter incest could well be not as unusual as we had
thought or hoped. (p. 569)

Russell (1984b) proposed a variety of reasons for the much larger number
of male molesters than female molesters. She stated,

Women are socialized to prefer partners who are older, larger, and
more powerful than themselves; men are socialized to prefer partners who are younger, smaller, innocent, vulnerable and powerless
. . . men are not only expected to take the initiative, but also to
overcome resistance . . . men appear to be more promiscuous than
women . . . men seem able to be aroused more easily by sexual
stimuli divorced from any relationship context. . . . Women, on the
other hand, rely more on a totality of cues, including the nature of

the relationship with the sexual partner. . . . Men appear to sexualize the expression of emotions more than women do . . . having sexual opportunities seems more important to the maintenance of self-esteem in men. . . . Men interact less frequently with young children so do not develop the kind of protective bonding that would make themselves sensitive to the harm of sexual contact, women's social role includes maternal responsibilities . . . sexual contact with children may be more condoned by the male subculture. (pp. 229–230)

Lastly, the readers should be cautioned against attempting to fit female sexual offenders into the same categorical groups as male offenders. To gain a better understanding of gender and female development, readers are encouraged to read the works of Belenky, Clinchy, Goldberger, and Tarule (1986), Gilligan (1982), Gilligan, Ward, and Taylor (1988), and Kaschak (1992).

SIBLING INCEST

Unfortunately fathers and mothers are not the only perpetrators in intrafamilial abuse. Brother–sister incest has been grossly underreported in the literature. However, as early as 1965, Gebhard, Gagnon, Pomeroy, and Christenson reported sibling abuse to be five times higher than father–daughter incest. Other researchers have substantiated the fact that sibling abuse is more common than father–daughter incest (deYoung, 1982; Finkelhor, 1979; Loredo, 1982). Russell (1983) found that 16% of her study population reported sexual abuse by a sibling. Finkelhor (1980) found in his study of 796 college students that 15% of the females and 10% of the males reported sexual activity with a sibling. Much of the research has been concentrated on either father–daughter incest or on incest between relatives such as older males victimizing younger females (Browning & Boatman, 1977; Cole, 1982; Finkelhor, 1980; Herman, 1981; Herman & Hirschman, 1977, 1981; Loredo, 1982; MacFarlane & Korbin, 1983; Meiselman, 1978; Russell, 1986; Smith & Israel, 1987).

Sibling incest connotes any type of sexual behavior that occurs between brother and sister, brother and brother, or sister and sister and is of a more inclusive nature than is generally included in normal child sexual exploration. Research studies on sibling incest are sadly lacking, which may be true for two reasons according to Cole (1982): (1) parents who discover their children engaging in sexual acts are usually not inclined to call child protective services, and (2) sibling incest has a myth surrounding it that labels it benign with no aftereffects.

Loredo (1982) discussed a variety of reasons for the occurrence of sibling incest. She contended it could be sexual experimentation that has progressed too far. Second, the incest could be a result of family dysfunctions, ill-defined and poor boundaries within the family, or parents can actually promote the sexual relations between siblings.

Sibling Incest Studies

Wiehe (1990) studied three kinds of sibling abuse—physical, emotional, and sexual—among adult survivors. For our purposes only the sexual abuse will be discussed. One hundred participants (67%) of the study population reported being sexually abused by a sibling. Wiehe included a discussion of how the adult survivors responded to the abuse. Some female survivors reported pretending to be asleep when the sibling approached her, while others reported that at the time they were too young to comprehend what was occurring. Some kept the abuse a secret because of threats, and none of the survivors reported fighting back against the abuser because none believed she had the power to do so.

Frequently survivors did not tell parents about the sexual abuse because the sibling abusers were baby-sitting the survivors and the child had been told (by the parents) to obey the perpetrator; the survivor had been threatened; he or she did not tell because of self-blame and guilt; or the parents were not receptive to hearing what the survivor attempted to communicate.

Parental responses in the studies were varied. Rarely did the parents in the study put a stop to the abuse. Sometimes the parents would placate the abused child by saying, "Boys will be boys," or "He'll outgrow it," or "He needs to get it out of his system." Frequently victimized children are blamed and then revictimized by the parents failure to intervene to protect them (Laviola, 1992; O'Brien, 1991; Wiehe, 1990). Parents would sometimes respond by physically abusing the abuser. This seemed to be predicated on the notion that if the sibling abuser knew what it felt like to be hurt then he would stop engaging in that behavior, an "eye for an eye" kind of thinking. Sometimes the parents would not believe the abused (Laviola, 1992; Loredo, 1982; O'Brien, 1991; Wiehe, 1990).

Wiehe (1990) proposed four reasons for sibling abuse occurring. First, inappropriate expectations were held by the parents that older siblings should be able to take care of younger children. In reality the older child may be old enough chronologically but not mature enough emotionally to act as a surrogate parent in a baby-sitting situation. Second, parents may be so caught up in their own problems that they are unable to effectively parent their children. Third, parents may not know how to put an end to the abuse and as a result of their ineffective parenting the abuse persists. Fourth, parents may believe the behavior is "normal."

O'Brien (1991) studied 170 adolescent male sex offenders who ranged in age between 12 and 19 years. Fifty adolescents met the criteria for sibling abuser. Almost 45% of the sibling offenders victimized a sibling for more than a year. Forty-six percent of the sibling offenders engaged in contact and intrusive sexual abuse such as sexual intercourse or sodomy. At least 53% of the adolescent offenders had sexually abused more than one sibling and 76% of the sibling offenders sexually abused a brother or sister less than 9 years of age. Sixty-one percent of the male sibling abusers reported their families as being physically abusive toward them. The sibling perpetrators reported 36% of their mothers and 10% of their fathers had been sexually victimized as children. Forty-two percent of the sibling perpetrators admitted to being victimized themselves. Sixty-eight percent of the adolescents who had been sexually abused by males chose boys to molest and only 7% of the sibling abusers who themselves were abused by females chose boys to victimize. Thus it seems there is some support for the notion that male adolescent perpetrators who were abused by a male will be more inclined to select male children to victimize.

Sarrel and Masters (1982) presented the following as a case example of sibling abuse:

> When he was between 10 and 12 years of age, this boy was repeatedly abused by his sister, who was 4 years older. She stimulated him manually and orally and then inserted his penis into her vagina. At first he only felt frightened and did not understand what was happening. She usually threatened to beat him or attack him with a knife if he told anyone. He does not recall if he ejaculated. He was too frightened to tell his parents. When he was 12, his sister was admitted to a psychiatric hospital. Subsequently, he became suicidal and was hospitalized for psychiatric treatment. (pp. 124–125)

Smith and Israel (1987) studied 25 cases of sibling incest. The oldest abuser was 20, the youngest was 9 years of age, the oldest victim was 13, the youngest was 3 years of age. Twenty percent of the abusers were females, 80% were males, 85% of the victims were females, and 11% were male. Seventy-two percent of the sexual abuse involved fondling or oral or genital contact; 28% of the abuse was sexual intercourse. Seventy-six percent of the abusers were from two-parent families (56% were stepfamilies) and 24% had only one parent in the household.

Smith and Israel (1987) found three factors specific to the families in which sibling incest occurred. Parents were distant and unavailable, both emotionally and physically; 88% of the fathers and 75% of the mothers fit this category. Second, the home environment was sexually stimulating. Forty-eight percent of the sibling perpetrators witnessed some form of sexual contact between parents or a parent and someone else. Fifty-two percent of the sibling perpetrators had been sexually abused and 32% of the sibling perpetrators had abused the same female member of the family that had been victimized by the father. Forty percent of the sibling perpetrators' mothers were labeled as "seductive" and 35% were rigid, authoritarian and described as sexually repressed. Third, over three quarters (76%) of the parents were engaged in extramarital affairs. Additionally, 72% of the parents in this study had been sexually abused as children.

Much controversy seems to focus on the existence of long-term negative effects on a sister victimized by an older brother. Certain writers speculate older brother–younger sister incest is a result of unresolved Oedipal issues in both the brother and the sister and suggest there is little damage to either sibling, especially if both are of close proximity in age and less than 18 years of age (Arndt & Ladd, 1981; Lukianowicz, 1972). Russell (1986) and Finkelhor (1980) theorized that sibling incest is detrimental if the brother is at least 5 years older than the sister. Some research suggests that harm is done even if the brother is the same age or older because of the nature of the patriarchal system in which the incest occurs (Brickman, 1984; Cole, 1982; Laviola, 1992; Wiehe, 1990).

Evidence is available to suggest that negative consequences do result from older brother–younger sister incest. Research on adult women who were molested by an older brother have reported the following issues: lowered sexual self-esteem (Finkelhor, 1980; Laviola, 1992; Wiehe, 1990), fear of being raped (Cole, 1982; Meiselman, 1978; Russell, 1986), depression and guilt surrounding sexual activity (Cole, 1982; Loredo, 1982; Wiehe, 1990), revictimization experiences (Cole, 1982; deYoung, 1982; Meiselman, 1978; Wiehe, 1990), suicide attempts, and substance abuse (Cole, 1982; Wiehe, 1990).

Prevention of Sibling Abuse

Although limited in scope, the study done by Wiehe (1990) does provide some prevention information that may be helpful in stopping this type of abuse from occurring or continuing. Wiehe (1990) asked his study participants to indicate what would be helpful in preventing sibling abuse. Almost all of the participants suggested that society and professionals need to be cognizant of the fact that sibling abuse occurs and that it is not harmless sex play. The participants suggested parents and others in the child's life should believe what the child is stating. Children should not be asked to keep secrets even if he or she has been threatened by the abuser. The parents then need to follow through on protecting the child once the abuse is revealed. Parents need to maintain adequate supervision for children in the family when they are away from home. Wiehe's study found that sibling abuse occurred most often when the parents were not at home and the perpetrator was baby-sitting the child. Parents need to discuss appropriate sexual matters with children based on the child's age and maturity level. Rules need to be established and maintained about the bathroom and body ownership. Violence-proof the home; be aware of the violence on the television and in the movies and set limits or do not permit children in the family to watch violent movies or television shows. Parents need to be aware of how children treat each other and notice and respond positively to healthy interchanges between siblings, for example, "Tom, I noticed how you played with Susie today and asked one another for your video games instead of just grabbing what you wanted." It is the parent's responsibility to protect the child.

Clinicians might want to reevaluate the importance that the impact of this type of sexual abuse may have on women, men, and children in treatment. Definitely the sibling incest needs to be explored and addressed, the impact of the abuse explored and then it needs to be determined if presenting issues, problematic behaviors, and past or current conflicts are affected by an incestuous brother–sister, sister–brother, sister–sister, or brother–brother relationship in childhood, adolescence, or even adulthood (Laviola, 1992). Clinicians should be careful to explore current relationships between siblings even if all family members are adults. In addition, the survivor's conceptualizations about the incest need to be taken into consideration. Adult male and female survivors of sibling incest need to consider how this places their own children at risk to be victimized. In other words, the survivor should not leave his or her own children alone with the brother (uncle) or sister (aunt) who sexually abused him or her. There is no reason to believe that a brother or sister who sexually abused a sibling in childhood would not continue the abuse cycle and abuse his or her nieces or nephews. Sexual offending is not a behavior an individual outgrows.

GRANDPARENTS AS PERPETRATORS

Grandparents who sexually abuse grandchildren or someone else's children do exist. A small segment of the grandparent population has been identified as being sexually abusive (Kendall-Tackett and Simon, 1987, $N = 4/224$; Kercher

& McShane, 1984, $N = 11/515$; Russell, 1986, $N = 11/190$). A number of other researchers have at least documented the occurrences of this phenomenon, but in extremely small numbers (Barry & Johnson, 1958; Bass & Thornton, 1982; Cupoli & Sewell, 1988; deYoung, 1982; Justice & Justice, 1979; Lukianowicz, 1972; Meiselman, 1978). According to Margolin (1992), grandfathers appear to be an overrepresented intrafamilial group, with only three grandmothers involved as perpetrators in the following studies (Barry & Johnson, 1958; Bass & Thornton, 1983; Cupoli & Sewell, 1988). Almost exclusively, female children were victimized in all of these studies.

Margolin (1992) reported on 95 children sexually abused by 76 grandparents. Seventeen of the grandparents molested more than one child, and 27 of the abusers were stepgrandparents. Margolin's (1992) findings are similar to those in Russell's (1986) study, where over 25% of the reported grandparent perpetrators in the study were stepgrandparents and 27% of the grandparents in the Kercher and McShane (1984) study were stepgrandparents. Based on available data there appears to be an overrepresentation of stepgrandparents as perpetrators.

Margolin's (1992) study was based on reports of child protective service workers. Twelve of the 95 children were less than 6 years of age when the abuse was brought to the attention of the authorities. Eighty-four of the child victims were female and 11 were male. Seventy-five of the perpetrators were male and 1 was female. Forms of abuse ranged from fondling (45%), fondling and penetration using the fingers (31%), being forced to touch the grandfather's genitals (16%), and intercourse (12%). Seventy percent of the children were molested 3 or more times by the same grandparents and at least 35% of the children were victimized for more than a year. Margolin presented some interesting data with regards to intergenerational abuse. Twenty-six of the grandparents who molested a total of 35 grandchildren also had molested their own daughters. This is not surprising since sexual victimization is frequently an intergenerational phenomenon. In at least 19 instances the mothers or grandmothers were aware the child was being victimized but made no attempts to protect the child. Other researchers have reported on intergenerational abuse occurring (deYoung, 1982; Meiselman, 1978). Margolin (1992) posited an explanation for this intergenerational phenomenon: "Individuals from families with a history of intergenerational abuse may either feel inured to these violations or feel there is little likelihood of successful intervention" (p. 740). In other words the survivors feel powerless to protect their own children. Some researchers have suggested sexual offenses perpetrated by grandparents as being less harmful and less violent than offenses committed by other adults (deYoung, 1982; Meiselman, 1978; Russell, 1986). Margolin (1992) reported the exact opposite finding in her study; 14 of the children reported being physically overpowered or threatened. Children were often victimized while sleeping. This disputes the myth that grandparents are more gentle in their victimizing acts. Most of the grandchildren who were sexually abused did not live or reside for long periods with their grandparents but were victimized during overnight sleep-overs at the grandparents. Margolin's (1992) findings suggest that a child is at increased risk for sexual victimization if the child is a female and the grandparent is male, if the grandparent has sexually abused his own daughter (the child's mother), and if the grandparent is a stepgrandparent. One of the major problems with the Margolin study is that the sexual abuse was substantiated from case records of child protection workers whose records present a biased sample population.

Mitchell (1992) has data that suggests that grandmothers as perpetrators of sexual abuse have been grossly underreported in the abuse literature, especially with regards to intergenerational abuse. All of the adult participants in Mitchell's study were abused in childhood by females, and many of the females were sexually abused by both the mother and the maternal grandmother. In her study not a single case was ever reported to the authorities.

Realizing that grandparents can be sexual abusers reinforces the need for the clinician to take as complete and extensive a family history as is possible from an adult in treatment or the parent of a child in treatment. An emphasis needs to be placed on family secrets by asking questions such as the following:

"What happened in your family while you were growing up that no one talked about?" or

"What would be some things everyone knew about in the family but no one discussed?" or

"What would be some things no one knew about in the family but you and perhaps one or two other persons?" or

"If you could have told one trusted adult something about your family when you were a child what would it have been?"

ADOLESCENT OFFENDERS

Adolescent offenders represent a special population for treatment centers, since frequently they are both a sexual abuse survivor and a sexual offender. The majority of sex offenders develop deviant sexual interests during adolescence, before the age of eighteen (Abel & Rouleau, 1990). Appropriate treatment of this particular offending group may be critical to breaking the cycle of molestation

(Longo & Groth, 1983; Stenson & Anderson, 1987). Negating and discounting adolescents sexually offending or sexually abusive behaviors has been a standard behavioral response by parents and professionals until just recently (Herman, 1990; Ryan, Metzner, & Krugman, 1990). Herman (1990) has suggested not ignoring adolescent's sexually acting out behaviors, not labeling it as experimental, and recognizing that sex offenders have little internal inducement to stop engaging in the offending behaviors. Therapeutic interventions need to center on the objectionable sexually offending behaviors. This includes treatment provider's knowledge of the abuser's sexual fantasies; who, what, where, when, and how the victims are procured; and repeatedly confronting the offender's cognitive distortions. Parents and professionals not intervening during the years when the sexual molesting is still in its infancy frequently seems to result in lifelong patterns of sexual offending for the adolescent perpetrator. Ryan et al. (1990) contended that adolescent sexual offenders have not been held "accountable" for their abusive actions. Rape by adolescents is viewed as a variation of the cultural maxim, "boys will be boys," and engaging in sexually abusive behaviors is often dismissed as the male adolescent's way of learning about sex. Frequently these behaviors are identified in the professional communities as "adolescent adjustment reactions," with the end result being that adolescent offenders do not get the necessary treatment at a point in their lives when it could be most beneficial. Intervention with adolescent sexual offenders seems to be critical if the cycle of sexual abuse is to be eliminated (Bengis, 1986; Perry & Orchard, 1989).

Groth and Loredo (1981) proposed a variety of reasons to suggest why the needs of the adolescent offender have been basically ignored. These authors stated:

> The first step in addressing the juvenile sex offender is recognizing that the problem exists and that the youngster himself is struggling with this problem in silence because it appears it is too uncomfortable for others to listen to and respond to. Instead, his behavior is minimized or dismissed on the supposition that whether it is not serious, or, if it is, it will with time spontaneously self-correct. Unless intervention is forthcoming the juvenile is in fact being professionally neglected or abandoned with the result that not only will there be more victims, but ultimately, when he reaches adulthood and faces the serious legal consequences of his behavior, rehabilitation my no longer be possible. (p. 39)

Cycles of Abuse in Adolescent Offenders

Sexual abuse cycle is a term created by Lane and Zamora (1984). This concept evolved as a result of the treatment providers identifying certain cognitive patterns and feelings of satisfaction among adolescent perpetrators. There appeared to be a commonality among offenders in their conduct or abusive actions, the process involved in choosing victims, and then enforcing the victim's participation in the molesting. Additionally there seemed to be a distinguishable antecedent process for most of the adolescents studied.

Development and refinement of the sexual abuse cycle model presented here is based on Issac, Lane, and Davis' clinical work with 2500 offenders (Lane, 1991). The word "process" best characterizes the sexual abuse cycle. Lane (1991) stated: "It is presented as a cycle due to the repetitive nature of the behavior sequence reported by many youths and the indication that previous offense incidents parallel and reinforce subsequent offense patterns." (p. 104)

A number of different components have been suggested to be a part of sexual molesting behaviors (Lane, 1991). Most molesters do not sexually abuse others on an impulse, but engage in molesting behavior after some thoughts or fantasies have occurred. Second, molesting is a vehicle for maintaining power over others, in addition to reducing escalating negative feelings of anxiety. Offending behavior enables adolescents to obtain mastery over their environment and some of the individuals in their world. Lane (1991) stated, "A power-based response does not resolve a situation, instead it retaliates against a situation. Power/control responses do not involve developing self-control or improve an individual's interpersonal coping skills" (p. 108) The author contended that certain erroneous cognitions underpin the offender's thoughts about their own proficiencies and capabilities. Some of these cognitive distortions include: engaging in prohibited, illegal acts and not getting caught is symbolic of competency in the world; and it is acceptable to coerce, control, and dominate others, especially when it results in proving one's abilities. These are just two of the many distortions that prevail in the minds of adolescent offenders. Ryan, Metzner, and Krugman (1990) discussed Berenson's (1982) report on the cognitive distortions of adolescent sexual offenders. These distortions are a result of erroneous suppositions, deductions, and judgments about the environment. Irrational thoughts mold the offender's demand for power and mastery, reinforce the advancement of the sexual abuse cycle, and vindicate offending behaviors. Cognitive distortions identified by Berenson (1982) are the "I'm unable to help myself" philosophy; inability to empathize with others; unwillingness to try; unwillingness to accept responsibility; poor ability in making appropriate decisions; inability to make future projections; fear of being humiliated; being power-oriented; demonstrating an unwillingness to show apprehensions; utilization of anger to dominate and manipulate people; distorted view of accomplishments and errors; ignorance about causing physical or psychological harm to others;

illogical expectations of self and others; unwillingness to compromise; lack of knowledge about loyalty; and belief in possession and infringement on others. Lane stated, "A power-based response style arises from these patterns of thinking, and sexually abusive behaviors are justified by these inaccurate beliefs" (p. 114). A number of other researchers have concluded that these type of thinking errors perpetuate the sexual molesting behaviors (Abel & Blanchard, 1974; Becker, Kaplan, Tenke, & Tartaglini, 1991; Ryan et al., 1990).

According to Lane (1991), the sexual abuse cycle has three phases: precipitating, compensatory response, and integrative. Precipitating phases include occurrences or happenings that result in the offender feeling victimized, expecting negative outcomes, and developing evasive behaviors (avoiding thoughts about the offending or staying away from the potential victim) in an attempt to deal with the trigger event. During the compensatory response phase the adolescent tries to augment his or her feelings of self-worth and lessen anxiety through sexual fantasies, which may be aggressive in nature. During the integrative phase the offender attempts to justify his or her actions so as to be able to continue feelings of entitlement and control: choosing to objectify the victim, determining the likelihood of accomplishing the victimization, manipulating or taking advantage of an occasion (to molest), reworking the plan, and deciding to proceed with the molestation.

Sexual abuse is believed to be compensatory in that feeling powerful and in control reduces anxiety. Adolescent molesters have recounted sustaining feelings of animation, intoxication, and exuberance during the antecedent phase and while the abusive incident is occurring. Events which trigger the offender's need to feel in control are any or all of the following (according to Lane, 1991): physical abuse, abasement, exclusion, or estrangement. One of the ways in which the offender then compensates for any of these negative feelings is by engaging in a behavior, such as molesting, which enables him or her to feel powerful and in control.

Adolescent offenders frequently become sexually aroused while thinking about the molesting and on reflection about the incident after it occurs. Couple this with the fact that becoming stimulated and achieving orgasm are physically and mentally gratifying and therefore become self-rewarding behaviors (Becker, Hunter, Stein, & Kaplan, 1989; Lane, 1991). A number of other researchers have reported the conditioning results of masturbation with sexual fantasies (Abel & Blanchard, 1974; McGuire, Carlisle, & Young, 1965; Lane, 1991). This conditioned behavior then becomes compensatory because it results in the lessening of the offender's anxiety and contributes, if only briefly, to his or her sense of well-being. Sexually offending then becomes a learned response to feeling anxious (Money, 1986, Lane, 1991). The more the pattern is repeated the more deeply ingrained the offending behavior becomes.

Adolescents admitted to attempting to stop their behaviors but were unable to do so. Lane (1991) discussed that it was not uncommon to find adolescents who rapidly developed a tolerance for their offending and fantasy behaviors. When this occurred, they had to continue to "up the ante" or offend more frequently to achieve the same feelings of power and control. This in turn results in adding additional rudiments of chance and danger (of getting caught) to the offender's behaviors or fantasies.

Classification of Adolescent Offenders

Bera (1989) has identified a classification system composed of 7 different types of male adolescent sex offenders. First is the *naive experimenter*. With this type of adolescent there is rarely a background of acting out behavior. He is sexually immature and inexperienced. Sexual experimentation may be quite limited and involve just one or a couple of sexual exploratory type activities with a child who is approximately 2 to 6 years younger in age.

The *undersocialized child exploiter* experiences exclusion from peers and is quite unskilled in social situations. Offending behaviors most often include control of the victim and bribes to keep the victims quiet about the abuse. Engaging in abusive behaviors provides temporary self-enhancement and a dysfunctional means to get closer to another person.

The *pseudo-socialized child exploiter* rarely has a background that includes asocial behaviors but is more likely to be a survivor of some type of long-term abuse. He experiences no contrition for his offending behaviors. The primary goal is to achieve sexual stimulation through abusing others.

The *sexual aggressive* offender's lifestyle is characterized by criminal or acting-out behaviors, alcohol or other drug abuse, and insignificant amounts of self-control. Offending provides him with feelings of power and a way to vent and displace his anger.

The *sexual compulsive* generally engages in compulsive, noncontact forms of abuse like voyeurism or exhibitionism. His abusive behaviors are primarily an attempt to deal with feelings of anxiety. This adolescent's family system is often characterized by poorly established boundaries between family members.

The *disturbed impulsive* is often psychologically impaired, abuses drugs or alcohol, is often learning disabled, and his family of origin is quite disturbed. His molesting is often spur of the moment or impromptu and he may also be delusional at times.

The *group-influenced* abuser engages in molesting with a group of his friends and may engage in sexually abusive behaviors because of peer pressure and to fit into his peer group.

Bera (1989) and O'Brien and Bera (1986) have created specific treatment plans for each one of the seven types of offenders. Perry and Orchard (1992) are quite supportive of this approach to treating adolescent offenders because these authors support the contention that adolescent offenders are a distinct population of offenders, and cannot be categorized or treated based on current treatment approaches utilized for adult offenders. Based on clinical experience Perry and Orchard (1992) believe that adolescent offenders do not fit appropriately into just one treatment group, but different types of offenders need different services. These authors wrote,

> Adolescent sex offenders are extremely poor predictors of their future sexual behaviors, and are poor managers in that sphere of their lives. Clinicians need to view the adolescent's sexually deviant behavior as a higher habitual sexual preference. They also need to realize that the offender without treatment is perpetually vulnerable to his deviant sexual preferences. He will fall prey to re-offense if he does not respect his vulnerability or if he ceases to manage his life in the ways necessary to prevent re-offense. Such a vulnerability model emphasizes that there is no cure, but rather a relative mastery of serious behavioral problems. (pp. 7–8)

Statistics on Adolescent Offenders

Abel, Mittleman, and Becker (1985) revealed that 57% of their sample of sexual offenders ($N = 411$) began molesting before the age of 19. Longo's (1982) evaluation of adolescent sexual abusers ($N = 17$) reported 76% had committed their first sexual offenses before age 12. Russell (1986) reported in her study of 930 women in the San Francisco area that almost 25% of the females who reported abuse had been victimized by an adolescent. More recently, Becker, Cunningham-Rathner, and Kaplan (1986) reported in their study ($N = 220$) of adolescent males alleged to have committed or found guilty of intrafamilial sexual offenses had a previous record of arrests for sexual offenses (63.5%), and some (9.1%) had a minimum of two or more arrests for sexual offending behaviors. Finkelhor's (1979) study of college students ($N = 796$) found one-third of the women reported having been sexually abused by a male aged 10 to 19.

A number of studies have examined the sexual histories of adolescents convicted of sexually abusing children. Longo (1982) reported that 47% of his sample of adolescent sexual offenders reported being sexually abused as a child. Forty-three percent in the study were labeled as child sexual abusers. Fehrenbach, Smith, Monastersky, and Deisher (1986) found that 18% of the adolescents in their study had been sexually abused as children and, of the 18%, 63% sexually abused other children. Becker, Cunningham-Rathner, and Kaplan (1986) found that 77% of their study's population of adolescent sex offenders committed the sexual offenses within their own families. Of the 77%, 23% had themselves been sexually abused as children.

The Vermont Department of Health (1985) collected data on 161 adolescent child sexual abusers. In the study, 90% of the adolescents were males. The median age for male abusers was 15 years, for female abusers, 13 years. More than two-thirds of the victims targeted by the adolescent offenders were less than 10 years of age and almost one-half were under the age of seven. In at least 60% of the cases penetration occurred. Other studies have indicated that at least 50% of reported cases of child abuse are perpetrated by persons under the age of 18 (Brown, Flanagan, & McLeod, 1984; Thomas, 1981).

Baby-sitting as a Situational Factor in Adolescent Abusers

Most sex offenders commit their first sexually abusive acts as adolescents. Baby-sitting is the most frequent setting for adolescents to sexually abuse others. Some other studies have confirmed that many sexual offenses take place when the molester is baby-sitting (Fehrenbach, Smith, Monastersky, & Deisher, 1986; Kournay, Martin, & Armstrong, 1979; Margolin, 1992; Wasserman, Kappel, Coffin, Aronson, & Walton, 1986). Adolescent babysitters have been found to commit sexual offenses against children more frequently and commit more serious sexual offenses than older extrafamilial babysitters. (Margolin & Craft, 1990; Margolin, 1991). Another study (Margolin & Craft, 1989) demonstrated that male adolescent baby-sitters sexually abused the children they were taking care of five times more often than the adolescent female sitters.

Research concerning adolescent sexual offenders has been on the increase. The vast majority of the research has focused on male adolescent offenders. A few studies have addressed the issue of female adolescent sexual offenders.

Fehrenbach and Monastersky (1988) studied 28 female adolescent sexual offenders. The sexual acts committed by females were divided into two groups: rape (53.6%), which included oral, anal, or vaginal intercourse; and object or digital penetration or indecent liberties (46.4%), which included sexual touching (anything just less than intercourse). All of the participants in this study acted alone. The average age of the female sexual offender was thirteen. All abused victims were younger than twelve years of age, except for one. The average age of the child that was victimized was five. Fifty-seven percent of the perpetrators abused only females, 35.7% committed offenses against males, and 7.1% abused both males and females. The offenders knew all the children they victimized. Sixty-eight percent of the time the victimization took place during the activity of baby-sitting. Twenty-one percent of the offenders reported being physically abused while growing up and 50% admitted to being sexually abused. Barnard, Fuller, Robbins, and Shaw (1989) also have reported baby-sitting to be the most common time for adolescent molestations to take place.

Etiologies of Molesting Behaviors in Adolescents

Researchers studying adolescent offenders frequently cite problems of low self-esteem, social isolation, and poor social skills (Becker, Kaplan, & Karoussi, 1988; Becker, Kaplan, Tenke & Tartaglini, 1991; Davis & Leitenberg, 1987; Katz, 1990; Ryan, Metzner, & Krugman, 1990; Walker, Bonner, & Kaufman, 1988). Richardson, Loss, and Ross (1988) suggested seven reasons for adolescents engaging in molesting behaviors: (1) to have power and control over another person; (2) to have a retaliatory mechanism against a specific individual or the world in general; (3) to vent angry feelings; (4) to frighten someone and cause the victim to feel negatively about himself or herself; (5) to have instant satisfaction for unmet needs; (6) to feel desirable; (7) to feel like someone admires him or her. Davis and Leitenberg's (1987) review of the literature on adolescent offenders reported a past history of physical abuse to be the most significant factor in the background of many of the adolescent sex offenders. Other researchers have concurred with this finding (Jackson, 1984; Lewis, Shanok, & Pincus, 1981; VanNess, 1984).

SEXUALLY REACTIVE CHILDREN

An increase has occurred in knowledge among the general public and professionals that adolescents do sexually molest others; however little attention has been paid to the preadolescent or "sexually reactive" children.

A sexually reactive child is usually eight-years-old or less. He or she engages in behaviors with other children that are hurtful or illegal. Most often this is because he or she is a victim of sexual abuse (Matsuda & Rasmussen, 1990). Sexual reactivity is not meant to be taken as a reference to self-masturbation or sexual curiosity, but behavior that involves some type of force on the part of the offending child.

Rasmussen, Burton, and Christopherson (1992) suggested there are five reasons children become sexually reactive with other children. The first reason is prior traumatization. These authors stated,

> The prior trauma may be an actual molestation, or another traumatic event coupled with early sexual awareness (e.g., witnessing the sexual activity of others). Prior to developing offending behavior, a young child must be made aware of sexual behavior. Exposure to pornographic material may lead to early sexualization. This enhanced sexual awareness coupled with anger associated with physical and/or emotional abuse can lead to an offense. The second precursor to a child acting out sexually is inadequate social skills. Children with effective social skills are less likely to offend sexually because they usually have a more extensive social network from which they can draw support. Both Johnson and Berry (1989) and Friedrich and Luecke (1988) have described their samples of sexually aggressive children as having problems with peer relationships. . . . A third precursor to offending in children is lack of social intimacy. . . . This relates to some degree with level of social skills, but represents a somewhat different dimension in that there are children who relate relatively well on a superficial basis, but feel lonely due to problems maintaining close friends. . . . We view impulsiveness as a fourth precursor to sexual reactivity in children. . . . In our experience, these children frequently have problems with stealing. Some of the children in our treatment program have attention deficit and oppositional disorders. . . . The fifth precursor to children offending appears to be a factor we have named lack of accountability. This precursor encompasses more than mere lack of accountability for sexual behavior, and describes an overall tendency to deny personal responsibility for actions. (pp. 36–37)

Rasmussen, Burton, and Christopherson (1992) developed a theory to aid clinicians in understanding and recognizing the thoughts and emotions that precede molestations. They classify their approach as the Trauma Outcome Process. This approach suggests a child has three potential responses to being traumatized, with the trauma being any way in which a child is victimized by any form of abuse. The responses are (1) recovery—where feelings are expressed and worked through; (2) self-victimization—where the hurt, anger, and shame is turned inward and the self of the child is violated in destructive ways; and (3) assault—reactive children act out and abuse other children. Rasmussen et al. (1992) suggested the child may display more than one kind of response to the abuse.

Entering the trauma outcome process occurs through an event in which the child feels victimized. Once a child has been traumatized, he or she may experience any or all of the following feelings: recriminations against the self, powerlessness, feelings of loss, reproachment, desolation, and dissociative reactions.

Rasmussen, Burton, and Christopherson also discuss Stickrod 's (1989) labeling of these symptoms of abuse as trauma echoes. Trauma echoes are the statements the perpetrator originally made to the child before, during, or after the abuse: "You really wanted this to happen, I know because you had an orgasm," or "This is really all your fault. You seduced me." After a time the survivor begins to believe and accept these cognitive distortions and incorporate them into his or her belief system. The distorted cognitions of the survivor then become the trauma echoes. Sgroi and Bunk (1988) have called this phenomenon rewriting the script.

The next part of the sexual assault cycle is the trigger point. A "trigger" can be anything that reminds the survivor of an abusive experience. It can be a sight, sound, or an odor. Almost anything can be a trigger. Rasmussen, Burton, and Christopherson (1992) reported that once the feelings have been brought to the surface by a trigger, the individual decides how he or she will react to these feelings. The authors called this the choice point. At the choice point the individual will either: (1) recover—work through the feelings of rage and betrayal and put the blame where it belongs, on the perpetrator; (2) self-victimize—repress the feelings, then discharge them in a hurtful way, which results in a lessening of self-esteem, and the thinking errors become more pervasive; or (3) assault someone else—in this process the traumatized individual begins to act out or experience "get even" fantasies with the end result being the molestation of a child.

Research Data on Sexually Reactive Children

Johnson and Berry (1989) reported on 13 female children referred to the Department of Children's Services for "developmentally inappropriate sexual behavior with children which was deemed to be outside of 'normal' limits and serious enough to require treatment" (p. 573). Female children in the study were between the ages of 4 and 12, and the average age was 7.5. The average age the female child began engaging in sexually reactive behaviors was 6.7 years (range 4 to 9); the average number of children molested per child perpetrator was 3.3 (range 1 to 15 children victimized). All of the victims were known to the sexually reactive children. Female children were admitted to the study if

> they had 1) acted in a sexual way with another child, and 2) there
> was a pattern of sexually overt behavior in their history, and 3)
> there was an age differential of at least two years, and 4) they used
> force or coercion in order to obtain the participation of the other
> child, or victims were too young to realize they were being violated
> and did not resist the sexual behavior. (p. 573)

The child and at least one parent were evaluated and assessed to determine if the female child met the criteria to be treated in a program for children who were sexually reactive to other children. The program was called SPARK (Support Program For Abuse-Reactive Kids). Thirteen female children were admitted to the program. Results indicated that none of the children were found to be psychotic, and all were depressed and anxious.

Twelve of the 13 mothers had been involved in physically abusive relationships with men, 85% ($N = 11$) of the mothers had been sexually abused as children. Fifty-four percent were involved in substance abusing behaviors at some point after the birth of the daughter who was in the SPARK program. Only two of the birth fathers were involved in the SPARK program. Five of the female child perpetrators had been sexually abused by their birth fathers, all 13 female children had been sexually abused by someone known to each. Twelve of the females were abused before age five.

Types of sexual behaviors the female children committed against other children are as follows: penetration of the vagina with a finger ($N = 6$); penetration of the vagina with objects ($N = 6$); anal penetration with a finger ($N = 8$); oral sex ($N = 12$); fondling ($N = 13$); genital contact excluding penetration ($N = 13$); mimic intercourse ($N = 11$); actually engaged in intercourse ($N = 1$); and French kissing ($N = 1$). Verbal coercion (54%) and excessive physical force ($N = 23$) were the most common types of intimidation tactics used by the female children.

Many of the sexual acts were intrusive and forceful in nature. Johnson (1988) presented a case example in which 4 female sexually reactive children restrained and performed fellatio on an 18-month-old male toddler. This child was so debilitated by the abuse he had to receive medical treatment. Prior to the male child's molestation each of the female perpetrators had been forced to fellate a father or an uncle.

Johnson proposed some suggestions as to why these female children externalized their pain and acted-out. She wrote,

> The sexual abuse which these children sustained was one of the most serious kind, in that the frequency was high, the degree of relationship between the perpetrators and the girls was very close, most of the abuse occurred over an extended period of time, and when the children disclosed the abuse they sustained, there was little support for them. The mothers of these children were highly dependent personalities who had themselves been physically of sexually abused as children or adults. Their stance vis-a-vis the world was one of victimization. The children had no stable, nurturing mother or father figure in their lives. Neither of their parents had the ability to protect them. The family structure was unstable and shifting. (p. 581)

Johnson continued by discussing the idea that the female children were not seeking orgasms or sexual satisfaction when they molested another child, but rather the child perpetrator was attempting to lessen feelings of rage, anxiety, and confusion. Johnson's study found that male children were twice as likely as female children to be molested by a female child perpetrator.

From this study's findings there appears to be a significant interrelationship between a previous history of sexual abuse and sexually reactive children molesting other children. Friedrich and Luecke's (1988) study on male reactive children support this conclusion. All 13 child participants in their study had a history of sexual abuse.

CONCLUSION

Both adult females and adult males abuse children. Sometimes the abuse occurs inside the family system, sometimes outside the family system, sometimes both inside and outside the family at the same time. Male and female adolescents are sexually abused and sometimes in turn become abusers. Small children, both boys and girls, are sexually molested and sometimes, beginning at a very early age, sexually victimize other boys and girls. Sexual abuse is but one of many violent acts that fall on a continuum of assaults to individuals in our society. Violence permeates the fabric of our entire society. Verbal and physical assaults on women and children are commonplace occurences in our society, as are physical and emotional abuse, rape, date rape, murder, and gang killings, which also fall on the continuum of violent, brutal acts.

It cannot be assumed that sexual abuse happens to someone else's children, especially with statistics suggesting one in every three females and one in every five males will at least be approached by a sexual offender before the age of 18. Unfortunately, no defining characterizations of an intrafamilial, extrafamilial, or adolescent abuser exist. Sexual abusers occur in all races, religions, socioeconomic, and occupational groups. Females abuse as well as males. No one set explanation can be written for what creates a sexual abuser. No easy answers exist with regards to preventing sexual abuse or even detecting abusers. The research literature is rich in establishing varying prevalence rates of abuse and the effects of abuse but is lacking in concrete criteria to utilize in identifying sexual offenders. Certainly a place for mental health professionals to begin is by taking a complete psychosocial and family history of any individual referred for treatment (use of genograms facilitates this process) to help identify any individuals who initiated sexual offending behaviors in adolescence or were victimized in childhood or adolescence by sexual offenders (inquire about current and past relationships with siblings, grandparents, and other family members in addition to exploring the issue of family secrets, family mottos, and family rules). Inquiries should also focus on the individual's current and past coping styles and those in the family of origin.

Once an individual has been identified as a sex offender, some researchers (Conte, 1985; Hollin and Howells, 1991) have suggested that he or she be appraised on the following: denial, sexual arousal, sexual fantasies, cognitive distortions, deficits in social skills, and other problems, such as depression and drug abuse. Keep in mind that sexual abusers have a tendency to minimize, rationalize, and distort their behaviors. Sexual offenders are not going to reveal deviant behaviors if the clinician does not ask pertinent questions relating to the aforementioned. Whether sexual offenders actually provide accurate information is questionable because of societal taboos against sexually abusing children, apprehensiveness about being punished, and the defense mechanism of denial (Hollin & Howells, 1991). Probably the factor that is most prohibitive in the study of pedophiles is that the abusers, offenders, molesters, or whatever name you choose to call them are not studied until they have become involved in the legal system. Almost all of the studies completed have been researched on men incarcerated for committing sexual offenses or men involved in outpatient treatment programs. Men in prison may be quite different psychologically than men who are sexual offenders who are never caught. For instance, the low self-esteem theory may be a result of being processed into the judicial system rather than the reason some pedophiles sexually abuse children. Almost nonexistent are studies that include female sex offenders. This may be because the incidences of sexual abuse by females for the most part go unreported. It does not mean that female child sexual abusers do not exist, it just means that they are not reported. Something that is known is how lacking professionals are in knowledge to identify the sexual abuser before he or she is brought to the attention of the legal system or child protective agencies.

Chapter **4**

THE HOWS AND WHYS
OF VICTIMIZATION

We can learn much from the children and adult survivors of abuse. The following is an exercise to help the reader get in touch with what it might feel like to be a child who is sexually abused.

> You are molested by . . . a police officer who arrested you for an unnamed offense, and he is alone with you in a cell. You have no knowledge of the law, no access to outside help, and no idea of your rights. When will you be released? You do not know. Do you push him away? Or then will he become more violent? Who will protect you from him? Who will even believe you when you get out of the situation? The chances are, however, at this point, that this last worry will not yet have occurred to you. Your overwhelming survival reaction undoubtedly will be fear. And until you are released from police custody you will never have complete access to the normal emotions of a free person, the freedom to express the anger that was yours by right, the indignation of an ordinary human being. . . . Your healthiest reaction—anger—has been confused and complicated by abuse of power and of access. (Driver, 1989, p. 26)

STAGES OF SEXUAL ABUSE

Sgroi, Blick, and Porter (1982) have stated that sexual abuse includes five different phases: the engagement phase, the sexual interaction phase, the secrecy phase, the disclosure phase, and sometimes a suppression phase. Each phase has it own characteristics. Hallmarks of each phase follow.

Engagement phase. The adult uses his authority and power over the child to begin initiating sexual activity with the child. This engagement phase may be subtle or it may be direct and inclusive of violence.

Sexual interaction phase. Usually the perpetrator penetrates the child either orally, vaginally, or anally.

Secrecy phase. It is paramount to the offender to keep the sexual activities secret. He may use blame, force, threats, anger, or anything else with the child that he believes will be effective in suppressing the truth about what is occurring.

Disclosure phase. This may occur because of discovery of the sexual activity by someone else, by pregnancy, or if the child tells someone else in anger. Male perpetrators rarely, if ever, disclose their victimization activities. Disclosure creates a crisis in the family, especially if the perpetrator is someone in the family system. Often family members will begin to take sides, and the child all too often is once again victimized by other family members.

Suppression phase. Parents and other family members often make every effort to negate, deny, minimize, and suppress what the child has disclosed (pp. 9-37).

Child Sexual Abuse Accommodation Syndrome

Roland Summit (1983) coined the term Child Sexual Abuse Accommodation Syndrome. This phrase was used to describe the most common reactions of children who have been sexually abused. Summit developed the model to better enable clinicians to understand and accept the child's point of view. The Child Sexual Abuse Accommodation Syndrome illuminates how the child survives within the family system. These survival mechanisms unfortunately result in society's questioning of the child's credibility, and a lack of empathy and acceptance of the truth about the child's victimization. The syndrome has five categories, two of which are circumstances that occur before the sexual abuse transpires. Summit (1983) states, "The remaining three categories are sequential contingencies which take on increasing variability and complexity" (p. 83).

The five categories of the Child Sexual Abuse Accommodation Syndrome, according to Summit (1983) are (1) secrecy; (2) helplessness; (3) entrapment and accommodation; (4) delayed, conflicted, and unconvincing disclosure; and (5) retraction. Each of these are discussed in the following paragraphs.

Secrecy.   One of the major factors that enables sexual abuse to thrive is secrecy. Most adults who were sexually abused as children never told anyone (Finkelhor, 1980; Gagnon, 1965a, 1965b; Herman, 1981; Russell, 1983). If the child did tell, more than likely no one listened. Information from adult retrospective studies (Finkelhor, 1980; Gagnon, 1965a, 1965b; Herman, 1981; Russell, 1983) indicate that most adults who were victimized as children did not tell anyone. Those who did report the abuse often found that their parents became hysterical, punished them, or denied the existence of what he or she had revealed (Finkelhor, 1980).

Sexual abusers are invested in keeping the abuse secret. The abuser may say to the child, "This is our secret, nobody else will understand." "Don't tell anybody!" "Nobody will believe you." (Summit, 1983, p. 181). Children do not know that it is okay to tell someone. They may fear being blamed, punished, or harmed in some way.

Helplessness.   This characterizes the child's relationship to adults. Children are allowed to ignore strangers but are taught and forced to be acquiescent, dutiful, docile, and compliant to any adult that they know. The research is consistent in noting that at least 75% to 85% of the time the child knows the offender (Finkelhor, 1979, 1980; Russell, 1983).

It is misleading to assume that because children do not report the sexually abusive incidents that they are giving consent to participating in these sexual acts A child is not in a position to say no to an adult caretaker, adult friend of the family, adult teacher, or Scout leader. The balance of power is too unequal. Sexual abuse is not a question of choice, because the child is never given a choice but to allow the abuse to continue.

Usually the victimization does not just happen, according to Summit (1983). The sexual abusiveness takes on a compulsive addictive pattern, a pattern that continues until the child can physically remove himself or herself from the relationship by running away or becoming pregnant by a boyfriend, or until the abuse is discovered (Herman, 1981). Discovery of abuse does not ensure the abuse will be stopped.

Entrapment and Accommodation.   The child has only one option and that is to learn to live with the abusiveness and somehow, and in some way, survive. Accommodation is what the child learns. The accommodation has a high price for the child—self-punishment, self-mutilation, and development of multiple personalities are just a few of the remnants of childhood sexual abuse.

The caretaker violates both the child's body and mind. To the child this is so unbelievable that the child rationalizes that the abuse is all his or her fault. This is then taken a step further, and the child begins to believe that if only he or she was "good enough," then the abuse would not happen.

Adults make good use of the child's self-blaming behavior. The adult gives the child the power to destroy the family: "If I don't do this to you then I will have to give this kind of attention to your sister or brother" or "Don't tell your mother about this, it would break her heart." The abuser also gives the child the power to keep the family together: "If you tell, then I will. have to go to prison, and you will have to live in a foster home." "This will break up the family if you tell anyone."

Delayed, Conflicted, and Unconvincing Disclosures.   Most sexual victimization is not discussed, reported, or investigated. The fourth component of Summit's model (1983) is delayed, conflicted, and unconvincing disclosure. He stated, "The child of any age faces an unbelieving audience when she complains of ongoing sexual abuse. The troubled, angry adolescent risks not only disbelief, but scapegoating, humiliation, and punishment as well" (p. 186).

However, not all adolescents are angry and rebellious. Sometimes they are the students voted most popular or most likely to succeed. Even so, if these adolescents reveal abuse, they are still likely to be disbelieved but for different reasons. For instance, if these adolescents are doing so well socially and academically, then people assume the abuse could not have been very severe or sexual abuse does not appear to be harmful. Summit stated, "Whether the child is delinquent, hypersexual, asexual, suicidal, hysterical, psychotic, or perfectly well-adjusted, and whether the child is angry, evasive, or serene, the immediate affect and the adjustment pattern of the child will be interpreted by adults to invalidate the child's complaint" (p. 187).

Retraction.   The fifth component of the Child Accommodation Syndrome is retraction. Whenever a child makes a disclosure about the sexual abuse, he or she will later be inclined to refute what he or she originally said happened. Disclosure creates chaos. The child is blamed for whatever happened. Again the child is placed in the position of maintaining or annihilating the family system. Telling the truth may result in the child being blamed for destroying the family. Maintaining the lie that everything is okay restores the homeostatic balance of the family. Does the child really have a choice? In many cases the child retracts what he or she originally revealed because the price is too high. The child is once again sacrificed.

Based on Summit's article, child care workers, teachers, clergy, Scout leaders, parents, relatives, and camp counselors need to be cognizant of the following when a child reveals he or she was abused. Listed below are some concrete guidelines to help if you ever find yourself in this kind of situation.

1. **Remain calm.** Do not become hysterical or enraged and start calling the perpetrator all types of names, and do not threaten to kill the molester. The child needs you to think straight at this point in time.

2. **Believe what the child or adolescent says.** Say to him or her, "I believe what you are telling me," or "Thank you for telling me," or "It must have taken a lot for you to tell me and I believe what you have said."

3. **Do not respond negatively to the child or adolescent.** Don't say "Oh, no!" or "Are you sure?" or "You are certain you are not making this up?" or "Maybe you just had a bad dream," or "Don't be saying things like that. Those kind of things never happen in our family."

4. **Understand that children have been humiliated, subdued, and are fearful of what will happen to them and the rest of the family.** Confusion and fear are just two of the many emotions the survivor experiences.

5. **Children do not have the ability to communicate with adults on an adult level.** Validate what they have lived through and experienced on a level they can understand.

6. **The child's fear about losing his or her family, or not being believed, can be more alarming than any abusive incidents that have happened to him or her.**

7. **Consistently and repeatedly confirm and reaffirm the child's innocence and lack of choice in being abused.** Say things like, "What has happened is not your fault, you did not have a choice," or "No matter what he or she said, you are not to blame," or "You are completely innocent."

8. **Provide unconditional caring and acceptance to the child or adolescent.**

9. **Know that as an adult you may have to prove again and again that you are trustworthy. Be consistent.**

10. **Tell the child you are going to have to call some professional people and let them know about what has happened.** Tell the child that some people are going to come and ask him or her some questions. If you can, reassure the child that you will stay with him or her throughout the process if you are allowed to do this. Do not make promises you cannot keep. If you do not know what is going to happen, tell the child you do not know. Again reassure the child that you believe him or her.

11. **Know that children and adolescents frequently retract their allega-tions of sexual abuse as a way to protect the family system.** State-ments of abuse are not reversed because they are lies, but the truth is often recanted to "save" the family.
12. **Recognize that the perpetrator is always responsible.** The fault is never the child's or adolescent's.
13. **Call Children and Youth Services or Child Protective Services.** The number is in the yellow pages. If unsure about how to proceed ask someone from one of these agencies what you should do or say until someone arrives.

RESEARCH STUDIES

Offender's attitudes toward children does not appear to have been the cen-tral issue in many research investigations. One study (Sattem, Savells, & Murray, 1984) examined male sex-offenders attitudes toward women and children. No statistically significant differences were established among offenders of chil-dren or of adults, or of offenders and nonoffenders on any of the three mea-sures administered.

To understand and perhaps gain some insight into stopping the abuse cycle, a better understanding of why and how children are victimized is needed.

Reasons Children or Adolescents Maintain Secrecy about Sexual Abuse

- Fear of not being believed
- Fear of being blamed
- Fear of retaliation from the abuser
- Fear of losing source of gifts and money
- Fear of losing perpetrator's affections
- Fear family will dissolve
- Fear of being sent away from the family
- Fear of perpetrator's showing pictures to other family members of child or adolescent engaged in sexual acts
- Very young child may not know the abuse is inappropriate
- Young child may lack the verbal skills necessary to report the abuse
- May experience sense of shame or embarrassment about reporting the abuse
- May believe that it really is his or her fault
- May have received the message that sexual issues should not be dis-cussed at home

One source of information lies within the offender population. Two studies interviewed sexual offenders about the process of selection, recruitment, and maintenance of children in a sexually abusive situation (Budin & Johnson, 1989; Conte, Wolf, & Smith, 1989). Conte et al.'s (1989) study of 20 male child molesters revealed the offenders identified and targeted "trusting, vulnerable, and friendly" children. The offenders stated, "First you would groom your victim by heavy handedness promoting fear. . . . The next step would involve making the child think that everything is okay so they wouldn't run and tell. You could convince them there is nothing wrong with it or pressure a child not to tell. . ." (p. 298).

Budin and Johnson (1989) explored how 72 incarcerated pedophiles garnered the child's participation in the victimization. Over 20% of the offenders utilized intimidation and over 25% employed techniques to prevent a child from revealing the abuse to anyone. A major deterrent for sex offenders appears to be fear of getting caught.

Participants in both studies indicated that parents could do something to prevent child sexual abuse. First, the offenders stated that they were able to identify vulnerable children. Vulnerable children were defined as those children living in a divorced home, being young, needy (physically or emotionally), passive, or quiet. The child's trust was gained in many of the incidences by the offender being a friend, playing children's games, giving the child gifts or money, or by the offender knowing another offender who had access to a child. Most often the offender would approach the child in a nonthreatening manner, by joking or complimenting the child.

The offenders in the Budin and Johnson (1989) study had some recommendations for parents who want to prevent sexual abuse from occurring: provide a home environment where children feel parents will listen to them and care about them; be involved and active in the child's life; let the child know they are loved and that what he or she says matters; directly ask children if they have been abused or approached—be specific when asking questions; parents should use the correct words for body parts; parents should ask questions like "Has anyone ever offered to give you money, toys, gum, or candy if you would show them your genitals or breasts [for females]?" or "Has anyone ever showed you their genitals?" or "Has anyone ever shown you videos, pictures, or magazines of adults or children naked?"; and parents should tell children if anyone ever does any of these things to come and tell the parents and they will handle the situation. Children need to learn to be assertive and parents need to be educated about sexual abuse prevention.

Offender's Cognitions

The idea of cognitive distortions has its roots in the cognitive behavioral literature. These cognitive distortions are how the offenders talk to themselves, which permit them to negate, gloss over, excuse, and explain their behavior. The cognitive distortions are not viewed as being the original source of aberrant sexual behavior, but as one of the vehicles sex offenders use to vindicate themselves from responsibility for their behavior (Abel, Becker, & Cunningham-Rathner, 1984; Rouleau, Abel, Mittleman, Becker, & Cunningham-Rathner, 1986; Wolfe, 1984).

Abel et al. (1984) explored sex offenders' thought processes in relationship to their sexually abusive behaviors. These authors proposed that the men in their study who were sexually attracted to children would respond to this perplexity by developing cognitive distortions that sustained the deviant behavior. Abel and Becker (1984) developed a cognition scale to measure child molesters' distorted thoughts. The scale has 29 statements on which persons taking the test rate from 1 (strongly agree) to 5 (strongly disagree). The following statements are a few of those listed on the cognition scale (Abel & Becker, 1984): "A child who does not physically resist really wants sex." "Having sex with a child is a good way to teach a child about sex." "A child doesn't tell anyone about having sex with an adult because he or she really enjoys it." "Society will someday condone sex with children." "An adult who fondles a child's genitals is not really sexually engaging the child, and so no harm is being done." "When a child asks about sex, it means that the child wants to see the adult's genitals, or to have sex with the older person." "The relationship between the child and the adult is enhanced by having sex." (pp. 88–89). The subscales appear to be able to delineate child sexual abusers from other groups of sex offenders.

A study by Stermac and Segal (1987) showed that Abel and Becker's scale (1984) could differentiate (in their study populations) between child sexual abusers, rapists of adult women, and control groups of nonsex offenders. The most significant problem with the scale is that the statements are evident and could be affected by the participants desire to appear socially acceptable and normal.

Nichols and Molinder (1984) developed another test, the *Multiphasic Sex Inventory,* to explore offender's cognitions. They suggested that two of the subscales on the inventory can be utilized for exploring sex offender's cognitive processes. These are the Justifications and the Cognitive Distortions and Immaturity subscales. The test appears to still be in its infancy and as yet does not have much data to substantiate the authors' suppositions.

Lastly, Stermac and Segal (1987) have reproduced actual case studies garnered from clinical files that differ on degrees of sexual encounters and the child's reaction to the encounters (smiling, not responding, or crying). Test participants were asked to rate the case studies on a couple of different scales, which included seeing the harm versus the helpfulness to the child, the child's willingness to participate, and adult accountability. The researchers found that child sexual abusers viewed the sexual acts as more helpful to the child, viewed the child as being more accountable for the abuse and the adult as less accountable, than did rapists or other nonsex offender control groups who participated in the study. Stermac and Segal (1987) have provided an unprecedented approach to tapping into the cognitive distortions of sex offenders, by presenting them with real-life situations and asking them to respond.

ATTRIBUTES OF THE CHILD OR ADOLESCENT

There are a number of attributes of the child and adolescent or their families which seem to promote the development and continuance of sexually abusive behaviors. This is in no way to be misconstrued that the child or adolescent is ever responsible for any abusive acts that take place. An emotional problem in the child or adolescent may cause him or her to view the sexual interaction as positive because it fulfills his or her need for affection, feeling loved, and feeling like a special person, regardless of the fact that being abused is the price he or she must pay to feel special (Halleck, 1965; Rush, 1980; Seghorn, Prentky, & Boucher, 1987; Storr, 1964; Summit, 1983).

Lack of interpersonal relationships and poor social interaction skills may make it difficult for the child or adolescent to develop relationships with persons their own age. They have a tendency to feel isolated. Children who have already been victimized by an adult or adolescent are at risk to be further victimized by other offenders (Gagnon, 1965a, 1965b; McGuire, Carlisle, & Young, 1965; Schwartz & Masters, 1983).

The child or adolescent's comfortableness with their own gender identity (degree to which he or she feels masculine or feminine) is believed to be another important variable in understanding the hows and whys of victimization. Stoller (1975, 1979, 1985) theorized that the more traumatized the child was by the sexual victimization experiences, the greater the chance that the child will reenact the experience with others when he or she is in a position to do so. Some authors have used this to explain why adolescents become sexually aggressive toward others who are viewed as weaker than themselves

(Burgess, Hartman, McCausland, & Powers, 1984; Burgess, Hartman, & McCormack, 1987; Carmen, Reiker, & Mills, 1984; Rogers & Terry, 1984; Rush, 1980).

A child is never to be blamed for being abused or for being a target of sexual abuse. The parents and extended families play a large role in the whole process. Parental histories of sexual abuse, emotional liabilities of the parents, isolation from the community, and family dysfunctionalism is theorized to place the child or adolescent at higher risk for victimization (Abel, Becker, & Cunningham-Rathner, 1984; Constantine, 1980; Halleck, 1965; Seghorn, Prentky, & Boucher, 1987).

TRAUMA AND SEXUAL ABUSE

Finkelhor (1984) theorized that four preconditions must be fulfilled for child sexual abuse to occur. These four conditions are: (1) the potential abuser needs to be motivated to abuse a child. This appropriate motivation on the part of the child sexual abuser has three parts: (a) the sexual abuse gratifies some emotional needs of the offender, (b) the child is an object of sexual excitement and fulfillment, and (c) other sources of getting sexual needs met are blocked or inhibited in various ways. (2) the potential abuser has to have overcome internal inhibitions against following through on the motivation. Some disinhibiting factors might be alcohol or other drug usage, or sociocultural factors such as society's tolerance of child sexual abusers and the difficulty in convicting offenders. (3) the potential abuser needs to have found a way to circumvent external factors to permit him or her to commit the abusive acts. (4) the potential abuser needs to overcome the child's resistance. This is frequently accomplished by use of force, threats, bribery, or exploiting a lonely or a needy child. Finkelhor has suggested two measures for categorizing child sex offenders: the strength of the individual's desire to have sex with children and the exclusivity, which refers to how much of the individual's entire sexual activities involve children.

COPING RESPONSES OF CHILDREN
WHO HAVE BEEN ABUSED

Roth (1993) discussed the coping strategies that children who have been abused employ. Again, some abused children might not display all of these phenomena.

Dissociation. The child acts depressed, disengaged, and removed. He or she may have the ability to tolerate a great amount of pain. Affect is often flat and the child may appear to be unable to enjoy anything. During sexual abuse experiences the child may actually have the sensation of leaving his or her body and "floating" away from what is happening to him or her.

Splitting or compartmentalizing. An abused child may develop two or more distinct selves. One self is the good child; the other self is bad. This bad self is the one who is abused. He or she is abused because of his or her badness; it is deserved. This helps the child rationalize any pain or degradation experienced.

Rigid thinking. The child attempts to understand why he or she is abused. It is an effort to provide some understanding of the chaotic world in which he or she lives. An effort is made by the child to gain some control over what is happening to him or her. Often the only way to gain control is by engaging in magical thoughts and behaviors; for example, since her father only abuses her in the dark she leaves on lights in her room to prevent the darkness, which in turn will prevent he father from abusing her.

Denial. An abused child may convince himself or herself that the abusive experiences are really just nightmares and what is happening to him or her takes on a surrealistic quality.

Overly responsible behavior. Again the abused child assumes that the abuse is his or her fault. Thus if he or she could improve and be a better child the abusiveness would end. Often the abused child becomes parentified. He or she becomes a small adult and takes on adult responsibilities, like cooking, cleaning, or child care.

Overly nurturant behavior. Abused children never have enough nurturing yet on some level he or she recognizes the need for love and caring. As a result the abused child often will be very tender, loving, and caring toward other children and animals. The secret desire is that someone will nurture him or her too.

Complete self-reliance. Because the abused child knows that adults really cannot be trusted he or she may do everything for himself or herself. As a result this child comes to depend only on himself or herself.

Self-nurturance. More often than not a child finds ways to soothe himself or herself, possibly by rocking himself or herself, have a very developed imagination, reading constantly, or overeating.

Hypervigilance. The abused child is continually on edge in a vain attempt to prevent himself or herself from being abused. The child is tuned in to smells, noises, and so on.

Self-abuse. When a child inflicts pain on himself or herself (e.g., self-mutilation, scalding self), at least he or she has control over what happens. Often for abused children physical pain is more manageable than emotional pain (pp. 19–22).

DISPELLING THE MYTHS

Myths about molesters are prevalent in our society. The following are some of the most prevalent myths in our society about child sexual abuse. Acceptance of these myths as truth seems to have three purposes: (1) to keep the survivor quiet, (2) to protect the molester, and (3) to aid in keeping society and professionals removed from the incidents (Driver & Droisen, 1989). If there is no truth to the accusations and reports, then no one has to deal with it.

Myth 1—Children Lie about Sexual Abuse

Summit (1983) most eloquently refutes this myth with the following statement: "Rather than being calculated or practiced, the child is most often fearful, tentative, and confused. . . . Of the children who were found to have misrepresented their complaints, most had sought to understate the frequency or duration of sexual experiences" (p. 190). If children lie about sexual abuse, the lies are not of their own making, but rather originated from adults involved in messy divorce cases or the like who may have coached the child into lying about sexually abusive incidents in order to gain custody or for other reasons.

Myth 2—Males Are Rarely Victimized

Male children who have been sexually abused are frequently more secretive about the abuse than females. There appears to be more of a stigma for males who have been victimized. In our culture males are taught to be "macho," that sex is power, and men are to be the aggressors rather than the victims. Our failures to address the fact that males are frequently and violently abused once again victimizes them.

Myth 3—Children and Adolescents Sometimes Ask for Sex
Because They Behave in a Seductive Manner

No child or adolescent has equal power to refuse to have sex with an adult. Most often the child or adolescent is described as "seductive" so that the adult victimizer will have a "logical" explanation for their behavior. Adults are always responsible for their actions. The child or adolescent who is abused is not to blame.

Myth 4—Sex Offenders Are Strange Looking

Movies such as "M" and cartoon characters like "Chester the Molester" in Penthouse magazine enable stereotypes to thrive. Often the offender is characterized as wearing a trench coat and carrying a bag of candy with which to entice children. Nothing could be further from the truth. No one can describe exactly what a sex offender looks like because sex offenders look just like everyone else. If there is one consistent research finding it is that sex offenders are found in every socioeconomic level, every race, every occupation, and both sexes. The only consistency is their individuality.

Myth 5—Child Molesters Are Dirty Old Men

Most child sexual abusers begin abusing others when they are adolescents or young adults. In addition, not all sexual abusers are males, some are females.

Myth 6—Sexual Abuse Is Usually an Isolated Incident

Sexual abuse is rarely a one-time occurrence, especially if it is occurring within the family system. Some sexual abuse may continue for years.

Myth 7—Children with Special Needs
(Physically or Mentally Challenged)
Have a Much Lower Percentage Rate of Abuse

Having a special need places a child or adolescent at greater risk for being sexually abused. Social bias about the sexual unattractiveness of persons with special needs permit those who are convinced that sexual abuse is a result of the attractiveness of the child to eliminate these children or adolescents. Secondly, abuse of special needs children or adolescents frequently goes unreported because families and other caretakers are sometimes unable to sort out symptoms of abuse from those symptoms that are a result of the child's or adolescent's physical condition. Very little money is allocated to teaching special needs children and their parents about prevention techniques, or what to do if sexual abuse is occurring.

Myth 8—Sexual Abuse Is Just a Symptom of Other Issues in the Life of the Abuser

Sexual abuse is not a symptom for anything else. Perpetrators may have low self-esteem, feel inadequate, or be a substance user and abuser. But this does not negate the fact that sexual abuse is still a "sexual" act. There is no research evidence to indicate that treating the problems mentioned (low self-esteem, feelings of inadequacy, addiction) reduces or eradicates the sexually abusive behaviors.

Myth 9—Individuals Who Sexually Abuse Their Own Children Do Not Seek Children outside the Family System to Abuse

For years this was thought to be true. However, current research suggests that some individuals who abuse their own children or stepchildren will also seek to abuse children outside the family. An intrafamilial abuser can also be an extrafamilial abuser.

Myth 10—Sexual Abuse Usually Occurs in Rural Areas or in the Inner City, among People Who Are Poor

Abuse is no respecter of socioeconomic status or demographics. This myth may originally have been perpetuated because the poor and minority cases were the ones seen in mental health clinics and brought to the attention of the authorities, and thus became overrepresented in the research studies. Wealthier abusers are better able to shroud the molestations in secrecy or pay private practitioners for assistance or hire expensive attorneys to plead their cases should they ever even be prosecuted in court.

Myth 11—Professional Persons Such as Doctors, Mental Health Workers, Teachers, and Clergy Members (Ministers, Priests, Rabbis) Do Not Sexually Abuse Children

Abusers are found in all types of occupations, blue collar as well as white collar. Molesters also thrive and survive in the helping professions.

Myth 12—Sex Offenders Are Mentally Ill or Retarded

A few convicted sex offenders have been found to be psychotic or of less than average intelligence, but this is not usually the case.

Myth 13—Women Never Sexually Abuse Children

While it is true that females do abuse children less frequently than males, females can and do sexually abuse children in much larger numbers than has been reported in the past. Again if professionals and others ignore this, then the female or male child survivor is once more victimized by society and the helping professions.

Chapter 5

RITUALISTIC ABUSE

A variety of terms have been used to describe ritualistic satanic abuse: ritual satanic abuse, satanic ritual abuse, ritualistic child abuse, cult ritualistic child abuse, and group ritualistic child abuse.

DEFINITION OF TERMS

Finkelhor, Williams, Burns, and Kalinowski (1988) suggested the following definition for ritualistic abuse:

> Abuse that occurs in the context linked to some symbols or group activities that have a religious, magical, or supernatural connotation, and where the invocation of these symbols or activities are repeated over time and used to frighten and intimidate the children. (p. 59)

The Los Angeles County Commission for Women (1989) provided the following definition of ritual abuse:

> Ritual abuse is a brutal form of abuse of children, adolescents, and adults, consisting of physical, sexual, and psychological abuse, and involving the use of rituals. Ritual does not necessarily mean satanic. However, most survivors state that they were ritually abused as part of satanic worship for the purpose of indoctrinating them into satanic beliefs and practices. Ritual abuse rarely consists of a single episode. It usually involves repeated abuse over an extended period of time. The physical abuse is severe, sometimes including torture and killing. The sexual abuse is usually painful, sadistic, and

humiliating, intended as a means of gaining dominance over the victim. The psychological abuse is devastating and involves the use of ritual/indoctrination, which includes mind control techniques and mind altering drugs, and ritual/intimidation which conveys to the victim a profound terror of the cult members and of the evil spirits they believe cult members can command. Both during and after the abuse, most victims are in a state of terror, mind control, and dissociation in which disclosure is exceedingly difficult. (p. 1)

There are two types of ritualistic abuse; one includes the worship of Satan or the devil, the other does not. Frequently individuals with multiple personality disorder have described abuses that would fit the category of satanic ritual abuse (Braun, 1986; Kluft, 1988; Putnam, 1989; Young, Sachs, Braun, & Watkins, 1991).

Young et al. (1991) defined satanic cults as and limited to

. . . intrafamilial, transgenerational groups that engage in explicit satanic worship which includes the following criminal practices: ritual torture, sacrificial murder, deviant sexual activity, and ceremonial cannibalism. The authors have specifically chosen the word "ritual" rather than "ritualistic" to describe satanic abuse. This is to emphasize that these patients are reporting abuse which occurred in connection with specific satanic rituals and to avoid any implication that the abuse was ritual-like. (p. 182)

Bromley (1991) suggested four degrees of satanic activity: (1) dabblers—persons who are involved with heavy metal rock music and fantasy games such as "Dungeons and Dragons"; (2) self-styled satanists—criminals who use satanic themes as the basis for their antisocial activities; (3) organized satanists—individuals who belong to public churches that worship Satan, (e.g., Church of Satan and Temple of Set); and (4) traditional Satanists—those persons that are part of a cult that involves child sacrifices. Bromley suggested that a "dabbler" may evolve into an organized satanist or a traditional satanist. He theorized that it is not uncommon for an individual to begin at a lower level and gradually become more involved in satanic activities.

HISTORY OF RITUAL ABUSE

Hill and Goodwin (1989) reviewed pre-Inquisition historical records that gave an accounting of 11 satanic rituals quite similar to current reports of rituals from modern-day satanic cult survivors. The rituals reported by the authors are as follows: clandestine nighttime banquets; sexual orgies; inversion of the Christian mass; ritualistic utilization of blood, urine, feces, and semen; infant sacrifice and cannibalism; animal sacrifices; ritualistic use of candles; repeated intonation of demonic names; drug usage and the drinking of elixirs; use of a "circle" to symbolize satanic involvement; and dissection of the heart. Goodwin and Hill do not conclusively state that current reports of satanic cult survivors are accurate but they do suggest examining the similarities between their documentation of pre-Inquisition satanic practices and modern day reports of satanic activities.

Katchen and Sakheim (1992) suggested that therapists need to have some comprehension of cult customs and suppositions in order to be helpful to satanic cult survivors. These authors contended that many of the satanic practices in America are a result of druid influence. Some of the occult customs of the southeastern United States have their origins in Spain. The Spanish developed their beliefs and practices from the Aztec, Mayan, and Lecumi religions. Currently Eliphas Levi and Aleister Crowley are the fathers of modern day occult practices. Crowley (1924/1976) popularized worship of the devil among high-class English men and women and American pleasure seekers. Even earlier, about the middle of the 19th century, a member of the French Catholic clergy by the name of Alphonse Constant altered his name and became Eliphas Levi. Levi made an undeniable impact on ideological thinkers in Europe, Britain, and America. In fact, Robert E. Lee, general of the Confederate Army, had a commander of military intelligence by the name of Albert Pike who became the most infamous of Levi's disciples in the United States. Pike was also one of the primary creators of the Ku Klux Klan (Lester & Wilson, 1972). The robes, cross burnings, peaked hats, and Klan terminology were grounded in the teachings of Eliphas Levi. (For more see Raschke, 1990, Chapter 2, "Murder on Mainstreet").

SATANIC PRACTICES

Many satanic practices in America are a reversal of Christian doctrine (Cook, 1991; Driscoll & Wright, 1991). These practices involve worshipping idols, incestuous relationships, sacrifice of living things and the consumption of body fluids. Cavendish, author of *The Black Arts* (1967) described the meaning of sacrifices:

> In occult theory, a living creature is a storehouse of energy, and when it is killed most of the energy is suddenly liberated. The killing is done inside the circle to keep the animal's energy in and concentrate it. The animal should be young, healthy and virgin so that its supply of force has been dissipated as little as possible. The

amount of energy is very great, all out of proportion to the animal's size and strength, and the magician must not allow it to get out of hand. (p. 272)

Power is further augmented by eating and drinking blood, urine, feces, and aborted fetuses (Katchen & Sakheim, 1992). Power is what satanism is about. Ryder stated,

Satanism, for the most part, is all about power, as are witchcraft, Druidism, Santeria and other practices sometimes associated with ritual abuse. (As the physical, sexual, and emotional abuse in these groups may be similar). . . . People involved with Satanism call upon the powers of Satan to be able to manipulate the world around them through prescribed ritual. (p. 11)

Satanists and other occult groups (e.g., Wiccans, who are not Satanic) divide the calendar year into two halves. Halloween is the beginning of the year. Days begin at midnight, based on Celtic traditions (Conway, 1990). Satanists celebrate many holidays: Baemhain (October 31), Candlemas (February 2), Preparation for Sacrifice (April 21–26), Beltane or Grand Climax (May 1), Demon Revels (July 1), Lammas (August 2), Marriage To The Beast Satan (September 7), both equinoxes (March 21 and September 22) and solstices (June 21 and December 22) (Ryder, 1992). In addition Satanists often perform matching ceremonies opposite Christian holidays like Easter, Christmas, and All Saint's Day. There is also reported ritual activity around full moon nights and on all Friday the 13ths.

Satanists are reputed to have many symbols. Katchen and Sakheim (1992) include discussions of pentagrams, which represent the head, arms, and legs of the human body; the colors black (symbolic of evil) and red (representing blood or life); and the "grimoire" (book of spells).

THE CONTROVERSY

The concept of ritualistic child sexual abuse continues to be one of the most controversial issues among mental health, legal, and law enforcement persons and agencies. One expert asserted that there is

. . . A vast international, multigenerational, conspiracy practicing religious worship of Satan through sex and death rituals involving torture, incest, perverted sex, animal and human sacrifice, cannibalism, and necrophilia. In addition to suffering rape, bizarre tortures and being forced to participate in victimizing others, alleged victims of satanic ritual abuse (SRA) are often reported to have been "brainwashed" with the aid of hypnosis and drugs and implanted with suggestions to kill themselves or commit other acts on command. These "triggers" allegedly can be activated by covert cues embedded in prosaic objects, e.g., flowers or greeting cards, in a manner strikingly reminiscent of scenes from the "The Manchurian Candidate," a famous movie about brainwashing during the Korean War. (Putnam, 1991, p. 175)

Other professionals deny the existence of ritualistic abuse. Professionals are divided into the believers and the nonbelievers. Greaves (1992) named four groups of professionals who are involved in this controversy. Group One, according to Greaves, is composed of the nihilists. Nihilists are those who "see their function as explaining how the presentations made by satanic cult survivors cannot be true" (Greaves, 1992, p. 46). Greaves identified Lanning as a member of the nihilist group based on Lanning's writings. To illustrate this point Lanning (1991) stated the following with regards to ritual satanic abuse,

One of the basic problems of discussing or publishing articles about "ritualistic" abuse of children is how to define it. After years of trying I have given up and prefer not to use the term. It is confusing, misleading, and counterproductive. The use of the word satanic is almost as confusing and certainly more emotional. I prefer the term multidimensional child sex ring. Not all ritualistic activity is spiritually motivated. Not all spiritually motivated ritualistic activity is satanic. In fact, most spiritually or religiously based abuse of children has nothing to do with satanism. Most child abuse termed "ritualistic" by various definitions is more likely to be physical and psychological than sexual in nature. Not all ritualistic activity with a child is abuse or a crime. (p. 171)

The nihilists are convinced that satanic cults do not exist and suggest that what survivors are reporting are based on the following hypotheses (Greaves, 1992): (1) *incorporation hypothesis,* which contends that individuals unconsciously incorporate material about ritual abuse that has been garnered from other sources, such as magazine articles, television, or newsletters, and believe it to be their own; (2) *screen memory hypothesis*, which occurs when the individual reports or describes genuine or imaginary memories symbolic of a deeper struggle; (3) *urban legend hypothesis,* which are stories originally told as a gag, then told and retold (e.g., the woman in West Virginia who tries to dry her cat's wet fur in the microwave and blows him to pieces); (4) *contamination hypothesis,* which occurs when the survivor is purported to unconsciously construct concepts from the verbal reports of other survivors, such as in a group therapy setting, and incorporates other survivors' stories as his or her own; (5) *ESP hypothesis*, which happens as a result of survivors who either unconsciously or consciously read the therapist's mind and obtain and acquire the therapist's knowledge of satanic rites and incorporate this information into their psyche; (6) *collective unconscious hypothesis,* which suggests that satanic cult survivors are translating their own unconscious imaginary thoughts into facts and believe them to be true; (7) *Chinese menu hypothesis,* which contends that anyone who has some knowledge of candles, colors, and other satanic paraphernalia can create a "menu" of satanic cult survivor stories; (8) *personal myth hypothesis,* which theorizes that individuals who have experienced trauma create "personal myths" as defense mechanisms; the myths have some underlying truth to them but for the most part are fabrications; and (9) *propagation of rumors hypothesis,* which contends that all survivors' stories are just "rumors" and nothing more (p. 46).

Apologists are those professionals who "seem to conceive their task as explaining why Satanic cult survivor productions must be true" (Greaves, 1992, p. 46). Greaves considered himself to belong to this group of individuals.

Greaves (1992) wrote,

> My particular research interest in the field has been in trying to close the circle of external validity issues. I have collected thousands of pages of writings on witchcraft, secret societies, occult history, sorcery, black magick, cults and cult-related crimes, ceremonial magick, kabbalism, sex magick, alleged satanic cult activities, possession states, and attended police seminars and psychiatric seminars from coast to coast that focused on the subject of transgenerational satanic cults. From an empirical standpoint I find an enormous amount of inductive, circumstantial evidence that such cults, in some form, do indeed exist. (p. 65)

Heuristics are the third group. Greaves (1992) stated that these individuals are "mainly a large group of clinicians who are un-committed to any objective conclusions about the whole matter, but who have found that treating their SCS patient reports in a confirming manner has resulted in favorable outcomes intreatment" (p. 47).

Methodologists are the fourth group of individuals, according to Greaves (1992). These persons provide "the least developed perspective in the Satanic cult survivor field, since in any scientific investigation observation always precedes method" (Greaves, 1992, p. 47).

Greaves (1992) reported the existence of 5 different groups who have been labeled satanic: (1) transgenerational satanic cults, which have had family members participate in satanic rituals for several generations; these cult members practice human and animal sacrifice and worship Satan; (2) neosatanic cults are cults who worship Satan, but deny utilizing sacrifices as part of their religion (e.g., Church of Satan and Temple of Set) (LaVey, 1969, 1972); (3) self-styled satanic cult leaders are those persons who often have been involved in other satanic groups and have left to start their own cult; (4) teen dabblers are adolescents who study books by LaVey and Crowley and listen to specific kinds of heavy metal rock music; and (5) solitary satanists are people who say they have been chosen to do the work of Satan. These people may make the evening news for committing perverse acts of violence against others (e.g., Charles Manson and Richard Ramirez, the Night Stalker, are two examples).

RITUAL ABUSE SURVIVORS

Two basic types of reports substantiate the claims of ritualistic abuse: those from adults who state they were abused as children (Cook, 1991; Driscoll & Wright, 1991; Young, Sachs, Braun, & Watkins, 1991) and children who report being victims of ritual satanic abuse (Edwards, 1990; Gould, 1988; Hudson, 1990). Certain common themes have emerged among the adults reporting satanic abuses in childhood: *sexual abuse* (Cook, 1991 [100%]; Driscoll & Wright, 1991 [93%]; Young et al., 1991 [100%]); *physical torture* (Cook, 1991 [97%]; Driscoll & Wright, 1991 [84%]; Young et al., 1991 [100%]); *observed or participated in animal sacrifices* (Cook, 1991 [97%]; Driscoll & Wright, 1991 [48%]; Young et al., 1991 [100%]); *received death threats* (Cook, 1991 [89%]; Driscoll & Wright, 1991 [73%]; Young et al., 1991 [100%]); *forced to ingest drugs or receive injections* (Cook, 1991 [88%]; Driscoll & Wright, 1991 [73%]; Young et al., [96%]); *observed or were coerced into participation in adult and infant sacrifices* (Cook, 1991 [88%]; Driscoll & Wright, 1991 [57%]; Young et al., 1991 [83%]); *cannibalism* (Cook, 1991 [82%]; Driscoll & Wright, 1991 [57%]; Young et al., 1991 [81%]); *live burial in coffins* (Cook, 1991 [unknown percentage]; Driscoll & Wright, 1991 [50%]; Young et al., 1991 [72%]); and *used as a breeder and then forced to sacrifice the child* (Cook, 1991 [33%]; Driscoll and Wright, 1991 [82%]; Young et al., 1991 [60%]). In all three studies of adult survivors the abuses began before the age of six; in the Cook (1991) study the majority of the participants indicated the abuse began before the age of three; and in the Driscoll and Wright study (1991) 80% of the abuse began before the participant was 2 years of age. All of the participants of the Young et al. (1991) study were given the diagnosis of multiple personality disorder or dissociative disorder not otherwise specified. In Driscoll and Wright's study (1991), 34% of the study participants were labeled as dissociative and 63% were reported to have multiple personality disorders (total N = 37). Cook (1991) reported the majority of her study participants (N = 33) also had multiple personality disorders.

Many of the perpetrators were family members, such as fathers (Cook, 1991 [58%]; Driscoll & Wright, 1991 [65%]); mothers (Cook, 1991 [42%]; Driscoll & Wright, 1991 [38%]); grandfathers (Cook, 1991 [33%]; Driscoll & Wright, 1991 [35%]); grandmothers (Cook, 1991 [21%]; Driscoll & Wright, 1991 [22%]); uncles (Cook, 1991 [24%]; Driscoll & Wright, 1991 [41%]); physicians outside the family unit (Cook, 1991 [30%]); Driscoll & Wright, 1991 [54%]); priests, ministers, or church members (Cook, 1991 [18%]; Driscoll & Wright, 1991 [35%]); and teachers (Cook, 1991 [15%]; Driscoll & Wright, 1991 [22%]).

The abuses took place in a variety of locations: the woods (Cook, 1991 [73%]; Driscoll & Wright, 1991 [64%]); churches (Cook, 1991 [58%]; Driscoll & Wright, 1991 [47%]); homes, their own or someone else's (Cook, 1991 [48%]; Driscoll & Wright, 1991 [43%]).

Child survivors of ritualistic abuse may have issues in the following areas: (1) obsession with urine and feces either in art work, language, or behavior (avoiding the bathroom, using inappropriate toilet skills, e.g., golden showers) (Gould, 1988; Hudson, 1990); (2) use of occult symbols—writing 666, drawing pentagrams (Gould, 1988; Grossman, 1987; Hudson, 1990; Warnke, 1986); (3) saying prayers to the devil (Gould, 1988; Hudson, 1990); (4) having fears of closets, being restrained, death, or the colors black and red (Hudson, 1990); (5) refusing to eat certain food that are red or brown (e.g., spaghetti or ketchup) as a result of being made to eat feces and drink blood or urine (Edwards, 1990; Gould, 1988; Hudson, 1990); (6) panic at the sight of blood and knowing that human and animal blood differ in taste (Edwards, 1990); (7) concern with phases of the moon (Edwards, 1990); (8) experience psychological liabilities—mood swings, agitation, hyperactivity, short-attention span, learning difficulties, or regressive behaviors (thumb-sucking or bed-wetting) (Gould, 1988; Hudson, 1990); (9) complaints of shadows in their mind (Edwards, 1990); (10) sleep disturbances or nightmares (Gould, 1988; Hudson, 1990); (11) fear that family members will be harmed or killed (Gould, 1988; Hudson, 1990); (12) disturbed play—acting out death, mutilations, attempting to harm other children or sexualized play (Edwards, 1990; Gould, 1988; Hudson, 1990); (13) fear of something unusual being put inside their body (e.g., Satan's heart, a bomb, etc.) (Gould, 1988); (14) becoming hysterical at the sight of bugs, spiders, ants, and earwigs (Edwards, 1990); and (15) having certain themes or symbols appear in their artwork: the penis, a lonely tree, a broken or cracked egg, huge open mouths, genitals, or hooded figures (Klepsch & Logle, 1985; Burns, 1982; Dileo, 1983). Satanic cult members are invested in breaking down a child's belief system about being able to trust professionals in the world, so it is not uncommon for cult members to dress-up as policemen, clergy, doctors, nurses, or priests. (Edwards, 1990).

Gould (1988) has developed a comprehensive checklist for identifying signs and symptoms of ritualistic abuse in children. The instrument is quite thorough and extensive. The following are the major headings (Gould lists symptoms under these headings, but these are not included here): (1) problems associated with sexual behavior and beliefs; (2) problems associated with using the toilet and the bathroom; (3) problems associated with the supernatural, rituals, occult symbols, or religion; (4) problems associated with small spaces or being tied up; (5) problems associated with death; (6) problems associated with the doctor's office; (7) problems associated with certain colors; (8) problems associated with eating; (9) emotional problems (including speech, sleep, and learning problems); (10) problems associated with family relationships; (11) problems associated with play and peer relationships; and (12) other fears, references, disclosures and strange beliefs (pp. 210–216).

Gould (1992) had this to say about diagnosis of ritual abuse in children:

> . . . ritually abused children very seldom disclose any part of their abuse spontaneously. First, ritually abused children are nearly always drugged before the assault occurs, precisely so they will be unable to consciously recall the abuse. Second, in the trance-inducing drugged state, hypnosis is often used to implant the suggestions that victims will be unable to remember what has taken place, and that if they do remember, they will have to harm or kill themselves. Third, the acts that children are forced to endure, witness, or participate in during the course of the ritual abuse are so intolerable that dissociation typically results. In other words, victims must split off the extremely traumatic events from awareness and encapsulate them psychologically in order to survive their horror. . . . These conditions taken together—drugging, hypnosis, dissociation-producing trauma, and terrorization of the child, combine to produce a dissociative barrier truly daunting to the clinician. It appears that such dissociative barriers can be effectively erected with virtually any child who is ritually abused under the age of six. That is to say, the immature personality structure in the child less than six years old cannot prevent amnesic barriers from being erected in response to abuse. (p. 208)

Both Gould (1992) and Hudson (1991) present excellent clinical guidelines for mental health professionals who work with children and their families who have been identified or where there is suspicion of a child having been ritually abused. Both clinicians advocate the use of specific play therapy modalities.

EFFECTS OF RITUAL ABUSE:
THE PHENOMENON OF DISSOCIATION

Frequently survivors will engage in a phenomenon called dissociation. Pierre Janet wrote an article in 1887 about the phenomenon of dissociation. He was the first person to use the meaning for the term that is used in the current literature (Crabtree, 1992). Steele and Colrain (1990) have called dissociation the "universal survival response" (p. 4). Gil (1988) has identified three kinds of individuals who often have dissociative phenomenon: (1) children who have been repeatedly physically and sexually abused; (2) children who have had multiple perpetrators of abuse; and (3) children exposed to ritualistic abuses.

Peterson (1991) had this to say about dissociation and children. He stated, "Dissociation is a common phenomenon in children. Under conditions of extreme stress, dissociation may be used to wall off traumatic memories. In extreme cases, dissociation may result in the development of multiple personality disorder" (p. 152). Putnam (1985) defined dissociation as a ". . . complex psychophysiological process, with psychodynamic triggers that produce an alteration in the person's consciousness. During this process, thoughts, feelings and experiences are not integrated into the individual's awareness or memory in the normal way" (p. 66). Lastly, Kluft (1985) had this to say about the phenomenon of dissociation:

> Highly traumatic events promote the use of dissociation as a psychological/behavioral defense in persons with an inborn biopsychological capacity to dissociate. If the dissociative individual's psycho-social environment is chronically and inconsistently permeated with traumatic events, then the individual instinctively reasons to dissociation as a defense because the trauma is simultaneously perceived as unpredictable and overwhelming. (p. 8)

Barach (1991) stated,

> The process of detachment protects the abused child from crying for help and finding out that he is alone. In traumatic situations such as 'active abuse,' a child feels pain, terror, and other overwhelming

feelings. Such feelings obviously make a child want his or her mother. But whether he or she fantasizes floating away and watching the abuse from somewhere else, or develops alters in order to imagine . . . that the abuse is happening to someone else (Ross, 1989, p. 55), the child detaches from the affect. . . . (p. 117)

Certain researchers are beginning to make a connection between childhood abuse and dissociation in both the clinical (Chu & Dill, 1990) and nonclinical populations (Briere & Runtz, 1988). Chu and Dill (1990) conducted a study on females hospitalized in a psychiatric facility. These women described sexually abusive incidents that occurred during childhood. When symptoms were compared to other hospitalized females at the psychiatric facility, the sexual abuse survivors had higher degrees of dissociative symptoms than the females who did not have a history of sexual abuse. Briere and Runtz (1988) found that 15% of 278 college women in their study were sexually abused before the age of 15. Contrasted to a sample population of nonabused college women the abused women presented with higher degrees of dissociation, somatization, depression, and anxiety.

Braun (1986) suggested that the level on which an individual dissociates falls along a continuum, with a "normal" level of dissociation at one end (e.g., going to work with the flu and ignoring the symptoms) and multiple personality disorder at the other end of the continuum. A high incidence of multiple personality disorder (MPD) has been reported among survivors of severe child sexual abuse (Braun, 1986; Cook, 1991; Kluft, 1988; Putnam, 1989; Young, Sachs, Braun, & Watkins, 1991). Primarily females have been identified as having multiple personality disorders. At this point in time the ratio of males to females with multiple personality disorder is about 1:4 or even higher (Coon & Stern, 1986; Horevitz & Braun, 1984; Putnam, Guroff, Silverman, Barban, & Post, 1986; Ross, Norton, & Wozney, 1989; Solomon, 1983; Stern, 1984). Putnam (1989) theorized that multiple personality disorder begins in childhood, although it is rarely diagnosed until adulthood (Kluft, 1985; Putnam et al., 1986). Peterson (1991), in his review of the literature, has documented 26 cases of children from different studies who were suspected of having symptoms of multiple personality disorder (Fagan & McMahon, 1984 [$N = 3$]; Gainer, 1989 [$N = 4$]; Kluft, 1984 [$N = 5$]; Malenbaum & Russell, 1987 [$N = 1$]; Riley & Mead, 1988 [$N = 1$]; Snowden, 1988 [$N = 4$]; Waters, 1989, [$N = 6$]; Weiss, Sutton, & Utecht, 1985 [$N = 1$]). Peterson (1991) identified the following symptoms in the children presented in the 26 cases: amnesia; trance states; child called himself or herself by another name; drastic changes in social, physical, and emotional behaviors; had imaginary companions; was sexually preoccupied; was depressed; and had auditory hallucinations. (Note: Not all the children presented with each symptom listed.) He discussed the difficulty of identifying multiple personality disorder in children and adolescents and proposed a new category for children called dissociation identity disorder (Petersen, 1991, p. 161).

Young, Sachs, Braun, and Watkins (1991) suggested a clinical syndrome of adult survivors of ritualistic abuse that was described as the adult experiencing "... unusual fears, survivor guilt, indoctrinated beliefs, substance abuse, severe post-traumatic stress disorder, bizarre self-abuse, sexualization of sadistic impulses, and dissociative state with satanic overtones" (p. 183). This syndrome has also been verified by Cook (1991) in her study of 33 ritual abuse survivors from thirteen different states and Driscoll and Wright (1991) discussed many of the same symptoms in their article.

CREDIBILITY

Ritual abuse involving satanic practices has been difficult to prove. It is noteworthy, however, that the survivors in the studies discussed (Cook, 1991; Driscoll & Wright, 1991; Hudson, 1990; Young, Sachs, Braun, & Watkins, 1991) described their experiences quite similarly even though the individuals came from different areas of the country. Cases are rarely reported to the police and based on the threats involved in the abusive practices, it is no wonder.

Some of the accounts of ritual abuse are phenomenal. It is difficult for the human psyche to comprehend the traumas that these children and adult survivors have suffered. However, simply because professionals are uncomfortable and frequently disbelieving of what they have been told by survivors does not mean that the incidents did not happen. If survivors are not believed, the end result is that the individual is revictimized by the very professionals from whom he or she sought help. Calof (1991) as presented in Golston (1992) has discussed this struggle of professionals to believe or not believe survivor's accounts of ritual abuse as "a premature attempt to resolve the ambiguity and conflict ... to form the question in the absolute terms of, 'is or isn't' ... is to parallel the processes of denial and splitting used by survivors to regulate the impact of abuse" (p. 9).

RITUAL ABUSE IN DAY CARE

Finkelhor, Williams, Burns and Kalinowski (1988) studied 267 day-care centers in which sexual abuse occurred, some of which was ritual abuse. Thirteen hundred children were directly affected by the abuse. (There were a total of 229,000 licensed day-care facilities in the United States when this study was conducted. Finkelhor, Williams, Burns Kalinowski [1988] did determine that a child has a greater chance of being sexually abused in his or her home than in a day-care center.) The authors stated,

> Clear-cut corroboration of ritualistic practices was available in a few cases, such as Country Walk, where ritual objects were found by police, and where the female perpetrator did admit to some of the sadistic practices alleged in the children's stories. . . . An allegation of ritualism was present in 66% of all multiple-perpetrator cases, compared to only 5% of single perpetrator cases. . . . Nonetheless most of the ritual cases in our sample involved groups of perpetrators. Females were involved in all the cases, and in some cases there were only female perpetrators. (pp. 60–61)

Finkelhor, Williams, Burns, and Kalinowski (1988) suggested that there are three groups of individuals who engage in ritualistic abusiveness with children: true-cult based, where sexual abuse is just one part of the child's complete encompassment in cult beliefs and rituals; pseudo-ritualistic, where sexual abuse is the most important activity and cult rituals are much less important; and psychopathological ritualism, where mentally ill individuals sexually abuse children within a framework of ritualistic activities.

Faller (1990) presented seven different typologies for those individuals who sexually molest children in day-care programs.

> (1) Circumstantial sexual abuse. Circumstantial victimization involves a perpetrator with no past history of sexual activity with children, but who because of physical or life circumstances, engages in sex with a child . . . (2) Naive pedophile abuse. Some persons with pedophilic tendencies are unaware of them. Often they feel an affinity for children but experience this as unrelated to any sexual attraction . . . (3) Induced sexual abuse. Some offenders who sexually abuse in daycare have no intention of doing so but are manipulated or coerced into these activities by other offenders who play leadership roles . . . (4) Calculated pedophilic abuse. . . . There are some sexual abusers whose primary sexual orientation is to children. They tend to abuse multiple children and often consciously choose to work or volunteer in settings where they have easy access to children for sexual purposes . . . (5) Entrepreneurial sexual abuse. In some cases, sexual abuse in daycare is done for profit. In these cases, there are reports of the production of pornography and child prostitution . . . (6) Sexual abuse by people who hate children. It appears that some

of the sexual abusers of children wish to do great psychological and sometimes physical harm to them . . . (7) Ritualistic abuse. . . . The term is limited to situations where the sexual abuse is part of some rite that appears to have significance related to a type of religion, Satanism, witchcraft, or other cult practice. (pp. 193–197)

Hudson (1991) found many similarities in reported abuses of children from nine day-care agencies in five separate states. In all the day-care centers, reports indicated that the children were (1) sexually assaulted by adult strangers and day-care personnel; (2) all were threatened that if they told anyone about the abuse, their parents, siblings, or pets would be killed; (3) all were photographed or filmed during the abusive incidents; (4) all children described their abusers as wearing robes, masks, or carrying candles; and (5) medical evidence in all the cases was consistent with actual sexual assaults. These reported abuses are consistent with the findings by Waterman, Kelly, Oliveri, and McCord (1993).

Finkelhor, Williams, Burns, and Kalinowski (1988) proposed that there are two explanations for the connection between sexual abuse and ritualism. The first contention the authors label mortification of a child's sexuality. Adults involved in ritualistic abuse view their own sexuality as defiled, debased, contaminated, and wicked. A consequence of this self-hatred may be the motivation to demoralize and pervert a "pure" child's sexuality. A second reason these authors suggested is identification with evil. Individuals who personify this ideological assumption may have been reared in extremely strict religious families and continually failed to emulate the perfectionism expected. This unsuccessful attempt to attain self-acceptance in the narrow righteous community may have caused the individual to embrace a dogma that rejoices in purposefully malevolent acts. Thus, sexual abuse of children enables the individual to engage in forbidden activities where the chances of being arrested for illegal activities are almost nil.

CHOOSING A DAY CARE

- Determine if the day care has a license. Ask to see the license if there is some uncertainty.
- Make certain the ratio of teachers or helpers is adequate (e.g., one adult caregiver per three infants, one caregiver for every four toddlers, one caregiver for eight children age 3 to 6.
- Explore the turnover rate when seeking an appropriate day-care facility. Children need consistency in caregivers.
- Determine the qualification and educational level of staff members. What

is the highest level of education obtained by the teachers and other caregivers in the center and what is the least amount of education any staff member has? Each state has different requirements for educational level of staff members.

- Ask if the day-care center does criminal background checks on employees (Act 33 and 34 clearance). You as the parent should get to know all the employees of the day-care center.
- Ask how children are disciplined (e.g., "What do you do with a child who bites, kicks, hits, or soils or wets their pants after he or she is completely potty-trained?")
- Determine when and how often the center is inspected. Ask for the last date of inspection. Again, each state has different legal requirements regarding inspections.
- As a parent, look for clearly marked and accessible fire exits, clean kitchen and restroom facilities, type of meals and snacks that are provided, appropriate toys for your child's age level, large play areas, child-proofed toys, play equipment, and so on. Pay attention to how the staff and administrators are responding to your questions and request a complete tour of the facilities.
- Please take the time to spend at least one day at the facility.
- Be certain that the day-care center has your work number and knows how to get in touch with you should there be an emergency of any kind. Ask what happens if you are late. For instance, if the day-care center closes at 6 p.m. and you get stuck in traffic and do not arrive until 6:25 p.m., what will happen to your child?
- Determine the day-care center's policy on allowing sick children to attend for the day. Ask if there is a nurse on the premises. What will happen if your child becomes ill during the day? Ask if the staff receives yearly medical check-ups and especially tuberculosis screenings.
- Become involved with your child's day-care center.

ASSESSMENT BY CLINICIANS

Clinicians involved in assessing children abused in day-care settings might want to be cognizant of the following information based on research by Faller (1988); Finkelhor, Williams, Burns, and Kalinowski (1988); Kelley (1989); and Waterman, Kelly, Oliveri, and McCord (1993).

- Physical abuse is often present in day-care settings in which sexual abuse has occurred (e.g., children may have been forced to eat feces or may have been physically hit or tied up).

- Sexual abuse may have occurred in a setting that could be classified as ritualistically abusive. That might include adults dressed in robes, wearing masks, killing small animals, or forcing the children to drink blood and urine.
- Be aware that more than just day-care personnel may be the perpetrators (e.g., family members of staff employed at the center could be involved, as well as others who are strangers to the children but are known to the other perpetrators.).
- Children may be given drugs, which could blunt the memories.
- Children are often sexually abused by more than one perpetrator.
- Be aware of the parental response to the child's disclosure about abuse in a day-care setting. Is there denial, minimization, or disbelief on the part of the parents?
- Children may be brought for assessment after describing (to their parents) abusive games that have taken place in day care, or if a child begins exhibiting some behaviors that are atypical for him or her and the parents are puzzled or concerned.
- If the child is acting in a precocious manner regarding sexual activities the clinician needs to determine if the child's knowledge is a result of sexual practices in the child's family or if the child has been exposed at home or in other's homes to sexually graphic materials in the form of magazines or videos.
- Clinicians need to know what is developmentally appropriate for a child to know about sexual matters (e.g., it is rare for a preschooler to have comprehensive knowledge about intercourse or oral sex unless he or she has been a part of or observed these types of activities).

Waterman et al. (1993) believed that the psychological evaluation of a preschool child

> . . . poses many special challenges to the clinician because of the psychological immaturity of the child, the often complex nature of the abuse suffered by the child, and the nature of a young child's reactions and accommodations to the abuse. Research data on the types and impact of preschool abuse is very helpful in guiding the clinician. In addition, research about young children's memory of trauma, normal sexual development, and preschoolers' emotional and behavioral reactions must guide the clinical assessment. . . . A single symptom is rarely diagnostic of an abusive situation. Rather the clinician should look for a pattern of symptoms of time correlated to context, development, and other life events of the child and family. (pp. 80, 82)

RITUAL ABUSE AS A SOCIAL ISSUE

Cook (1991) contended that the societal scourge of ritual abuse of children should be viewed, in part, as a social problem. Conflict theory, she believes, provides a partial explanation for how and why ritual abuse continues to thrive and survive in modern day society. She stated,

> Conflict theory describes labels of deviance as an attempt by those in power to maintain their positions of control. Ritual abuse survivors who are talking about their experiences are deviant in the eyes of society because they threaten the power structure of both.
>
> The first initial assumption of conflict theory suggests that those in power are the people who have control over labeling what is deviant behavior. . . . The norms dictate that those who are victimized by the system are somehow to blame for their misfortune. In this way the social structure is not questioned. . . . Believing ritual abuse survivors makes people very uncomfortable because it not only makes people question their own spiritual beliefs, but it also makes them question the social structure and integrity of those who have power and control over them. . .
>
> Conflict theory may also help explain why cults commit the crimes they do. False consciousness, a term used by conflict theorists, is the norms and values in a society that blame poor social conditions on something other than the social structure. . . . There is also a false consciousness the cult groups teach to keep their members silent and loyal. (pp. 28–29)

Conflict theorists suggest that by discerning what false consciousness (which is a plot by those in authority to uphold current societal beliefs and conditions) is all about, individuals are empowered to move beyond the power that at one time was maintained over them.

RELIABILITY OF RITUAL ABUSE MEMORIES

Comstock (1992) believed that "The question of the reliability of ritual abuse memories is the most significant question in a list of several facing therapists in the field of multiple personality disorder (MPD) and dissociative disorders (DD) today. . . . It is the issue of reliability of patient memories which dominates the clinical discourse today" (p. 23).

Invalidating and questioning many of the mores and values our society perpetuates against sexually or ritually abused children will only happen if each of us becomes more involved in confronting and accepting these realities and atrocities. Survivors of ritual abuse need to be believed. Society can lend support and caring to those persons who have been victimized and survived. Societal acceptance and belief that ritual abuse does occur can only facilitate these survivors in their journey of healing.

Chapter 6

PARENTS AS PROTECTORS

Prevention, according to Kehoe (1988), needs to address three areas. First, a prevention approach suggests that everyone who takes care of children (parents, parents-to-be, baby-sitters, day-care personnel, pediatricians, Scout leaders, ministers, rabbis, priests, psychiatrists, psychologists, and so on) needs to learn to dismiss stereotypes regarding child abuse, recognize the signs and symptoms of high risk situations or situations in which abuse is already occurring, and learn how to talk to children about discussing a situation with a trusted adult if the child is confused about what others have said or done to him or her, has been asked to keep a secret, or if someone has been touching the child's private parts. These adult persons need to know whom to contact once an abuse situation is revealed. Once the recognition factors are in place the next step is to respond. Parents, child care workers, schools, churches, Scout groups, and everyone involved with children can become a part of this prevention process, can learn to be more protective of children, and can learn what to do if abuse is suspected.

Second, prevention must concentrate on societal elements that encourage child sexual abuse, such as advertisers exploiting children's sexuality to sell products and services, and the predominance of violence in television, movies, and magazines (Kehoe, 1988). Everyone is responsible for his or her part in maintaining and legitimizing the abuse of children.

The third prevention method is developing healthy parenting skills and increasing a child's self-esteem (Kehoe, 1988). Building self-esteem in children makes them less vulnerable to being abused. If a child feels positive about himself or herself and has his or her physical and emotional needs met, then he or she is less likely to be abused.

Parents can begin by teaching a child some basic safety rules in a number of different areas, such as safety away from home, at school, in religious meetings, in public restrooms, at public swimming pools, in movie theaters, and in doctors' offices. Children can also learn to use a special word to indicate to the parent that he or she (the child) is in a dangerous situation. The following are some guidelines to facilitate this process. All of what is presented is based on an active parenting model.

Parents, mothers, fathers, grandparents, and other extended family members need to take as much responsibility as possible to ensure children grow up feeling protected and loved. Learning some safety rules does not ensure that the child will be protected from others, but making sure that a child knows to tell a trusted adult about what has happened is a place to begin. This is especially true since the research literature indicates that the offender's major concern seems to be getting caught or having the child tell others about the sexual activity. Knowing that a child would tell an adult may be an effective deterrent for extrafamilial abusers. All the young child needs to remember is to tell a trusted adult about what has happened. This is simple and easy to remember, and it also places the burden of responsibility on the adult to respond and to resolve the issue.

Intrafamilial abusive situations are much more complex, but once again, adults need to be better educated about recognizing the signs and symptoms of abuse and how to intervene by bringing the abuse to the attention of Children and Youth Services or the proper organization or agency. Family members talking to the abuser about stopping the abuse is not effective, and it will not prevent the abuse from occurring again. Keeping the abuser in the home will not help the situation, nor will denial or minimization of what has occurred.

Parents and others can use puppets, dolls, and stuffed animals to teach safety rules for young children around the ages of 6 or 7. These objects have many uses. Playing with puppets, dolls, and stuffed animals provides a safe environment to engage young children and to teach them safety rules. Puppets can represent a friend, stranger, parent, or child. Puppets and dolls can be used to teach the child about body ownership, strangers, telling secrets, and how to answer the telephone or the door. These objects can also be helpful in teaching a child what to do if an adult asks the child for assistance or an adult asks a child to keep a secret. If the child has a special need, have the puppet or doll have the same need. Listen to the child. Hear what he or she has to say, both verbally and nonverbally.

SAFETY AWAY FROM HOME

Mall or Grocery Store

Parents should keep their hands on young children at all times; never allow the child to go to the bathroom alone. Do not use video arcades as a baby-sitter while shopping, and do not permit young children to go to other aisles or go alone to the toy section of a store. Do not allow the child to speak to strangers and never leave a child at the checkout counter alone. A parent or caretaker can engage older children by asking them to push the cart, if in a grocery store.

School

Parents should know the exact route the child takes to school. Help the child identify restaurants, small businesses, and homes of friends where the parent knows that the child could run to if help was needed. In our community we have big yellow stickers placed on the doors of some of the restaurants and small businesses that say, "Safeplace." Children in our community know that if they are frightened by someone and need a safe place all they have to do is go to a place where the special yellow sticker is on the door. We encourage parents to help children identify these stickers on trips to the mall, grocery store, or restaurants.

Determine if absenteeism is reported in your school district. If not, attend a PTA meeting and ask to discuss this issue. It is important that the parent be contacted if the child is absent from school. Provide the school with a work number as well as the home number. Never give universal approval to a school to remove your child from school property; insist that the child bring home a permission slip to be signed each and every time he or she will be removed from school grounds. If a parent gives permission for his or her child to attend a function at the school, the parent needs to determine the specifics, time, location, who will be in charge, and who will chaperon. Introduce yourself to your child's teachers, coaches, the principal, and all other school personnel involved with your child. Volunteer and become involved in your child's school activities; be present at all your child's afterschool activities, like sporting events and plays. Parents of Girl Scouts, Boy Scouts, or Campfire Girls should note that children spending nights away from home can be prime targets for molesters. If a parent is not welcome on campouts, question and investigate. Sexual abusers can be Scout leaders.

Religious Meetings

Meet and become familiar with your child's Sunday School, CCD (Catholic Christian Development), catechism, or youth group leaders. Make unannounced visits to your child's classroom or nursery. If you have concerns about leaving your child with a Sunday School teacher or nursery worker, don't; trust your gut instinct. Never leave a baby or child in a dirty nursery or Sunday School classroom.

Public Restrooms

Parents should always go along with a child to use the facilities in a public restroom. If a male child is too old to go with a female parent or caretaker, she can stand outside the door of the men's restroom and wait. Fathers can knock on the door of the women's restroom to determine if it is empty before entering with the female child. If a child goes to the restroom unattended and you become concerned, speak to the child through the door to find out if he or she is okay. If the child fails to respond, enter the restroom and if the door is locked, have one of the employees obtain the key to unlock the door.

Public Swimming Pools

Parents should remember that lifeguards are not responsible for baby-sitting a child. Talk to and discuss with your child what to do if someone approaches them in the dressing room area. Be specific. If possible, go with the child to the dressing area; pay attention to strangers who seem drawn to or are paying special attention to your child.

Movie Theaters

Parents should teach children to adhere to the same rules for public restrooms while in movie theaters. Teach children to identify persons (e.g., ushers or the manager) to approach if he or she should need to inform an adult of some inappropriate incident that has occurred. Teach children to say "No" if someone offers them candy or other treats in exchange for leaving the theater with them, and attend movies with your child. Be aware of what he or she is viewing. Censor what the child is permitted to view.

Doctor's Offices

Parents should not leave the child alone with the doctor or the nurse. As a parent, you have the right to question all procedures and ask for a complete explanation of anything that is being done to your child. If you do not understand, then ask the doctor or nurse to repeat the explanation. It is okay to ask questions about anything that involves your child; this includes medications that are being prescribed.

SAFETY WHILE AT HOME

Answering the Door

Children (if home alone) should never answer a knock on the door. If the person persists and is a stranger, tell the child to call the police. If the person persists and states he or she is in distress, call the police who will help the person. If the person tries to carry on a conversation with the child through the door, the child should not respond, should ignore the person's solicitations, and should call the police. Teach the child to keep the doors locked at all times. Parents should set an appropriate example for the child by doing the same thing when they are home. A locked door will not deter a professional but may stop a small-time thug.

Children and Telephones

Children need to be taught to use all types of phones: cellular, car phones, rotary, push-button, and pay telephones. Parents need to tape a list of emergency phone numbers to the phone or someplace where the child knows how and where to find them. If the child is young, under the age of six or seven, draw a police hat for the police, fire truck for the fire company and an ambulance for medical emergencies. Unplug the phone and have the child practice dialing the numbers and speaking into the telephone, giving the police or ambulance the correct information about address and phone number. Children can learn how to answer the phone. The child should not carry on conversations with strangers regardless of how charming or friendly the caller seems. If parents are not at home and someone calls and asks to speak to one of the parents, the child can learn to reply, "Mom and Dad are unable to come to the phone right at this time. They told me to take your name and number and they will call you." Children should never give out any other type of information. Remember, a child does not automatically know how and what to do in a given situation; he or she needs to be taught. All of these safety rules can teach a child how to deal more effectively with situations.

Presents

Parents should find out who is giving the child presents, and exactly what is contained in the presents. Ask questions, know the specifics. Pay attention to what the child says about earning gifts, and determine exactly how the child earned the gifts.

Photography or Videotapes

Parents can teach children that taking pictures by family members is permissible only if the family members do not ask the child to take off their clothes or engage in sexual behaviors while taking the pictures. Acknowledge that it is acceptable to take school pictures for the yearbook or church directory pictures. Never allow strangers to photograph the child.

IMPORTANT MESSAGES FOR PARENTS TO SEND TO CHILDREN

Convey to a child that he or she is loved. Reinforce to a child that if adults need assistance, adults should ask other adults for help, never children. One of the serial killer Ted Bundy's favorite ploys for engaging young women to help him was to go to a mall, use crutches, and ask teenage girls to help him carry his packages to his car. He was quite successful in his attempts, and most of the young women did not live to tell about it.

Teach a young child that anytime anyone asks the child to keep a secret then he or she should tell a trusted adult. Teach a child (by age 4) the difference between a surprise and a secret. Surprises are okay to keep, because the person eventually finds out about the surprise (birthday parties and presents at the holidays, for example). Secrets are not okay to keep.

A Special Word

Parents should teach a child that the special word is only used to identify an emergency situation. The special word can be a unique animal name, a place, person, shape, or color. It is a word only to be used when there is a threat to the child's safety on any level. By the age of 6 or 7 the child can developmentally understand the ramifications of using a special word. This word can be used for years, or a new one can be identified beginning in adolescence. Remember, it is not just small children that are in potentially dangerous situations, but adolescents as well—date rape is on the rise. This special word can be used in a variety of ways.

If a child is left in the care of a baby-sitter, always ask to speak to the child. Should the child use the word, ask for clarification or ask the child if there is a problem and if the answer is "yes," then parents, return home immediately. If you suspect a problem, then a helpful procedure is to ask the child questions to which he or she can respond with an affirmative or negative reply, such as "Are you okay?" or "Are you in a situation where you need me to come to where you are?"

If a child is visiting friends, call the child and ask how everything is going. If the child uses the distress word, ask if the child is in trouble and if the answer from the child is "yes," then go pick up the child immediately. This follows for adolescents as well. Do not assume that because an individual is a teenager, he or she can handle any situation. Adolescents still need to feel safe and believe their parents will be available if needed.

If in any situation the child uses the special word, ask him or her if there is trouble and if he or she is in distress, then phrase the question again so that it can be answered in a "yes" or "no" format. If the answer is "yes," immediately get to the place where the child or adolescent is. If you are unable to go to the child, call the police.

PUPPET PLAY

The following are some suggestions for puppet play with a child at least 6 years of age.

The Trust Game (Adopted from Adams & Fay [1987] and Hart-Rossi [1984])

The puppet is to supply a "yes" or "no" answer to the questions about whom the child can trust.

Can you trust everybody?
Can you trust your neighbors?
Can you trust your friends?

Can you trust friends of your parents?
Can you trust your teachers?
Can you trust your minister, your rabbi, or your priest?
Do you always know whom to trust?

The answer to every question above is "no." Parents then need to provide some explanation as to why all of the above cannot be trusted. Help the child to understand that just because the child knows someone does not mean that person would not abuse them. Even adults do not always know whom to trust. Just because a person is in an authority position does not imply he on she can be trusted. However, it is important to emphasize to the child that most people can be trusted and do care about the child; the problem is that children as well as adults do not know the difference between who is safe to trust and who is not.

The Game of "What If?"

The following game can be played utilizing puppets, dolls, stuffed animals, or whatever object the child relates to most significantly. Simply ask the puppet, "What would you do if?" Allow the puppet (the child has one of the puppets and the adult has another puppet) that is asking the questions to answer.

What would you do if?

1. (a). A man or a woman asks to take your picture? (Say no and move away from the person.)
    (b). A man or a woman just photographs you without your permission? (Tell a trusted adult.)
2. If an adult man or woman asks for your help to find their missing dog, cat, or other pet? (Say "No. My mother [or father] says I can't help you." This puts the responsibility on the parent.)
3. An adult man or woman asks your help to find an address of someone on your street? (Say "No, I can't. But I'll go ask my mother or father to come help you.")
4. An adult man or woman told you he or she was lost? (Tell them to ask an adult to help them find their way.)
5. An adult man or woman gives you candy, food, ice cream, money or presents? (Don't accept them.)
6. An adult man or woman asks you to help him or her in any way. (Respond, "No, I can't help you but I will ask an adult.")
7. A car, truck, motorcycle, or any type of vehicle pulls up beside you when you are playing or walking and asks if you would like to go for a ride, or tells you one of your parents is hurt and they will take you to them? (Don't go.)

8. Anyone, either an adult, adolescent, or child, asks you to touch his or her private body parts and tells you that it is okay to do this? (Say no and move away. Tell a trusted adult.)

9. An adult, adolescent, or another child tells you a secret and asks that you not tell anyone? (Tell a trusted adult that you were asked to keep a secret.)

10. Someone invites you to go inside their yard or house and your parents have not said that it is okay? (Don't go. Ask you mother or father or caretaker if it is okay to go.)

11. You feel scared while visiting at someone else's house and you want to talk to a parent? (Ask to call home. Make sure child knows his or her home phone number and his or her parents' work numbers. Also make sure the child knows how to use all types of phones.)

12. You are at home by yourself and someone knocks on the door? (Don't answer the door. If the knocking persists and the person will not go away, call the police.)

13. You are at home alone and the phone rings, what would you say to the caller? (Say, "My Mom [Dad] can't come to the phone right now but give me you name and number and I will have them call you.")

14. (a). A minister, rabbi, priest, teacher, doctor, or a police officer touches your private body parts or asks you to touch their private body parts? (Tell the person no and then tell a trusted adult.)
    (b). The person tells you that if you tell anyone, they will hurt you, and this is a secret? (Tell a trusted adult.)
    (c). The person gives you money not to tell anyone? What would you do? (Tell a trusted adult.)

15. A baby-sitter tries to touch your private body parts, or asks you to touch his or her private body parts? Your parents told you to listen to the baby-sitter before you left; what would you do? (Say no and tell your parents or another trusted adult.)

16. Someone asks you to tell them your name? (Don't tell them unless your mom or dad or caretaker says that it is okay.)

17. (a). An aunt, uncle, or cousin tries to touch your private body parts? (Say no, move away from them and tell a trusted adult.)
    (b). What would you do if the relative said he or she would be angry with you or your Mom or Dad would be angry with you if you did not listen to them and touch them like they asked? (Say no and tell your parents or another trusted adult.)

18. A stranger asked you what are the names of your parent's friends? (Don't tell them.)

19. What would you do if one of your parents tried to touch your private body parts or asked you to touch their private body parts? (Say no and then tell a trusted adult.)

20. (a). You are selling candy for a school project and have to go knock
        on people's doors. What would you do if a man or woman in-
        vited you inside? (Say "No, my parents don't allow me to go in
        other people's homes.")
    (b). A stranger shows you his or her private parts? (Tell your parents
        or another trusted adult.)
    (c). A family friend or neighbor tells you he or she will give you
        candy, money, or presents if you will show him or her your pri-
        vate body parts? (Say no and tell a trusted adult or parent.)
    (d). A family friend or neighbor asks you if you can keep a secret?
        (Say "No, we don't keep secrets at our house.")

21. You come home from school or a meeting and your parents are not
    home and you find the door unlatched? (Do not go in the house. Go
    to a neighbor or other trusted adult's house and tell them what has
    happened.)

22. (a). Your teacher or Scout leader asks you to stay after school or
        after a meeting and wants you to touch his or her private parts.
        (Say no and tell a trusted adult.)
    (b). What if he or she threatens to harm you? (Tell a trusted adult.)
    (c). What if this person says he or she will tell your family bad things
        about you? (Tell your parents or other trusted adult.)
    (d). What if he or she offers to give you money and asks you to keep
        a secret, what would you do? (Refuse the money, say no, and tell
        a trusted adult.)

23. Someone you know offers you pills or a drink of alcohol? (Don't take
    them.)

24. You tell your parents someone has touched your private body parts or
    someone has asked you to touch theirs. Your parents act as if they do
    not believe you. What should you do? (Tell another adult you can
    trust. Keep telling until someone listens.)

25. You are lost in a park, a toy store, a grocery store, or a mall, what
    should you do? (Go find a police officer, a security guard, or a clerk
    and tell them you are lost.)

CHILD ABUSE SUSPECTED: SUGGESTIONS
FOR PARENTS/CARETAKERS/TEACHERS
(Hart-Rossi, 1984; Hillman & Solek-Tefft, 1988)

1. **Talk to the child in a private place.** If behavioral changes have
   occurred (regressiveness or changes in eating and sleeping habits), comment

to him or her on the behavior changes. "I notice that you are not sleeping as well and you are avoiding certain foods you always loved before. I would appreciate your telling me if someone has been asking you to keep a secret." It is appropriate to ask questions, like "Has someone been asking you to keep secrets?" or "What has he or she asked you to keep secret?" or "Has someone asked you to touch their private parts (penis, vulva, or breasts)?" or "Has someone shown you their private parts?" or "Has someone shown you videos of children or adults being sexual with one another?"

2. **Remain calm and believe the child.** Children rarely lie about being sexually abused. Take the time to be alone with the child and listen to what the child has to say. Say, "I believe what you are telling me," "Thank you for telling me," or "It was the right thing to do by telling. That took a lot of courage for you to tell me."

3. **Reassure the child.** If the child reveals he or she has been abused, tell the child he or she did right by telling you. "Thank you for telling me. I believe what you said." Demonstrate reassurance by talking, hugging, holding hands, playing, or whatever seems appropriate. Ask the child what he or she wants. "You have just shared a lot of things with me. Could I hug you, hold your hand, sit close to you, or do something else that will make you feel better?" The child may want to play and want you to play with him or her. Remember that children deal with feelings and the world through play.

4. **Call Children and Youth Services or Child Protective Services.** Inform the child that you have to call and report the abuse. Tell the child that someone is coming to hear their story. Reassure the child that you will stay with him or her while the people ask him or her some questions about what has happened.

5. **Reinforce verbally and behaviorally that the child acted appropriately.** Please know that the child may feel guilty and overwhelmed as a result of telling about the abuse. The child may be both relieved and scared. These are normal feelings. Be consistent in what you tell the child. Again tell the child he or she was right to tell you. "You did the best thing by telling me." Don't make promises you can't keep.

6. **Be sensitive to what has happened to the child.** If you are a parent, tell the child's brothers and sisters briefly what has happened. Ask the siblings not to question the child. Reinforce to other family members that it is not the child's fault. He or she is blameless. The offender is the one at fault. Ask the siblings the same questions about secrets. Siblings may feel scared and overwhelmed and be fearful of what their friends will think if others find out what has happened.

7. **Seek support for the parents (if they have not been involved in the**

abuse). During this difficult time allow friends, relatives, professional counselors, support groups, and 24-hour crisis agencies to be support-ive.

8. **Recognize that the child is NEVER at fault.** This needs to be rein-forced again and again to the child and other family members. The offender is completely responsible for what has happened.

9. **Reassure the child that you will be there for him or her, regardless of what happens (Please say this only if you can follow through and be available to him or her.)** Be certain you follow through on any statements or promises made to the child.

10. **Offer to answer any questions the child has.** If you do not know the answer, assure the child you will find someone who can answer the question.

11. **If the child wants to talk about the abuse, encourage him or her to do so.** Never force the child to talk about the abuse; allow him or her to make that decision. See that there are dolls, crayons, paper, and figures for the child to play with. Play helps children deal with issues and feelings.

12. **Seek professional help for yourself, the child, and the family.** If you are unsure about whom to contact professionally, call your local 24-hour hotline or Childhelp USA (800-422-4453), and they can direct you where to seek professional help for the family.

Note: If a parent is the sexual offender, the situation can become quite complex. Sometimes the nonoffending parent will express an un-willingness to believe the child or will ignore what the child has said. This is especially true if the child is making accusations about a mother's boyfriend or a stepfather. Mothers are more inclined to believe reports of abuse about the natural father. The child should be and needs to be believed and protected. Just because the accused offender vehemently denies and protests that he or she is innocent does not signify that he or she has not molested or abused the child. Do not be persuaded by the denials of the accused. His or her protests do not mean that no abuse has occurred. An offender will lie to protect him- or herself. Offenders lie even when there is physical evidence to indicate other-wise. Ignore pleas or promises not to do it again. Contact Child Pro-tective Services.

THE CHILD SURVIVOR

Children do not always loath or fear adults who have sexually abused them. The child may enjoy certain areas of the relationship. Any pleasurable feelings the child has experienced may cause intense guilt feelings. If the abuser is a parent, the child may be more afraid of losing the parent if the abuse is reported than of the abuse continuing. The child may have been told "I won't get to see you ever again if you tell about our secret," or "Your mother will be very hurt if she finds out what has happened,"or "No one will believe you because this is all your fault," or "You must really like it based on how you responded when I touched you."

Parental Coping Behaviors with Children Who Have Been Abused

Parents, caretakers, day-care personnel, and extended family members can learn how to handle and respond appropriately to the child's feelings. Survivors often experience denial, dissociation, confusion, or fear (child may be fearful the perpetrator will follow through on threats). The threats should never be trivialized. The child needs reassurance again and again. Know that children may experience depression, sadness, and grief. None of these should be ignored. These feelings may be manifested in stomachaches, headaches, or eating disorders. Children do not say, "Gee, I am depressed or anxious." In a situation where a child is a survivor of sexual abuse, his or her physical symptoms can be a barometer of unexpressed feelings. A child survivor usually believes he or she is responsible for the sexual abuse that occurred and for other family members' distress. Responsibility for the abuse is with the perpetrator regardless of what he or she told the child and whether or nor the child experienced any pleasurable feelings from what occurred. These matters can and should be discussed with the child more than once.

Attempt to keep the child's routine as much the same as possible. A certain security exists in "ordinariness." If a child's routines are disrupted, then he or she may feel as if he or she is being punished. If the child always went to bed at 9 p.m., maintain that bedtime. If the child had to do his or her homework after school, keep this routine. Seeking professional help is crucial in helping parents and other family members deal with their own feelings and respond effectively to the child. Children who have been abused forcefully might experience temper tantrums and acting-out behaviors, all of which is normal. Parents can learn how to respond and set limits for and with the child regarding appropriate behavior. Sometimes children deal with feelings of powerlessness and loss of control by reenacting the abusive behaviors. In these instances the child who was victimized now becomes the perpetrator. He or she may act aggressive toward other children, try to force other children into sexualized play, or be seductive with adults. All of this is an attempt on the child's part to gain some control and mastery over his or her feelings. The adults in the child's life can be aware of this possibility of sexually acting-out behaviors and decide how to respond to the child should these behaviors occur. Professional direction and support can be helpful in managing a child's aggressive and sexualized behaviors. Do not hit the child as a technique to manage acting-out behaviors. If the abused child attempts to act in a sexual manner with other children, the adult should intervene and redirect the play without making a big deal out of the situation. Consistency, limit-setting, and structure are important issues, especially since aggressive acting-out is a real possibility. Children who have been abused are often frightened to experience any type of negative or positive feelings. Adults have the responsibility to model the appropriate way to express feelings. All adults involved can learn to redirect the child's behavior without making a big deal out of it. Be consistent. There is a definite need for teamwork among school, family, and mental health professionals.

When a child has been abused, the siblings also need to be in individual treatment or family therapy. This accomplishes two things: (1) nonabused children can learn how to deal with potentially abusive situations, and (2) treatment provides an opportunity for any of the other siblings to reveal if they have also been abused.

BUILDING A CHILD'S HOUSE OF SELF

Kehoe (1988) and Hillman and Solek-Tefft (1988) suggested the following for helping to positively build children's house of self. Building a child's house of self requires parents to have some knowledge and understanding of child development concepts and what is appropriate behavior for a 2-year-old child, a 3-year-old, a 7-year-old, and so on. Having age-appropriate expectations of a child can go a long way toward responding appropriately to situations with the child and lessening the frustrations and expectations surrounding parenthood. Use positive parenting, which includes physical and emotional nurturing like hugs and praise. Never use the negative parenting behaviors: humiliation, name-calling, or denigrating the child. Hillman and Solek-Tefft (1988) suggested encouraging a child to attempt something new or untried, whether it be a new flavor of ice cream, a new fruit, or a new sport. If the child is unsuccessful in his or her attempts, do not criticize the child but encourage the child to try again. Do not use physical punishment like spanking, slapping, or hitting. Using physical punishment places a child at risk for being abused because the child may fear being punished if he or she reports the sexual abuse to anyone.

Hunt (1991) published an article on reasons not to hit children. She suggested the following as reasons: Children who are hit can and do become adults who are violent and hurt others. (The most consistent finding to date on adolescent males who sexually abuse is that these males, as children, were physically abused again and again.) What children learn from the use of physical punishment is that whoever is bigger and stronger wins. Hitting conveys the message that striking out is an effective way to solve problems. Hitting only produces fear-based responses from children, and anger internalized from this kind of physical abuse in childhood may be expressed as rage in adolescents. Striking a young child on the buttocks can set the stage for a later association between pain and pleasure and result in sexually dysfunctional behaviors in adulthood. And of course, hitting can cause physical harm or even kill the child. It also escalates. Once an individual begins to hit he or she may find it difficult to stop hitting. Children's acting-out behaviors may be the only manner in which the child can convey that he or she feels neglected and ignored, or it may be the only way to deal with feelings he or she is experiencing. All of us, including children, need love and understanding. Finally, hitting causes a child to shift his or her focus from what was the actual problem to dealing with feelings around being hit, like anger, pain, fear, or retaliation. Hitting is not helpful in teaching a child how to resolve problems and solve conflicts (Hunt, 1991, pp. 168–171). Other tactics such as removing the child from a situation or taking away privileges are far more appropriate.

Children can learn and do need to be taught the proper names for the parts of their bodies, including their genitals. Respect for one another is an important concept to communicate to a child. It is a concept that is learned. Respect for a child's body needs to be apparent in the family. Respect can be communicated to a child by permitting him or her to decide when and where he or she wants to give and receive hugs and kisses. If a child does not want to hug and kiss, he or she can shake hands, draw the person a picture, smile, or wave. Parents can explain to relatives who are overly affectionate that the child is given a choice in expressing affection. Parents, support your children, especially if they don't want to give kisses and hugs.

Teach children to recognize the difference between behavior and self. A parent should acknowledge that he or she is angry with the child's behavior, but not with the child. Just because a behavior is unacceptable does not make the child unacceptable. Acknowledge that it is okay to feel sad, mad, glad, happy, or angry. Children need to know that feelings are not hurtful, it is how one expresses what he or she feels that can be hurtful, for example, feeling sad is okay, crying in response to feeling sad is okay, but throwing dishes or toys is not an appropriate way to express feeling sad. Anger is okay, but it is not okay to hit another person when feeling angry. (Parents need to be certain that they do not hit the child.)

Give words to feelings. The child needs to know the parent will listen to what he or she is trying to communicate. Teaching children to identify feelings is important. This can be accomplished in a variety of ways. A feeling chart can be utilized. To draw a feeling chart, take a sheet of blank, unlined paper and ask the child to draw circles on the paper and then draw a happy face, a sad face, a mad face, a scared face, and so on. Put the feeling chart in a prominent place in the house, perhaps on the refrigerator. Kehoe (1988) suggested asking the child to choose a feeling and then drawing a picture to illustrate it, and if the child is old enough she or he can add a story to the picture. A complete text including many different feelings may take weeks to complete. Children can learn that how they show their feelings is through their behaviors or actions: by crying when feeling sad, hitting a pillow when feeling mad, or laughing when feeling glad. Behaviors are what can be seen and described by other people.

Part of educating children about protecting themselves from sexual abuse is helping the child to build his or her self-esteem. It is important to encourage parents and caretakers to teach children to say, "Don't touch me!" and "No, I won't touch you! I don't like it" (Hart-Rossi, 1984, p. 21). Assertive behavior involves looking the person in the eye while speaking. Maintaining eye contact communicates to the other person (1) that you are sincere in what was communicated, (2) that you are not fearful of him or her, and (3) that you are comfortable with what is being said. When communicating with a child, maintain frequent eye contact with the child and place your face at the child's eye level, which might require bending down. Teaching children about sexual abuse and other safety issues should be accomplished in a calm, relaxed way.

Chapter 7

DEVELOPMENT OF THE CHILD: ORIGINS OF THE SELF

One of the core tenets in the development of the child is the evolution of his or her sense of self. Chess and Thomas (1987) defined the self as ". . . made up of the identity, character, and essential qualities of a person, which tend to be enduring in nature. In essence, the self is one's own person or being, as distinct and apart from all others" (p. 155). Both Bowlby (1969) and Stern (1985) were convinced that the child's sense of self develops from his or her interactions with significant others.

As the child develops a sense of self, he or she either feels positive or negative about himself or herself, about his or her capabilities in relating to others in various settings, and about being proficient in overcoming difficult tasks. High self-esteem enables a child to greet opportunities and obstacles with a belief in his or her capacity to surmount them effectively. Low self-esteem in a child is manifested in part by the child's uncertainty of his or her abilities to effectively deal with new challenges, in addition to his or her concern about present and past accomplishments when compared to others. Children exhibiting low self-esteem have a tendency to constantly compare themselves to others.

Infancy is when a sense of self begins to form. For the self to begin to emerge the baby needs to be capable of distinguishing himself or herself as a unique person, different from his or her parents and other things in his or her environment (Chess & Thomas, 1987).

STAGES OF LIFE

Erik Erikson (1959) believed the "self" began to form during the first months of life. Erikson (1968) stated, "At birth the baby leaves the chemical exchange of the womb for the social exchange system of his society, where his gradually increasing capacities meet the opportunities and limitations of his culture" (p. 92).

Kohut (1977) viewed the evolution of the self as the earliest and most intricate task of childhood. Erikson (1959) believed that an individual, beginning in infancy, has to work through eight crises of development throughout his or her lifetime. (For our purposes, only the first five will be discussed.) As each stage or crisis is resolved the individual's identity is reaffirmed on a new level.

Trust versus mistrust is the first stage of an infant's development. It takes place from birth through the first year of life (Erikson, 1959, 1968). Erikson (1968) defined basic trust as "an essential trustfulness of others as well as a fundamental sense of one's own trustworthiness" (p. 96). The child forms a relationship with the parent or a primary caretaker and then begins to discover the difference between self and other. Erikson contended that some mistrust is necessary for development but, if the infant is more mistrustful than trustful, the infant, child, and later the adult will lack in feelings of confidence. He or she will experience low self-esteem and be withdrawn and suspicious of everyone with whom he or she comes into contact. The major task accomplished in this stage is giving and receiving.

Bowlby (1969) determined close proximity during infancy and toddlerhood necessary for bonding and avoiding incestuous relationships. Erickson (1993) stated,

> The adult who bonded securely in childhood should have stable intrapsychic boundaries between sexual and familial feelings. As parent, he or she is therefore able to respond spontaneously and appropriately to a child's affectional needs, naive sexuality, and assertiveness. In contrast, the parent who experienced impaired bonding as a child may have relatively unstable boundaries between sexual and familial feelings. In this latter case, a child's display of affection or flirtatiousness may either be rebuffed, because it is psychologically threatening, or be misinterpreted and responded to in an inappropriately sexualized manner. (p. 415)

A caregiver who is responsive to the infant's needs reinforces the infant's worthiness and trust that his or her needs will be met by the caregiver. Bowlby (1969) has suggested that children develop working models of their world based on relationships formed in infancy and toddlerhood with primary caregivers.

Cole and Putnam (1992) defined the tasks of infancy and toddlerhood as,

> (a) the discovery of a world of people and objects, (b) the establishment of secure social relationships within the family, (c) the establishment of a basic sense of self, (d) the development of an agentic or autonomous awareness, and (e) the acquisition of an initial sense of right and wrong (or good and bad). (p. 176)

Stage two is conceptualized by autonomy versus shame and doubt (Erikson, 1959). This stage lasts from approximately 1 year to 3 years of age. This stage is characterized by the child beginning to walk and talk, experiencing anxiety during times of separation from parents, gaining control of the bowels, and having to come to terms with failure, which can in turn affect the child's self-esteem depending on how parents respond when the child attempts to master tasks. The positive aspect of this stage is in the development of autonomy; the negatives are shame and doubt. Shame and doubt generally revolve around the child's ability to be potty-trained and have some independence from the parents. If the basic trust between parent and child is faulty, then the child may experience feelings of shame and doubt about himself or herself and the world in general. Major tasks to accomplish are holding on and learning to let go. In this stage the child is quite self-oriented. The child is governed by external controls, not internal rules.

Erikson (1959) stated that stage three usually begins around 4 years of age. It is the initiative versus guilt stage of development. During this stage the child progresses in physical abilities, language, thought processes, and creativity, especially in imaginative play. But the most important issue for the child during this phase, according to Erikson, is the identification with his or her parents. He stated, "he wants to be like his parents, who to him appear very powerful and very beautiful, although quite unreasonably dangerous" (Erikson, 1959, p. 74). The child's main concern at this developmental stage is to avoid getting into trouble. If he or she does get blamed he or she does not want to accept responsibility for any of his or her negative actions.

Cole and Putnam (1992) described the child's tasks of these preschool years as,

> to learn to integrate its secure sense of an agentic self with the restrictions of the social world. Preschool age includes setting limits

> on one's own behavior (Kopp, 1982), cooperating with others (Hartup, 1983), and being accountable for rule violations. Preschoolers sense of self tends to be restricted to concrete observable attributes, e.g., I am a girl. . . ." (p. 177)

During this time period it is not possible for a preschooler to understand that persons possess both positive or negative qualities. People are seen as either all good or all bad.

Industry versus inferiority is the fourth stage of development according to Erikson (1959), lasting from about 6 years to puberty. Entering school is the most significant task of this stage. The child is exposed to learning all kinds of new and wonderful things. If the child is able to feel successful in learning, he or she will experience a sense of industry and a belief in his or her ability to achieve and acquire new skills and new levels of thinking. Too many failures during this period will result in the child believing himself or herself to be inadequate or less than other children.

By the time a child reaches first grade he or she is aware of his or her gender-type. Throughout the elementary school years the child becomes more cognizant of his or her thoughts and feelings. By the time a child reaches 8 or 9 years of age, he or she is aware that the self and others can possess both positive and negative traits. If intrafamilial abuse is occurring during this stage of development, the child may find it difficult to seek friendships and may experience feelings of guilt, shame, and confusion, that may be pervasive for a child at this time (Cole & Putnam, 1992). Obviously it becomes more difficult for a child to learn self-control behaviors if the parents are lacking in self control themselves. A parent who is sexually abusive with his or her child has obvious deficits in self control. A child at this age may struggle with the blurring of boundaries because his or hers are continually being violated.

Stage five, according to Erikson, is the identity and repudiation versus identity diffusion phase of development. This stage occurs during adolescence. A central task of this stage is for the adolescent to develop a more complete, integrated identity, based on the different roles or selves from childhood. If the adolescent is incapable of incorporating these identities, the result will be "identity diffusion." This struggle may be complicated enormously if the adolescent is from a different ethnic or minority culture, has questions about his or her sexual preference, or is too emotionally dependent on a parent. Erikson (1959) has defined the developmental tasks of later adolescence as attaining autonomy from parents, internalizing moral values, choosing a career, and identifying with and having a well-grounded sense of one's sex-role identity. Blos (1979) described adolescence as a time of "shedding family dependencies." However, according to Erikson (1968) a female's adolescence is held in check until she attracts a husband. The husband is how she defines her self and she, according to Erikson, does not form a separate identity but rather defines herself through her husband.

Perhaps another way of looking at autonomy for women is that a woman is able to make choices for herself, but does not have to negate or deny her needs for connectedness and affiliation. Kaschak (1992) wrote,

> There is not one certain kind of self for all women. Instead there are differences as a function of race and class, differences between women in these groups as a result of unique combinations of experience and unique meanings made of those experiences. And the differences within a woman in different situations depends on the meanings they evoke for her. (p. 155)

Gilligan, Ward, and Taylor (1988) addressed the issue of autonomy:

> To see self-sufficiency as the hallmark of maturity conveys a view of adult life that is at odds with the human condition, a view that cannot sustain the kinds of long-term commitments and involvements with other people that are necessary for raising and educating a child or for citizenship in a democratic society. (p. xii)

They continued with,

> Being dependent, then, no longer means being helpless, powerless, and without control; rather, it signifies a conviction that one is able to have an effect on others, as well as the recognition the interdependence of attachment empowers both the self and the other, not one person at the other's expense. (p. 16)

Adolescence marks the beginning of puberty and the development of secondary sex characteristics. There is a real move to develop and establish relationships with members of the opposite sex. Adolescents begin to understand and integrate the various aspects of their personalities with both how they see and experience themselves, and how others view them. If the adolescent is being sexually abused during this critical phase of development and if he or she is engaging in denial and dissociative behaviors to cope with the abuse, then these phenomena will certainly impact on his or her ability to integrate aspects of the self and form opposite sex relationships.

Erikson and Kohut are a sharp contrast to Freud (1965), who believed infants were only born with primitive instincts, called the "id." Freud (1933) described the id as ". . . a cauldron of seething excitement" (p. 104). The newborn, according to Freud, did not begin to be a real part of the human race until the ego and superego had evolved, suppressed, regulated, and subdued the culpable id.

Margaret Mahler's (Mahler, Pine, & Bergman, 1975) views on the new-born were even more negative than Freud's. She and her colleagues described the infant in the following manner: "During the first few weeks of extrauterine life, a stage of absolute primary narcissism, marked by the infant's lack of awareness of a mothering agent, prevails. This is the stage we have termed "normal autism" (Chess & Thomas, 1987, p. 98). She and her associates labeled the first four months of the first year of life as the biological birth of the infant. Mahler et al. (1975) continued by describing the second phase of the newborn's life, beginning in the second month, as ". . . a phase of normal symbiosis, in which the infant behaves and functions as though he and his mother were an omnipotent system" (Chess & Thomas, 1987, p. 98). She postulated that not until 5 or 6 months of age does the baby make his or her debut in the world by "hatching out" and viewing himself or herself as a distinct entity from the mother (Chess & Thomas, 1987, p. 98). Mahler et al. (1975) suggested there are four subphases in the separation–individuation phase, which occur from about 5 to 6 months to 36 months. Somewhere between 5 and 8 months the infant recognizes others besides his or her mother (according to Mahler et al.); this has been called the differentiation subphase. By 7 to 8 months, Mahler suggested the infant will engage in crawling behavior and physically moving away from the caregiver a little bit, but will turn his or her head to see where his or her caregiver is located. Mahler et al. (1975) called this "checking back to Mother, "which has been formally titled the practicing subphase. By 8 to 9 months the infant is aware that strangers are different from the caregiver and some "stranger anxiety" may develop. The infant may turn away, cling to the caregiver, or cry if approached by a stranger.

Kagan (1984) saw this fearfulness of strangers as a new level of cognitive advancement in the infant, an indicator that the child has the ability to discriminate between parents and unknown persons. Some researchers have indicated that fearfulness of strangers is frequently transitory and does not have an impact on long-term development of the child's sense of self (Bretherton, 1978; Lamb, Thompson, Gardner, Charnov, & Estes, 1984; Sroufe, 1977).

Somewhere between 16 and 25 months the toddler learns that he or she is not the center of the world and recognizes that he or she is very small in a very large world. Mahler et al. (1975) have called this the rapprochement subphase of development. As a result of recognizing his or her smallness and vulnerability, the child may feel anxious and insecure. He or she may cling to the mother and then distance himself or herself from her if she attempts to hold him or her. In every sense the child is learning to separate and reunite himself or herself with the parents, learning to know more about himself or herself and learning to trust his or her parents. From the ages of 25 to 36 months (called the object constancy phase), the child is capable of longer times apart from the mother by using transitional objects like bears, dolls, or blankets, that symbolically represent the mother. Eventually the child is able to recall from memory a loving image of his or her mother and no longer needs a transitional object.

Mahler's child development theories were not universally accepted by all members of the professional community, although her formulations had a significant impact on many professionals. A number of researchers took great issue with her developmental stages of an infant's first six months of life (Bowlby, 1982; Peterfreund, 1978; Stern, 1977). More recently, Stern (1985) has postulated four stages in the infant's development of the "self." Emergent self is the first step of development. During this stage the baby has distinct, unconnected encounters. After this time the baby begins to synthesize and arrange these individual isolated experiences into some form of meaning for him or her. Core self is Stern's second stage of development, which takes place between 2 and 6 months of age. During this time the baby begins to understand that he or she has some mastery of his or her movements (e.g., your foot moves when you want it to) and that his or her movements have outcomes (if he or she kicks a blanket, the blanket moves). Subjective sense is the third level of development, which occurs when the infant is between 7 and 15 months of age. In this stage the toddler recognizes that communication is possible and begins to make requests. Verbal self is the fourth area of development. This stage occurs after the first 15 months of the child's life. This stage enables the child to communicate more effectively than he or she was able to previously. He or she is also able to begin to play at this stage of development. As the child progresses through each stage, one level of development does not supplant the other; all the stages build on one another. As the child grows he or she is becoming more and more integrated and complex (Stern, 1985).

Understanding how and when a sense of self begins to develop is important. Viewing the infant as a functioning human being rather than as an undifferentiated object who "hatches" into a human being may enable parents and other caregivers to respond and interact more effectively with the infant and in turn enhance the infant's development of self (Chess & Thomas, 1987). How parents perceive the baby impacts on how each of the parents responds to the child and influences the child's psychological growth. Increased knowledge of how a child develops will impact on how children's behavior is labeled and perceived by others. Implications of this could be far-reaching and could result in a much healthier and more positive view of an infant and his or her interactions with the world. Once the child's sense of self has been developed, the formation of self-esteem is the next step in the progressive development of the self.

DEVELOPMENT OF SELF-ESTEEM

Garbarino, Stott, and the faculty at the Erikson Institute (1989) have written that "Out of the interaction of a child's experiences and characteristics comes a perspective on himself, or self-esteem, and a set of strategies and tactics for dealing with the world, or coping mechanisms. . ." (p. 18). Self-esteem influences how children behave and communicate. Erikson (1959) believed that for children's self-esteem to flourish, they needed to continually recognize that they were accomplishing the tasks necessary to be a part of their environment. Erikson believed it was not the mastery of the tasks that was paramount to the child's development of the self, but rather the continued recognition of the accomplishments. Self-esteem is not an all-encompassing quality. Sometimes self-esteem is dichotomous, meaning that an individual may have high self-esteem in some areas of his or her life, perhaps in academics, but low self-esteem in other areas, such as musical abilities (Chess & Thomas, 1987).

Parents are the cornerstone in promoting development of healthy self-esteem in their child. Acknowledging, appreciating, and acclaiming a child's mastery of developmental tasks helps to form the core of a child's self-esteem. Parents and other caretakers are instrumental in fostering a healthy sense of development and high self-esteem in a child, but environment and culture are critical factors in the child's development of self. Racism, sexism, or religious and ethnic biases can strongly impact on a child's self-esteem.

Chess and Thomas (1987) presented a concept that impacts on the child's development of self. It is called "goodness or poorness of fit." They described it in the following manner:

> Goodness of fit exists when the demands and expectations of the parents and other people important to the child's life are compatible with the child's temperament, abilities, and other characteristics. With such a fit healthy development for the child can be expected.
>
> Poorness of fit, on the other hand, exists when demands and expectation are excessive and not compatible with the child's tem-

perament, abilities, and other characteristics. With such a fit, the child is likely to experience excessive stress, and healthy development. (pp. 56–57)

Chess and Thomas (1987) also described others who have developed the same concept but labeled it a little differently than "goodness of fit," or as in Hunt (1980), "problem of the match."

Chess and Thomas (1987) described what "goodness of fit" is not. These authors contended that it is not necessary for parent and child to have analogous dispositions; it does not mean there will be a lack of stress, pressure, or contention when the child attempts to surmount new tasks. Chess and Thomas suggested that "goodness of fit" may change with time, since both parent and child continue to evolve and grow, and that "goodness of fit" may have a different meaning in a different culture. To illustrate the cultural meaning of this, Chess and Thomas (1987) presented a study by de Vries (1984), an anthropologist who studied 47 infants who lived Kenya, ranging in age between 2 and 4 months. de Vries rated all the children's dispositions. His data collection began when a harsh drought was starting to affect the region in Kenya where he was collecting the data. He labeled ten of the babies as having an "easy" personality, and ten as having an irksome personality. He left the region and returned five months later. At this point in time almost all of the cattle had died from the famine. de Vries could only locate 7 of the families with the babies he had labeled as having an easy personality and 6 with the families of the babies he had labeled as having an irksome personality. Of the 7 families with the"easy" babies, 5 of the infants had died. This is in marked contrast to the irksome infants, all of which had survived. de Vries was not certain why this phenomenon had occurred. He speculated that an infant who cried more frequently and more vehemently was perhaps regarded as more important than another infant who cried less. He also posited that "goodness of fit" occurred in a distressingly dismal environment where the infants who cried loudest received the most care. Losel and Bliesener (1990) would have called this infant a "resilient child."

Parents' failure to respond in cases of sexual abuse can be understood by examining Bowlby's (1969, 1973, 1980, 1988) theory of attachment. Attachment behaviors are defined as crying, clinging, following, sucking, and smiling, which in turn produce a caretaking response from the mother-figure.

A child begins to form attachments as soon as he or she is born. Bowlby was convinced that in the first three months of life, babies respond to different people the same way. By about 5 or 6 weeks, a baby will actually smile openly,

and until about 3 months of age, he or she will smile at any face. But according to Bowlby (1982), the baby smiling at the caretaker helps to solidify the
bonding and attachment process (e.g., baby smiles, so the caretaker smiles,
talks to the baby, or strokes the baby's face). During this time the baby will
begin babbling as well. Crying signals to the caretaker that the infant is dis-
tressed and needs something. Between 3 and 6 months babies become more
selective in who will receive their smiles. Generally during this period the child
responds most significantly to two or three persons or often one special person. This person could be the mother or the father. It is the person who is
the most in tune with the baby's needs and who is most responsive to him or
her. By about 6 months of age the child becomes intensely attached to one
person and may cry when that person leaves the room. By 7 or 8 months,
according to Bowlby, the child will crawl after the caretaker and hold out his
or her arms to be picked up. If the attachment between the child and the mother-
figure is secure, the toddler can then begin to explore his or her world but
continue to return to the mother when afraid or to reinforce that the mother-
figure is available and is a constant. By the time the child has reached five
years of age he or she should have been able to internalize that a secure base
exists and should feel secure that the mother-figure is always there or returns
if he or she goes away (Bowlby, 1969, 1973). This knowledge enables the
child to form attachments with others outside his or her family. Research studies have supported the notion that parents of neglected and abused children
frequently are not emotionally available to their children, and the parents do
not respond to their children's needs. Barach (1991) proposed that adult attachment relationships reflect the situation that occurred during childhood. Parents
fail to protect the child from abuse and the parents detach from emotional involvement with the child.

Bowlby discussed the three phases of a child's response to separation. First,
the child protests the loss (usually by crying) and uses attachment behaviors to
bring back the mother. If the mother does not return the child despairs but
continues to remain vigilant for her return. Finally, he or she appears to detach
and seems unconcerned about the mother-figure's return. If the separation period is not too long the child will reconnect with the figure upon his or her
return, if the parent has been caring and responsive to the child's earlier needs.
The child may cling to the parent and display anxious behaviors at any signs of
separations. Bowlby (1973) viewed the phenomenon of anxious attachment stem-
ming from real or temporary abandonment by caretakers during childhood. If
the child is aware and cognizant of a secure base he or she will be able to deal
effectively with separations and will have the ability to enter new situations
with a sense of confidence. If he or she has an insecure base it may make him
or her more vulnerable to being sexually abused.

Alexander (1992) contended that insecure attachment (based on Bowlby's theories) of a parent to a child then results in insecure attachment of the child to the parent. This insecure attachment is a precursor to abuse of the child. A child who has experienced insecure attachment will feel unloved and have of sense of not being wanted. The parent in this instance is often both physically and psychologically unavailable to the child and is unwilling or unable to meet the child's needs.

A second situation often found in sexually abusive homes is parentification of the child (Alexander, 1992). Sometimes there is almost complete role reversal between parent and child; the child assumes parental roles of nurturing, taking care of the other children, and cooking. The parent may also expect this parentified child to meet his or her sexual needs. Obviously the parentified child's needs for love and caring are not even recognized or are ignored. Being in a sexual relationship with one of the parents may be the only way he or she can receive any form of caring or nurturing. A secure attachment between parent and child ensures that sexual boundaries are not violated.

Lastly, a parent who is sexually abusing his or her child may have fears of abandonment by others, and he or she may be a survivor of childhood sexual abuse and thus did not have a secure attachment to his or her own parents. He or she may lack any coping abilities to stop the abuse from occurring. Alexander (1992) stated, "Thus, insecure attachment may either help set the stage for sexually abusive behavior or may interfere with its termination" (p. 189).

COGNITIVE DEVELOPMENT

The infant is born with the capacity and capability of learning. According to Kagan (1984) infants have visual, auditory, olfactory, and tactile senses, even though these senses are not fully developed.

One of the pioneers in the study of cognitive development was Jean Piaget, a Swiss epistemologist, who was interested in how children think at different ages. The first stage in Piaget's theory of cognitive development is called the sensorimotor intelligence phase (from birth to 2 years of age). It encompasses the baby learning to synchronize sensory and motor stimuli. This first stage was comprised of six separate phases.

Phase 1 (reflex responding), which lasts from birth to 1 month, focuses on the child's reflexes and how using them to suck, grasp things, and so on helps him or her to become better acquainted with the world. Phase 2 (primary circular reactions), which occurs when the child is 1 to 4 months old, is characterized by the infant engaging in circular activities like grasping objects, scratching, and so on. Piaget labeled the behaviors as circular because the infant will engage in the behavior again and again. He stated, "I note how definitely the spontaneous grasping of the sheet reveals the characteristics of circular reaction-groping at first, then regular rhythmical activity (scratching, grasping, holding, and letting go), and finally progressive loss of interest" (Piaget, 1952, p. 92). Phase 3 (secondary circular reactions) is characterized by the baby's interest in cause and effect motions ("I shake the rattle and it makes noise."). He or she develops a repertoire of actions to use to get reactions. Phase 4 (coordination of secondary schemes), according to Piaget, takes place during the first 8 to 12 months of the infant's life. This stage is characterized by the infant's acting specifically with a goal in mind. He or she demonstrates more curiosity at this stage, and if a toy is hidden under a blanket, he or she will seek to find the lost object.

Phase 5 (tertiary circular reactions) begins at 12 months and ends around 18 months of age. This stage is characterized by experimentation. Toys and other objects are explored and examined in new ways. The child experiments through trial and error to give activities new meanings, like pulling a blanket toward him or her to get cracker from the other side of the blanket. During this stage, somewhere between 15 and 18 months of age, the child develops what is known as symbolic function. Symbolic functions enable a child to utilize menial symbols, which result in the ability to grasp and begin to effectively use language. Phase 6 (invention of new means through mental combinations), which occurs when the child is 18 to 24 months of age, centers on the child beginning to form mental pictures of objects, actions, and situations. He or she begins to understand symbols and their meanings. According to Piaget's theory the child must successfully master the tasks in each developmental stage before he or she is able to progress to the next level.

Preoperational is the second stage of cognitive development according to Piaget. This stage occurs in the time period from 2 to 7 years of age. This stage is characterized by egocentrism, in which the child is unable to distinguish between himself or herself and the world at large, for example, the child may have an inability to delineate between a nightmare and reality; centration, in which the child is able to only focus on one aspect of an object at a time; lack of reversibility, when a child is able to understand lemonade poured from a pitcher into a glass but cannot mentally visualize the now full glass of lemonade being poured back into the pitcher; and limited moral reasoning ability, such as judging the wrongness of actions based on the amount of harm or damage done (the intent is ignored, and the boy who wants to be helpful and decides to fill his father's ink bottle but makes a mess on the tablecloth is considered more guilty than the child who was simply playing with the ink bottle and spilled a little bit on the table). People are viewed as either all good or all bad. It is difficult for a child in this stage to believe and understand that a caretaker would sexually abuse him or her.

Concrete operations is the third stage, lasting from about 7 years of age to 12. During this stage the child engages in the processes of constructing and synthesizing his or her cognitions into an understandable framework: He or she categorizes objects; comprehends and describes the concept of time, dimensions, bulk and mass, distance, and width; learns to use multiplication and division; and learns to put objects into order. According to Piaget, after 11 or 12 years of age the adolescent has the capacity of formal operations, although Piaget acknowledged that some adults will not even be able to achieve this level of logical reasoning.

Formal operations, the fourth stage, has sometimes been called being able to think in a scientific method form. It is characterized by the adolescent being able to think logically, abstractly and hypothetically. For example, an object is attached to a piece of string and the assignment is to find out what determines how fast the object oscillates, or, determine why five colorless liquids when mixed together become yellow in color. Changes in the child's thought processes and experiences facilitate the accommodation and assimilation of the child's movement from one stage to the next.

Children's thought processes are quite different than those of adults; the younger the child the greater the difference between adult and child. Thinking is always influenced by the cultural, social, physical, and emotional environment in which a child lives. This includes the individuals who surround the child and the expectations placed on the child. Many factors need to be considered in terms of utilizing prevention models effectively. It is a necessity for the clinician and those who work in the helping professions with children to have an understanding of normal child development that includes developmental milestones and an understanding of the features of each age group, and some conceptualization about what is necessary for the child to advance developmentally. It is simply not possible to comprehend a child's abilities and performance if taken out of the cultural context in which it occurs. Context can mean the physical, social, or cultural meaning of an event that causes and results in certain behaviors. Garbarino, Stott, and the faculty at the Erikson Institute (1989) suggested two major classes of contexts: (1) the physical surroundings, the importance of the event to the child, and the social exchange that occurs between

child and adult; and (2) a child's family, education, and culture. A child's interactions and performance may be affected by an adult's race, ethnic background,
gender, clothing (e.g., a uniform), tone of voice, gestures, mannerisms, adults'
conscious and unconscious agendas, and adults' expectations of the child.

LANGUAGE DEVELOPMENT

Language is one of the primary ways human beings communicate thoughts
and feelings. This is true for both children and adults. By the time a child is 2
years old he or she generally understands about 200 to 300 words; by the age
of 5 the child comprehends about 2,000 words (Sprinthall & Sprinthall, 1987).
Children age 7 or younger are limited in their ability to use language solely as
a way of communicating their thoughts and feelings. Children communicate in
a number of different ways: nonverbally through play, facial expressions, gestures, and mannerisms. Garbarino, Stott, and the faculty at the Erikson Institute
(1989) suggested the following to be helpful in verbally communicating with a
child: never assume anything; depend on other methods of communication besides language that is known to the child; and continually be aware of the
likelihood of miscommunication on the part of both the adult and the child.
These authors go on to present some basic facts that are known at this point in
time about preschoolers' cognitive abilities. Garbarino et al. (1989) suggested
that preschoolers do not have recall memory skills as advanced as those of
adults; preschoolers are more inclined to be open to suggestions about a situation (especially after it occurred); they are less capable of synchronizing complicated perceptual information; they are less inclined to employ intentional
recall; they are more inclined to use magical thinking; and they are less likely
to be aware of what they do or do not have knowledge (metacognition).

One of the most productive ways to appraise a child's cognitive abilities is
by observing him or her while he or she is involved in play, such as assem-
bling a puzzle, constructing designs from blocks, or drawing pictures. It is equally
important to pay close attention to a child as he or she is involved with other
more competent children or adults who are also engaging in problem-solving
activities (Garbarino, Stott, and the faculty at the Erikson Institute, 1989).

Young children do not remember a concept after it has been presented
verbally; the ideas need to be presented again and again (Cowan, 1978). Simply because a child can parrot back to the adult what he or she has learned
does not signify that the child has comprehended the concepts taught. Verbal
recall does not imply understanding (Elkind, 1976). Children seem to learn best

when material is presented using concepts and words they can comprehend (Donaldson, 1979; Elkind, 1976). If a child attempts to synthesize information that is developmentally beyond his or her comprehension, he or she often distorts the information; a fact that is not of small consequence when discussing the topic of sexual abuse.

STORIES AND PLAY AS WAYS TO MAKE MEANING IN A CHILD'S WORLD

Play

Garbarino, Stott, and the faculty at the Erikson Institute (1989) have suggested that the mechanisms of play enable adults to have a better understanding of the world of a child. These authors concluded that play does this in three distinct manners. First, play provides information about the child and his or her developmental level and capabilities at a particular point in time. Second, play reveals and gives the adult insight into the child's internal world. Third, play and stories are mechanisms that enable children to reenact traumatic events that have occurred in their lives. Garbarino, Dubrow, Kostelny, and Pardo (1992) had this to say about play: "Children seek to understand external reality in play. It is a process that has no assigned or expected product. Children cannot fail when they engage in free play" (p. 205).

Interpretation of children's play should be done cautiously. Many times an unskilled and untrained observer makes invalid and incorrect assumptions about the meaning of a child's play. These authors contend that there are two common mistakes made in trying to understand children's play or telling of stories: (1) not comprehending what it is the child is attempting to communicate, which can be caused by a lack of information or lack of skill on the part of the clinician; and (2) use of interpretations about the child's play without having more knowledge about the home situation or cultural or ethnic background, or use of interpretation to permeate the child's defenses before a child is psychologically and emotionally ready to do so, especially during a time of crisis.

Sexually Anatomically Correct Dolls

One of the areas that has of late produced much controversy is the use of play and sexually anatomically correct dolls. Underdeveloped language skills and lack of concrete physical evidence may make it difficult for young children who have been sexually abused to be identified (Britton & O'Keefe, 1991; Showers & Johnson, 1988). Anatomically correct dolls have been utilized to better enable children to describe potentially abusive acts (Boat & Everson, 1986; Friedemann & Morgan, 1985; Jones & McQuiston, 1986; Leventhal, Hamilton, Rekedal, Tebano-Micci & Eyster, 1989; White, Strom, Santilli, & Halpin, 1986). Any clinician considering using dolls in the assessment process of children needs to be certain to receive the proper training. Specific guidelines for using dolls are available and should be utilized in addition to the clinician being trained in using dolls (Boat & Everson, 1988; Dillon, 1987; White & Santilli, 1988). Untrained clinicians can and do make interpretive mistakes just as untrained and unskilled play therapists can and do make errors when attempting to make interpretations about children's play. Clinical interpretations from the child's interactions with dolls is not enough to legally substantiate a claim of sexual abuse made by a child (Cohn, 1991; Realmuto & Wescoe, 1992). Other evidence can augment use of the dolls, such as a child's verbal disclosures, artwork (human figure drawings), or any abnormal physical evidence like sexually transmitted diseases or a torn or damaged vagina or anus (Cohn, 1991). Britton and O'Keefe (1991) asserted that dolls' efficacy in the interview with a child are important for several reasons: (1) dolls are a vehicle that help in a child's expression of what has transpired; (2) dolls can help a child to reenact what he or she is yet unable to verbally communicate; (3) using dolls enables the clinician to observe the child as he or she plays with the dolls; and (4) doll play is a known and nonthreatening manner for the child to relay to the clinician what has happened in his or her world. Unfortunately, the data available on the reliability and validity of using anatomically correct dolls is sparse (Aman & Goodman, 1987; August, 1986; Boat & Everson, 1988; Leventhal, Hamilton, Rekedal, Tebano-Micci, Eyster, 1989; Sivan, Schor, Koeppl, & Noble, 1988; White, Strom, Santilli, & Halpin, 1986). The debate over using these dolls as clinical evidence that abuse occurred continues and may be challenged in courtroom presentations (Freeman & Estrada-Mullaney, 1988; Yates & Terr, 1988).

Value of Play

Play enables children to remove themselves from situations that generate anxiety by pretending the problems presented during play are someone else's. Play enables children to express the forbidden. Play provides meaning-making to a child's life (Erikson, 1977). Paley has written a number of books on the play of preschoolers entitled *Boys and Girls: Superheroes in the Doll Corner* (1984), *Bad Guys Don't Have Birthdays: Fantasy Play at Four* (1988), and *The Boy Who Would Be a Helicopter* (1990). Paley provides fascinating accounts of the manner in which children extrapolate characters from television, fairy tales, and other stories and incorporate them into their playtime activities. Timely insight is provided by these books with regards to children's cognitive development and struggles with societal issues, and the books demonstrate how child's play is reflective of the influence of the media in our culture, especially that of television and movies.

Storytelling

Storytelling is another vehicle that can be utilized to understand and communicate with children. Most children love stories. Garbarino, Stott, and the faculty at the Erikson Institute (1989) discussed three different clinicians use of storytelling as a way of communicating with children: Winnicott, Claman, and Gardner. Winnicott (1971) has suggested play as an activity that enables children to create their own world, to withdraw from their external surroundings and recreate or reinvent events that have occurred in their world. He developed a squiggle drawing technique in which he asked the child to invent stories about squiggles. A squiggle is drawn on a piece of paper by an adult. The paper is then given to the child and he or she is asked to draw a picture from the squiggle. When the child completes this activity he or she is asked to create a story about the squiggle drawing. The purpose of this activity is to provide the adult some information regarding the child's thoughts and feelings. In turn, the adult then asks the child to create a squiggle and the adult then draws a picture. The adult tells a story about the drawing that is similar to but different than the child's story. The adult's story is different because it suggests other ways a child might handle a situation than he or she discussed when telling his or her story about the squiggle picture.

Claman (1980) combined Winnicott's method with the storytelling technique of Gardner (1971) to produce the squiggle-drawing game. Claman's format of the squiggle-drawing game asks the child to draw a squiggle, relate a story about the doodle, and then respond to inquiries from the adult about the story.

Gardner (1971) also maintained an active role with the child in the storytelling process. Part of Gardner's method involved a child telling a story and then Gardner repeating the story by creating another ending for the story that is healthier, thus enabling the child to see different answers to issues the child described in the stories without the child having to admit to his or her own issues or struggles. Another variation is mutual storytelling (Gardner, 1971). This is when the child makes up a story that has a beginning, middle, and end. The story is taped and then replayed and discussed with the child.

Telling stories, just like playing, enables children to express what is occurring in their lives while removing themselves from objectionable feelings by assigning those feeling, thoughts, or actions to the figures in the story. The figures, whether human or animals, permit the child to ascribe unacceptable feelings, thoughts, and behaviors to these figures. It gives the child permission to express himself or herself in a safe manner. Storytelling can be quite empowering for a child. Creating stories allows a child to manufacture a scenario the way he or she wishes it could be. Stories also provide a way for a child to retaliate against individuals who have acted in hurtful ways toward him or her.

Drawing

The Event Drawing Series was developed by Burgess and Hartman (1993). This series of drawings is described by the authors as "a graphic presentation of the child's thinking about a specific event and can be used in several ways" (p. 164).

A child is asked to draw seven pictures using pencils, crayons, colored pencils, or pens. As the child is drawing the therapist chronicles (on paper) what the child is saying and his or her actions throughout the drawing exercise. A child is asked to draw: (1) his or her favorite weather; (2) a picture of his or her self at an earlier age; (3) a picture of himself or herself currently; (4) a picture of his or her family with everyone engaging in an activity together; (5) a picture of what has happened to him or her; (8) a house and a tree; and (7) a picture of whatever the child would like to draw (pp. 164–165).

After each drawing, Burgess and Hartman (1993) suggest specific questions to ask the child about the drawings. These authors also provide guidelines for analysis of each of the drawings. They had this to say:

> Drawings are useful in assisting children to discuss frightening and threatening information and perceptions about events in their lives. They give information about how memories have been stored at sensory, perceptual, and cognitive levels. The drawings provide insight into the dysregulation of memory and critical discontinuities between the child's labeling and comprehension of what has occurred. The child is presenting direct experience, not a secondary elaboration of the experience. This appears unique to the recollection of traumatic events and is important for assessment and diagnostic purposes. It becomes the basic level of information that has to be dealt with before recovery can occur. (p.176)

Puppetry

Puppetry is another way to interact with children. Renfro (1984) said, "Puppetry has almost unlimited potential as a therapeutic medium because it represents the integration of sculpture, design, movement, expression, and other elements of the arts" (p. 16). A puppet helps a child to feel at ease, since it redirects the focus of attention away from the child and serves as a protective shield behind which a child may temporarily take refuge and assume a new persona. The puppet helps the shy or inhibited child to focus on the puppet rather than his or her own actions or statements by encouraging emotional release. Puppets offer a wide variety of socially acceptable outlets for discharge of stress-related emotions. Additionally, the child, through puppet play, experiences alternative emotions and actions.

Fairy Tales

Fairy tales are also a way to convey messages to children about many real-life situations. Rush (1980) contended that there are fairy tales that portray females as heroines and tales in which mothers and daughters are involved in caring, loving relationships. She suggested reading *Cantenella* (Lang, 1900), a story about a father who forces his daughter, Cantenella, to marry an evil man. At the conclusion she is rescued by her friends and her horrible husband is killed. *Sunchild* (Lang, 1900) is another positive fairy tale in which a 12-year-old-female child plans (on her own) how to escape from an evil spirit. She is successful, returns to her mother, and the two live happily ever after. One fairy tale certain to intrigue, according to Rush (1980), is *The Marriage of Sir Gawain* (Corcoran, 1968). This tale is about King Arthur's quest for the answer to the question, "What is it every woman desires?" Eventually a very ugly woman provides him with the answer in exchange for marriage to one of Arthur's knights. Sir Gawain offers to marry the woman, kisses her, and she turns into a beautiful woman for half of the day. The other half of the day she reverts back to her ugly self. The woman asks her husband to decide which half of the day he would like her to be beautiful. He tells her to decide, which breaks the spell completely (this was the answer to the question—a woman wants to be able to make her own decisions) and the couple lives happily ever after (Corcoran, 1968). Rush (1980) suggested works by Robert Louis Stevenson and Mark Twain to enable male children to feel empowered in a healthy way.

Mythology and Folktales

Mythology and folktales are replete with stories about incest (e.g., Oedipus, and Phaedra). These tales can provide an opportunity for discussion about sexual abuse in a down-to-earth and nonintimidating manner. In addition, the tales explore and present a number of ways to respond to the topic of sexual abuse.

The myth of Oedipus recounts the penchant to sacrifice everything to save the family, the suicidal despondency, and the self-proscribed exile, all of which can face the incest survivor (Raglan, 1933). Phaedra's endeavoring to seduce Hippolytus illuminates the issues of stepparents and sexual abuse and the resultant feelings of panic and despair, which concluded in his running away from home (Aldington & Ames, 1977).

Utilizing myths and folktales can facilitate parents' or clinicians' discussions with children about the issues surrounding sexual abuse. Communication can take place indirectly through the figures in the story or fairy tale.

But again, whether it be with myths, folktales, or puppets, all of these methods require the parent to become actively involved in discussing sexual abuse issues with the child.

Chapter 8

PREVENTION PROGRAMS FOR PRESCHOOLERS, PRIMARY GRADERS, AND ADOLESCENTS

It is difficult to believe that someone known to us would abuse and manipulate the children in our society. Summit (1990) wrote,

> Since we cannot imagine these everyday realities of child sexual abuse we tend to be no better prepared than children to recognize, comprehend and prevent adult sexual incursions. Instead of facing the unthinkable, people have relied (until recently) on protective stereotypes. They reason that innocent children could not appeal to their friends and neighbors; only seductive ones. The worry is not about trusted associates anyway; only strangers. We seek to cloak the most likely child molesters with prejudicial innocence. We shift the blame to the victim rather than allowing ourselves to feel the terrible, tailor-made vulnerability of a child trapped in the underworld of pedophilia. The child is helpless to thwart the strategies of the sexual invader, less able to shatter the conspiracy of silence and the ignorant wisdom of protective adults. Much as adults think they are wise and protective, they are more protective of each other. They would rather question their children's credibility than challenge their own adult protective idealisms. (p. 59)

Prevention programs appear to have two major objectives: primary prevention (to prevent the abuse from ever happening), and secondary prevention (enabling disclosures of previous or current sexual abuse by children, to help them receive intervention and protection.)

Berrick and Gilbert (1991) wrote the following about sexual abuse prevention programs: "The conventional metaphor is that of providing a universal inoculation that injects skills into children's cognitive systems, which strengthen their abilities to ward off physical or psychological hazards" (p. 7).

PRESCHOOLERS

Some of the research has shown that preschoolers learn less sexual abuse prevention skill concepts than older children (Borkin & Frank, 1986; Gilbert, Daro, Duerr, LeProhn, & Nyman, 1988). Younger children have difficulty in understanding the more complicated concepts of secrets and confusing touches (Gilbert, Berrick, LeProhn, & Nyman, 1990). Borkin and Frank (1986) studied 84 preschoolers. These authors discovered that almost none of the 3-year-olds questioned retained anything (that was measured) from a prevention program a week later and less than 45% of the 4- and 5-year-olds retained any of the prevention skills over a week's time. Thirty-one percent of the children could correctly respond to the question, "What would you do if someone tries to touch you in a way that doesn't feel good?" (p. 75).

Gilbert, Berrick, LeProhn, and Nyman (1990) studied the pretest and posttest scores of 118 preschool children in California. These preschoolers were asked specific questions about how they would handle touches, secrets, and strangers. Based on the results of the tests, some slight increases were obtained regarding assimilation of the sexual abuse prevention material as measured by the posttest questionnaire.

Yet some research studies in the last couple of years have demonstrated that children under the age of seven can learn prevention skills (Harvey, Forehand, Brown, & Holmes, 1988; Wurtele, 1990; Wurtele, Gillispie, Currier, & Franklin, 1992; Wurtele, Kast, Miller-Perrin, & Kondrick, 1989). Liddell, Young, and Yamagishi (1988) examined the posttest scores of 183 preschoolers following a 20-lesson prevention program (Talking About Touching). Results indicated an average score of 47% correct responses on a 13-question posttest evaluation instrument.

Gibson and Bogat (1993) suggested the best manner to address pretest sensitization programs is to utilize a Solomon four-group design (Solomon, 1949). In Gibson and Bogat's study 121 preschoolers were administered a modified version of the *What-If Situation Test* (Wurtele, 1990, 1993). This study used four stories with pictures to determine a child's understanding of prevention concepts. In this particular study children did have difficulty in recognizing inappropriate touch. Comprehending that a situation could become sexually abusive is the basis for many of the prevention programs. Yet adults sometimes have difficulty determining if a touch is inappropriate; it is much more difficult for a child to discern the intent of a touch.

Children in Gibson and Bogat's study were divided and placed into four groups. In the first group children did not participate in a sexual abuse prevention program but received a pretest and a posttest. The second group of children took posttests but were not involved in any kind of program involving sexual abuse prevention. A third group of children participated in a pretest, a posttest and sexual abuse training. The fourth group of children were posttested and participated in the sexual abuse training program.

Children in the pretest groups were less able to comprehend appropriate and inappropriate touch situations on the posttest when compared to the groups that received the posttest only. Gibson and Bogat (1993) had this to say about the results:

> Although the idea of good and bad touch is presented, it is not well-elaborated (e.g., explanations that would clearly define bad touch as a violation of a moral code are not presented) and children do not get a chance to practice these skills. When recognition was not adequately explained to the pretested experimental children, their confidence in their responses may have been undermined. Similarly, given the novelty of the recognition questions, the pretest control group may have had doubts about the veracity of their pretest answers, and with no additional clarifying information, they may have remained confused at posttest. (p. 28)

Gibson and Bogat (1993) suggested the following for future prevention and evaluation of a sexual abuse curriculum:

> Future evaluations of sexual abuse prevention programs, analyzing separate skill components, employing true Solomon four-group designs, and using longer follow-up periods, are needed to replicate these findings. Often, studies, which indicate that young children learn less from prevention programs than do older children, use a

composite skill score as the dependent variable (Conte, Rosen, Saper-stein, & Shermack, 1985; Middleton, 1989). Results may then sim-ply reflect young children's lack of competency on the skill of rec-ognition, a deficit that may be enhanced when pretesting occurs. We need to understand whether the increased difficulty pretested chil-dren have learning to recognize good and bad touch is a ubiquitous problem, or if it is unique to the particular curriculum used in this project. (p. 29)

Issues to Consider with Preschoolers

Children have little ability to understand abstract concepts at the preopera-tional stage of development (2 to 6 years), according to Piaget. Many preven-tion concepts being taught involve nebulous concepts such as secrets, children's rights, and intuition, to name just a few. Berrick and Gilbert (1991) discussed the concept of secrets in a preschooler's view of the world. They wrote,

> If one were to ask a preschool child to define a secret, the child's response would focus on the description of a concrete action. That is, the child would probably say that secrets involve the act of whis-pering in someone's ear or cupping a hand over one's mouth; the content of the secret would be lost, especially if it had been commu-nicated in inaudible tones. (p. 50)

A preschooler, according to developmental theory, is going to have diffi-culty in comprehending an idea or construct that has more than one dimension (Abound, 1985; Cowan, 1978; Flavell, Green, & Flavell, 1983). Based on these tenets deYoung (1988) has suggested that preschool children are going to find it difficult to sort out the different kinds of touches. Cowan (1978) and Flavell (1985) contended that preschoolers do not recognize experiencing more than one emotion at a time, thus the child is not capable of experiencing simulta-neous feelings like, "Mommy is wonderful when she plays with me, I hate Mommy when she says no." The child's feelings during this stage are all black or all white (Cole & Putnam, 1992). Thus a confusing touch would be incom-prehensible to a child. Piaget (1962) has called this phenomenon of the child only being able to think about one concept at a time as centration.

Gilbert, Berrick, LeProhn, and Nyman (1990) discussed how children are expected in many of the prevention programs to comprehend the relationship between being touched and the feelings around that occurrence. The authors contended based on their study of preschoolers that most children developmen-tally are unable to comprehend and discern the meaning of this concept.

Some of the arguments for maintaining preschool prevention programs have centered on the "sleeper" element (Berrick & Gilbert, 1991). Basically this sleeper element suggests that, although preschool children are unable to comprehend most of the prevention curricula presented, some part of the concepts are retained and when the child is later exposed again in the primary grades to these prevention concepts the knowledge stored will increase the child's ability to comprehend the information that is disseminated. There is no empirical validation for this contention either way. High pretest scores received by children in the primary grades could be a result of parents being better educated about sexual abuse prevention; messages conveyed through television, radio, books, pamphlets, magazines, or billboards; and children coming into contact with other children who have received this prevention information.

Some other factors need to be considered, which will influence the cognitive development of the child (Fischer & Silvern, 1985). These include environment, as well as the internal influences of temperament, desire to succeed at the given tasks presented, and ability to synthesize and translate environmental expectations into behaviors. Another area to be considered in child abuse prevention training is the concept of children's memory. Researchers (Cole & Loftus, 1987; Flavell, 1985; Kail, 1986; Saywitz, 1987; Schneider, 1987) have demonstrated that children's recognition memory is as good as older children or even some adults. With recognition memory there are some built-in reminders, but with recall memory the child is expected to determine and acknowledge his or her own reminders. The child's ability to utilize deliberate recall is not as effective as adults until between 10 and 12 years of age (Kail, 1984; Loftus & Davies, 1984). Again, part of sexual abuse training programs is expecting small children to be able to recall what they are supposed to do in certain situations. Children younger than 6 or 7 years of age have not yet developed "metacognition," or understanding and recognizing things about which they do not have knowledge (Flavell, 1985). Basically metacognition is knowing what you know.

Moral Development of Preschoolers

Berrick (1991) asked the question, "How does preschooler's moral development relate to their ability to process, understand, and respond to prevention concepts that are taught?" (p. 61). She continued by discussing Piaget (1932/1962), the first researcher to study the moral development of children. Berrick discussed how Piaget presented moral dilemmas to children in a story format. Children were presented two different stories and asked to choose which child was "naughtier" and why. Piaget used six stories to explore the child's level of moral reasoning. There were three story pairs, and in each pair one child had good intentions but the results were quite damaging, and in the other story the child did not have good intentions but little harm resulted from the child's actions.

From his work, Piaget theorized that children's responses were a reflection of their cognitive development. A 4-year-old child who is developmentally at the preoperational stage of cognitive development would conclude (based on the story presented) that the child in the stories who did more damage is naughtier, because the child at this level of development is unable to consider intentions. Piaget labeled this type of reasoning (based on how much damage has occurred) objective responsibility.

Subjective responsibility is the second stage of moral development, according to Piaget (1932). The preschooler is not able, based on subjective responsibility, to distinguish between what is external versus internal. Based on this tenet, Berrick (1991) concluded that children believe most actions originate from themselves, even though in reality the child is not responsible for the actions of others, especially adults. Because of this type of objective reasoning, it may be impossible for a child to believe that he or she has not precipitated the sexually abusive incidents. If this is true, then the child will be emotionally impacted by what the adult or adolescent offender tells him or her about the sexual abuse. Thus, nonpenetrating forms of sexual abuse (e.g., fondling, petting, or exhibitionism) may not be viewed by the child as being negative, but when exposed to prevention concepts the child may begin to recognize that what has happened to him or her is wrong. Based on Piaget's theory of moral development, the child may start to feel guilty. (Keep in mind, the child also may not have the developmental ability to deal with the feelings of humiliation and guilt.)

Kohlberg (1969) developed a prototype of moral development that is somewhat more intricate than Piaget's, although his stages one and two are analogous to Piaget's first two stages. In Kohlberg's first stage of moral development a child is focused on punishment, obedience, and physical and "reward" power.

Preschoolers are frequently taught in prevention programs that they need to tell an offender "No," runaway from the situation, and tell someone. Consider this with regards to Kohlberg's model in which the child is basically more concerned with obedience to avoid punishment. If a child fears he or she will be punished for revealing a secret between himself or herself and the molester, chances are the child will not tell (Berrick, 1991).

In Kohlberg's second stage of moral development the child is influenced by the positive or negative remunerations he or she will receive for doing what is asked. Recognizing this tenet, it becomes easier to understand what motivates a child who is being sexually abused to keep silent. Obviously children are vulnerable to presents or treats and also to threats and punishments (Berrick, 1991). Additionally, most children want to please adults.

Kohlberg's six stages of moral development evolved as a result of his research on male adolescents. Kohlberg believed very few adults ever achieve the sixth stage of moral development. Kohlberg believed (1978) that moral development transcends all cultures and class structures.

Kohlberg's work has not gone unchallenged. Gender is not an issue that can be discounted in developmental theory. Gilligan (1982) suggested the presence of undeniable differences between male and female children that are not innate, but rather a result of women being the primary caretakers of young children. Gender identity for male children involves separating and beginning to individuate from the mother in order to form the masculine self. Female children do not have to separate from the mother to form the feminine self. Gilligan (1982) contended that both Kohlberg and Piaget completely negated the differences between males and females in their theories of moral development. She was not convinced that males and females developed in the same manner. She believed moral development was different for each gender as a result of different socialization experiences for each group. Kohlberg's model for determining stages of moral development involved presenting the research participants with a succession of moral quandaries and then investigating and exploring the participant's reasoning abilities utilized to determine the outcome of each problem presented. Gilligan (1982) replicated some of Kohlberg's studies but used both male and female study participants, whereas Kohlberg used only males in his study. Based on Gilligan's research on moral development she does not believe males are superior to females or vice versa in moral reasoning and development, but rather that each gender group is unique in their response to moral dilemmas.

Piaget's (1932/1962) theory of moral development inferred that if a child's primary concern is to be obedient to an adult caretaker, he or she may not report any sexual abuse that is occurring. Thus if a child is told not to tell by a trusted adult and is exposed to the opposite admonition (to tell) in a prevention class taught by an adult not known to the child, he or she will be more inclined to be obedient to the offender.

Prevention programs discuss and present the concept of different types of touches (Beland, 1986; Gilbert, Daro, Duerr, LeProhn, & Nyman, 1988; Smetana, 1984). It appears to be quite challenging to teach preschoolers what constitutes confusing touches. deYoung (1988) contended that if a child is manipulated by an abuser to engage in fondling and other kinds of sexual abuse that do not involve force and is told that this is an expression of love, the young child will not believe this kind of touching is bad.

Child sexual abuse is a multifaceted problem that is obviously not going to be eliminated simply by employing school prevention programs. Berrick (1991) wrote,

> . . . it is, as discussed earlier, an issue of mutuality, power, consent and exploitation. The immorality of the act is not only defined by the physical act of touch. Therefore, prevention education should be viewed from a broader perspective; one that includes a more thorough understanding of morality, in general. (p. XX)

> Children cannot be expected to incorporate a healthy moral attitude with brief, isolated programs that teach a litany of conventional rules. For whatever reason, adults are often more eager to enforce conventional rules than they are to intervene in immoral acts. Children are often reminded to say "please" or "thank you," but many adults allow children to resolve acts of aggression among themselves. Parents should be active in regularly enforcing moral standards so that children are clear about the boundaries of acceptable behavior. Consistent positive reinforcement for moral acts will allow children to internalize their behavior and will help them recognize when they are being treated unfairly. Teachers who encourage justice and equality among children and those who set boundaries on acts of aggression and violence will influence childrens' total sense of morality, thereby clarifying the moral issues involved in abuse (p. 72).

SCHOOL-AGE CHILDREN

Programs designed for children usually present the following basic prevention concepts:

1. Child sexual abusers are more likely to be someone the child knows and trusts than a stranger.
2. Body ownership concepts (e.g., the child's body is his or her property, and no one has the right to touch the child without his or her permission).
3. The different types of "touches" a child can encounter that make the child feel good, bad, or confused.

4. Assertiveness—specific actions the child can use in an attempt to stop the "bad" or "confusing" touching behaviors. These actions include saying, "No, don't touch me!"; running away; telling another adult about the behavior; teaching that secrets should not be kept, but told to a trusted adult; and the child should keep telling until someone believes him or her and intervenes (Conte, Rosen, Saperstein & Shermack, 1985; Finkelhor, 1986).

Prevention programs generally seem to focus on a children learning to protect themselves. The concept of "bad" touches sometimes feeling good is also rarely addressed.

A school-age child is better able (based on moral development theory) to determine and understand what is happening to him or her and whether or not it is sexual abuse. A school-age child also is less fearful of the molester's power and size than a preschool child (Berrick, 1991). However, while children are able to think more concretely and are able to determine nightmares from reality, the child at 6, 7, and 8 is still unable to determine facts from hypotheses. Rules are critical in this stage of development and there is a right way and a wrong way, situations are black and white (at least at the early part of this stage) with no shades of gray. During this age children become more aware of how to not tell the complete truth as a protective mechanism for self and for others, such as family members. This is different than a preschooler who does not tell about sexual abuse because he or she does not exactly understand what has happened to him or her or has a fear of being punished for telling a secret.

In the concrete operations stage (according to Piaget) the child would be old enough to comprehend the prevention techniques to which he or she is exposed and better understand the ramifications of what telling about the abuse might mean. The abused child would be able to understand what an offender may have told him or her about being removed from the family.

Some social learning theorists believe moral judgments made by a child are variable over time and in different situations. Rosenthal and Zimmerman (1978) reported that there are not stages to moral development but changes in moral reasoning based on many different factors, like the child's views of the amount of harm or damage done on certain occasions, how punishments and rewards are given at other times, adult or authority figure's expectations, and peer pressure.

Bandura and McDonald (1963) studied 5- to 11-year-olds who were placed in one of two groups based on the child's response to Piaget's (1932) stories about moral dilemmas. An example of one set of stories follows:

There was once a little girl who was called Marie. She wanted to give her mother a nice surprise, and cut out a piece of sewing for her. But she didn't know how to use the scissors properly and cut a big hole in her dress.

A little girl called Margaret went and took her mother's scissors one day that her mother was out. She played with them for a bit. Then as she didn't know how to use them properly she made a little hole in her dress. (Piaget, 1932, p. 118)

In each pair of stories one child has good intentions but his or her behavior results in a large amount of damage, and in the other story the child does not have good intentions but little damage is done. One group of children was identified as having an objective moral stance, the second group of children were labeled as having a subjective moral orientation based on their response to the stories.

In the second phase the children who were found to be the most subjective or the most objective were then placed in one of three situations. In the first group the adult responded first but always chose the exact opposite answer from what the child had responded in the first stage. The experimenter praised the adult's response and then praised the child if he or she changed his or her answer after listening to the adult's response. In the second group the child was not verbally praised for changing his or her answer to match the adult's response. In the third group there was no adult but the experimenter praised the child if he or she changed his or her response from the first stage. Following this, the children were told different stories and asked to make a judgment about the characters' intentions in the stories, and no praise or reinforcement were utilized. Social learning theorists suggested that the implications of this study are that children learn and incorporate the moral judgments of other individuals. This assumption was found to be correct with all the children in the study regardless of whether verbal reinforcement was utilized.

ADOLESCENTS

Probably the one group that has been sadly neglected in the teaching of prevention skills is adolescents, a group of individuals who are still at risk for sexual abuse and additionally for date rape victimization. Barth and Derezotes (1990) conducted a survey by mail of 86 prevention programs in California. Sixty (70%) of the programs returned the questionnaires. The questionnaire focused on the content areas of high school sexual abuse prevention programs.

Programs surveyed were requested to identify all subject matter in the particular program utilized. Participants also were asked to list two or three key subjects their program deemed important. Twenty-seven different themes were recognized in response to this question. The topic of acquaintance rape as listed as not important in 30% of the programs; descriptions and explanations of child abuse were most emphasized in 27% of the programs; utilization of assertiveness skills was found to be most important in 22% of the programs; self-empowerment was most important in 22% of the programs; and rights of the adolescent was most important in 18% of the programs.

The five topic areas covered most frequently but not deemed most important in the programs surveyed were: 90% of the prevention programs discussed rape by a stranger (but 0% listed this topic as being emphasized); 90% of the programs discussed oppression (only 3% emphasized this area); 90% discussed how to assist a friend who had been abused or raped or who is at risk for this to happen (again only 2% emphasized this topic); 88% discussed how to deal with physical abuse from adults (only 2% deemed it important); and 88% of the programs discussed neglect by adults (10% emphasized this area). The majority of prevention programs lasted less than two hours total, and the average length of time each topic was addressed (from the 27 topics identified) was about 5 minutes, with an average of 24 topics covered in a 2-hour presentation.

These authors had some concrete suggestions to be included in a prevention curriculum for children K–12th grade.

1. Incorporating and utilizing prevention materials for children based on appropriate age and developmental level of the child (e.g., determining when it is or is not destructive to present to the child the concept that parents and other caretakers can and do sexually abuse children). Barth and Derezotes (1990) discussed the dangers inherent in presenting programs too early but also the risk of introducing relevant topics too late to be of any benefit to the child or adolescent (e.g., acquaintance rape).
2. Barth and Derezotes (1990) suggested reinforcing again and again the prevention concepts that have been introduced. Social learning theory suggests this approach will maximize learning (Bandura & McDonald, 1963). The following are some of the prevention concepts that Barth and Derezotes (1990) believed should be addressed in programs: child abuse prevention, spouse abuse prevention, acquaintance rape and violence prevention, and prevention of abuse of aging populations (p. 136).
3. Exposing and educating all school employees about prevention skills, and expecting them to utilize the skills learned by modeling conflict resolution skills and intervening appropriately in fights between children.

4. Using peer counselors in prevention endeavors.
5. Combining developmental theory and the most current research on abuse prevention to enhance prevention teaching methods.
6. Recognizing the differences in various ethnic, cultural, gender, language, and family groups (p. 137).

Barth and Derezotes (1990) suggested having clear-cut objectives, teaching techniques, and evaluation techniques for each grade. Three broad areas of prevention have been suggested: prevention of abuse by adults and older children, prevention of abuse by children their own age, and prevention of children being abusive to other assailable populations, such as the aged, children, adults with special needs, and ethnic minorities.

Chapter 9

ISSUES AND COMPONENTS
OF PREVENTION PROGRAMS

PROGRAM LENGTH

In considering prevention programs, several issues and components must be taken into account. Prevention programs vary in time requirements from one program to another. The content and presentation format are somewhat different depending on the program utilized. The goals of most prevention programs are similar. Also, the extent to which parents are to be involved needs to be planned. The research findings on different programs with different content for different age children must be considered. The contents of this chapter are applicable to these issues and components.

PROGRAM CONTENT

Prevention programs are of varying lengths. Some programs are only one session, others are longer. One of the longest is composed of 38 segments (Committee for Children, 1983). Length of sex abuse prevention programs is variable, depending on the age of the child and the prevention program utilized. Preschool programs generally last for 15 to 30 minutes and are presented either once weekly for 1 to 3 weeks, or 1 to 3 consecutive days. School programs from first grade on are usually about 1 hour in length and are presented from 1 to 3 days. The Talking About Touching Program varies from 2 to 27 lessons depending on the grade level of the children.

PROGRAM FORMATS

Many of the programs in the United States are modeled after the Child Assault Prevention Program (1983), which was one of the very first sexual abuse prevention curricula designed for children. This program's information is usually presented by volunteer or paraprofessionals from the community. Program length is three days. Types of touches are not discussed, secrets are described as being either good, which means it can be told eventually, or bad, which are secrets the child cannot tell or that the child supposedly feels bad about. If the child is told to keep a secret, he or she is to tell someone immediately. Children are taught body ownership concepts. The child is told via role-play that someone he or she knows could abuse him or her. Children are taught coping skills that include running away and telling someone, such as a teacher or parent. Children are instructed how to stand when they meet someone new, how to use yelling as a prevention skill, and how to use physical force to deter an incident (e.g., biting, scratching, stomping, or punching). Private parts are described with the correct anatomical terms, like breast and penis. This program does not address when it is okay to be touched, bribes, abductions, and guilt or blame.

Some of the most extensively utilized prevention materials are the following: a curriculum guide titled *Preventing Sexual Abuse* (Plummer, 1984a); a coloring book, *My Very Own Book about Me* (Stowell & Dietzel, 1982); the book *No More Secrets* (Adams & Fay, 1981), which provides clear, concise information about preventing sexual abuse for parents and teachers; a special edition of a Spiderman comic book on preventing sexual abuse (National Committee for the Prevention of Child Abuse, 1986); a coloring book, *Red Flag/ Green Flag People* (Williams, 1980); the Behavioral Skills Training Program (Wurtele, 1986); the Safe Child Program (Kraizer, 1990); the film *Touch* (Illusion Theater Company & Media Ventures, Inc., 1984), developed to teach children in K–6th grade a variety of personal safety skills; the play, *Bubbylonian Encounter* (Mackey, 1983); and *Talking about Touching: Personal Safety for Preschoolers and Kindergartners* (Committee for Children, 1983), which provides concrete rules for children to utilize in a variety of situations. The last named program has 27 sessions and includes fire and safety rules in addition to sexual abuse prevention guidelines like, "No one should touch your private parts and if someone does you should tell an adult." This program is quite specific in teaching children what appropriate and inappropriate touches are and does not expect children to rely on their own intuition, especially in relation to confusing touches.

Some evidence is available to suggest that active participation in child sexual abuse prevention programs through behavioral modeling and role-playing is more effective than observing plays or films (Fryer, Kraizer, & Miyoshi, 1987a, 1987b; Wurtele, Marrs, & Miller-Perrin, 1987).

SPECIFIC PROGRAMS

Frequently the preventive education materials use are dictated by economics, depending on how much money has been allocated to be spent on child sexual abuse prevention.

Talking about Touching—A Program for Preschoolers

This program is comprised of 27 lessons presented in the classroom by a teacher who has been trained specifically to use this prevention material. Touches are defined as safe, confusing, or unsafe. The concept of secrets is dealt with by describing secrets that can be surprises, like secrets about gifts or dress up or when no one is hurt. Bad secrets are explained as involving touch or concealing something. If a child is asked to keep a secret he or she is instructed to tell, tell, tell. Body ownership is presented in the classroom as the child's body belonging only to him or her. Children are taught that someone he or she knows could be sexually abusive (examples provided in the training involve stories in which the baby-sitter, friend of the family, or a stranger sexually abuse a child.) The child is not taught to yell or utilize self-defense techniques. Private parts are presented as those body parts covered by a bathing suit. Children are taught that it is not okay to be touched by an adult unless it is for health reasons. Health reasons are specifically delineated. Bribes are discussed, abduction is not. Children are told that if someone touches his or her private parts it is not the child's fault.

Behavioral Skills Training Program (Wurtele, 1986)

There are two versions of the Behavioral Skills Training Program (BSTP) —one for parents and another for teachers. The program is three days in length, and it teaches children prevention skills from a behavioral viewpoint. If taught by teachers, the children are arranged into small groups (from four to seven participants per group). Teachers present the following concepts to the children:

> . . . [that] they are the bosses of their bodies; to identify the location of their private parts; that it is appropriate for doctors, nurses, or parents to touch children's private parts for health or hygiene reasons, but that otherwise it is not okay to have their private parts touched or looked at by a bigger person, especially if the person wants them to keep it a secret; that it is wrong to be forced to touch a bigger person's private parts; and that an adult's inappropriate touching of the child's private parts is never the child's fault. (Wurtele, Gillispie, Currier, & Franklin, 1992, p. 151)

The children then practice deciding between acceptable and unacceptable situations. Practice involves utilizing the skills of modeling, behavioral rehearsal, and using the appropriate behavioral and verbal responses (e.g., moving away from the potential perpetrator and telling a trusted adult). Teachers provide verbal approval and feedback regarding the children's responses.

The BSTP for parents includes a script with pictures, a package of tokens (with a sticker for each time the child meets one of the 27 program objectives), and stickers and crayons, all to be utilized in the home environment. (For evaluation of the program's effectiveness, see Wurtele, 1990; Wurtele, Kast, Miller-Perrin, & Kondrick, 1989)

What-If Situation Test (Saslawsky & Wurtele, 1986; Wurtele, 1993)

The What-If Situation Test (WIST) is a test designed to measure a child's capability of determining if a situation is abusive and then reacting to the situations. Six short stories are contained in the WIST. Three stories include scenarios in which acceptable requests to touch are asked of the child; for example, a physician requests to examine a child's genitals. Three scenarios portray unacceptable requests, like a neighbor wanting to photograph a child's genitals. The child is then asked after each story is presented, "Would it be okay for [the person in vignette] to [do the activity requested]? (p. 68). Correct responses are given one point. Children who can identify an inappropriate touch situation are then asked, "(a) What would you say to [person in vignette]?" "(b) What would you do?" "(c) Would you tell anyone [about the situation]? If so, who would you tell?" and (d) "What would you say to [person named in answer to question c]?" Each of these questions are then scored and receive either zero, one, or two points. The maximum number of points is eight points per story for a total of 24 points for the three inappropriate-request-for-touch stories.

The Safe Child Program (Kraizer, 1990)

The Safe Child Program (Kraizer, 1990) is a detailed child abuse prevention curriculum. This particular program teaches children to think for themselves, improve their communication skills, learn to be assertive, and know how and when to seek adult intervention in situations. This program obviously goes well beyond the realm of just teaching children prevention skills with regards to sexual abuse.

This program has two separate formats—preschool and K–3. Both program formats include parent and teacher instruction videotapes, children's videotapes, and teacher classroom guides. Preschool and kindergarten curricula each have two separate programs consisting of five sessions per program. The first program centers on body ownership. If the child's appeal ("No, don't touch me.") is denied, the child is instructed to physically move away from the person and state, "I'm going to tell." The second program focuses on "Stranger Danger," and includes specific, concrete guidelines to follow if the child is alone at home, or lost in a store, for example.

Starting in first grade, the program uses a single, five-session format that includes a more comprehensive approach to issues about touching and stranger danger. At the second grade level the program is entitled "The Choice Is Yours," and discusses making choices, breaking promises, and determining when to seek trusted adult interventions in situations. The third grade program is called "Being Your Own Best Friend." This program reiterates the concept of making choices and provides more explicit examples of appropriate touches than those presented in the earlier grades. Detailed examples are provided of how to effectively respond in coercive situations, and the importance of breaking promises in certain situations is stressed.

The younger children are given easy to understand, global rules. A clear distinction is made between the touch programs and stranger danger. This is important since at least 85% of the time, the child knows the individuals who are inappropriately touching him or her, thus it is important to teach the child that because he or she knows someone does not ensure that the known adult will not inappropriately touch the child. (For studies evaluating this program's effectiveness, see Kraizer, Witte, & Fryer, 1989.)

PARENTAL INVOLVEMENT

A number of books have been published that present a vast array of information specifically for parents to assist them in talking to a child about preventing sexual abuse (Adams & Fay, 1981; Kraizer, 1985; Sanford, 1980, 1982).
Nibert, Cooper, and Ford (1989) studied 223 Ohio parents whose children were
exposed to the Child Assault Prevention Program. Almost 65% of the parents
reported having discussed sexual abuse with his or her preschooler before the
child's exposure to the program. What each child was told specifically is not
known. Finkelhor's (1984) survey of parents in New England reported that less
than 30% of parents in the study had broached the issue of sexual abuse with
their children. If the matter was discussed, most of the information conveyed to
the child related to "stranger danger." This was in keeping with these parents'
beliefs that at least 50% of sexual offenses were perpetrated against children by
unknown persons. These parents obviously did not know that less than 15% of
abuse is perpetrated by strangers. This fact alone causes one to consider what
other types of misinformation may have been relayed to the child surrounding
issues of sexual abuse. Thus, a real need exists for parents to be educated about
how to talk to their children about these kinds of issues. Some of the unin-
tended negative effects of teaching prevention concepts to children at school
may be the parents developing a false sense of security about a child's ability
to protect himself or herself after exposure (Berrick & Gilbert, 1991). Parents
are unaware that there is a real lack of evidence regarding program efficacy in
preventing abuse from taking place. The professional community is divided on
the validity of these programs.

Finkelhor, Araji, Baron, Browne, Peters, and Wyatt (1986) emphasized the
usefulness of prevention programs involving parents and other professionals.
Programs designed to include parents accomplish two agendas: (1) they enable
parents to recognize symptoms of abuse, and (2) they teach parents how to
respond in a facilitative manner if abuse is revealed. In addition, if parents are
the instructors, children will have the opportunity to be exposed to the information again and again.

Wurtele (1993) suggested the following reasons for having parents teach
children a personal safety curriculum in the home:

> Involving the family in the educational process may help reduce the
> secrecy surrounding the topic of child sexual abuse, and may stimu-
> late parent child discussions about sexuality in general. Parents can
> be sensitive to their children's abilities with regard to comprehen-
> sion and rate of skill acquisition. (p. 66)

Her comments address the very issue that has for the most part been neglected. Tutty (1993) wrote,

> The influence that parents might have on the learning of prevention concepts has largely been ignored. . . . We might come to understand more about how and when young children learn and remember prevention concepts by looking at them in the context of their most important social system, the family. Since attitudes regarding sexuality and, hence, sexual abuse are first developed in the home, ignoring the influence of parents and concentrating solely on teaching children may well be a mistake. (pp. 84–85).

Tutty (1990) studied 284 parents whose children were in kindergarten or first grade. These parents were asked to predict their children's responses to sexual abuse prevention concepts. He found that many of these parents significantly exaggerated their child's ability to comprehend these concepts. These findings suggest that parents may not continue to augment prevention concepts taught at school because parents believe the child knows, understands, and can use the information to protect himself or herself. He follows this with, "It is essential to stress to parents that their young child will need repetition and support in order to learn the concepts and that parents must maintain considerable responsibility for this process" (Tutty, 1993, p. 100).

Despite the advantages of involving parents, not much is being done in this area of prevention work. Part of the reason some parents do not discuss sexual abuse with their children is that the parents feel uncomfortable with the topic, do not know how to bring the subject into conversation for discussion, do not feel qualified to discuss the subject, believe their child is safe and that sexual abuse could not happen, and believe in their ability to provide a safe environment for their child. With regards to safety, Finkelhor (1984) surveyed parents and found that the majority believed their own children were closely watched and therefore would not have the opportunity to be harmed. Additionally, parents expressed concerns about needlessly frightening their children. Lastly, parents who are inclined to become involved in this type of educational program may be more informed and inclined to educate their children about such matters anyway.

Obviously more parents need to be involved in teaching their children about sexual abuse. If a larger segment of the parental population is to be reached, this could involve parents being taught at their places of employment and through groups such as the Kiwanis, the Lions, and Rotary Clubs (Haugaard & Reppucci, 1988). Until now parents have been involved only peripherally with school-based prevention programs. Often the prevention programs involving parents will include one meeting with parents (in a group format) before the child receives the presentation of prevention skills training at the school. Brassard, Tyler, and Kehle (1983) have suggested parent education programs for understanding and preventing child sexual abuse should be offered through Parent-Teacher Associations and should include definitions, predominance rates and abuser profiles, short-term and long-term effects of incest, intergenerational transmission of incest and abuse, referrals for abusers and survivors, the signs and symptoms of sexual abuse, and the rights of both parents and children.

Hopefully the more parents become involved and the more safety skills are taught at home the less anxiety will be produced and as a result more material and subject matter will be available for parents (Adams & Fay, 1986). A skill that is taught at home has the advantage of being reinforced again and again by someone the child loves and trusts implicitly.

For example, in the state of Illinois, the Ounce of Prevention Fund (1987) has created a program entitled "Heart to Heart" to increase adolescent parent's capabilities in preventing both the mother and the child from being victimized by sexual abuse. The program format includes sessions with 3 major objectives: increasing awareness of child development in conjunction with sexual abuse issues; augmenting and implementing positive parenting skills; and providing information about community resources available for the new parent.

Williams and Finkelhor (1990) reported a number of problem areas that place a child at risk for sexual abuse from the father: lack of understanding of the child and his or her needs; a lack of participation in child care responsibilities; and incompetency in using social supports or lack of appropriate support systems.

Berrick (1988) reviewed some of the components of the more popular sexual abuse prevention programs aimed at the parents' informational meetings. She wrote the following:

> All programs cover much of the same content, yet there are several differences in their emphases which stand out. Some programs used the parent meeting, in part, as an opportunity to teach parents how to protect their children from abuse. These programs stress the weight of parents personal obligations to their children. In contrast, other programs expect children essentially to protect themselves, placing emphasis on the child's responsibility for her/his own safety. Still other programs recognize parents' potential to abuse their children and use the meeting, in part, as a forum to discuss parenting skills,

methods of stress reduction, and appropriate disciplining techniques. (p. 544)

She continued by suggesting that parents should be reached on a national level through newspapers, periodicals, television, and in-service training at work. A definite need also exists for prevention programs for teachers, pediatricians, day-care workers, clergy, and police. Training would teach these professionals to identify sexual abuse and intervene constructively and appropriately.

Wurtele and Miller-Perrin (1992) stated that

> . . . prevention programs operating on one level can and do affect other systems. For example, teaching children to be assertive regarding their personal rights may cause problems if the family system is unresponsive to or critical of such changes. Instructing children in a classroom to disclose their abuse is being irresponsible if school personnel have not been helped to feel competent responding to such disclosures and/or if reporting agencies are not equipped to handle the increase in the number of reports. Clearly, prevention efforts do not operate in a vacuum. (p. 51)

Current Research

Over 25 research studies evaluating the efficacy of child sexual abuse prevention programs for preschool and elementary school children have appeared in the literature since 1981 (Tutty, 1991; Wurtele, 1987). Some criticisms of the studies have emerged (Tutty, 1992). These include scant use of control or comparison groups, a lack of statistically reliable and valid testing instruments, and small sample populations.

In the 26 studies reviewed (Tutty, 1992), only eight utilized control groups (Conte, Saperstein, & Shermack, 1985; Dube, Heger, Johnson, & Herbert, 1988; Fryer, Kraizer & Miyoshi, 1987a, 1987b; Kolko, Moser, Litz, & Hughes, 1987; Nelson, 1981; Saslawsky & Wurtele, 1986; Volpe, 1984; Wolfe, MacPherson, Blount, & Wolfe, 1986). Many of the test instruments utilized had only 7 to 13 questions in the posttest segment of the training: Personal Safety Questionnaire (Sigurdson, Strang, & Doig, 1987), What-If Situations Test (Saslawsky & Wurtele, 1986; Wurtele, Marrs, & Miller-Perrin, 1987), 9-item questionnaire (Kolko, et al., 1987), 13-question assessment instrument (Binder & McNeil, 1987), and an assessment instrument designed specifically for preschoolers (Gilbert, Berrick, LeProhn, & Nyman, 1989). Tutty (1992) questions whether the tests can sufficiently measure children's understanding of prevention concepts with this limited number of assessment questions at the posttest level.

A few programs did find statistically significant improvement (posttest) in children's comprehension after involvement in a prevention program (Conte, Rosen, Saperstein, & Shermack, 1985; Downer, 1984; Fryer, Kraizer, & Miyoshi, 1987b; Saslawsky & Wurtele, 1986; Sigurdson, Strang, & Doig, 1987; Wolfe, MacPherson, Blount, & Wolfe, 1986). The statistically significant differences between children's pretest and posttest knowledge scores were not large in any of the studies. Conte et al. (1985) determined that children older than 6 years of age recalled more prevention knowledge and concepts regarding sexual abuse prevention than children younger than 6 years of age. Gibson and Bogat (1993) suggested that sexual abuse prevention programs need to use a Solomon four group design to determine if there are any pretesting effects.

Long-term retention of the safety skills has not been extensively studied. Saslawsky and Wurtele (1986) found kindergartners in their study were able to retain some of the prevention concepts over a 3-month period. Other authors have found children able to retain some of the material after 6 months (Fryer, Kraizer, & Miyoshi, 1987a; Kolko, Moser, Litz, & Hughes, 1987; Ray & Dietzel, 1985).

The research on the effectiveness of prevention programs for preschool children has been contradictory (Borkin & Frank, 1986; Gilbert, Berrick, LeProhn, & Nyman, 1989; Poche, Brouwer, & Swearingen, 1981), reporting preschoolers were not able to retain safety skills after just one week. Children in second grade and above were better able to retain the prevention information (Conte, Rosen, Saperstein, & Shermack, 1985; Garbarino, 1987; Saslawsky & Wurtele, 1986). This would certainly follow the child development literature, which suggests that older children are better able to recall prevention concepts presented in sexual abuse training programs.

Learning and retaining prevention concepts obviously is one of the core tenets of any program. Children cannot implement a skill if it is not yet acquired. Repetition is a key in the learning process for adults as well as children.

Means of Assessing

Determining how preschoolers synthesize information and then designing and implementing programs based on this seems to be a key ingredient in the success of any program to which the child is exposed (Krivacska, 1990). Currently skills are assessed by asking the child to answer multiple choice, true/false, or yes/no questions, for example, "If an older child touched your private parts, would you tell?" (Binder & McNeil, 1987; Conte, Rosen, Saperstein, & Shermack, 1985; Plummer, 1984a; Wolfe, MacPherson, Blount & Wolfe, 1986). Another form of assessment involves presenting vignettes that include examples of "good" and "bad" touches. The child is then asked how he or she should respond in the drama presented: "Marc is Alexander's baby-sitter. Marc asks Alexander to touch his private parts one day while he is baby-sitting and Alexander's parents are not home. What should Alexander do?" (Harvey, Forehand, Brown, & Holmes, 1988; Kenning, Gallmeier, Jackson, & Plemons, 1987; Kolko, Moser, Litz, & Hughes, 1987; Wurtele & Miller-Perrin, 1987). Touches have been labeled in different ways: good, bad, or confusing (Anderson, 1986); safe or unsafe (Beland, 1986); heart touches, question mark touches, and not nice touches (Children's Self-Help Project, 1981; Tobin, Levinson, Russell, & Valdez, 1983); or red light, yellow light, and green light touches (Patterson, 1986). Some programs focus on the use of intuition or gut feelings to label the touch: good or bad, okay or not okay, or makes the child feel uncomfortable inside (Child Assault Prevention Program, 1983); makes the child experience a funny feeling (Children's Self-Help Project, 1981); or gives the child an "uh-oh" feeling (The Touch Program, 1987).

CORE ELEMENTS

A core element of most prevention programs is that children have rights and their bodies belong exclusively to them. A majority of the sexual abuse prevention programs usually address the private parts issue in an attempt to ensure children know clearly where he or she should not be touched. Often the private parts are identified as parts of the body "covered by a bathing suit." Berrick and Gilbert (1991) contend that the bathing suit analogy can impart misinformation to children because a one-piece bathing suit may cover a child's back, which is not considered a private part. All prevention programs encourage children to say no to anyone who attempts to hurt them and for the child to tell a trusted adult about the incident. The Child Assault Prevention Program (1983) teaches, "*No* is a safe, strong and free word" (p. 151); Children's Self-Help Project (1981) encourages the child to say "No" or "Stop" (p. iv); The Touch Program (1987) tells the child to say, "Stop, I don't like that" (p. 3). Two programs advocate using a "safety yell" (Child Assault Prevention Program, 1983; Children's Self-Help Project, 1981). The Child Assault Prevention Program (1983) teaches children to physically fight back by kicking, using the elbow, stomping on the instep, or pulling his finger back (p. 163). Unfortunately children have not been educated as to how and what the offender may do in response to the child's behavior.

From the research studies reviewed it appears that the most successful way to teach prevention skills is when children participate in the learning process through role-playing, modeling, and behavioral rehearsals (Chadwick, 1988; Ray & Dietzel, 1984; Wurtele, Marrs, & Miller-Perrin, 1987; Wurtele, Kast, Miller-Perrin, & Kondrick, 1989).

Impact on Program Effectiveness

Increased involvement on the part of both teachers and parents would hopefully increase long-term effectiveness of children understanding prevention skills and help reduce parental and teacher anxieties about the subject matter (Binder & McNeil, 1987; Hazzard, 1984; Miltenberger & Thiesse-Duffy, 1988; Porch & Petretic-Jackson, 1986). But again this is not known, it is merely speculation.

All of the following considerations will impact on program effectiveness:

1. Content and scope of the prevention programs
2. Age and grade level at which the material is presented
3. The type of instructor—a teacher, a child abuse prevention specialist, a police officer, or a parent
4. Time allotted to programs (how many minutes per session, number of sessions, and number of weeks of training)
5. Type of setting in which the material is presented
6. Persons involved (children, parents, teachers, and caretakers)
7. Techniques utilized (talks, films, role-playing, puppets)
8. Skills taught (assertiveness, communication, decision making)
9. Cultural background
10. Family rules and values

Kolko (1988) believed that parents and teachers need to be included, with booster or review sessions added to preventive education formats. In addition, children need to be provided with the opportunity to utilize behavioral rehearsal skills and receive feedback on skills used. Obviously, the training materials need to meet the child's cognitive abilities (Coppens, 1986). This point cannot be overemphasized.

Secondary Prevention Goals

Some researchers have reported success in achieving secondary prevention goals. Kolko, Moser, Litz, and Hughes (1987) revealed that in five out of six schools where prevention programs were instituted, 20 confirmed reports of inappropriate touching were reported in the intervening 6 months after the prevention programs were presented. No reports were made from the control group in which no prevention programs were instituted. Hazzard, Webb, and Kleemeier (1988) found that 28 children reported either current or past sexual abuse in less than a 2-month period after receiving a three-session prevention program.

Children need to be taught assertiveness skills, decision making, conflict resolution, and communication skills that are useful in everyday situations as opposed to just being used to prevent sexual abuse.

IMPROVING PREVENTION PROGRAMS

Daro (1991) stated, "Child assault prevention programs need to expand their explicit outcomes. Knowledge regarding child sexual abuse, the need for a child to tell an adult if he or she is threatened or abused, and the need for a child to avoid risky situations are all important messages" (p. 293).

Teacher Training

Most of the programs for teacher training include only a short instructional component (1- to 2-hours) on prevention program goals and objectives, indicators of sexual abuse, and appropriate replies to disclosures. The training may or may not incorporate child abuse reporting laws and the process involved in reporting (Kolko, Moser, Litz, & Hughes, 1987). A definite need exists to supply concrete guidelines for teachers and school counselors on how to handle disclosures, issues of confidentiality, and reporting procedures to child protective services.

Booster Sessions

Children need booster sessions following exposure to the concepts of sexual abuse (Borkin & Frank, 1986; Plummer 1984b; Ray, 1984; Ray & Dietzel, 1984). In California, the Child Abuse Prevention Training Act has legally declared that all children in publicly funded schools have the chance to receive prevention training at least 5 times during their public school education experience. Daro (1991) emphasized the necessity for taking a multifaceted approach to preventing child sexual abuse. She suggested the following: prevention education for children should be available intermittently throughout their school years with prevention concepts and education about all kinds of abuse; increased training programs for those professionals whose work is with children—the training should include how to recognize abuse and to whom the abuse should be reported and how to do so; education for children on how to prevent abuse from occurring, including a parental education component; training for employees and volunteers, including adding questions on topics of sexual abuse and prevention to licensing tests for different professional groups; education for parents on early attachment and bonding issues between parent and child; assistance in teaching parents about the need to communicate with the child about sexual matters, including sexual abuse; and increased public awareness that preventing and reporting sexual abuse is everyone's responsibility.

NEGATIVE REACTIONS

A number of studies (Garbarino, 1987a; Kraizer, 1986; Leventhal, 1987; Swan, Press, & Briggs, 1985) evaluated negative effects on children after exposure to child sexual abuse prevention material. Swan et al. (1985) contacted parents within a week of the child seeing a presentation of the play *Bubbylonian Encounter*. The parents were interviewed regarding children's adverse reactions to the play. Adverse reactions were defined as sleep or appetite disturbances, nightmares, or increased fearfulness. Five percent of the parents reported these adverse reactions on the part of their children. Garbarino (1987a) evaluated responses to the special edition Spiderman comic book. The comic book includes two stories about sexual abuse. In the first story a female child runs away from home because her father is sexually abusing her and the mother will not believe her statements about the abuse. Ultimately the girl meets a group of children who have extraordinary powers. These children convince her to tell their parents about her father's sexual abuse. She does and is believed. The parents of her new friends promise to help her and her family with the incest. The second story involves Spiderman finding a male child who is being sexually abused by his adolescent female baby-sitter. Spiderman shares with the boy his own experiences of being sexually abused as a child. The story concludes with the boy relating the abusive incident to his parents. Garbarino found that up to 50% of male and female children reported feelings of worry or fear after reading the comic book. Thus it does appear that there are some negative reactions associated with exposure to the prevention concepts. Haugaard and Reppucci (1988) suggested that instead of viewing the results as negative, perhaps another way to think about this is that the prevention concepts presented have a long-lasting effect on the children. They stated, "As with fairy tales, the most enduring stories are frequently those that are somewhat disturbing to their young audience because they provide a warning about some harmful event that could happen" (p. 326).

Cohn (1990) evaluated the Spiderman comic and believed it would be a helpful tool for both children and their parents, since both age groups like to read comics. She believed the comic could facilitate conversations about sexual abuse between parent and child.

Ray-Keil (1989) suggested the benefits of teaching prevention concepts certainly outweigh any negative effects that occur after the training. She cited examples where other safety training programs (e.g., fire safety programs) may result in the child experiencing anxiety and other negative reactions. The real problem lies in no one knowing the effectiveness of these prevention programs.

After reviewing the curricula of over 40 prevention programs, Tharinger, Krivacka, Laye-McDonough, Jamison, Vincent, and Hedlund (1988) suggested that schools should not use any program that suggests children should be taught to trust their own feelings. Finkelhor and Strapko (1992) have suggested that children may develop the idea from prevention programs that all sex and touch behaviors are negative. Quite a message to convey to young minds. Both authors contended that researchers and educators have not addressed these kinds of issues. Elsewhere it has been suggested that because of the experimental nature of the sexual prevention programs, schools need to employ the same "standard procedures for informed consent used by institutional review committees for the protection of human subjects" (Berrick & Gilbert, 1991, p. 96).

POINTS TO PONDER

As previously noted, child sexual abuse takes many different forms. It has been suggested that some skills that are necessary to prevent one kind of abuse from occurring may not be useful in another kind of situation in which prevention is needed. The same can be said for different age groups of children; what might be helpful to a 4-year-old would not provide the same benefits to an 11-year-old (Haugaard & Reppucci, 1988).

Within the last couple of years quite a controversy has occurred in California regarding the efficacy of sexual abuse prevention programs for preschool children. In 1988, a 14-member Preschool Curricula Task Force was formed to study preschool sexual abuse prevention programs by examining research results, monitoring prevention programs, and hearing professional opinions on the issues. By the fall of 1989 the task force had made its recommendations. Although the task force did not suggest that all preschool prevention programs be eliminated, the task force did make recommendations that would eliminate some of the core elements from the preschool programs for sexual abuse prevention training; suggested to be eliminated from the programs were assertiveness components, body is private property components, and children's rights. Task force recommendations strongly suggested that primary prevention at the preschool level should involve training and educating parents and teachers (Berrick & Gilbert, 1991).

Melton (1988) had this to say about prevention programs:

> . . . the history of public health shows that prevention programs designed to change individual risky behavior are relatively ineffective. . . . Research confirms what common sense tells us: childproof caps and lead-free paint prevent poisoning much more effectively than efforts to increase parents' vigilance or diminish children's risk-taking; highway engineering usually has substantially greater effects on pedestrian safety than does safety education; legal regulation of the marketplace affects teenagers' drinking and smoking habits much more than does health education. . . . As a general matter, as noted earlier, environmental change is the most effective approach to prevention. However, structuring the environment in order to diminish opportunities for sexual abuse is not an easy task. . . . Finally, it should be recognized that prevention of sexual abuse is an extraordinarily difficult, indeed improbable exercise. . . . Ultimately we may reach the unhappy conclusion that our resources are better invested in remediating the effects of abuse than preventing its occurrence. (pp. 181, 185–186)

Translating Skills into Life Situations

The assumption is that children will be able to translate the skills acquired in prevention training into real-life situations when and if necessary. This supposition has not been proven in the research literature. A study conducted by Downer (1985) determined that although 94% of the children in her study could provide a correct definition for assertiveness (after a training class) only 47% could accurately state an appropriate assertive reply to an abusive predicament. Again there are no certainties that the 47% who knew what an assertive response would entail would respond in that manner if confronted with an abusive situation. Tharinger, Krivacka, Laye-McDonough, Jamison, Vincent, and Hedlund (1988) reviewed 41 sexual abuse prevention programs in the United States and determined that only 2% of the programs utilized child development concepts as a basis for program design and implementation and only 2% utilized learning theory concepts. Two percent increase in knowledge for sexual abuse prevention programs when comparing pretest and posttest information is not impressive. (Binder & McNeil, 1987; Harvey, Forehand, Brown, & Holmes, 1988). Because a child demonstrates an increase in knowledge about preventing a sexually abusive incident from occurring is not indicative that the child will be able to translate the learning into behavioral responses (Stillwell, Lutzker, & Greene, 1988). Some reported increase in knowledge about preventing sexual abuse following the prevention training has been reported (Fryer, Kraizer, & Miyoshi, 1987a; Wurtele, Saslawsky, Miller, Marrs, & Britcher, 1986). Conte, Rosen, Saperstein, and Shermack (1985) reported an increase in knowledge by 40% of the participants in their studies.

Achievement of Primary Prevention

There does not appear to be any evidence to indicate that the goals of primary prevention (preventing sexual abuse from occurring) have ever been accomplished. Professionals and parents want to believe that programs are effective in prevention but no study to date has provided concrete proof that primary prevention is effective (deYoung, 1988; Gilbert, Daro, Duerr, LeProhn, & Nyman, 1988; Reppucci & Haugaard, 1989). Reppucci and Haugaard (1989) suggested that many prevention programs are based on concepts that have not been researched, and adults teach children what adults think would be helpful in deterring abusive incidents.

Achievement of Secondary Prevention

In contrast, there are some studies that have indicated success in meeting the goals of secondary prevention (children who are currently or in the past have been abused reveal what has occurred). Garbarino (1987b) presented the following:

> At the conclusion of a standard interview evaluating a prevention program using the Spiderman comic on the prevention of sexual abuse, a fourth grade boy said, "This is just what happened to me!" And he proceeded to tell of being sexually molested over a period of a year and a half starting when he was in the second grade. He was silent over that period to protect his mother from the harm the neighbor threatened to inflict upon her if he told. The boy concluded, "He said he would put soap suds in her eyes and put her in the washing machine and he has a black belt in karate and he said he would get her." Finally the boy was asked if having had the Spiderman comic at the time would have made a difference. "Yes," he replied, "I would have told my Mom about it. I wouldn't have been so afraid. I would have known that it was right to tell." (p. 148)

Negative Effects

The assumption cannot be made that prevention programs are effective and do not cause some negative reactions in the child. Quite possibly the prevention programs will negatively affect the child's relationships with adults or provide the foundation for children to worry or become fearful. At this point in time, this information is unknown. Nor can it be assumed that children are safe from sexual abusers as a result of experiencing prevention training (Wald & Cohen, 1986).

Addressing a Broader Societal Group

As Finkelhor (1990b) pointed out, "It is both morally unfair and pragmatically ineffectual to put the full responsibility for prevention on children themselves. We need to devise approaches for stopping offenders before they get to the children" (p. 385).

Finkelhor (1990b) believed that prevention of child sexual abuse needs to be addressed on a broader societal level than has been done in the past. He suggested having fathers take a more active parenting role, which involves the father caring for the child by feeding, bathing, and dressing him or her. Also Finkelhor suggested that the following be addressed: (1) "altering the male sex role" to include teaching men to express their needs for affection and love in other ways besides sex; (2) "sexual socialization," which relates to the issues of how and what children are taught directly and indirectly about their sexuality, especially by the parents; (3) "deterrence" includes increasing the risk for getting caught (If a molester is caught, Finkelhor suggested increasing publicity for the consequences of child sexual abuse.); stopping the sexualizing of children in advertising, films, and pornography; (4) "identifying high risk social groups" by targeting specific groups for prevention (e.g., blended families, especially since stepfathers have a much higher incidence of sexual abuse toward stepchildren than do natural fathers); and by focusing on adolescents who have been sexually molested to prevent the survivor from becoming the molester at a later point in time. Finkelhor also suggested that alcohol treatment groups should include strategies to prevent sexual abuse since alcohol is frequently utilized in cases of sexual abuse.

Other Factors

Other factors to consider when designing and implementing abuse prevention programs include tailoring the program to suit the presenter's age, gender, ethnic background, level of education, and previous experience (e.g., should the programs use one presenter or two; should the presenter be someone familiar to the child, such as a teacher; should both genders be present and involved in the presentation; how could parents and other caretakers be involved; and what is the optimal length of a prevention program with regards to efficacy for learning and retaining concepts taught?) (Barth & Derezotes, 1990). All of these are important concepts to consider when teaching children about something as important as preventing sexual abuse.

Lastly, Garbarino, Dubrow, Kostelny, and Pardo (1992) had this to say:

> Approaching children developmentally means that we recognize the child's capacity for change. It also means that we recognize the social environment's power to produce change. The child's life is not fixed in some unalterable genetic code that predetermines what and who he or she will be. Each child contains the potential to be many different children, and caring adults can help to determine which of those children will come to life. (p. 9)

Selected Versus All Children

Child sexual abuse prevention programs have employed an all-encompassing approach to include every child in programs rather than identify high-risk groups. Herman (1990) suggested that certain high-risk groups known to be sexist should be targeted for preventive education; this includes the military, college fraternities, and sports teams. She also contended that there needs to be much greater regulation of the organized sex industry, including child pornography.

PREVENTION PROGRAMS FOR YOUNG CHILDREN

Inherent Problems

Two problems are inherent in prevention programs for young children, especially involving preschoolers and the early primary grades (K–3). First, consider the realistic dynamics of teaching young children to distinguish between different kinds of touches when adults cannot adequately do that for themselves. Also saying no to adults (most often those in caretaking positions) and then physically repelling someone older, bigger, and stronger may set the child up to be harmed even further. Assuming that prevention classes enable a child to be responsible for their safety is questionable at best. Adults need to assume the responsibility for a child's safety (Berrick & Gilbert, 1991). Secondly, an all-encompassing approach to prevention programs teaching preschool children that parents and other caretakers can and do sexually abuse is an upsetting message, especially at the age in children's lives when they need to believe they will be taken care of and protected by those adults in their world (Berrick & Gilbert, 1991).

Empowerment Versus Prevention

Butler (1985) has identified two factions within the prevention movement—empowerment versus prevention. Berrick and Gilbert (1991) are proponents of moving away from the empowerment model and moving toward a protection model. In the protection model adults are given the primary responsibility to protect children. This model of protection encapsulates four areas: (1) body awareness (teaching appropriate names for body parts beginning in first grade); (2) communication (talking about feelings of self and other's feelings; teachers are expected to model communication and conflict resolution skills); (3) secret touching (all touching of any kind should be reported to an adult); and (4) adult responsibility (adults are held accountable for their behaviors and it is adults who need to keep children safe from victimization).

SUMMARY

Prevention programs have been developed from every conceivable format. Using audiovisual technology (film, video, audiotape, filmstrips) and the written word (storybooks, coloring books, songs, plays, board games), all different types of programs exist. These programs and materials are based on a set of core assumptions: that many children do not know what sexual abuse is, that sexual touch need not be tolerated, that adults want to know about sexual touching by older persons, and that telling a trusted adult about sexual abuse will cause it to cease. These prevention programs assume children can be taught the difference between a safe and an unsafe touch, who to tell about these touches, and that saying no assertively will be useful in preventing or escaping the experience of abuse (for reviews see Conte & Fogarty, 1990; Kolko, 1988).

Differences exist among prevention programs and materials in the scope of material presented, the amount of time used to present the prevention program to the children, the words used to identify and explain concepts, the location in which the material is presented (home or school), the format of the presentation (video, instruction by adult trainers, printed material), the amount the child interacts with the materials (reads a book, colors, listens and asks questions of an instructor, observes someone demonstrating a prevention behavior and then role-plays situations), and the occupation of the trainer.

Summit (1990) stated, "We will learn to protect children when we learn to stop protecting ourselves. Children will be reasonably safe in adult society when we are willing to expose and control those adults who are most frequently dangerous. Children will be less vulnerable when we, as protective adults, can understand how exquisitely vulnerable they are" (p. 73).

Oates (1990) stated that prevention of sexual abuse is a complex issue. Both she and Finkelhor (1990b) contended that teaching children how to protect themselves is only part of the answer to eliminating sexually abusive behaviors. Oates believed children need to learn to translate the information learned in prevention programs into action. An area that has been somewhat neglected in prevention programs is how to respond to children who disclose sexual abuse. She continued by discussing how unfair and imponderable it is to place children in the position of complete responsibility for their preservation. Adults hold the greatest accountability in protecting children from sexual abuse, even though teaching a child to say, "No I won't keep secrets," is an important concept for children to learn.

What do we know about child sexual abuse? Child sexual abuse is a multifaceted complex issue. Unfortunately, it is also one that has been present for centuries and occurs in societies all over the world. Origins of sexually abusive behaviors seem to have their roots in both individual dysfunctionalism and societal tolerance of abuse and the exploitation of children. Current understanding of the dynamics of sexual abuse, features of the perpetrators, qualities and traits of the abused, and the most effective interventions for all involved, is nebulous at best. More information is available today on all of the aforementioned topics than was available ten years ago, yet so much more needs to be known and understood.

No one particular type of individual emerges as a classic example of a perpetrator. Molesters are engaged in all kinds of occupations, they come from all socioeconomic groups and every kind of ethnic background, and are both male and female. Likewise, no outstanding characteristics have been determined to be unique to those victimized by sexual abuse. Research studies have indicated that frequently molesters begin victimizing others during adolescence, sometimes after the adolescent himself or herself has been victimized, but not always.

Intervention needs to take place during a time when the abuse is just beginning and before the offending behaviors become entrenched. The presence of physical abuse in the home seems to be a large contributing factor in the lives of adolescent perpetrators. Yet it cannot be said that everyone who has been physically abused becomes a sexual offender. Reasons for molesting behaviors involve both sex and power, but these are not the only two issues. Sexual gratification is part of the reward of molesting and abusing others. Other factors come into play.

Cognitive distortions are abundant among offenders. Molesters have a plethora of erroneous beliefs about what is appropriate sexual behavior, in addition to incredible denial about their molesting behaviors. But again, everyone who has erroneous beliefs about sexual matters does not become an offender.

Sexual offenders rarely seek professional help for their abusive behaviors and only become involved with the mental health or legal system as a result of getting caught. Treatment is challenging at best; the more conditioned the behavior the more difficult to control. Viewing sexual abusers within an addiction framework is helpful especially in terms of treatment. There is no cure, only hope for control and abstinence.

Lastly, we as clinicians, therapists, psychologists, psychiatrists, social workers, and clergy need to listen to the survivors. They have much to teach us and there is so much to learn. We need to give them a voice and hear what they are saying. One way to do this is to read a number of different survivor newsletters. (Some of these newsletters are listed after the Reference and Bibliography sections.) Sexual abuse continues to thrive and survive, in part because of the messages communicated through the media about violence against women and children, and the use of pornography, which devalues both women and children. Society has for every purpose concerned legitimized sexual abuse of children.

Chapter 10

CHILD SEXUAL ABUSE
AND PORNOGRAPHY

The invention of photography revolutionized the manner in which children and women could be victimized on a large-scale basis. This technological development facilitated the production of pornography in a way never before possible (Tyler & Stone, 1985). Schultz (1982) documented the availability of purchasing sexually explicit photos of children in Europe before 1865. These exploited children were photographed engaging in graphic sexual acts with other children, adults, and animals.

DEFINITION

Child molesters are frequently collectors of child pornography. Kenneth Lanning (1984) defined child pornography as "any visual or print medium depicting sexually explicit conduct involving a child" (p. 83). Another way of describing child pornography is to say that it is photographs, films, or videos of children being sexually molested. These acts of molestation can include sexual intercourse, bestiality (performing sex acts with animals), masturbation, sadomasochism, or exhibitionism. The act of photographing or filming children in sexual poses or children engaging in sex acts is itself a form of sexual abuse (Faller, 1988; Lanning, 1984).

MOTIVATING FACTORS
FOR COLLECTING CHILD PORNOGRAPHY

There has been some speculation as to why child sex offenders collect child pornography. In reality there are probably a variety of reasons. Collecting pornography may enable child molesters to gratify and support sexual fantasies about children. This may also be a way for a child molester to validate his or her behavior. The pedophile rationalizes that if so many other individuals are "collecting," then there must not be anything wrong with the behavior. Frequently pedophiles will exchange pornographic materials (Crewdson, 1988). This seems to reinforce and further validate their behaviors. Trading is also a vehicle to promote bonding between pedophiles.

Often pedophiles will collect the names, addresses, and phone numbers of other pedophiles who have the same sexual interests. Pedophiles continually endeavor to update and augment their list. Names of potential pedophiles are garnered from "swinger" and pornographic magazines. Pedophiles are quite cautious when they first begin corresponding with a new person. This is because there is a fear of getting caught with illegal materials and arrested for sexually victimizing and molesting children.

Another motivating factor for amassing child pornography is that in the picture, film, or video the child will always be a certain age (Newberger & Newberger, 1984). When the pedophile looks at that child in the picture, the child will forever be 6, 7, 8, or whatever age the pedophile finds most appealing.

The pictures symbolize the pedophile's sexual relationship with the child. Although the child may reach an age when he or she is no longer attractive to the pedophile, the pedophile will always have the pictures or videos that keep the child at the age the pedophile finds most attractive and exciting.

UTILIZATION OF CHILD PORNOGRAPHY

Child pornography is utilized in a variety of ways by the pedophile. It is used to arouse the pedophile and gratify sexual fantasies (Faller, 1988). The second way it can be used is to desensitize other children (O'Brien, 1983). Desensitization, as utilized by child sexual abusers, is a process of seduction. Tyler and Stone (1985) discussed the desensitization process. In the beginning the child or the children are given attention, friendship, and sometimes even gifts. As the child becomes more comfortable with the adult, the adult may begin to touch the child in a nonsexual manner (e.g., rubbing the child's back or head, etc.) Following this behavior is handling, or fondling. This is when the adult may pretend to accidentally touch the child's buttocks or genitals. The process is very gradual and may occur over many months. While the child is being handled or fondled the molester may suggest that he or she watch a video together and place an X-rated movie in the video recorder. The pedophile and child might only watch the X-rated video for a couple of minutes the first time. Each time the X-rated video is watched a little longer. This is done until the child is able to sit and watch the videos without becoming too uncomfortable. Variations on the grooming process are many but the end result is desensitizing the child to engaging in sexual acts with the perpetrator, other children, or other adults.

The child and pedophile also look at a pornographic magazines (O'Brien, 1983). Children are often shown books, films, or magazines of other children engaging in sexual acts. Pedophiles often want children to participate in the type of sexual acts shown in the magazines, knowing that children are impressed and influenced by books, films, and videos. Children think that if it is published, taped, or filmed, then it must be legitimate. The process of desensitization is utilized to lower the child's inhibitions. Children are exposed to sexually explicit materials as an attempt by the pedophile to make them comfortable with seeing nakedness and sexually explicit acts. The more comfortable the child becomes in viewing these sex acts the easier it becomes for the pedophile to manipulate the child into performing these acts. Adult pornographic materials are frequently used to desensitize adolescents during the grooming process.

Blackmail can be the third use of child pornography (Lanning, 1984). Once the pedophile has established a relationship with the child, he or she wants it to continue. What better way to force the continuation of an abusive relationship than to blackmail the child. This can be done by threatening to reveal the pictures to the child's parents, friends, or teachers. (Hunt & Baird, 1990). It then becomes important for the child to preserve the secret.

Barter can be another reason for collecting child pornography (Goldstein, 1984). Certain pedophiles trade photographs of children. This is done in exchange for photographs of different children. Pedophiles exchange phone numbers of children who are used for sexual gratification. Whatever information the pedophiles exchange, it is usually a duplicate of what he or she already has in his or her collection.

Selling pictures, films, or videos for profit can be a fifth use of child pornography, although everyone involved in making a profit from this material is not a pedophile. Sometimes individuals get involved with pornography because it is profitable. It is also possible that a pedophile may begin by only collecting and trading child pornography. After awhile he or she needs more money to deal with the escalating costs of continually updating his or her collection. To increase their monetary resources, pedophiles begin selling pornography either to commercial collectors who will then publish it in kiddy porn magazines, or to other collectors willing to pay for the photos or videos.

Frequently the pedophile will have their own photographic equipment and darkroom because getting the pictures printed or reproduced can be a problem. Legitimate film developers will not reproduce sexually explicit photos. (It is important to note that those persons involved in incestuous relationships may also collect child pornography. Pictures of family members can be photographed and then traded or exchanged for photographs of other children.)

Pedophiles are known for the meticulous notes kept on each child used (Wilson, 1981). These notes include the type of activities engaged in; where the encounter took place; and the child's name, address, and phone number. This information is stored in computer files or in handwritten or typed diaries.

COLLECTORS AND SEX RINGS

Just as there are different reasons for collecting child pornography there are different types of collectors. Sometimes these collectors will become involved in sex rings. Commercial sex rings supply the staples (movies, videos, photos) that form the cornerstone of the commercial child pornography industry (Tate, 1990; Tyler & Stone, 1985).

Collectors are those individuals who acquire, amass, preserve, cherish, and value child pornography (Lanning, 1984; Tate, 1990). The literature (Burgess, Hartman, McCausland, & Powers, 1984) has suggested that there are four different types of collectors: closet collectors, pedophile collectors, cottage collectors, and commercial collectors who have access to many groups of children. Collectors and some individuals who operate sex rings have much in common. A sex ring is a group of children who are molested by the same adult individual (Burgess, 1984; Crewdson, 1988; Faller, 1988; Hunt & Baird, 1990). Rings are of three specific types: solo, transition, and syndicated.

A closet collector is one who maintains secrecy about his or her involvement with children (Burgess, 1984). Rarely are pictures, film, or videos sold or traded to other collectors. Closet collectors are not involved in sex ring operations.

The pedophile collector (Burgess, Hartman, McCausland, & Powers, 1984) generally engages in sexual activity with one child at a time, but the pedophile collector is almost always involved with more than one child throughout the pedophile's life. The children molested can be his or her own, relatives such as nieces or nephews, friend's children, students, and so on. A prevalent belief that this type of collector upholds is that they are not harming the child.

The cottage collector (Burgess, 1984) is one who sexually abuses children in a group setting; pictures and videos are often taken during the sexual molestations. Cottage collectors intend the pornography to be used for the relationship it generates between themselves and other collectors. This type of collector represents the largest group of collectors. These collectors have access to children in a variety of ways. Frequently the parents trust this individual. They may even allow this person to take care of the child or give the child permission to stay over at the adult's house. The parents may even believe that this person can spend more quality time with their child than they can. Second, the cottage collector may have a respected position in the community; he or she may be a coach, Scout leader, or youth activities director. Third, this type of collector will frequently use children in the group to recruit other children. The goal is to have children outside the group become members and participate in the activities of the group. New children are often sisters, brothers, cousins, friends, or acquaintances. Most of the pornography the pedophile collector and the cottage collectors are involved in depicts the adult engaging in sexual acts with a child or in reciprocal exhibitionism between child and adult.

Cottage collectors are sometimes involved in solo sex rings. A solo ring (Burgess, Groth, & McCausland, 1981) is usually operated by one adult who has access to several children. Usually the children know the adult, know one another, and are knowledgeable about one another's sexual acts with the pedophile. The children are initiated into the adult activities of cigarettes, beer, liquor, or other drugs in exchange for sexual acts. Often a child already involved in the group is used to invite other children to come into the group. Geiser (1979) discussed a male sex ring in Houston that involved thirty boys, 27 of whom were tormented, tortured, and then murdered. The solo ring leader often holds a respected position in the community. If the parents do not know them directly, they know of them, enough so that a child spending time with this person is not questioned. Sexual activity is usually introduced in an indirect fashion, either by using pornography, showing pictures of children undressed, asking the child to get undressed to play a game, or the adult engaging in the act of handling. Again desensitization is utilized. Offenders may use sexual games and peer pressure to promote group cohesiveness. Children keep the secret because of fear that they or someone they love will be harmed, fear of being blackmailed by the adult, and peer pressure. The adult or other children apply pressure by saying things like, "If you tell, then you will miss all the fun," or "If you tell, it will ruin it for the rest of us. Don't be a baby."

Cottage collectors can also be involved in transition rings. With transition rings more than one adult is sexually involved with a group of children (Burgess, Hartman, McCausland, & Powers, 1984). In transition rings, most of the children have gone through puberty. Just as *pedophile* means love of children, *pederast* is someone who loves adolescents. The word "loves" once again is used to connotate someone who wants to have a sexual relationship with an adolescent. Pederasts have a sexual preference for adolescents. Burgess et al. (1984) suggested that children become involved in transition rings in a variety of ways: (1) incest victims who have runaway from home, (b) abused adolescents from dysfunctional families, (c) adolescents who have been kidnapped and coerced into a life of prostitution, and (d) children who were once involved with pedophiles who have gone through puberty and are no longer sexually exciting to the pedophile, but are just the right age for pederasts.

Pornography usage seems to have three identifiable functions. First, the sex offender hopes that it will help the child to become aroused. Second, the pictures can help teach children how to perform and participate in certain sex acts. Finally, the photos, films, or videos can be used to desensitize the child to being photographed.

The fourth type of collector is the commercial collector. This collector can be a sex offender who has his or her own cache of children. These children are sexually exploited by a pedophile who also has access to other collector's groups of children. Commercial collectors are organized and are frequently into child pornography as a profit-making venture. A commercial collector may quite easily be a part of a syndicated ring. Syndicated rings are very well organized. These rings involve a variety of activities including enlisting children for the production of pornography, and providing sexual services to a large clientele of adults (prostitution) who have a sexual preference for children or adolescents. Items that are for trade or for sale are photographs, films, videos, and audiotapes of children in varying degrees of sexual activities. Some photos may be of children in bathing suits, while others include very explicit sexual acts. The material is often circulated through the mail (which is illegal) or by computer networks (Crewdson, 1988).

If the pornography is circulated through the mail it may be ordered from another country and then mailed to the United States; however, the material frequently was originally produced in this country. This procedure makes it difficult to trace the initial source of the magazines (Campagna & Poffenberger, 1988).

Those persons who supply syndicated rings with pornographic material may be pedophiles who have access to children or groups of children, or professional distributors who have access to a photographer, a photo lab, a film processor, or video cameras. Sometimes adult magazines will advertise that they develop photos confidentially. Finally, parents, foster parents, and group home workers will sometimes supply children for pornography and prostitution.

In today's society it has become increasingly easy to reproduce pornographic materials. The availability of video equipment has greatly enhanced these clandestine operations. Equipment is not expensive and does not require a developing laboratory to reproduce the videos, thus making it much easier to produce child pornography films (Faller, 1988).

Study of 55 Sex Rings (Burgess, Hartman, McCausland, & Powers, 1984)

Based on information available, sex rings are a prevalent part of an underground network in our society. Gathering information about sex rings is difficult because of the clandestine nature of the activity. Individuals are happy to appear on the major talk shows and discuss divorce, ESP, and so on, but rarely, if ever, are talk shows aired that deal with the subject of sex rings. Sexual abuse almost always seems to be presented with one victim and one perpetrator. As discussed below, this is frequently not the case with sexual abuse victims. Often the victim is just one of many children who have been abused (Hunt & Baird, 1990).

Burgess, Hartman, McCausland, and Powers (1984) obtained information on 55 sex rings. This information was acquired from research consultants who had access to data on sex rings. These consultants were mailed a questionnaire and asked to complete it, based on their information about sex rings. Before beginning to discuss the study's results, several flaws in the study need to be noted. First, the study is not scientific because the information about the sex rings was not obtained by using statistical procedures. The Russell, Finkelhor, and Wyatt studies discussed in Chapter 1 did utilize statistical methods to generate the information provided. Secondly, sometimes all the data needed to complete the questionnaires were not available to the consultants. Finally, 55 rings is a small number, so the information presented should be viewed as mostly descriptive for the 55 rings studied, with the possibility that the information discussed could be used in an attempt to understand other sex rings.

The 55 rings were classified into the three types of sex rings previously discussed: 31 were solo rings, 6 were transitional rings, and 17 were syndicated.

Based on this small sample of 55 sex rings, it can be stated that the sex offenders who sexually exploited the children were primarily middle-class and middle-aged males. Fifty-three of the 55 rings studied were organized by males. Their economic status reflected mostly middle- and upper-class occupations. Thirty-five of the rings were handled by skilled, white collar, or professional people (63.6%). Only 11 of these sex rings were handled by unskilled or blue collar persons (20%). The average age of the offender was 45, but the ages of the offenders ranged from 25 to 74. Ninety percent of the pedophiles were between the ages of 30 and 59. Their initial access to children was through their jobs (38.2%), living arrangements (27.3%), and other children (14.5%). Many did not have previous sexual offenses (41.8%). A significant number did have previous sexual offenses (34.6%). Data were unavailable on the other 23.6%. Almost half the pedophiles were referred for psychiatric help (36.4%), but no data were available on how many followed through and the length of time they were in treatment.

More of the rings involved male children than female children. Forty-nine percent had only boys, and 23% had only girls, and 27% had both sexes of children in their rings. Almost all the rings participated in handling and fondling (89.1%) and in oral sex (80%) with the children. In 73% of the rings the pedophile used his or her home as the established place where the sexual activities occurred. Adult pornography was presented to over half of the children. Syndicated rings were more likely to be involved in the prostitution of children and in using the pictures, films, or videos for monetary gain.

The information garnered from this study on 55 sex rings has quite a message to tell. Frequently members of our society have had a mistaken notion that abuse only occurs in poor, socioeconomically deprived families; in families that live in extremely rural, isolated areas; or families that live in the inner city. The study by Burgess, Hartman, McCausland, and Powers (1984) has shown that this is simply not the case.

Two of the findings that should be noted are the fact that the rings were operated 73% of the time in the individual's home and that 38% of the time the pedophile had access to the child because of their job situation. Parents and other caretakers need to take responsibility for what is happening to their children, learn how to talk to their children about sexual abuse, and learn ways they can better protect their children.

DIMENSIONS OF DENIAL

Summit (1990) contended there were seven dimensions of denial in our society that enable child victimization to flourish. Negation is the first dimension. He proposed that society negates the fact that guileless children are exposed to something as inconceivably repulsive as pornography. Second, frequently a small child such as a preschooler does not have an adequate conceptualization that he or she is being abused and therefore does not report the crime. Third, the customary methods of garnering information about criminal activities definitely are lacking in the area of child sexual abuse; police and government agencies do not infiltrate families or day-care facilities. Children are the only source of information on abuse that occurs in these settings. Fourth, crimes of a sexual nature need state and federal criminal penalties levied against the offending parties, thus giving children validation that child pornography and other forms of child sexual abuse will not be tolerated. As yet this has not happened. Fifth, defense attorneys contend that in many cases, children reporting incidents of sexual abuse are lying at the prompting of adults. This once again promotes the myth of denial. Sixth is what Summit called deliberate deception, in which the professionals involved in the legalities of a case may also be a part of a network that commits atrocities against children, so in order to cover up their activities, the professionals dismiss what the child has stated regarding the abuse or pornography. Seventh, mental health professionals do not have a clear-cut classification and understanding of the etiologies and treatment for children and their offenders.

PORN INDUSTRY

Raschke (1990) wrote,

> The kiddy porn industry grosses 3 billion a year in the United States. The worldwide gross is twice that amount. Kiddy porn in which children are sexually abused before cameras, made to perform degrading acts, and sometimes snuffed has become as common and as popular as eating out. (p. 351)

He estimated that 300,000 children a year are victimized by the kiddy porn industry.

Pierce (1984) believed that the child pornography industry, sometimes called kiddy or chicken porn, continues to thrive and grow. Prostitution and pornography are linked to one another (Giobbe, 1993). Chickenhawks is a slang word for men who enjoy sexual exploits with male children. The children are sometimes called chickens (Rush, 1980). These adult male chickenhawks cruise specified areas of large cities for young boys to pick up, molest, and sometimes pay for the abuse of their bodies. Lloyd (1976) graphically recounts the world of the male child prostitute in his book, *For Money or Love*. Sometimes the chickenhawks will make contact with boys through computer bulletin boards or personal columns in publications like *Hermes* or *Straight to Hell*, or call boy services in large cities. Usually these young male prostitutes are between 12 and 16 years of age. For molesters who prefer younger male children, ages 6 to 12, there are the publications *Boy Howdy* or *O Boy* (Rush, 1980). Dudar (1977) reported in an article for Ms. Magazine that naked children are shown in pastoral settings exposing their genitals. He continued by discussing the more graphic material involving children in orgies, and sex with adults and with animals. (See Ennew & Milne, 1989; Ireland, 1993; Lee-Wright, 1990; Moorehead, 1989; Truong, 1990; and United Nations, 1992, for information about child prostitution in other countries.)

CHILD PORNOGRAPHY AND THE LAW

Before 1977 most states did not have laws that regulated the production and distribution of child pornography. In 1977, the Protection of Children Against Sexual Exploitation Act—Public Law 92-225, 18 U.S.S. 2251-53 was enacted (Nash, 1981). This law gave the federal government the legal authority to arrest and try those who published magazines, films, and so on, as well as those who distributed child pornography. According to the law it was illegal to take children across state lines to engage in this type of activity and it was illegal for adult persons to allow a child to participate in pornographic activities (Nash, 1981).

FEMINIST PERSPECTIVE ON PORNOGRAPHY

Feminists have long contended that child pornography and the media are interconnected (Densen-Gerber, 1983; Rush, 1980). These authors suggested that the process of becoming sexually desensitized to children is in fact a type of culturally learned behavior. Rush (1980) stated, "The more we are exposed to pornography, as to all forms of brutality, the more we become desensitized to its dehumanizing influence" (p. 64).

SEXUAL OFFENDING AND PORNOGRAPHY

Murrin and Laws (1990) have suggested two different theoretical explanations for the existence of the relationship between pornography and sex crime. These theories are the pornography–rape theory and the culture–rape theory (p. 79). The pornography–rape theory maintains that the easier it becomes to purchase soft-core pornography materials the more uninteresting and bland soft-porn becomes. If the purchaser of porn becomes bored with the product, it becomes necessary to include topics the consumer will be drawn toward, such as those portraying men as aggressive and fearless, and those portraying violence, sadomasochism, and males tyrannizing and degrading women. These are frequently some of the themes noted in pornographic materials produced and presented in current magazines. In effect, society, according to this theory, becomes desensitized to violent sexual acts. As pornographic materials increase in violent themes the number of rapes in a society will escalate. The greater the demand for pornography the higher the rate of sex crimes.

The culture–rape theory (Murrin and Laws, 1990) suggested that, as pornography becomes more widely accepted, the pornography laws become more liberal and this creates a greater demand for pornography . As attitudes change and society becomes more inclined to decriminalize pornography, there will be an increase in consumers purchasing pornography and an increase in crimes that are sexual in nature.

One method of determining the part pornography plays in sex crimes is to explore sex offenders' use of pornography and compare that data with other population groups' usage of pornography. Twenty years ago Goldstein, Kant, and Hartman (1973) reported descriptions of pornography usage among three groups of sex offenders: homosexual pedophiles, heterosexual pedophiles, and rapists. A control group was used by the researchers. Almost 70% of each group was exposed to pornography before age 12, 45% were first exposed between the ages of 9 and 12, and 22% were exposed to it before reaching the age of 9. Thus there were few differences between when the sex offenders and the normal control group were first exposed to pornographic materials. Differences did exist in the use of pornographic materials between the rape offenders and the control group: 30% of the rapists and only 2% of the controls viewed graphic sexual material (hard-core porn). Soft-core porn was described as pictures of naked bodies not engaged in sexual acts.

Marshall's (1988) study involved groups of sex offenders receiving outpatient treatment and a matched control group of nonoffenders. By the time each of the groups had reached puberty, 33% of both the rapists and heterosexual pedophiles, 39% of the homosexual pedophiles, and 21% of the control group reported having viewed hard-core pornography. None of the incest offenders reported viewing this type of material. All of the information was based on retrospective self-reports. After reaching adulthood many sex offenders reported having engaged in masturbatory acts after viewing pornography (Cook, Fosen, & Pacht, 1971; Marshall, 1988). Marshall reported the sexual offenders who masturbated more than two times a week (42% in the sex offender group) reported using pornographic materials as a stimulus as compared to the group who masturbated less than two times per week. Marshall (1988) reported over 33% of his study population of rapists and child sexual abusers had utilized hard-core porn before offending, and 53% of the child sexual offenders and 33% of the rapist group made a conscious decision to view pornographic subject matter in preparation for victimizing a child or an adult.

Carter, Prentky, Knight, Vanderveer, and Boucher (1986) studied groups of rapists and imprisoned pedophiles. Pedophiles had higher indices of viewing pornography in adulthood than the rapist group. When asked what importance pornography played in their lives, less than 7% of the pedophile group reported that pornography had little importance in their lives. In contrast 39% of the rapists stated that it had little importance for them. The child sexual abuser group had double the reported incidence of using pornography before molesting, during the molestation, or to deal with the desire to molest.

Laws (1988), as reported in Murrin and Laws (1990), questioned pedophiles during a written intake interview about pornography usage. Fifty-two of the 55 (95%) pedophiles reported viewing pornography involving adults a minimum of one time, and less than 10% ($N = 5$) admitted exposure to child pornography. Eight of the offenders in this study acknowledged photographing the victims for individual possession. If the eight offenders who reported photographing children are included, the number who admitted viewing child pornography is 20% ($N = 8$).

Silbert and Pines' (1984) study of 200 female prostitutes confirmed that some sex offenders use pornography as a stimulus. Of the 200 prostitutes interviewed, 193 reported having been raped, and 24% stated the rapist alluded to certain pornographic images that portrayed the woman as wanting to be raped. Studies presented in this section ascertain that pornography usage is a component in the lifestyle of some sex offenders and seems to preclude some offenders committing sexually victimizing acts. Adult sex offenders reported masturbating to pornography more often than nonoffenders in the studies presented.

Societies that have a high incidence of rape are patriarchal, genderize males and females proscribed roles, and foster violent acts against females (Sanday, 1981). Murrin and Laws (1990) stated, "In a cultural environment where people are not considered to be sexual objects, pornography use probably would have little effect on sex crime. Ironically, in such a culture, pornography itself would most likely not exist" (p. 89). Marshall and Barbaree (1990) contended that the type of pornography available in our society legitimizes sexual offending and promotes sexual stimulation, which in turn creates disinhibition in the sex offender after repeated exposure.

One of the greatest problems inherent in utilizing sex offenders as a study population and then extrapolating broad generalizations from the information garnered is that convicted and incarcerated sex offenders account for less than 10% of the total sex offender population group (Herman, 1990). Most of the reports on offenders using pornography are self-made and obviously there are some real methodological problems in this type of data collection with a population known to lie about their behaviors. Thus the offenders could be grossly underreporting their involvement with pornography. Much more research needs to be done in this area, but meanwhile children continue to be victimized by sex offenders and society continues to legitimize these acts.

Chapter 11

MINORITY CHILDREN

Sexual abuse of minority groups is one of the most neglected areas of research and study in relation to prevention and intervention. This chapter begins by providing some basic definitions of culture, ethnicity, and race, followed by the discussion of the need for prevention program designers and trainers to consider culture when creating and teaching programs; how to develop a multicultural awareness; the indexical versus the referential self and the implications of these concepts in cultural groups; and lastly a discussion on other ways in which minority children are abused simply because of their skin color.

Culture is inclusive of nationality, ethnic origins, religion and language. Pedersen (1988) has stated that culture is basic similar patterns of "learned behavior that is transmitted to others in the group" (p. 54). It also can encompass age, gender, domicile, and educational and socioeconomic status (Hines & Pedersen, 1980). Race generally refers to innate genetic differences of physical traits (e.g., skin color) that distinguish between groups of individuals (Pedersen, 1988). Ethnicity refers to religions and customs haeded from one generation to the next.

MULTICULTURAL SKILLED COUNSELORS

Pedersen (1988) posited that culture is internal, not external to the self. He further suggested that it is imperative in the development of the self that all of us recognize, accept, and form a multicultural identity, incorporating and blending many cultures into our everyday lives. Sue et al. (1982) suggested multicultural skilled counselors need to develop awareness, knowledge, and skills (but the same could be said for prevention trainers or prevention program developers). This three-component approach to training counselors has been echoed elsewhere (Compton & Galaway, 1984; Lum, 1986; Pedersen, 1988). Awareness includes the mental health professional or prevention trainer being able to acknowledge and respect his or her own culture, and cultures other than his or her own. The mental health professional or prevention trainer needs to have developed a sensitivity to and a conscious awareness of his or her values and stereotypes in addition to an understanding of how these may impact on interactions with ethnic minority children. Also, mental health professionals and prevention trainers need to have a sense of ease or satisfaction with the differences in other cultures' and ethnic groups' values and principles, with neither person having to forsake his or her cultural beliefs. Every culture does not employ the same definition for "normal behavior" (Kelly & Scott, 1986).

Sue et al. (1982) suggested that the second area of development needed for a multicultural mental health professional or prevention trainer in this instance is an increased knowledge regarding the United States' socioeconomic and sociopolitical response to ethnic minority groups; an understanding of the specific ethnic minority groups that they may come into contact with; and comprehension of how mental health services, educational programs, and institutions are viewed by the minority groups.

The third component of a culturally competent mental health professional or prevention trainer identified by Sue et al. (1982) is skill. These authors suggested that a mental health professional or prevention trainer should be able to demonstrate proficiency in interacting verbally and nonverbally with others from different cultural groups; this includes being capable of both sending and receiving messages, and of being competent in intervention skills within the culture. Sue and Sue (1990) remind us that becoming a culturally skilled professional "is ongoing, and that it is a process that never reaches an end point" (p. 146).

Sue, Arredondo, and McDavis (1992) have suggested

> that all forms of counseling are cross-cultural, that cultural issues need to be seen as central to cross-cultural counseling (not ancillary), and that by focusing just on ethnic minority issues, we may be 'ghettoizing' the problem. Yet we believe that multicultural counseling is a specialty area as well. (p. 478)

Sue and Sue (1990) remind us that culture, race, and ethnicity are a part of each of us and not just indigenous to ethnic minorities.

DEVELOPING A MULTICULTURAL AWARENESS

Pedersen (1988) has suggested 10 points of reference appropriate for mental health professionals and prevention trainers in learning to develop a multicultural awareness, but these could be adapted to prevention trainers working with children from different cultures or to those who are attempting to develop prevention programs. He suggested the person should possess the

> . . . ability to recognize direct and indirect communication styles; sensitivity to nonverbal cues; awareness of cultural and linguistic differences; interest in the culture; sensitivity to the myths and stereotypes of the culture; concern for the welfare of persons from another culture; ability to articulate elements of his or her own culture; appreciation of the importance of multicultural teaching; awareness of the relationships between cultural groups; accurate criteria for objectively judging "goodness" and "badness" in the other culture. (p. 9)

Barna (1982) listed a number of factors that effect cross-cultural communication: (1) language; (2) nonverbals (e.g., voice volume, rate of speech, gestures, and eye contact); (3) stereotypes and preconceived notions about the culture; (4) constantly evaluating communication with others in an "all or none" framework; (5) feelings of considerable anxiety based on the unknown and ambiguousness of situations that produce stress; and (6) organizational barriers or sociopolitical and economic barriers.

A number of authors have proposed varying developmental theories for minority groups in their adaptation to a White-ethnic culture: Vontress (1981) discussed adaptation of African Americans, and Sue and Sue (1972) discussed Asian Americans. Certain other models have been criticized (Helms, 1984) because the person from the minority or ethnic group is left to assume total responsibility for resolving the struggle of adaptation to the prevailing culture. Second, the majority of identity models, as these are called, center on the person from the minority group developing an ultimate distaste for his or her own ethnic minority group. Third, an assumption is made that a minority identity model is fluid, with little attention given to the fact that adaptation is rarely a contiguous process.

A model that is quite refined is the Minority Identity Developmental Model designed by Atkinson, Morten, and Sue (1983). This model explains the external and internal stands an individual develops in relation to his or her own culture and in response to the dominant culture. Development is considered to occur in five separate stages: (1) conformity, (2) dissonance, (3) resistance and immersion, (4) introspection, and (5) synergetic articulation and awareness (Atkinson et al., 1983, p. 198).

A current model of multicultural counseling (Sue, Arredondo, & McDavis, 1992) suggested that clinicians need to be aware that it is not deviant or pathological to be culturally different; that often racial and ethnic minorities are bicultural; biculturality is positive; and individuals are a part of a larger whole, society, and oppression and racism are negative functions of society. As a whole mental health professionals more often than not reflect the values of society as a whole. These authors stated,

> What is needed is for counselors to become culturally aware, to act on the basis of a critical analysis and understanding of their own conditioning, the conditioning of their clients, and the sociopolitical system of which they are both a part. Without such awareness, the counselor who works with a culturally different client may be engaging incultural oppression using unethical and harmful practices. (Sue, Arredondo, & McDavis, 1992, p. 480)

Sue and Sue (1990) defined a culturally competent counselor as one who continually seeks to understand his or her beliefs about human behavior, values, and stereotypes, and who has knowledge about personal and professional capabilities. Second, a culturally skilled counselor does not judge his or her culturally different client but accepts and seeks to gain a better understanding of how he or she perceives the world. Third, a culturally skilled counselor is one who seeks to develop and practice timely, pertinent, and germane intervention strategies in his or her work with culturally different clients.

PREVALENCE RATES

Wyatt's (1985) retrospective study of African American and Caucasian women did not determine any statistically significant differences between these two groups on reported incidents of sexual abuse during childhood. Sigel, Sorenson, Golding, Burnam, and Stern (1987) found reported incidents of sexual abuse to be higher for non-Hispanics than Hispanics. This is in direct contrast to Russell (1986) who reported lower incidences of childhood sexual abuse in

Asian and Jewish women and higher rates for Hispanic women. Kersher and McShane (1984) also reported higher prevalence rates for Hispanics.

CULTURAL CONTEXT OF THE SELF

Wyatt (1990) contended that researchers and clinicians may be unaware of other types of victimizations that are occurring in addition to sexual abuse. The cultural context in which an individual grows up impacts on all areas of his or her life. To effectively work with children from different ethnic backgrounds one needs to understand the significance of a child's culture in relationship to verbal and nonverbal interactions with adults. Both verbal and nonverbal communications between a child and an adult need to be understood within the child's cultural framework, which may be different than the adult's (e.g., a child may not maintain eye contact with an adult because in the child's culture maintaining eye contact is a sign of disrespect toward the adult). An adult in the dominant culture may perceive this behavior on the part of the child to imply he or she has something to hide, is uncomfortable, or has low self-esteem. Landrine (1992) stated: "the task of increasing cross-cultural understanding is made difficult by the fact that cultural differences are not primarily differences in behavior, but rather in the meanings attached and attributed to the 'same' behaviors" (p. 401).

Garbarino and Gillian (1980) suggested that both ethnic minority and socioeconomic class need to be addressed with regards to prevention programs. Korbin (1980) contended that different cultures cannot and should not be excluded in sexual abuse prevention programs. According to Wyatt (1990) researchers have not addressed a connection between ethnic origins and the different types of child abuse.

Landrine (1992) had this to say about the concept of self: ". . . culturally determined assumptions about the self are beneath all Western cultural clinical concepts and understandings of normalcy, psychopathology, and psychotherapy . . ." (p. 402). According to Western culture one assumes the self can be distinguished and recognized from the nonself. Behaviors, thoughts, feelings, and observations originate from the self. A belief that someone or something external controls one's thoughts, actions, or feelings would be labeled as delusional or schizophrenic. Self is then differentiated from human and nonhuman. Thus, if an individual experiences their "self" as lifeless or more automated than alive, Western culture labels the individual as experiencing depression, dysthymia, or depersonalization. Anything not retaining or endowed with a construct of self is considered less than human, or flora, fauna, other elements occurring in nature, and entities such as emotions and time. Believing that occurrences that are nonself events (accidents, death, etc.) are caused by one's cognitions and wishful thinking is viewed by Western culture as delusional (Landrine, 1992). Crapanzano (1981) and Gaines (1982) have called this the referential self. Landrine (1992) had this to say about the referential self: ". . . [it] is a god that creates, explains, and takes responsibility for its free actions" (p. 406).

The concept of the referential self is an unrecognizable, obscure tenet among minorities (Gaines, 1982; Marsella, Devos, & Hsu, 1985; Marsella & White, 1982; Nobles, 1976; Strauss, 1977). Ethnic and minority groups uphold what has been called the indexical self. The indexical self is based on ". . . social interactions, contexts and relationships. The self is created and re-created in interactions and contexts, and exists only in and through these" (Landrine, 1992, p. 406). In sociocentric cultures, family and the culture are who and what has needs and ambitions. The individual has obligations to the culture. Failure to uphold the cultural traditions and obligations results in the death of the self. Often children will not tell anyone about abuse because they believe it is their role to protect and maintain the family and cultural system (Driver & Droisen, 1989).

Successfully working with minorities involves addressing the larger needs of the family and culture in which the individual lives. Failure to do this usually produces dismal therapeutic results (Christensen, 1989; Grevious, 1985; Padilla, Ruiz, & Alvarez, 1975; Root, 1985).

Landrine (1992) inferred that in our society the nonself domain is something to be regulated and dominated by the self. Those individuals who are unable to master tasks, control their lives, and regulate their emotions are labeled passive, socially impaired, having poor impulse control, or a victim of learned helplessness. All of which may be in direct contrast to some ethnic minorities belief systems about the appropriate response by an individual to a given situation.

This culture is rife with stereotypes about people of color. Wyatt (1990) recounted some of the more pervasive ones: "All Latinos are hot-blooded," or "Asian women have secret knowledge about increasing a man's sexual pleasure." She contended that children of color incorporate and accept these stereotypical images of their sexuality (garnered from the media) as fact and "act as he or she is expected" to act according to societal misnomers, rather than act according to the values and mores their culture or religion teaches (Wyatt, Strayer, & Lobitz, 1976).

FAILURES TO DISCLOSE

Fontes (1993) described a number of factors that impede children's disclosures of sexual abuse. First, discrimination by the dominant culture, which includes discrimination by the police, the judicial system, and the schools. Second, poverty prohibits children from telling. These children are often isolated from available support systems (extended families, friends, or someone else who could be told about the abuse) because of violence in their communities. They become virtual prisoners in their own homes. Poverty places children at risk because offenders often can provide candy, clothes, toys, and other things the child desires but is too poor to afford. Third, a language barrier may exist that prevents children from telling about the abuse; there is a lack of service providers who are fluent in Spanish, for example. Fourth, the child-rearing practices of specific cultures may prohibit disclosure. Fontes described how children are viewed in a Puerto Rican culture:

> In Puerto Rico, children are not part of society. You become part of society when you turn 15 or 16. Before that, well, as is commonly said in Puerto Rico, "You speak when the hens pee." That means that you cannot speak. Children are completely isolated, rejected until they turn 16. (p. 29)

Our understanding of cultural norms such as these can only enhance prevention and treatment efforts. Other values center on the high regard for virginity in the Puerto Rican culture and females who have been sexually abused are seen as dishonored. Knowing this it is easy to understand why females who have been abused would not choose to reveal this information. Additionally, sex is a forbidden topic in the home; it is simply not discussed.

Thompson and Smith (1993) had this to say about African Americans and sexual abuse:

> The judicial system response to African American victims may affect the willingness of African American families to disclose sexual abuse. . . . In addition, victims and their families may have had experiences with negative police response to sexual assault and other crimes in the African American community. (p. 7)

INTERVENTIONS

Fontes (1993) suggested some interventions for Puerto Rican children who have been abused. She stated,

Large numbers of bilingual personnel at all levels of the educational, social service, medical and legal systems would immediately reduce the isolation of Puerto Rican children. . . . Providers who are serving low income Puerto Ricans must be aware of and respectful toward Puerto Rican history and culture, aware of their client's socioeconomic context, and skilled in working with issues of sexual abuse. . . . Programs which educate and support identified leaders are apt to be more readily accepted than those which try to impose "alien" authorities. Finally, and most importantly, the social service, medical and legal providers who work with abused Puerto Rican children need to prove themselves worthy of the community's trust. Child victims and their families are not going to disclose if they perceive the authorities as intent on destroying or disgracing, rather than empowering, Puerto Rican families. (p. 33)

Fontes (1993) suggested research is needed to determine how each separate ethnic group determines what constitutes and encompasses sexual abuse, how pain is conceptualized in each group, who are the current resource persons in each community, and how current treatment services are utilized in each group. Heras (1992) had this to say,

Cultural consideration in assessing sexual abuse is crucial when working with ethnically diverse groups and includes the following: (1) understanding the context of the abuse, (2) understanding how family structure impacts therapeutic assessment of sexual abuse, and (3) understanding what is culturally congruent and what is dysfunctional. It is important to remember that generally incest is taboo in most cultures. However, among people from developing nations (third and fourth world peoples), it is not uncommon that family values take priority over the concern of molestation. (pp. 120–121).

Heras (1992) discussed how misunderstanding the family structures in Asian and Hispanic cultures can result in American clinicians reaching incorrect assumptions especially with regards to incidents of sexual abusiveness that may or may not have occurred. She discussed how the male is the dominant figure in both cultures (Asian and Hispanic) and parental rights take precedence over children's rights. These ethnic families value a sense of unity more than individual needs. Allegiance to the family is seen as more important than allegiance to the self. (Heras cites her clinical work with over sixty Asian families in which the father was the perpetrator. In these sixty families the nonoffending mother left the father in only four of the cases.) The marital relationship is different in Asian and Hispanic cultures than in American culture. In both Asian and Hispanic cultures the emphasis is between mother and child, not mother and father. Sometimes therapists attempt to shift this balance by focusing on the husband and wife dyad. Other differences are the manner in which Hispanic and Asian clients attempt to save face by negating or projecting the blame for their actions on something or someone outside the self. The family may see no merit in continuing to discuss the abuse, what led up to the abusive incidents, and so on. These families may instead want to focus on what comes next or how to get on with family life. Another difference between American and Asian and Hispanic cultures is styles of communicating. Communication is carried out in these ethnic families through more indirect methods. Nonverbal behaviors may play a significant role, especially with anger and love. Lastly, Heras reminded us that many times

> . . . our ethnic clients usually come from histories where institutions are not trustworthy, or where discrimination and racial bias exists in institutions, so their lack of trust in the system reflects healthy, reality based paranoia and not resistance. At other times what we see as resistance could be our inability to join with this family either through misinterpretation of culturally congruent dynamics, or our inability to provide them with tangible and practical evidence of our usefulness. (p. 124)

The Hmong, a group of Asian people, were relocated to this country after the Vietnam War. The Hmong are described as "a Southeast Asian mountain dwelling tribe that lived primarily in North Vietnam, Laos and Thailand" (Cerhan, 1990, p. 88). They live in a patriarchal system with the oldest male in the family having the most status, position, and power.

Clinicians need to know that showing emotions, expressing feelings, and self-disclosure are viewed quite negatively by the Hmong people (Voigt, 1984). Cerhan had some specific suggestions to help mental health professionals work effectively with the Hmong. Her first suggestion involved not making generalizations about having a broad-based knowledge about Asian people, because the Hmong may not have the same priorities as other groups from Southeast Asia (e.g., the Hmong did not place a high value on formalized education in their country of origin, whereas many other Asian cultures have this value). Second, insight-oriented techniques are probably not appropriate for the Hmong. Focusing on and discussing feelings would be quite strange as this is not done in their culture, especially with strangers (which mental health persons would be). The Hmong have a strong cultural value around independence. Clinicians need to facilitate their client's understanding that the goals of treatment are not to make them more dependent. Goals of treatment need to be discussed and framed in a concrete way that is respectful of Hmong values and culture. Third, interventions may be facilitated and enhanced by utilizing a therapist who is Hmong or asking a shaman to participate in the therapy process. Cerhan did not recommend using children (who may have a much better command of the English language) as interpreters for older Hmongs because of the way the family unit is structured. Fourth, one of the most helpful services the therapist can provide is basic education and information about American culture. Fifth, the clinician needs to gather as much information as possible about the client or family's experiences in their country of origin; their immigration process; current and past experiences in this country; and if any family members or friends have been affected by the unexplained death syndrome affecting many Hmong's since being relocated to this country. Sixth, mental health services should be channeled into already existing mental health programs. Cerhan stated, "separate service may undermine the appropriate goals of integration and psychological adjustment" (Cerhan, 1990, p. 91). Cerhan quoted Westermeyer and Williams (1986), who contended that exclusive refugee programs are not helpful because they "contribute to isolation, paranoia and lack of familiarity of life in the mainstream society—precisely the clinical problems that must be overcome with refugee patients" (p. 91). For a better understanding of the Hmong culture, see the following authors: Downing and Olney (1982), Nishio and Blimes (1987), Westermeyer (1986), and Westermeyer and Williams (1986).

ASSESSMENT

Gomez (1992) suggested the following information should be gathered when doing an interview that involves or may involve sexual abuse:

1. Severity of abuse
2. Length of abuse (chronicity)
3. Number and severity of symptoms
4. Age of child (Could they tell you if it happened to them again?)
5. Cultural expectations of the family
6. Assessment of the proposed interventions to determine whether they will actually exacerbate the problem by being perceived by the patient as abusive
7. Family constellation, interdependency, and support system
8. Stressors (past, current, and future)
9. Determination of what the family, as a group and as individuals, want and expect of the process (p. 126)

Gomez reminded us that

> Each professional must represent and protect each patient's rights as a human being to live in safety and nonabusive environments. Any

time there is conscious or unconscious collusion with abuse by not confronting, or ignoring the mistreatment, the cycle of abuse continues. It is important to note that while not all patients may leave psychotherapy as child abuse experts, the ideas encountered in psychotherapy are often the seeds for future insights and growth. Thus while cultural variations exist with regards to human rights issues, these should not constitute excuses for actions such as dismissing or ignoring abusive behaviors, delaying or failing to notify the proper authorities, or active or passive support of inequality between the sexes, races and individuals. (p. 126)

THE MANY FORMS OF VICTIMIZATION

According to Wyatt (1990) researchers have not addressed a connection between ethnic origins and different types of child abuse. Certain researchers and authors have contended that ethnic minority children are often survivors of more than one form of victimization (Courtois, 1988; Wyatt, 1990). These authors have theorized that exposure to violence and crime in the child's neighborhood as well as natural disasters can affect a child's feelings of safety and security.

Wyatt (1990) believed an ethnic minority child begins to experience feelings of betrayal when he or she first realizes that he or she is not the same as other children. Being different is often brought to the child's attention by other children or adults vocalizing racial slurs; being physically victimized by others because of color or ethnic origins; being segregated from activities in which his or her peer's participate in; or becoming a target for mockery and derision based on "skin color, hair texture, facial features, and spoken language" (Wyatt, 1990, p. 339).

To determine that racism is alive and thriving in the 1990s one needs only to turn on the television or read the newspaper and see burning crosses, swastikas, and rallies of people in white peaked hats throughout the country. Few communities have been left untouched by brutal forms of racism and hatred. All of us are affected, especially those most vulnerable, the children, who look to adults for safety and guidance. Children, especially young children, have a need to believe their parents have the power and ability to protect them. Sometimes, when children are victimized by racism, the child blames the parents (Wyatt, 1990). Often a child's feelings of confusion, anger, and betrayal are not addressed by parents, teachers, clergy, or police; instead the child is told to overlook and disregard others who are verbally abusive (Wyatt,

1990). Failing to address the issues of hate and racism do not cause them to go away.

Minority children are frequently caught in a no-win situation; if they try to get ahead in the current system, they may be stigmatized by their White ethnic peers for being different or "less than," and may be treated as pariahs in their own ethnic group for attempting to achieve status and success in a White culture. In turn the individual often experiences segregation from his or her internal sense of self as well as his or her ethnic sense of self (Driver & Droisen, 1989).

Powerlessness is also a feeling ethnic minority children frequently experience (Wyatt, 1990). Wyatt (1990) has suggested that powerlessness is manifested in several different ways. First, it is a Herculean task for a child to believe he or she can be empowered when the adults in the ethnic milieu do not have the opportunity or prerogative to be educated, employed, or live in a place of their choosing. Second, it is difficult to feel empowered when the champions and role models in society are from a different ethnic group. During the 1960s and 1970s minority groups were provided role models on television. Unfortunately most of the role models were, according to Wyatt (1990), felons, maids, butlers, hookers, or drug dealers. She continued by pointing out that most world history classes ignore or do not include the work and achievements that people of color have made throughout the world. Third, it is challenging to feel empowered if personal boundaries are constantly violated or negated (e.g., when ethnic groups are the last to be waited on or served by store clerks and waitresses, or minority individuals are continually assumed to be service workers in shopping centers, colleges, or restaurants). Ethnic minority adolescents are most often portrayed as high school dropouts rather than as doctors, lawyers, scientists, and researchers. Societal messages to ethnic minority children are often negative and do not encourage empowerment.

Ethnic minority children, according to Wyatt (1990), may have been victimized by the pervasiveness of violence, often witnessing it first-hand where they live (e.g., homicides, domestic violence, crimes related to gangs, and drug deals). Wyatt (1990) discussed how children need to have some kind of meaning for what they see in their world. A steady diet of violence may result in the child acting out the anger and confusion he or she is experiencing. Children may blame themselves or others for a world out of control. Behavioral and verbal reactiveness by minority children might be a result of more than one type of victimization. Manifestations of symptoms may be indicative of cataclysmic, destructive, and oppressive events in the child's life that he or she has observed, witnessed, or been a part of. All of which most White, middle-class mental health professionals cannot even begin to comprehend. Clinicians and other professionals need to be aware of the kinds of multiple victimizations that can occur. Wyatt (1990) said,

> This can be accomplished by asking children if they have (a) ever had a bad or upsetting experience because of their skin color, facial features, hair texture, or cultural or religious values; (b) ever witnessed someone being beaten, shot, or killed; (c) ever been in an area that was bombed or where people were frightened or, (d) ever witnessed an earthquake, tornado, or hurricane. (p. 344)

Mental health professionals need to recognize that they alone might not be able to meet the needs of the child, but together as a team they might. A team that includes members from the child's own ethnic minority group would best facilitate the process of counseling. Garbarino, Dubrow, Kostelny, and Pardo (1992) have written an excellent book entitled, *Children in Danger: Coping with the Consequences of Community Violence.* It discusses the effects and interventions for children living in chronically violent communities.

PREVENTION CONCEPTS

Children of all colors need to have their self-esteem fostered in addition to learning to develop an affirmative appreciation for his or her own ethnic identity. Paramount to effective prevention and intervention is conferring with the designated healers and elders in the child's cultural environment (Landrine, 1992). Garbarino and Gillian (1980) stated that both ethnic minority and socioeconomic class need to be addressed with regards to prevention programs. Korbin (1980) contended that different cultures' values and mores cannot and should not be excluded in sexual abuse prevention programs. Individuals from the ethnic minority group need to be a part of any presented prevention programs for parents and children.

One of the few programs designed specifically for ethnic minorities is Levy's (1988). He developed the "Taking Care of Me" program for prevention of sexual abuse in the Hispanic community. Levy stated, "The underlying assumption of this program was that any prevention approach must strengthen the capability of the Hispanic family to deal with the stresses and social conflicts encountered" (p. 393). This program was utilized with 3,935 teachers, parents, and children age 6 to 18, over an 18-month period. The parental component focused on three areas: (1) general information about sexual abuse; (2) information about what the children were going to be presented; and (3) discussion of sexual abuse with children in the home environment. Program content included components of presenting sexual abuse as a safety issue rather than a sexual matter. Prevention concepts involved children's rights, assertiveness, and trusting feelings. Other content components included coping, encouraging children to speak out about any potentially abusive situation that arises, defining abuse, and denouncing the myths about sexual abuse.

The children's component focused on not keeping secrets, how to stop the abuse (e.g., yell, run away, say the word "Stop," tell a trusted adult), and how to take care of themselves when others in the community believe he or she is not showing respect for elders. Severity of the impact of sexual abuse was not presented to children under the age of 12.

Presenters utilized various teaching aids: stories with discussion (e.g., child was to share about a time when he or she had to take care of himself or herself), hand puppets for children K–3rd grade, flannel boards, and so on. Evaluation involved a posttest for children in the 7th grade or above. Both parents and teachers were asked to complete postprogram questionnaires. Presentations were provided in Spanish to both parents and children. (No statistical information regarding posttest questionnaires was provided by the author.)

As Levy (1988) has attempted to demonstrate there is a real need to include parents in any prevention program for children. Seemingly the focus has been on an empowerment model for children, while ignoring a more protective stance, especially for younger children. Perhaps prevention programs that are taught should target the parents and teach them how to recognize signs and symptoms of abuse and how to talk to their children about protecting themselves. Or perhaps training would be most effective if children and parents were trained together. It would facilitate the training process if a minimum of one facilitator for each group was from the child and parent's own ethnic group. Again, it needs to be reinforced that the child development literature and literature on each specific ethnic minority's culture must be examined. The knowledge available from these areas should be incorporated into any prevention programs that are being designed and implemented for children and parents. Program designers, program trainers, and program implementers also might want to examine and utilize the traumatic stress literature, because it is obvious that many ethnic minority children are survivors of more than one type of abuse. If the goal is to protect children and empower them perhaps the same also could be offered conjointly to the parents.

Chapter 12

CHILDREN
WITH SPECIAL NEEDS

Children with special needs are in greater jeopardy of being sexually abused (Finkelhor, 1984; Kelly, 1992; Mayer, 1988; Morgan, 1987; O'Day, 1983; Sobsey, 1993; Sobsey & Doe, 1991; Sullivan & Scanlon, 1988; Zirpoli, 1986) than able-bodied children. All children in Western cultures are at risk to be sexually abused, but the population of children with special needs appear to be even more vulnerable to abuse (Brookhouser, Sullivan, Scanlan, & Garbarino, 1986; Gill, 1970; Jaudes & Diamond, 1985; Krents, Schulman, & Brenner, 1987; Sangrund, Gaines, & Green, 1974; Sullivan & Scanlan, 1987). Sullivan, Brookhouser, Scanlan, Knutson, and Schulte (1991) suggested that sexual abuse is the most common form of abuse experienced by children with special needs.

PREVALENCE RATES

Supplying a correct prevalence rate among this population group is unlikely. The estimate is at least 50% higher for the child with special needs than the able-bodied child (Sobsey & Varnhagen, 1988). One of the problems in this particular group is how all-encompassing the term "special needs" has become. "Special needs" includes a vast array of physical and mental states including amputees and the learning disabled, as well as those afflicted with deafness, mental retardation (mild, moderate, or severe), cerebral palsy, blindness, juvenile arthritis, attention deficit disorder, and spina bifida, to name a few. Each child with special needs has his or her own specific set of circumstances as a consequence of his or her incapacities, which increases the child's chances for victimization (Westcott, 1991). Sullivan, Scanlan, Brookhouser, Schulte, and Knutson (1992) and Garbarino (1987a) contended that a society that treats its children with special needs inhumanely and with little respect is giving its members permission to abuse those children. Degener (1992) stated,

> Even before the disabled child is abused, his or her experience is one of oppression. . . . People with disabilities experience many different forms of discrimination. A major one is exclusion; individuals with disabilities are excluded from the mainstream of society through denial of social services and education within integrated settings. (p. 151)

She continued,

> The very first experience of a disabled child is a perception that he or she shouldn't be the way they are. . . . If a child has never been allowed to say "No" to being touched by doctors, nurses or even parents, how can we expect the child . . . to resist a sexual attack? (p. 154)

Kelly (1992) stated,

> Apart from not knowing how common abuse of children with disabilities is, we know even less about how those who are abused cope with it. . . . How can safety and protection be developed for children and young people with different/limited communication skills and who require institutional care? Or to put this another way how do we prevent skilled abusers using paid work to get access to vulnerable populations of children? (p. 165)

Sullivan, Scanlan, Brookhouser, Schulte, and Knutson (1992) had the following to say about the dearth of research literature and programs for children with special needs:

> The current state of research with nonhandicapped victims of child sexual abuse leaves much to be desired. Unfortunately, the state of affairs with handicapped populations is worse. Although handicapped children may be at increased risk to be sexually victimized (Garbarino, 1987; Sullivan, Brookhouser, Scanlan, Knutson, & Schulte, 1991), few studies have addressed the topic of treatment of sexually abused children within the handicapped population. The handicapped population is heterogeneous, and incidence as well as therapy efficacy data are scarce for the various conditions (i.e., mental retardation, visual impairment, hearing impairment, speech and language

disorders, emotional–behavioral disturbance, learning disabilities, and the physical disabilities. (p. 248)

In addition, myths have prevailed that suggest that children with special needs are not at risk for sexual abuse because these children or adolescents are pitied, or are seen as undesirable (Anderson, 1982; O'Day 1983). One of the biggest myths still perpetuated in modern day society is that children and adults with special needs are not sexually abused (Ammerman, VanHasselt, & Hersen, 1988; Anderson, 1982; Brown & Craft, 1989; O'Day, 1983).

CHARACTERISTICS OF SITUATIONS THAT PLACE SPECIAL NEEDS CHILDREN AT RISK

Characteristics that place children with special needs at an increased risk for being sexually abused are:

- reliance on others for essential needs and companionship;
- insufficient regulation and mastery over his or her life;
- malleability and submissiveness fostered as evidence of pleasing;
- worthwhile conduct;
- misconstruing inappropriate sexual behaviors committed by the perpetrators;
- segregation and exclusion by society, which augments responsiveness to attentiveness of others;
- incapacity to alert others to what has occurred; and
- incompetence in differentiation between what is and is not abusive behavior (Brown & Craft, 1989; Craft, 1987).

It has been suggested that children who are mentally retarded and lack general social acceptance are anxious to please adults (Zigler & Hodapp, 1986). The research literature has found that mentally retarded children who feel socially neglected from interactions with adults are more needy and inclined to engage in more interactions with supportive adults (supportive adults could include intrafamilial and extrafamilial sexual abusers) than mentally retarded children who are not socially neglected (Balla & Zigler, 1975; Zigler, 1961; Zimler, Balla, & Butterfield, 1968). The implications of this information are far-reaching in terms of compliance between a victimized child and perpetrators.

Ammerman, VanHasselt, and Hersen (1988) discussed the fact that most research investigating qualities of children that may cause them to be more susceptible to being abused ignore children with special needs. These children may be placed in certain circumstances that provide greater opportunities for them to be abused (e.g., attending special schools that require lengthy bus rides to and from home, living in residential centers, and being institutionalized). In addition, it is sometimes difficult to determine if the disability was present prior to the abuse or if the abuse created the disability (Garbarino, 1987; Morgan, 1987).

A number of authors have suggested that children with special needs be taught skills in the following areas: assertiveness, empowerment, and distinguishing between proper and improper solicitations and propositions from others (Craft, 1987; Hames, 1990; Kennedy, 1989, 1990; Krents, Schulman, & Brenner, 1987; Martin & Martin, 1990; Sobsey & Varnhagen, 1988; Sullivan, Vernon, & Scanlan, 1987; Trevelyan, 1988). Two researchers, Hames (1990) and Trevelyan (1988), have adjusted current abuse prevention programs for learning disabled students.

Yet to suggest to a child with multiple challenges that he or she say, "No, Go, and Tell," is ridiculous. If a child is completely dependent on his or her adult caretakers to do everything for him or her and they are the abusers, who is he or she going to tell, especially if communication is difficult?

Emphasis needs to be placed on improving communication skills between adults and children with special needs. Sobsey and Varnhagen (1988) contended that most physically and mentally challenged children are not going to report abuse, especially abuse that occurred in residential settings. This is distressing in light of the fact that some researchers have documented the increased risk for these children who live in group homes or institutions (Garbarino, 1987).

Recognizing sexual abuse in able-bodied children is complicated and challenging; it becomes even more so when the child has special needs. First, because the child may not understand he or she is being molested, and second, because of the child's condition he or she may find it difficult to tell others about the molesting (Westcott, 1991).

RESEARCH STUDIES

Jaudes and Diamond (1985) have identified four areas to be considered when determining the abuse and neglect of a child with special needs: (1) disabilities which are a result of abuse; (2) disabled children who are abused; (3) a child with special needs who does not receive adequate care or is neglected, and as a result, doctors, nurses, lawyers, and caseworkers become involved; and (4) a disabled child who is removed from the home and placed with foster families, in residential or institutional settings. In 1983 Diamond and Jaudes wrote an article that reported on 86 children with cerebral palsy, eight of whom became disabled as a result of physical abuse. As early as 1946, Caffey documented that physical abuse can result in developmental disabilities. Two other researchers in the 1950s and 1960s (Berenberg, 1968; Silverman, 1954) reported child abuse as a cause of developmental problems. More recently, eight studies have documented the relationship between child abuse and other disabilities (Brandwein, 1973; Ellison, Tsai, & Largent, 1978; Kogutt, Swischuk, & Fagan, 1974; Martin, Beezley, Conway, & Kempe, 1974; O'Neil, Meacham, & Griffin, 1973; Ryan, Davis, & Oates, 1977). Diamond and Jaudes (1983) suggested that part of the problem with the special needs child receiving adequate care is the poor coordination and communication between the diverse service provider groups, the medical, social services, legal, educational, and state agencies. Sometimes, if the abuse occurs in the home, the child continues to remain in the parents' care because adequate placements cannot be found. Multiple placements appear to be the rule rather than the exception whenever special needs children are removed from the home. Jaudes and Diamond (1985) reported that when 19 of 23 children who were abused were put in foster homes, six of the children had multiple placements, six were returned to their homes, three were put in institutions, and one child died. None of the children were adopted at the time of the study's completion. The children who were placed back in the home for the most part were once again at an increased risk of being victimized. Certain problems have been identified with placing children in foster homes, such as lack of adequate health care for the disabled child (Schor, 1982). Another problem is that foster parents have not been educated on how to meet the needs of the special child (Lahti, 1982). Jaudes and Diamond (1985) wrote,

> Further problems result from impermanence of placement: lack of continuity with previous health care providers, lack of planning for future health care, lack of planning for future education, lack of financial support, lack of adequate selection of appropriate foster parents. (p. 345)

In Jaudes and Diamond's (1985) study, 23 of the children with cerebral palsy were abused by the parent or caregiver after the physical disability had been diagnosed: Fifteen of the 23 were grossly neglected, and of the remaining eight, three were sexually abused, two were burnt, and three were physically abused. An earlier study conducted by Johnson and Morse (1968) found that of 101 abused children, 70 of the children had disabilities prior to the abuse. Being disabled seems to place children at an even greater risk for being abused. The other 31 children were able-bodied. Morse, Sahler, and Friedman (1970) determined in a follow-up study of the same children that 32% of the study population who had been abused would fit the criteria for mental retardation. Frisch and Rhoads (1982) studied 420 children with learning disabilities. Almost 7% of this study's population had been reported to state agencies that monitored child abuse. This was a rate 3.5 times higher than that for children not identified as having special needs.

Two studies have reported on the incidence of abuse and neglect in a multiple-handicapped population. Ammerman, VanHasselt, and Hersen (1988) reviewed the medical records of 150 multiple-disabled children admitted to a psychiatric facility. Results showed that 35% ($N = 58$) of the study population had been abused or neglected. Sixty nine percent ($N = 33$) of the children had been physically abused. The mother was the perpetrator in 15 of the cases, the father in 13 of the cases, a stepfather or boyfriend in 12 cases, a neighbor or friend in two cases, and a relative in two cases. Neglect occurred in 45% ($N = 26$) of the children by the mother ($N = 16$), father ($N = 6$), stepfather or boyfriend ($N = 1$), or a relative ($N = 1$). Sexual abuse occurred in 36% ($N = 23$) of the study population. The children were sexually abused by mothers ($N = 4$), fathers ($N = 6$), stepfathers or boyfriends ($N = 3$), neighbors or friends ($N = 3$), strangers ($N = 2$), or relatives ($N = 5$). Over 50% of the children experienced more than one form of abuse. Parents were more often than not the offenders in either abuse or neglect cases. Forty percent of the reports of sexual abuse involved multiple offenders. Sixty-six percent of the sexual abuse involved penetrating forms of abusiveness. The authors presented three case examples of different forms of abuse. Results from this study suggested very high prevalence rates of all types of abuse and neglect in multiple-disabled children. It may be even more difficult for children with multiple handicaps to report incidents of abuse. Additionally, multiple-disabled children may have more accidents that result in bruises and contusions, which makes identification of physical abusiveness even more difficult (Ammerman, VanHasselt, & Hersen, 1988). Review of medical records does have some limitations that are prohibitive in generalizing the research findings to other populations of children with special needs.

In another case record review study Benedict, White, Wulff, and Hall (1990) studied medical records of 500 children who were developmentally and functionally impaired in more than one area and who had been identified as being at risk for abuse or neglect. Figures by the U. S. Department of Health and Human Services (1988b) reported the national incidence of abuse at 16.3 per 100 children. Benedict et al. (1990) found only 10 cases per 1,000 children. This study's results were substantially lower than those statistics reported on a national level Four hundred eighty-four (96.8%) of the children were moderately to profoundly mentally retarded, 82% of the population had additional disabilities, 425 had cerebral palsy, and 39% had seizures, other disabilities, or visual or auditory impairments. These authors suggested that children who have less severe disabilities may be at risk for abuse and neglect because of increased parental expectations for more able-bodied children (Murphy, 1982; Willner & Crane, 1979). Benedict et al. (1990) suggested that the families of the more severely impaired children need to receive more monitoring by professionals than families of able-bodied children. These authors suggested close monitoring might be a deterrent for a parent who fears getting caught. Of the 500 children who were identified as being at risk for being abused, only three were identified as being sexually abused. Fifty-three children were identified as either abused (64%, $N = 34$) or neglected (36%, $N = 19$). Why the discrepancy exists between Ammerman, VanHasselt, and Hersen (1988) and this study (Benedict et al., 1990) is unclear. It may be a result of underreporting in the Benedict et al. (1990) study based on the medical records reviewed and how the data were charted. Any time data are garnered in a case review format from medical records the possibility exists for error because of the vast number of variables involved (e.g., the researcher doing this type of record review may be unsure of what may not have been documented in the chart, the ability and knowledge of the professional evaluating the child may make a difference, and so on).

The Mentally Retarded Child

Tharinger, Horton, and Millea (1990) discussed the vulnerabilities of the mentally retarded population to being sexually abused. They stated,

> Thus, children and adults with mental retardation appear to be extra vulnerable to abuse and exploitation. . . . They often are dependent on caregivers their whole life, are relatively powerless in society, are easily coerced, are emotionally and socially insecure and needy, and usually are not educated about sexuality and sexual abuse. This combination of enhanced risk factors helps to explain the suspected high incidence of sexual abuse among this population. (p. 305)

The Deaf Child

Deaf children are at risk because often family members and others cannot effectively communicate with these children (Ridgeway, 1993). Ridgeway suggested some factors that place deaf children at a greater risk for being abused than nonhearing impaired children:

(a) deprivation of early language development; (b) no exposure to other deaf people; (c) conflict or disagreement in the family over education and communication; (d) low self-esteem and social isolation; (e) lack of deaf peer group; (f) lack of deaf consciousness and deaf awareness; (g) poor or inappropriate parental involvement; (h) unrealistic expectations (by parent), low aspirations (by child); (i) rejection of deaf identity, discouraged from learning about deaf people in the community. One factor alone would not be evidence of abuse, but a combination of some of these factors might suggest that the deaf child is at risk (Ridgeway, 1993, pp. 170–171).

White, Benedict, Wulff, and Kelley (1987) have identified some specific research problems with current studies about children with special needs: Study populations have been determined to lack a comprehensive, encompassing definition of special needs children; no determination if there are different types of abuse which occur more frequently among the different special need population groups; lack of replication of the studies; and specification of the level of functioning of the special need children in the studies (e.g., Are all children with mental retardation placed in one research group?). These researchers stated, "Multiple additional factors also need investigation, such as specific and social environment strengths, community resources, public awareness and measurement of societal values relative to disabilities and maltreatment" (p. 99).

FAMILIES OF CHILDREN WITH SPECIAL NEEDS

Caring for a child who has special needs places considerable stress on the family. Many factors need to be considered: the child's degree of impairment, level of functioning, type and amount of care required, the family's level of functioning (both physically and emotionally), and the monetary resources and knowledge of community resources. All of the aforementioned impact on both the child and his or her family (White, Benedict, Wulff, & Kelley, 1987).

Dunst, Cooper, and Bolick (1987) discussed the needs of parents of disabled children. These authors pointed out that most of the information provided to parents is negative, centering on the child's limitations as opposed to a more positive yet realistic outlook for the child and his or her future. Negativity breeds negativity.

Solnit and Stark (1961) in a landmark article discussed the process of mourning families go through when a child's disability is first recognized. Research has suggested that families experience guilt, anger, grief (Trout, 1983), diminished self-esteem, depression, stress (Breslau, Staruch, & Mortimer, 1982; Cummings, 1976; Crnic, Friedrich, & Greenberg, 1983; Gath, 1985; Murphy, 1982; Shapiro, 1983), and marital discord (Friedrich & Friedrich, 1981; Kazak & Clark, 1986; Tew & Laurence, 1975).

Jones and Garfinkel (1993) discussed how special needs children are at higher risk for being abused in the family system than children who are not physically or mentally challenged. These authors wrote the following about these families:

> . . . [there are] added stresses brought on by having a child with a disability in regard to isolation, misinformation, unrealistic expectations that are ability-specific, and the limited resources available to many families. . . . The physical and emotional energy that some children with disabilities require is difficult for families where other stressors are present and/or there exists a prior history of abuse. . . . In families with a child who has a disability, the critical issues of physical boundary awareness can become muddled, in part because of the children's reliance on others for assistance in toiletry and in other intimate aspects of their lives. For some children, the question of comprehending the nature of sexuality and the need for self-protection does not even exist. (p. 128)

TREATMENT AVAILABLE

Boys Town National Research Hospital has a Center for Abused Handicapped Children. One of their programs is residential and is called Therapeutic Education for Abused Children with Handicaps (Sullivan, 1993). This program is for persons age 3 to 21 who have been abused, the nonoffending parent, and all brothers and sisters living at home. It is a six-week residential program. Individual, group, and family therapy are provided for the child who has been abused. Parents also participate in therapy sessions (Sullivan, 1993).

Sullivan (1993) and Sobsey (1993) both advocate intervention that is ecologically grounded. Sobsey (1993) had this to say:

> . . . If a child was abused by a family member, or is a member of a severely dysfunctional family, individual therapy for the abused client without addressing family issues in some way is not likely to be of significant benefit to the child. Such ecological issues are often equally essential and more complex for children with disabilities. . . . Clearly treatment programs must consider the entire life-ecology

of such children and ensure that environmental influences are consistent with therapeutic objectives. (pp. 132–133)

PREVENTION SUGGESTIONS

First, clinicians and all types of professionals need to be aware that all forms of abuse exist in children with special needs. Secondly, a distinct need exists for more basic information regarding the characteristics of abuse in the special needs population (Ammerman, VanHasselt, & Hersen, 1988). Third, all professionals need improved assessment techniques in identifying families in which abuse is most likely to occur. Lastly, once again it seems that prevention measures are targeted on the child or the disabled individual, putting the responsibility for their safety on them rather than on the parents, other caregivers, and society in general. Prevention programs need to be designed and implemented to target the parents and the staff of residential care centers and institutions, not once, but again and again. Knowledge of child development literature needs to be addressed when programs are being designed and implemented.

Improving Communication between Special Needs Children and Others

Kennedy (1992) has suggested some guidelines for working with children who have special needs. Deaf children should be taught sign language as opposed to using an oral or aural approach. For children who are deaf and blind telephones (called HASICOM) can be utilized to enable them to communicate with others. For children who have below average intelligence, Kennedy suggested the Rebus and Makaton symbol boards. Children with learning disabilities could be benefited by teaching them to use Makaton signs and symbols. (Makaton has a vocabulary base of about 350 language concepts.) Children with cerebral palsy could use communication boards like Blissymbolics, Makaton symbols, or Rebus symbols. (Blissymbolics is the most advanced symbol system and should only be utilized with the most able children who have cerebral palsy). Children and youth service workers need a working knowledge of the different communication models described and need to have access to an interpreter who is proficient in whatever augmentative communication format is to be utilized to conduct the interview. Interviews, assessments, therapy, and teaching modules need to rely on communication methods other than verbal types.

Some special needs exist for physically and mentally challenged children that must be taken into consideration when there is a question of abuse. Marchant and Page (1992) stated,

A disabled child may have difficulties with communication (perhaps reliant on others to take a lead); differences in physical experiences of intimate physical care; different life experiences, maybe living life in a very different setting than other children; and differences in learning and knowledge, perhaps having very limited access to information. (p. 180)

Prevention Program for the Mentally Retarded

Sgroi, Carey, and Wheaton (1989) designed and field tested a sex abuse prevention curriculum for the mild to severely mentally retarded population to better enable them to avoid being sexually abused by others. The program is designed to teach each individual he or she has rights, can run away if someone tries to touch him or her, and should tell someone if he or she is being touched. The authors have recommendations for developing and screening individuals to participate in the group, choosing training facilities, involving staff, rewarding participation, establishing rules for the group members (e.g., not engaging in disruptive behavior), following contractual agreements between trainers and participants (e.g., starting and finishing training sessions on time), paying attention to participants' behaviors (noting anyone who seems scared or uncomfortable), training staff to continue to reinforce materials that have been presented, and establishing a time frame for presenting the material (suggested to be spaced one week apart, or two to five days for those persons with moderate retardation). These authors provided suggested teaching aids (using anatomically correct dolls; the song, "It's Okay To Say No"; and large scale toys, like cars and buses). Sgroi et al. (1989) detail two other curricula for individuals who are severely retarded and another for adults who are moderately retarded. Group exercises are provided for each meeting.

INVESTIGATING CASES
WHERE CHILD ABUSE IS SUSPECTED

If a child with special needs is suspected of being abused he or she needs to have a trusted adult present with him or her throughout the interview process. This trusted person can facilitate the interview process. He or she may have questions about how to be helpful to the child, the next step in the process, and so on. It is also important that the investigative team offer support to him or her (Marchant & Page, 1992).

Marchant and Page (1992) suggested that the interviewer needs to know as much as possible about the child's daily routine, his or her social and language capabilities, and needs to garner as much information as possible regarding the child's family situation and the environment in which the child lives. They suggested the interviewer or team members gather as much support as is possible because this work is overwhelming and stressful at times.

Last are recommendations for professionals and others who are involved in sexual abuse investigations in which medical examinations are conducted, legal processes are involved, and photographs are taken. Cross (1992) has made these suggestions: (1) Everyone involved in the investigation should try to develop a relationship based on trust and respect. (2) Any and all medical and legal processes should be explained to the child on a level he or she can understand (recognize that an interpreter may be necessary, especially if the child speaks a language different than the interviewers). What will happen before, during, and following the procedure needs to be explained. (3) If photographs are to be taken, have a trusted adult beside the child. Explain what is going to occur at each stage of the investigative process. Ask the child's permission and ask all non-necessary persons to leave the room. Introduce the photographer to the child and allow the two of them a chance to get to know one another. (4) Never tell a child or adolescent that he or she has to sit in a room and view pictures or slides of himself or herself naked. Give the child a choice; offer to give the photos to him or her first for viewing. Suggest to him or her that he or she does not have to see the photos or even stay in the room. (5) Respect that we can all be different and look different, yet all of us have the same rights. (6) Do not leave the child unclothed and uncovered when it is not essential for him or her to be naked. Do not permit staff members to wander in and out of the examining room. (7) If the female adolescent has to wear equipment close to the urogenital area have a nurse talk to the girl and the mother or other caregiver about how to handle menstrual periods and what is the most effective way to keep the equipment clean. Convey the information in a direct manner. Do not talk down to the adolescent or use a disrespectful or condescending tone. Be sensitive to her and the situation. (Think about how you would feel if it were you in this person's situation). Cross (1992) stated,

> Professionals should not fool themselves that their attitude of only being interested in the leg or caliper is enough to protect the young person from embarrassment. A lot will depend on the young person's previous experiences, in and out of medical settings. The presence of a safe adult is very important, but professionals also need to remember that children and young people may need as much privacy as may be afforded to adults. (p. 196)

CONCLUSION

No easy answers or solutions exist to this multifaceted problem, but on some level I cannot help but wonder if part of the problem is lack of respect. Respect for everyone's right to be safe from any form of victimization; to be treated as individuals, not as property; to not be defined by socioeconomic status, religion, or skin color, or by who is bigger and stronger; to be respected as individuals, especially for those who are different, either culturally or developmentally; and probably most importantly, to be respected for one's self. To abuse and use others is not an indicator of respect for the self or the self of another person. The issue is not so much to tell a child that he or she has rights or that his body belongs to him or her; a far greater impact will be made if we as individuals and as members of a collective society respect children's rights. To accomplish that it must begin with each of us today.

AFTERWORD

As this book is completed, I reflect on Thoreau's statement, "It takes two to tell the truth—one to speak it, another to hear it." Survivors have spoken about abuse for centuries. Do we as professionals and the lay public respectfully hear and listen to what they have to say? Our best source of prevention information may very well come from the survivors. Offenders lie and deny and have nothing to gain by telling the truth. Survivors have lived the abuse. Let us as professionals, researchers, family members, and friends give them a voice to be heard, for there is much for us to learn. Perhaps the real question is, "Who will listen and hear them?"

Barrett (1993) has so eloquently put this in perspective. She wrote,

> The researchers, writers, and clinicians in the field of child sexual abuse are repeating the same dysfunctional patterns as some of the people we are treating, writing about, and/or researching. The pattern that we are repeating is that we are not fully exploring all the options for our professional lives. . . . Child sexual abuse is about power, control, and connection. What the professionals in the field need to do is stop fighting for the power of who is right and who is wrong about how they understand and treat the sexual abuse of children but rather to connect with one another and learn from each other. . . . The sheltered view of abuse that develops from not hearing all the information that is available to us results in closed repetitive patterns that can easily become dysfunctional. When we, as professionals, begin to believe that we have the "right" way to conceptualize and treat the abuse, then we run the risk of becoming abusive ourselves. . . . It is our responsibility to be open to listen to

other professionals' experiences and their teachings so that we can stay open and flexible to change. (pp. 142–143)

DEFINITION OF TERMS

Abuse of sexuality model—Used by Bolton, Morris, and MacEachron (1989) to describe various types of sexually abusive environments in the home. Included are three kinds: sexually permissive, negative and seductive environment, and overtly sexual.

Abused/Abuser hypothesis—Individuals who have been sexually abused who then sexually abuse others (Finkelhor, Araji, Baron, Browne, Peters & Wyatt, 1986; Kempe & Kempe, 1984; Lanyon, 1986).

Affimal incest—"Involves individuals who do not have genetic ties but are related due to contract or statute, as in the case of relatives by marriage or adoption" (Courtois, 1988, p. 21).

Androphilia—"Erotic preference for mature males" (Freund, Watson, & Dickey, 1990, p. 559).

Asymmetrical incest taboo—Ward's (1985) term, which emphasizes the double standard of incestuous abusers. Abuse by a male is considered more "normal" and acceptable than sexually abusive acts committed by females.

Automonosexualism—Original concept by Hirschfeld (1948) and expanded by Blanchard (1989) who stated, "All gender dysphoric males who are not sexually oriented toward men are instead sexually oriented toward the thought or image of themselves as women" (p. 23).

Bestiality—Having intercourse with animals.

Betrayal—"The dynamic by which children discover that someone on whom they were vitally dependent has caused them harm" (Finkelhor & Browne, 1985, p. 531).

Blockage theories—"Theories about pedophilia which focus on the propositions that individuals are blocked in their ability to get their sexual and emotional needs met in adult heterosexual relationships and thus turn to children" (Araji & Finkelhor, 1985, p. 26). Psychoanalysts say the blockage is a result of "castration anxiety." (Fenichel, 1945; Hammer & Glueck, 1957). Other developmental theorists say the "blockage" is a result of poor social skills and a lack of assertiveness (Storr, 1964).

Breeders—"Young girls who are kept as virtual slaves, they are terrorized, brainwashed, and repeatedly impregnated. Their babies are taken from them at birth for use in ritual sacrifices" (Bromley, 1991, p. 59).

Buggery—Penetration of the anus by a penis. (Driver & Droisen, 1989)

Bunnying—Fondling a child's or adolescent's genitals.

Candaulism—"Is named after a Greek historic figure and is a man's erotic preference for viewing (or listening to) his spouse interacting sexually with another man or disrobing where other men might observe her" (Freund & Watson, 1990, p. 590).

Ceiling effect—Many children answer a high percentage of questions accurately even before participating in a sexual abuse prevention program.

Chickens—Children who perform in child pornography films as actors.

Child abuse industry—"Is the term applied to the collection of professionals who, one way or another, earn livelihoods from investigating, treating, prosecuting, or otherwise dealing with those involved in child abuse" (Jones, 1991, p. 276).

Child pornography—"Photographs or films of children being sexually molested. This includes photos or films of sexually explicit conduct that includes sexual intercourse, bestiality, masturbation, sadomasochistic abuse, and lewd exhibitions of the genitals or pubic area" (Lanning, 1984, p. 83).

Child sexual abuse—Any male or female child under the age of eighteen who is engaged in "contacts or interaction between the child and an adult where the child is being used for the sexual stimulation of the perpetrator or another person" (National Committee for the Prevention of Child Abuse, 1988, p. 2).

Child Sexual Abuse Accommodation Syndrome—"The syndrome is composed of five categories, of which two define basic childhood vulnerability and three are sequentially contingent on sexual assault: (1) secrecy; (2) helplessness; (3) entrapment and accommodation; (4) delayed, unconvincing disclosure; and (5) retraction" (Summit, 1983, p. 177).

Closet collector—"Keeps secret their interest in pornographic pictures of nude children engaged in a range of behaviors and denies involvement with children" (Burgess, Hartman, McCausland, & Powers, 1984, p. 93).

Collectors—"Persons who collect, maintain, and prize child pornography materials" (Burgess, 1984, p. 93).

Commercial collector—"Is a pedophile who has his or her own group of children that he uses sexually and who has wide access to other collectors with their own groups" (Burgess, 1984, p. 104).

Consanguinal incest—Any type of "sexual contact between blood relatives" (Courtois, 1988, p. 21).

Contact victimization—A professional individual who works with incest survivors may experience symptoms of posttraumatic stress disorder as a result of his or her work with survivors, or as a result of triggering his or her own history of childhood abuses, or because of overwork (Courtois, 1988).

Cottage collector—"Is a pedophile who sexually exploits children in a group" (Burgess, 1984, p. 104).

Courtship disorder—"Hypothesis maintains that voyeurism, exhibitionism, toucherism-frotteurism, and the preferential rape pattern are expressions of the same disorder called the courtship disorder" (Freund, Watson, & Dickey, 1990, p. 589).

Cross-generational incest—"Involves sexual contact with a partner of a considerable age difference who is a parent, stepparent, in-law, grandparent, aunt, uncle or second cousin" (Courtois, 1988, p. 23).

Cult split—An individual who has a multiple personality disorder or who has an alter personality that is satanic; the cult has purposefully brought this alter into being. This is accomplished through the use of sensory deprivation, which creates a dissociative state. A member of the cult summons an alter, gives it a name, and assigns the alter certain functions (Ryder, 1992).

Cunnilingus—The mouth and tongue touches, licks, sucks, or bites the vagina (Faller, 1990).

Desensitization—In the context of child sexual abuse, it is the process of lowering a child's inhibitions to nakedness and sexually explicit acts so that the perpetrator can more readily sexually abuse the child.

Disinhibition—"According to these theories some mechanism, process, or condition works to disinhibit pedophiles so that they are able to sexually interact with children" (Araji & Finkelhor, 1985, p. 18). These disinhibitions include: lack of impulse control (Gebhard, Gagnon, Pomeroy, & Christenson, 1965; Hammer & Glueck, 1957); alcohol (Aarens, Cameron, Roizen, 1978; Rada, 1976); and failure of incest avoidance mechanism (Finkelhor, 1980; Russell, 1984a). Also three other reasons are suggested: situational stress, cultural tolerance, and patriarchal attitudes.

Dissociative disorder—"Dissociation always seems to be a response to traumatic life events. Memories and feelings connected with the trauma are forgotten and return as intrusive recollections, feeling states (such as overwhelming anxiety and panic unwarranted by current experience), fugues, delusions, states of depersonalization, and finally in behavioral reenactments. . . ." (van der Kolk & Kadish, 1987, p. 185). The DSM-IV (American Psychiatric Association, 1994) lists five types of dissociative disorders: dissociative amnesia, dissociative fugue, depersonalization disorder, dissociative identity disorder, and dissociative disorder not otherwise specified (p. 477).

Dyadic sex—Sexual abuse that involves one abuser and one child (Faller, 1990).

Emotional congruence—One of Finkelhor and Araji's (1985) four factors to explain why pedophiles are attracted to children. "Pedophiles choose children for sexual partners because children have some especially compelling emotional meaning for them. This conveys a 'fit' between the adult's emotional needs and the characteristics of children" (p. 20).

Ephobophile—Those persons only sexually interested in adolescents (See *pederast*).

Erotic gender differentiation—"Denotes the difference between an individual's sexual arousal effected by the body shape of the erotically most preferred gender age group and the sexual arousal effected by the body shape of the corresponding age group of the less preferred gender" (Freund, Watson, Dickey, & Rienzo, 1991, pp. 555–556).

Exploitative assault—An individual "uses the child as an object of sexual relief; he makes no attempt to engage the child in any emotional way" (Groth & Burgess, 1977, p. 259).

Extrafamilial sex offenders—Sexual abusers who could be neighbors, friends of the family, day-care workers, school teachers, camp counselors, mental health persons, pediatricians, nurses, clergy members, or Scout leaders (Faller, 1990).

Fellatio—Mouth contact with the penis that involves licking, kissing, biting, or sucking it (Faller, 1990).

Fixated heterosexual pedophile—A person who is experiencing a "temporary or permanent arrestment of psychosocial maturation resulting from unresolved formative issues that persist and underlie the organization of subsequent phases of development" (Burgess, Groth, Holmstrom, & Sgroi, 1978, p. 6).

Fixated pedophile—"An individual who from adolescence has been exclusively attracted to children or adolescents who are unrelated to them" (Burgess, Groth, Holstrom, & Sgroi, 1978a, p. 176).

Frottage—Individual receives sexual gratification by rubbing his or her genitals against the child's skin or clothing (Faller, 1990).

Gynephilia—"Erotic preference for mature females" (Freund, Watson, & Dickey, 1990, p. 559).

Handling or Fondling—Sexual offender touches the child's breasts, penis, vagina, or buttocks (Faller, 1990).

Hebephile—"Sexually attracted to young teenagers or adolescents" (Ingersoll & Patton, 1990, p. 20).

Identification with the aggressor—A molester who was sexually abused as a child or adolescent then sexually abuses a child, which enables him or her to deal with his or her own trauma by reversing roles. He or she becomes the aggressor in this reversal of roles and feels empowered (Araji & Finkelhor, 1985).

Implied incest—Term coined by Calof (1987) to describe family members' failure to respond to abuse that is committed by a person in a close relationship to the family.

Incest avoidance mechanism—Stepfathers who are not exposed to stepchildren from an early age are more prone to develop sexual feelings toward the child and to act on those feelings than the biological father (Araji & Finkelhor, 1985).

Incest envy—A sibling in the family constellation who is aware that incest is occurring between the father and sister or brother, and the sibling not involved is envious of the incestuous relationship (Berry, 1975).

Incest—"The imposition of sexually inappropriate acts, or acts with sexual overtones or any use of a minor child to meet the sexual or sexual/emotional needs of one or more persons who derive authority through ongoing emotional bonding with that child" (Blume, 1989, p. 4).

Inclusive pedophilia—Any type of sexual interest or sexual contact with a child even if the interest lasts only a short time (Araji & Finkelhor, 1985).

Interfemoral intercourse—Intercourse that happens when the penis is moved between the victim's upper legs. Also called dry intercourse (Faller, 1990).

Intrafamilial sex offenders—Is when someone related (by blood or marriage) to the child sexually abuses him or her. This can be stepfathers, fathers, grandfathers, uncles, mothers, grandmothers, aunts, or brothers and sisters of the child (Faller, 1990).

Kiddy snuff films—Pornographic films or videos where the child actors are actually murdered on the film.

Lovemap—Term proposed by Money (1984) in reference to each individual's personal template that describes the perfect lover. Money contends that paraphilias develop because something interferes with the person's normal process of developing the "lovemap."

Male monopoly—Research data and clinical reports that suggest males to be sexual offenders at least 90% of the time (Finkelhor, 1986; Finkelhor & Hotaling, 1984).

Maltreatment—"The commission or omission of an act which results in non-accidental injury or harm to the child. This includes physical abuse, sexual abuse, or neglect" (Ammerman, Van Hasselt, Hersen, McGonigle, & Lubetsky, 1989, p. 335).

Marionette syndrome—Ritual abuse survivors who have, because of repeated traumas to the body and the psyche, become puppets for the cult. The abuse may involve components of electroshock therapy and other types of abuses that occur in simulated laboratories (e.g., medical experiments).

Myth of mutuality—The unfounded belief that sibling incest occurs because both persons want to engage in the sexually explorative behaviors.

Nondifferentiating pedophiles—Pedophiles who have sexual contact with both male and female children (Freund, Watson, Dickey, & Rienzo, 1991, p. 557).

Nontouching sexual behavior—Obscene phone calls, exhibitionism, voyeurism, viewing sexually explicit films, videos, or magazines (National Committee for the Prevention of Child Abuse, 1988).

Paraphilia—Sexually deviant behavior. The paraphilia has the essential features of "recurrent, intense sexually arousing fantasies, sexual urges, or behaviors generally involving (1) nonhumanobjects, (2) the suffering or humiliation of oneself or one's partner, or (3) children or other nonconsenting persons that occur over a period of at least 6 months" (American Psychiatric Association, 1994, pp. 523–524). The DSM-IV (American Psychiatric Association, 1994) lists the following paraphilias: (1) Exhibitionism, (2) Fetishism, (3) Frotteurism, (4) Pedophilia, (5) Sexual Masochism, (6) Sexual Sadism, (7) Transvestic Fetishism, (8) Voyeurism, and a category, "Paraphilia Not Otherwise Specified" (p. 524).

Parentified child—A child who takes on parental responsibilities in the family while his or her own needs are neglected.

Pederasty—Translated from Greek, literally means love of adolescents. Used in today's society to describe an individual's exclusive sexual preference for adolescents.

Pedophile—Adults who have sexual contact with children.

Pedophilic sex object choice—Some pedophiles have a sexual preference for either a male child or a female child (Gebhard, Gagnon, Pomeroy, & Christenson, 1965; Goldstein, Freud, & Solnit, 1973; McCaghy, 1971).

Peer incest—"Involves sexual contact between individuals who are close in age and from the same age cohort (includes step- and half-siblings and cousins)" (Courtois, 1988, p. 24).

Penile plethysmography—This research method measures penile tumescence after being submitted to different sources of stimulation (e.g., photographs or oral or written accounts of sexually offensive behaviors) (Marissakalian, Blanchard, Abel, & Barlow, 1975).

Phaedra complex—When sexual attraction occurs between stepparents and stepchildren (Messer, 1969).

Phallometric test—"The original method measures penile volume directly and the indirect method measures penile circumference" (Freund, Watson, Dickey, & Rienzo, 1991, p. 556).

Powerlessness—"The dynamic of rendering the victim powerless . . . the process in which the child's will, desires, and sense of efficacy are continually contravened" (Finkelhor & Browne, 1985, p. 532).

Preference versus situational bias—The sexual offender always chooses a child for sex, regardless of the availability of adult partners.

Pseudo-ritualistic abuse—"Sexual abuse is the primary activity and cult rituals are secondary" (Jones, 1991, p. 164).

Quasi-relative incest—There are no blood relationships between abuser and child but he or she is involved in the family, possibly as a live-in lover or foster parent (Courtois, 1988).

Regressed pedophile—"An individual who usually preferred adult partners. He has a crisis that may be physical, social, sexual, marital, financial, or vocational. One of these crises or a combination of [two or more] occurs before a sexual encounter takes place with child, who is unrelated to him" (Groth & Birnbaum, 1978, p. 178).

Rewriting the script—Term coined by Sgroi and Bunk (1988). Survivors of sexual abuse deal with feelings of anxiety about being sexually abused by convincing themselves the abuse happens because he or she wants it to happen. This causes him or her to believe he or she is in charge of a stressful event, and thus the feelings of anxiety are allayed for the moment.

Ritualistic abuse—"Abuse that occurs in the context linked to some symbols or group activities that have a religious, magical, or supernatural connotation, and where the invocation of these symbols or activities are repeated over time and used to frighten and intimidate the children" (Finkelhor, Williams, Burns, & Kalinowski, 1988, p. 59).

Sadistic assault—Those children who "symbolize everything the offender hates about himself and thereby become an object of punishment" (Groth & Burgess, 1977, p. 261).

Second injury—A second injury happens when the victim of the crime (sexual abuse) is not believed or helped by the agencies and persons who should by all rights be there for him or her (Symonds, 1980).

Secondary elaboration—"Is a characterological adaptation to traumatization that includes depression, avoidance of intimacy and relational distortions. These features are most evident when the trauma has been neither acknowledged nor treated as such" (Krugman, 1986, p. 128).

Secondary secrets—If the sexual abuse resulted in the child experiencing sexual pleasure or gaining personal power, often the child will feel guilty and responsible for the abuse (Bass & Thornton, 1983).

Sexually schizophrenic home—A home where sexual victimization of a child or adolescent is taking place and people are aware of it but deny its existence.

Single-case victimizers—"Offenders against only one child" (Freund, Watson, & Dickey, 1991, p. 410).

Situational offender—Another name for an incest offender who does not particularly prefer children but takes advantage of easy sexual access to children (Marshall, 1988; Quinsey, 1977).

Sleeper effects—"Symptoms which occur in adulthood as a result of childhood sexual abuse, e.g., sexual dysfunction" (Beitchman, Zucker, Hood, daCosta, Akman, & Cassavia, 1992, p. 102).

Solo rings—"Adult operates alone with a small group of children" (Burgess, 1984, p. 51) with regards to sexually abusing children.

Stigmatization—"The negative connotations, e.g., badness, shame, and guilt, that are communicated to the child around the experience and that then become incorporated into the child's self-image" (Finkelhor & Browne, 1985, p. 532).

Syndicated ring—"Well-structured organization formed for recruiting children, producing pornography, delivering direct sexual services and establishing an extensive network of customers" (Burgess, 1984, p. 51).

Touching sexual behaviors—Handling (fondling); oral sex; anal sex; vaginal penetration with penis, finger, or objects; touching the genitals; incest; prostitution; or rape (National Committee for the Prevention of Child Abuse, 1988).

Transition rings—"Adult has begun to exchange or sell pornographic photographs of children and tries to pressure the child into the next ring level—the syndicated ring" (Burgess, Hartman, McCausland, & Powers, 1984, p. 51).

Trauma theory—Alice Miller (1984) relabeled Freud's "seduction theory" the trauma theory.

Traumatic sexualization—"Process in which a child's sexuality (including both sexual feelings and sexual attitudes) is shaped in a developmentally inappropriate and interpersonally dysfunctional fashion as a result of the sexual abuse" (Finkelhor & Browne, 1985, p. 531).

Traumatic transference—"The patient unconsciously expects that the therapist, despite overt helpfulness and concern, will covertly exploit the patient for his or her own narcissistic gratification" (Spiegel, 1986, p. 72).

Triolism—"A preference for watching humans or animals being maltreated—is a variant of sadism proper, the voyeur or rapist not being the patient himself, but a substitute in the person of a strange male" (Freund & Watson, 1990, p. 590).

True cult-based ritualistic abuse—Sexual abuse is one component of the child's total immersion in cult rituals and beliefs (Jones, 1991).

Victim precipitation—"Attributing some causal responsibility to the victim" of sexual assault (Collings & Payne, 1991, p. 519).

REFERENCES

Aarens, M., Cameron, T., & Roizen, J. (1978). *Alcohol casualties and crime.* Berkeley, CA: Social Research Group.

Abel, G.G., Becker, J.V. (1984). Complications, consent, and cognitions in sex between children and adults. *International Journal of Law and Psychiatry, 7,* 89–103.

Abel, G.G., Becker, J.V., Cunningham-Rathner, J., Mittleman, M., & Rouleau, J.L. (1988). Multiple paraphiliac diagnoses among sex offenders. *Bulletin of the American Academy of Psychiatry and Law, 16,* 153–168.

Abel, G.G., Becker, J.V., Mittleman, M., Cunningham-Rathner, J., Rouleau, J.L., & Murphy, W.D. (1987). Self-reported sex crimes of non-incarcerated paraphilias. *Journal of Interpersonal Violence, 2,* 3–35.

Abel, G.G., Becker, J.V., Murphy, W.D., & Flanagan, B. (1981). Identifying dangerous child molesters. In R.B. Stuart (Ed.), *Violent behavior* (pp. 116–137). New York: Brunner/Mazel.

Abel, G.G., & Blanchard, E. (1974). The role of fantasy in the treatment of sexual deviation. *Archives of General Psychiatry, 30,* 467–475.

Abel, G.G., Gore, D., Holland, C., Camp, N., Becker, J., & Cunningham-Rathner, J. (1989). The measurement of cognitive distortions of child molesters. *Annals of Sex Research, 2,* 135–153.

Abel, G.G., Mittleman, M.S., & Becker, J.V. (1985). Sexual offenders: Results of assessment and recommendation for treatment. In M.H. Ben-Aron, S.J. Huckle, & C.D. Webster (Eds.), *Clinical criminology: The assessment and treatment of criminal behavior* (pp. 191–205). Toronto: M & M Graphic.

Abel, G.G., & Rouleau, J. (1990). The nature and extent of sexual assault. In W.L. Marshall, D.R. Laws, & H.E. Barbaree (Eds.), *Handbook of sexual assault: Issues, theories, and treatment of the offender* (pp. 9–21). New York: Plenum Press.

Abound, F.E. (1985). Children's application of attribution principles to social comparisons. *Child Development, 56*(3), 682–688.

Achenbach, T., & Edelbrock, C. (1983). *Manual for the child behavior checklist and revised child behavior profile.* Burlington, VT: Department of Psychiatry, University of Vermont.

Adams, C., & Fay, J. (1981). *No more secrets: Protecting your children from sexual assault.* San Luis Obispo, CA: Impact Publishers.

Adams, C., & Fay, J. (1986). Parents as primary prevention educators. In M. Nelso & K. Clark (Eds.), *The educators guide to preventing sexual abuse* (pp. 93–97). Santa Cruz, CA: Network Publications.

Adams-Tucker, C. (1981). A socioclinical review of 28 sex-abused children. *Child Abuse & Neglect, 5,* 361–367.

Adams-Tucker, C. (1982). Proximate effects of sexual abuse in childhood: A report on 28 children. *Child Abuse & Neglect, 5,* 361–367.

Alexander, P.C. (1985). A systems theory conceptualization of incest. *Family Process, 24,* 79–87.

Alexander, P.C. (1992). Application of attachment theory to the study of sexual abuse. *Journal of Consulting and Clinical Psychology, 60,* 185-195.

Alexander, P.C., & Lupfer, S.L. (1987). Family characteristics and long-term consequences associated with sexual abuse. *Archives of Sexual Behavior, 16,* 235–245.

Allen, C.M. (1991). *Women and men who sexually abuse children.* Orwell, VT: Safer Society Press.

Alter-Reid, K., Gibbs, M.S., Lachenmeyer, J.R., Sigal, J., & Massoth, N.A. (1986). Sexual abuse of children: A review of the empirical findings. *Clinical Psychology Review, 6,* 249–266.

Aman, C., & Goodman, G.S. (1987). *Children's use of anatomically detailed dolls: An experimental study.* Unpublished manuscript, University of Denver, Denver, CO.

American Humane Association. (1981). *National study on child neglect and abuse report.* Denver, CO: Author.

American Psychiatric Association. (1994). *Diagnostic and statistical manual of mental disorders* (4th ed.). Washington, DC: Author.

Ammerman, R.T., VanHasselt, V.B., & Hersen, M. (1988). Abuse and neglect in handicapped children: A critical review. *Journal of Family Violence, 3,* 53–72.

Ammerman, R.T., VanHasselt, V.B., Hersen, M., McGonigle, J.J., & Lubetsky, M. (1989). Abuse and neglect in psychiatrically hospitalized multihandicapped children. *Child Abuse & Neglect, 13,* 335–343.

Anderson, C. (1982). *Teaching people with mental retardation about sexual abuse prevention.* Santa Cruz, CA: Network Publications.

Anderson, C. (1986). A history of the touch continuum. In M. Nelson & K. Clark (Eds.), *The educator's guide to preventing child sexual abuse* (pp. 26–41). Santa Cruz, CA: ETR Network Publications.

Anderson, C., & Mayes, P. (1982). Treating family sexual abuse: The humanistic approach. *Journal of Child Care, 1,* 41–46.

Araji, S., & Finkelhor, D. (1985). Explanation of pedophilia: Review of empirical research. *Bulletin of the American Academy of Psychiatry and Law, 13(1),* 17–37.

Armentrout, J.A., & Hauer, A.L. (1978). MMPI's of rapists of adults, rapists of children, and non-rapist sex-offenders. *Journal of Clinical Psychology, 34,* 330–332.

Armstrong, L. (1978). *Kiss Daddy goodnight: A speak-out on incest.* New York: Hawthorne Books.

Arndt, W.B., & Ladd, B. (1981). Sibling incest as an index of Oedipal conflict. *Journal of Assessment, 45,* 52–58.

Atkinson, D.R., Morten, G., & Sue, D.W. (1983). *Counseling American minorities: A cross-cultural perspective* (2nd ed.). Dubuque, IA: William C. Brown.

Atteberry-Bennett, J., & Reppucci, N.D. (1986, August). *What does child sexual abuse mean?* Paper presented at the 94th annual meeting of the American Psychological Association, Washington, DC.

August, R. (1986). *Differences between sexually and non-sexually abused children in their behavioral responses to anatomically correct dolls.* Unpublished doctoral dissertation, University of Miami, FL.

Bagley, C., & Ramsey, R. (1986). Sexual abuse in childhood: Psychosocial outcomes and implications for social work practice. *Journal of Social Work and Human Sexuality, 4,* 33–47.

Baldwin, L. (1984). *Ourselves.* Fayetteville, NC: McFarland.

Balla, D., & Zigler, E. (1975). Institutional social deprivation, response, social reinforcement and IQ change in institutionalized retarded individuals: A six year follow-up study. *American Journal of Mental Deficiency, 80,* 228–230.

Bandura, A., & McDonald, F. J. (1963). The influence of social reinforcement and the behavior of models in shaping children's moral judgements. *Journal of Abnormal and Social Psychology, 67,* 274–281.

Banning, A. (1989). Mother–son incest: Confronting a prejudice. *Child Abuse & Neglect, 13*(4), 563–570.

Barach, P.M. (1991). Multiple personality disorder as an attachment disorder. *Dissociation, IV*(3), 117–123.

Barbaree, H.E., Marshall, W.L., & Connor, J. (1988). *The social problem-solving of child molesters.* Unpublished manuscript, Queen's University, Kingston, Ontario, Canada.

Barna, L.M. (1982). Stumbling blocks in intercultural communication. In L. Samorar & R. Porter (Eds.), *Intercultural communication: A reader* (pp. 330–338). Belmont, CA: Wadsworth.

Barnard, C.P., & Hirsch, C. (1985). Borderline personality and victims of incest. *Psychological Reports, 57,* 715–718.

Barnard, G.W., Fuller, A.K., Robbins, L., & Shaw, T. (1989). *The child molester: An integrated approach to evaluation and treatment.* New York: Brunner/Mazel.

Barrett, M. J. (1993). Mother's role in incest: Neither dysfunctional women nor dysfunctional theories when both are explored in their entirety. *Journal of Child Sexual Abuse, 2,* 141–143.

Barrett, M.J., Trepper, T., & Stone Fish, L. (1990). Feminist informed family therapy for the treatment of intrafamilial child sexual abuse. *Journal of Family Psychology, 4*(2), 151–165.

Barry, M.J., & Johnson, A.M. (1958). The incest barrier. *Psychoanalytic Quarterly, 27,* 485–500.

Barth, R.P., & Derezotes, D.S. (1990). *Preventing adolescent abuse.* Lexington, MA: Lexington Books.

Bass, E., & Thornton, L. (Eds.). (1983). *I never told anyone: Writings by women survivors of sexual abuse.* New York: Harper & Row.

Bays, J., & Chadwick, D. (1993). Medical diagnosis of the sexually abused child. *Child Abuse & Neglect, 17,* 91–110.

Becker, J.V., Cunningham-Rathner, J., & Kaplan, M. (1986). The adolescent sexual offender, demographics, criminal history, victims, sexual behavior and recommendations for reducing future offenses. *Journal of Interpersonal Violence, 1,* 431.

Becker, J.V., Hunter, J., Stein, R., & Kaplan, M. (1989). Factors associated with erection in adolescent sex offenders. *Journal of Psychopathology and Behavioral Assessment, 11*(4), 343–350.

Becker, J.V., Kaplan, M., Cunningham-Rathner, J., & Kavoussi, R. (1986). Characteristics of adolescent incest sexual perpetrators: Preliminary findings. *Journal of Family Violence, 1,* 85–97.

Becker, J.V., Kaplan, M., & Karoussi, R. (1988). Measuring the effectiveness of treatment for the aggressive adolescent sexual offender. *Annals of the New York Academy of Sciences, 528,* 215–223.

Becker, J.V., Kaplan, M.G., Tenke, C.E., & Tartaglini, A. (1991). The incidence of depressive symptomatology in juvenile sex offenders with a history of abuse. *Child Abuse & Neglect, 15*, 531–536.

Beitchman, J.H., Zucker, K.J., Hood, J.E., da Costa, G.A., Akman, D., & Cassavia, E. (1992). A review of the long-term effects of child sexual abuse. *Child Abuse and Neglect, 16*, 101–118.

Beland, K. (1986). *Talking about touching II.* Washington, DC: Committee for Children.

Belenky, M.F., Clinchy, B.M., Goldberger, N.R., & Tarule, J.M. (1986). *Women's ways of knowing: The development of self, voice, and mind.* New York: Basic Books.

Bell, A.D., & Hall, C.S. (1971). *The personality of a child molester.* Chicago: Aldine.

Bender, L., & Blau, A. (1937). The reactions of children to sexual relationships with adults. *Journal of American Orthopsychiatry, 7*, 500–518.

Benedict, M.I., White, R.B., Wulff, L.M., & Hall, B.J. (1990). Reported maltreatment in children with multiple disabilities. *Child Abuse & Neglect, 14*, 207–217.

Bengis, S.M. (1986). *A comprehensive service delivery system with a continuum of care for adolescent sexual offenders.* Orwell, VT: Safer Society Press.

Bera, W.H. (1989, April). *Adolescent sex offenses and their family systems.* Paper presented for Treatment of Adolescent Sex Offenders, sponsored by Canadian Child Welfare Association, Toronto, Ontario, Canada.

Berenberg, W. (1968). Toward the prevention of neuromotor dysfunction. *Developmental Medicine and Child Neurology, 11*, 137–141.

Berenson, D. (1982). Adolescent offenders. In F.H. Knopp (Ed.), *Remedial intervention in adolescent sex offenses.* Orwell, VT: Safer Society Press.

Berliner, L., & Conte, J.R. (1993). Sexual abuse evaluations: Conceptual and empirical obstacles. *Child Abuse & Neglect, 17*, 111–125.

Berrick, J.D. (1988). Parental involvement in child abuse prevention training: What do they learn? *Chid Abuse & Neglect, 12*, 543–553.

Berrick, J.D. (1991). Sexual abuse prevention training for preschoolers: Implications for moral development. *Children and Youth Services Review, 13,* 61–75.

Berrick, J.D., & Gilbert, N. (1991). *With the best of intentions: The child sexual abuse prevention movement.* New York: Guilford Press.

Berry, G.W. (1975). Incest: Some clinical variations on a classical theme. *Journal of the American Academy of Psychoanalysis, 3,* 151–161.

Binder, R., & McNeil, D. (1987). Evaluation of a school-based sexual abuse prevention program: Cognitive and emotional effects. *Child Abuse & Neglect, 11,* 497–506.

Blanchard, G. (1985). The addictive personality in child sexual abuse. *Protecting Children, 2,* 15–16.

Blanchard, R. (1989). The classification and labeling of nonhomosexual gender dysphorias. *Archives of Sexual Behavior, 18,* 315–334.

Bliss, E.L. (1984). A symptom profile of patients with multiple personalities, including MMPI results. *Journal of Nervous and Mental Diseases, 172,* 197–202.

Blos, P. (1979). *The adolescent passage.* New York: International Press.

Blume, E.S. (1989). *Secret survivors: Uncovering incest and its aftereffects in women.* New York: John Wiley & Sons.

Boat, B.W., & Everson, M.D. (1986). *Using anatomical dolls: Guidelines for interviewing young children in sexual abuse investigations.* Chapel Hill, NC: Department of Psychiatry, University of North Carolina.

Boat, B.W., & Everson, M.D. (1988). Research and issues in using anatomical dolls. *Annals of Sex Research, 1,* 191–204.

Bolton, F.G., Morris, L.A., & MacEachron, A.E. (1989). *Males at risk: The other side of child sexual abuse.* Newbury Park, CA: Sage.

Bonaparte, M., Freud, A., & Kris, E. (Eds.). (1954). *The origins of psychoanalysis, letters to Wilheim Fliess, drafts and notes: 1887–1902.* New York: Basic Books.

Borden, T.A., & LaTerz, J.D. (1991). *Mother/daughter incest and ritual abuse.* Unpublished manuscript.

Borden, T.A., & LaTerz, J.D. (1993). Mother/daughter incest and ritual abuse: The ultimate taboo. *Treating Abuse Today, 3*(4), 5–8.

Borkin, J., & Frank, L. (1986). Sexual abuse prevention for preschoolers: A pilot program. *Child Welfare, 65*(1), 75–81.

Bowlby, J. (1969). *Attachment and loss, Volume I: Attachment.* New York: Basic Books.

Bowlby, J. (1973). *Attachment and loss, Volume II: Separation, anxiety, and anger.* Middlesex, England: Penguin Books.

Bowlby, J. (1980). *Attachment and loss, Volume III: Loss: Sadness and depression.* Middlesex, England: Penguin Books.

Bowlby, J. (1982). *Attachment and loss.* London: Hogarth.

Bowlby, J. (1988). *A secure base: Parent–child attachment and healthy human development.* New York: Basic Books.

Bradford, J.W.M. (1985). Organic treatments for the male sexual offender. *Behavioral Science and the Law, 3,* 55.

Brandwein, H. (1973). The battered child: A definite and significant factor in mental retardation. *Mental Retardation, 11,* 50–51.

Brassard, M., Tyler, A., & Kehle, T. (1983). School programs to prevent intrafamilial child sexual abuse. *Child Abuse & Neglect, 7,* 241–245.

Braun, B.G. (1984). Towards a theory of multiple personality and other dissociative phenomenon. *Psychiatry Clinics of North America, 7,* 171–193.

Braun, B.G. (1986). Issues in the psychotherapy of multiple personality disorder. In B.G. Braun (Ed.), *Treatment of multiple personality disorder* (pp. 1–28). Washington, DC: American Psychiatric Press.

Breslau, N., Staruch, K., & Mortimer, E. (1982). Psychological distress in mothers of disabled children. *American Journal of the Disabled Child, 136,* 682–686.

Bretherton, I. (1978). Making friends with one-year-olds: An experimental study of infant–stranger interaction. *Merrill-Palmer Quarterly, 24,* 29–51.

Brickman, J. (1984). Feminist, non-sexist, and traditional models of therapy: Implications of working with incest. *Women & Therapy, 3,* 49–67.

Briere, J. (1984). *The effects of childhood sexual abuse on later psychological functioning: Defining a post-sexual abuse syndrome.* Paper presented at the Third National Conference on Sexual Victimization of Children, Washington, DC.

Briere, J. (1989). *The Trauma Symptom Checklist for Children (TSC-C).* Los Angeles: University of Southern California.

Briere, J., & Runtz, M. (1986). Suicidal thoughts and behaviors in former sexual abuse victims. *Canadian Journal of Behavioral Sciences, 18,* 413–423.

Briere, J., & Runtz, M. (1988). Symptomatology associated with childhood sexual victimization in a nonclinical adult sample. *Child Abuse & Neglect, 12,* 51–59.

Britton, H.L., & O'Keefe, M.A. (1991). Use of nonanatomical dolls in the sexual abuse interview. *Child Abuse & Neglect, 15,* 567–573.

Broadhurst, D.D. (1986). *Educators, schools and child abuse.* Washington, DC: National Committee for Prevention of Child Abuse.

Bromley, D.G. (1991, May/June). The satanic cult scare. *Culture and Society,* 55–65.

Brookhouser, P.E., Sullivan, P.M., Scanlan, J.M., & Garbarino, J. (1986). Identification of the sexually abused deaf child: The otolaryngologist's role. *Laryngoscope, 96,* 152–158.

Brown, D. (1985). Historical perspective on child abuse. In A. Downer (Ed.), *Prevention of child sexual abuse: A trainer's manual* (pp. 3-50). Seattle, WA: Seattle Institute for Child Advocacy Committee for Children.

Brown, E., Flanagan, T., & McLeod, M. (Eds.). (1984). *Sourcebook of criminal justice statistics–1983.* Washington, DC: Bureau of Justice Statistics.

Brown, H., & Craft, A. (1989). *Thinking the unthinkable: Papers on sexual abuse and people with learning difficulties.* London: Family Planning Association Education Unit.

262   *References*

Browne, A., & Finkelhor, D. (1986). Impact of child sexual abuse: A review of the literature. *Psychological Bulletin, 99*, 66–77.

Browning, D.H., & Boatman, B. (1977). Incest: Children at risk. *American Journal of Psychiatry, 134*, 69–72.

Brownmiller, S. (1975). *Against our will: Men, women, and rape.* New York: Simon & Schuster.

Bryer, J.B., Nelson, B.A., Miller, J.B., & Krol, P.A. (1987). Childhood sexual and physical abuse as factors in adult psychiatric illness. *American Journal of Psychiatry, 144*, 1426–1430.

Budin, L.E., & Johnson, C.F. (1989). Sex abuse prevention programs: Offenders attitudes about their efficacy. *Child Abuse and Neglect, 13*, 77–87.

Bullough, V. (1964). *The history of prostitution.* New Hyde Park, NY: University Books.

Burgess, A.W. (Ed.). (1984). *Child pornography and sex rings.* Lexington, MA: Lexington Books.

Burgess, A.W., Groth, A.N., Holstrom, L.L., & Sgroi, S.M. (Eds.). (1978a). *Sexual assault of children and adolescents.* Lexington, MA: Lexington.

Burgess, A.W., Groth, A.N., Holstrom, L.L., & Sgroi, S.M. (Eds.). (1984b). Child pornography and sex rings. In A.W. Burgess, A.N. Groth, L.L. Holstrom, & S.M. Sgroi (Eds.), *Sexual assault of children and adolescents* (pp. 111–126). Lexington, MA: Lexington Books.

Burgess, A.W., Groth, A., & McCausland, M. P. (1981). Child sex initiation rings. *American Journal of Orthopsychiatry, 5*, 110–118.

Burgess, A.W., & Hartman, C.R. (1993). Children's drawings. *Child Abuse & Neglect, 17*, 161–168.

Burgess, A.W., Hartman, C.R., McCausland, M.P., & Powers, P. (1984). Response patterns in children and adolescents exploited through sex rings and pornography. *American Journal of Psychiatry, 141*, 656–662.

Burgess, A.W., Hartman, C.R., & McCormack, A. (1987). Abused to abuser: Antecedents of socially deviant behavior. *American Journal of Psychiatry, 144*, 1431–1436.

Burns, R.C. (1982). *Self-growth in families.* New York: Brunner/Mazel.

Butler, S. (1978). *Conspiracy of silence: The trauma of incest.* New York: Bantam Books.

Butler, S. (1985). *Conspiracy of silence: The trauma of incest* (2nd ed.). San Francisco: Volcano Press.

Caffaro-Rouget, A., Lang, R. A., & vanSanten, V. (1989). The impact of child sexual abuse. *Annals of Sex Research, 2,* 29–47.

Caffey, J. (1946). Multiple fractures of the long bones of children suffering from subdural hematoma. *American Journal of Roentgenology, 56,* 163–173.

Calof, D. (1987). *Treating adult survivors of incest and child abuse.* Workshop presented at the Family Network Symposium, Washington, DC.

Calof, D. (1991). Editor's desk: Regarding the credibility of ritual abuse reports. *Treating Abuse Today, 1,* 4.

Campagna, D., & Poffenberger, D. (1988). *The sexual trafficking of children.* Dover, MA: Auburn House.

Carmen, E., Reiker, P.P., & Mills, T. (1984). Victims of violence and psychiatric illness. *American Journal of Psychiatry, 144,* 1431–1436.

Carnes, P. (1983). *Out of the shadows: Understanding sexual addiction.* Minneapolis, MN: Compcare Publications.

Carter, D.L., Prentky, R., Knight, R.A., Vanderveer, P., & Boucher, C. (1986). *Use of pornography in the criminal and developmental histories of sexual offenders.* Unpublished manuscript.

Cavallin, H. (1966). Incestuous fathers: A clinical report. *American Journal of Psychiatry, 122,* 1132–1138.

Cavendish, R. (1967). *The black arts.* New York: G. P. Putnam and Sons.

Cerhan, J.U. (1990). The Hmong in the United States: An overview for mental health professionals. *Journal of Counseling and Development, 69*(1), 88–92.

Chadwick, M.W. (1988). *A comparison of two approaches to child sexual abuse prevention training.* Unpublished doctoral dissertation, University of California, Irvine.

Chaffin, M. (1992). Factors associated with treatment completion and progress among intrafamilial sexual abusers. *Child Abuse & Neglect, 16,* 251–264.

Chasnoff, I., Burns, W., Schnoll, S., Burns, K., Chisum, G., & Kyle-Spore, L. (1986). Maternal–neonatal incest. *American Journal of Orthopsychiatry, 54*(4), 577–580.

Chess, S., & Thomas, A. (1987). *Know your child.* New York: Basic Books.

Child assault prevention program: Strategies for free children. (1983). Program materials available from CAPP, P. O. Box 02084, Columbus, OH 43202.

Children's self-help project. (1981). Program materials available from Children's Self-Help Project, 170 Fell Street, Room 34, San Francisco, CA 94102.

Christensen, E.W. (1989). Counseling Puerto Ricans: Some cultural considerations. *Personnel and Guidance Journal, 55,* 412–415.

Chu, J.A., & Dill, D.L. (1990). Dissociative symptoms in relation to childhood physical and sexual abuse. *American Journal of Psychiatry, 147,* 887–892.

Claman, L. (1980). The squiggle-drawing game in child psychotherapy. *American Journal of Psychotherapy, 34*(3), 414–425.

Cohen, F.W., & Phelps, R.E. (1985). Incest markers in children's artwork. *Arts in Psychotherapy, 12,* 265–283.

Cohen, M.T., Seghorn, T., & Calmas, W. (1969). Sociometric study of the sex offender. *Journal of Abnormal Psychology, 1,* 74–85.

Cohn, A.H. (1990). Education as a means of prevention. In R. K. Oates (Ed.), *Understanding and managing child sexual abuse* (pp. 373–384). Philadelphia: W. B. Saunders.

Cohn, D.S. (1991). Anatomical child's play of preschoolers referred for sexual abuse and those not referred. *Child Abuse & Neglect, 15,* 455–466.

Cole, C.B., & Loftus, E.F. (1987). The memory of children. In S.J. Ceci, M.P. Toglia, & D.F. Ross (Eds.), *Children's eyewitness memory* (pp. 41–62). New York: Springer-Verlag.

Cole, E. (1982). Sibling incest: The myth of benign sibling incest. *Women & Therapy, 1,* 79–89.

Cole, P.M., & Putnam, L.W. (1992). Effect of incest on self and social functioning: A developmental perspective. *Journal of Consulting and Clinical Psychology, 60*(2), 174–184.

Collings, S.J., & Payne, M.F. (1991). Attribution of causal and moral responsibility to victims of father–daughter incest: An exploratory examination of five factors. *Child Abuse & Neglect, 15,* 513–521.

Committee for Children. (1983). *Talking about touching: A personal safety curriculum.* Available from the Committee for Children, P. O. Box 15190, Seattle, WA 98115.

Compton, B., & Galaway, B. (1984). *Social work processes.* Homewood, IL: Dorsey.

Comstock, C.M. (1992). Believe it or not: The challenge to the therapist of patient memory. *Treating Abuse Today, 2*(6), 23–26.

Condy, S.R., Templer, D.I., Brown, R., & Veaco, L. (1987). Parameters of sexual contact of boys with men. *Archives of Sexual Behavior, 16,* 379–394.

Constantine, L.L. (1980). The impact of early sexual experiences: A review and synthesis of outcome research. In J. Samson (Ed.), *Childhood and sexuality: Proceedings of the International symposium* (pp 150–172). Montreal: Editors Etudes Virentes.

Conte, J.R. (1985). The effects of sexual abuse on children: A critique and suggestions for future research. *Victimology, 10,* 110–130.

Conte, J.R. (1986a). Child sexual abuse and the family: A critical analysis. *Journal of Psychotherapy and the Family, 2,* 113–126.

Conte, J.R. (1986b). *A look at child sexual abuse.* Chicago, IL: National Committee for the Prevention of Child Sexual Abuse.

Conte, J.R. (1989). *An incest offender: An overview and introduction.* Unpublished manuscript, University of Washington, School of Social Work, Seattle.

Conte J.R., & Berliner, L. (1981). Sexual abuse of children: Implications for practice. *Social Casework, 62,* 601–606.

Conte, J.R., Berliner, L., & Schuerman, J. (1986). *The impact of sexual abuse on children* (Final Report No. MH 37133). Rockville, MD: National Institute of Mental Health.

Conte, J.R., & Fogarty, L. (1990). Sexual abuse prevention programs for children. *Education and Urban Society, 22,* 270-284.

Conte, J.R., Rosen, C., Saperstein, L., & Shermack, R. (1985). An evaluation of a program to prevent the sexual victimization of young children. *Child Abuse & Neglect, 9,* 319–328.

Conte, J.R., & Schuerman, J. (1987). The effects of sexual abuse on children: A multidimensional view. *Journal of Interpersonal Violence, 2*(4), 380–390.

Conte, J.R., Sorenson, E., Fogarty, L., & Rosa, J. (1991). Evaluating children's reports of sexual abuse: A survey of professionals. *American Journal of Orthopsychiatry, 61,* 428–437.

Conte, J.R., Wolf, S., & Smith, T. (1989). What sexual offenders tell us about prevention strategies. *Child Abuse & Neglect, 13,* 293–230.

Conway, D.J. (1990). *Celtic magic.* St Paul, MN: Llewellyn Publications.

Cook, C. (1991). *Understanding ritual abuse: Through a study of thirty-three abuse survivors from 13 different states.* Unpublished document available from RA Project, 5431 Auburn Blvd, Suite 215 Sacramento, CA. 95841.

Cook, R., Fosen, R.H., & Pacht, A. (1971). Pornography and the sex offender: Patterns of exposure and immediate arousal on effects of pornographic stimuli. *Journal of Applied Psychology, 55*(6), 503–511.

Coons, P.M., & Milstein, V. (1986). Psychosexual disturbances in multiple personality: Characteristics, etiology, and treatment. *Journal of Clinical Psychiatry, 47,* 106–110.

Coons, P.M., & Stern, A.L. (1986). Initial follow-up psychological testing in a group of patients with multiple personality disorder. *Psychological Reports, 58,* 43–49.

Cooper, I., & Cormier, M. (1982). Intergeneration transmission of incest. *Canadian Journal of Psychiatry, 278,* 231–235.

Coppens, N.M. (1986). Cognitive characteristics as predictors of children's understanding of safety and prevention. *Journal of Pediatric Psychology, 11,* 189–195.

Corcoran, J. (1968). *Folk tales of England.* Indianapolis, IN: Bobbs-Merrill.

Cormier, B.N., Kennedy, M., & Sancowicz, J. (1972/1973). Psychodynamics of father–daughter incest. In C.D. Bryant & J.G. Wells (Eds.), *Deviance and the family* (pp. 97–116). Philadelphia: F. A. Davis.

Courtois, C.A. (1979). The incest experience and its aftermath. *Victimology, 4,* 337–347.

Courtois, C.A. (1988). *Healing the incest wound: Adult survivors in therapy.* New York: W. W. Norton.

Cowan, P. (1978). *Piaget with feeling.* New York: Holt, Rinehart, & Winston.

Crabtree, A. (1992). Dissociation and memory: A two-hundred-year perspective. *Dissociation, 1,* 150–154.

Craft, A. (1987). *Mental handicap and sexuality: Issues and perspectives.* Kent, England: Costello Publishers.

Crapanzano, V. (1981). Text, transference, and indexicality. *Ethos, 9,* 122–148.

Crewdson, J. (1988). *By silence betrayed.* Boston: Little, Brown, and Co.

Crnic, K., Friedrich, W., & Greenberg, M. (1983). Adaptation of families with mentally retarded children: A model of stress, coping, and family ecology. *American Journal of Mental Deficiency, 88,* 125–138.

Cross, M. (1992). Abusive practices and disempowerment of children with physical impairments. *Child Abuse Review, 1,* 194–197.

Cross, W.E., Jr. (1989). Nigrescence: A nondiaphanous phenomenon. *The Counseling Psychologist, 17*(2), 273–276.

Crowley, A. (1976/1924). *Magick in theory and practice.* New York: Dove.

Cummings, S. (1976). The impact of the child's deficiency on the mother: A study of mothers of mentally retarded and of chronically ill children. *American Journal of Orthopsychiatry, 36,* 595–608.

Cupoli, J.M., & Sewell, P.M. (1988). One thousand fifty-nine children with a chief complaint of sexual abuse. *Child Abuse & Neglect, 12,* 151–162.

Daro, D. (1991). Prevention programs. In C.R. Hollin & K. Howells (Eds.), *Clinical approaches to sex offenders and their victims,* (pp. 285–305). New York: John Wiley.

Davis, G.E., & Leitenberg, H. (1987). Adolescent sex offender. *Psychological Bulletin, 101,* 417–427.

Deblinger, E., McLeer, S.V., Atkins, M.S., Ralphe, D., & Foa, E. (1989). Posttraumatic stress in sexually abused, physically abused, and nonabused children. *Child Abuse & Neglect, 13,* 403–408.

Degener, T. (1992). The right to be different: Implications for child protection. *Child Abuse Review, 1,* 151–155.

DeJong, A., Emmett, G.A., & Hervada, A.A. (1982). Epidemiological variations in childhood sexual abuse. *Child Abuse & Neglect, 7,* 155–162.

DeJong, A.R., & Finkel, M.A. (1990). Sexual abuse of children. *Current Problems in Pediatrics, 20,* 490–567.

DeJong, A.R., Weiss, J.C., & Brent, R.L. (1982). Condyloma acuminata in children. *American Journal of Diseases of Children, 136,* 704–706.

Densen-Gerber, J. (1983). Why is there so much hard-core pornography nowadays? Is it a threat to society or just a nuisance? *Medical Aspects of Human Sexuality, 17,* 30–35.

de Vries, M. (1984). Temperament and infant mortality among the Masai of East Africa. *American Journal of Psychiatry, 141,* 1189–1194.

deYoung, M. (1982). Self-injurious behavior in incest victims: A research note. *Child Welfare, 67,* 577–584.

deYoung, M. (1988). The good touch/bad touch dilemma. *Child Welfare, 67*(1), 60–68.

Diamond, L.J., & Jaudes, P.K. (1983). Child abuse in the cerebral-palsied population. *Developmental Medicine and Child Neurology, 25,* 169–174.

Dileo, J.H. (1983). *Interpreting children's drawings.* New York: Brunner/Mazel Inc.

Dillon, K.M. (1987). False sexual abuse allegations: Causes and concerns. *Social Work, 32,* 540–541.

The Discreet Gentlemen's Guide to the Pleasures of Europe (1975). New York: Bantam Books.

Donaldson, M. (1979). *Children's minds.* New York: W. W. Norton.

Dover, K.J. (1978). Greek homosexuality and initiation. In K.J. Dover (Ed.), *The Greeks and their legacy: Collected papers* (pp. 115-134). Oxford: Basil Blackwell.

Downer, A. (1985). *Prevention of child abuse: A trainer's manual.* Seattle, WA: Seattle Institute for Child Advocacy Committee for Children.

Downing, B.T., & Olney, D.P. (Eds.). (1982). *The Hmong in the West.* Minneapolis, MN: Center for Urban and Regional Affairs.

Driscoll, L.N., & Wright, D. (1991). Survivors of childhood ritual abuse: Multigenerational Satanic cult involvement. *Treating Abuse Today, 5,* 5–13.

Driver, E. (1989). Introduction. In E. Driver & A. Droisen (Eds.), *Child sexual abuse: A feminist reader* (pp. 1–68). New York: New York University Press.

Driver, E. & Droisen, A. (Eds.). (1989). *Child sexual abuse: A feminist reader.* New York: New York University Press.

Dube, R., Heger, B., Johnson, E., & Herbert, M. (1988). *Child sexual abuse prevention: A guide to prevention programs and resources.* Montreal, Canada: Hospital Sainte-Justine.

Dudar, T.S. (1977). America discovers child pornography. *Ms. Magazine, 80,* 45–47.

Dunst, C.J., Cooper, C.S., & Bolick, F.A. (1987). Supporting families of handicapped children. In J. Garbarino, P.E. Brookhouser, & K.J. Authier (Eds.), *Special children–special risks: The maltreatment of children with disabilities* (pp. 291–304). New York: deGruyter.

Dworkin, A. (1983, March). *Pornography and male supremacy.* Address presented at the University of New Hampshire, Durham.

Edwards, L.E. (1990). Differentiating between ritual assault and sexual abuse. *Journal of Child and Youth Care, Special Issue, 67–90.*

Einbender, A.J., & Friedrich, W.N. (1989). Psychological functioning and behavior of sexually abused girls. *Journal of Clinical and Consulting Psychology, 57,* 155–157.

Elkind, D. (1976). Formal education and early childhood: An essential difference. *Phi Delta Kappan, 67*(9), 631–636.

Ellis, H. (1933). *Psychology of sex.* London: Pan Books Limited.

Ellison, P.H., Tsai, F.Y., & Largent, J.A. (1978). Computed tomography in child abuse and cerebral contusion. *Pediatrics, 62,* 51.

Elwell, M.E., & Ephross, P.H. (1987). Initial reactions of sexually abused children. *Social Casework, 68*(2), 109–116.

Emery, R.E. (1982). Interparental discord and the children of discord and divorce. *Psychological Bulletin, 92,* 310–330.

Ennew, J., & Milne, D. (1989). *The next generaton: Lives of Third World children.* London: Zed Books.

Erickson, M.T. (1993). Rethinking Oedipus: An evolutionary perspective of incest avoidance. *American Journal of Psychiatry, 150*(3), 411–416.

Erickson, W.D., Walbek, N.H., & Seely, R.K. (1988). Behavior patterns of child molesters. *Archives of Sexual Behavior, 17,* 77–86.

Erikson, E. (1959). Identity and the life cycle. *Psychological Issues,* (Monograph 1). New York: International Universities Press.

Erikson, E. (1968). *Identity: Youth and crisis.* New York: W. W. Norton.

Erikson, E. (1977). *Toys and reasons.* New York: W. W. Norton.

Everson, M., Hunter, W., Runyan, D., Edelsohn, G., & Coulter, M. (1989). Maternal support following disclosure of incest. *American Journal of Orthopsychiatry, 59*(2), 197–207.

Fagan, J., & McMahon, P.P. (1984). Incipient multiple personality in children. *Journal of Nervous and Mental Disease, 172,* 26–36.

Fagot, B.I., Hagan, R., Youngblade, L.M., & Potter, L. (1989). A comparison of the play behaviors of sexually abused, physically abused, and non-abused preschool children. *Topics in Early Childhood Special Education, 9,* 88–100.

Faller, K.C. (1987). Women who sexually abuse children. *Violence and Victims, 2*(4), 263–276.

Faller, K.C. (1988). *Child sexual abuse: An interdisciplinary manual for diagnosis, case management, and treatment.* New York: Colombia University Press.

Faller, K.C. (1990). *Understanding child sexual maltreatment.* Newbury Park: Sage.

Farber, E.D., Showers, J.C., Johnson, C.F., Joseph, J.A., & Oshins, L. (1984). The sexual abuse of children: A comparison of male and female victims. *Journal of Clinical Child Psychology, 13,* 294–297.

Fehrenbach, P.A., & Monastersky, C. (1988). Characteristics of female adolescent sexual offenders. *American Journal of Orthopsychiatry, 58*(1), 148–151.

Fehrenbach, P.A., Smith, W., Monastersky, C., & Deisher, R.W. (1986). Adolescent sexual offenders: Offender and offense characteristics. *American Journal of Orthopsychiatry, 56,* 225–233.

Feinauer, L.L. (1989). Comparison of long-term affects of child abuse by relationship of the offender to the victim. *The American Journal of Family Therapy, 17,* 48–56.

Feldman, W., Feldman, E., & Goodman, J.T. (1991). Is childhood sexual abuse really increasing in prevalence? *Pediatrics, 88*(1), 29.

Fenichel, D. (1945). *The psychoanalytic theory of neurosis.* New York: W. W. Norton.

Finch, S.M. (1973). Adult seduction of the child: Effects on the child. *Medical Aspects of Human Sexuality, 1,* 170–187.

Finkel, M.A. (1991). Assessing anogenital trauma in children. *Medical Aspects of Human Sexuality, 10,* 56–63

Finkelhor, D. (1979). *Sexually victimized children.* New York: Free Press.

Finkelhor, D. (1980). Risk factors in the sexual victimization of children. *Child Abuse & Neglect, 4,* 265–273.

Finkelhor, D. (1982). Sexual abuse: A sociological perspective. *Child Abuse & Neglect, 6,* 95–102.

Finkelhor, D. (1984). *Child sexual abuse: New theory and research.* New York: Free Press.

Finkelhor, D. (Ed.). (1986). *A sourcebook on child sexual abuse.* Beverly Hills, CA: Sage.

Finkelhor, D. (1988). The trauma of child sexual abuse: Two models. In G.E. Wyatt & G.J. Powells (Eds.), *Lasting effects of child sexual abuse* (pp. 61–82). Newbury Park, CA: Sage.

Finkelhor, D. (1990a). Early and long-term effects of child sexual abuse: An update. *Professional Psychology: Research and Practice, 21*(5), 325–330.

Finkelhor, D. (1990b). New ideas for child sexual abuse prevention. In R.K. Oates (Ed.), *Understanding and managing child sexual abuse* (pp. 385–396). Philadelphia: W. B. Saunders.

Finkelhor, D. (1993). Epidemiological factors in the clinical identification of child sexual abuse. *Child Abuse & Neglect, 17,* 67–70.

Finkelhor, D., & Araji, S. (1985). Explanations of pedophilia: Review of empirical research. *Bulletin of American Academy of Psychiatry and Law, 13*(1), 17–37.

Finkelhor, D., Araji, S., Baron, L., Browne, A., Peters, S.D., & Wyatt, G.E. (1986). (Eds.). *A sourcebook on child sexual abuse.* Beverly Hills, CA: Sage.

Finkelhor, D., & Baron, L. (1986). Risk factors for childhood sexual abuse: A review of the evidence. In D. Finkelhor, S. Araji, L. Baron, A. Browne, S.D. Peters, & G. Wyatt (Eds.), *Sourcebook on child sexual abuse* (pp. 60–88). Beverly Hills, CA: Sage.

Finkelhor, D., & Browne, A. (1985). The traumatic impact of child sexual abuse: A conceptualization. *American Journal of Orthopsychiatry, 55,* 530–541.

Finkelhor, D., & Browne, A. (1986). Initial and long-term effects: A conceptual framework. In D. Finkelhor (Ed.), *A sourcebook on child sexual abuse* (pp. 180–198). Beverly Hills, CA: Sage.

Finkelhor, D., & Hotaling, G. (1984). Sexual abuse in the national incidence study of child abuse and neglect. *Child Abuse & Neglect, 8,* 222–232.

Finkelhor, D., Hotaling, G., Lewis, I.A., & Smith, C. (1990). Sexual abuse in a national survey of adult men and women: Prevalence, characteristics, and risk factors. *Child Abuse & Neglect, 14,* 19–28.

Finkelhor, D., & Strapko, N. (1992). Sexual abuse prevention education: A review of evaluation studies. In D. Willis, E. Holden, & M. Rosenberg (Eds.), *Child abuse prevention* (pp. 150–167). New York: Wiley.

Finkelhor, D., Williams, L.M., Burns, N., & Kalinowski, M. (1988). *Nursery crimes: Sexual abuse in day care.* Newbury, CA: Sage.

Fischer, K.W., & Silvern, L. (1985). Stages and individual differences in cognitive development. *Annual Review of Psychology, 36,* 613–648.

Fish, V., & Faynik, C. (1989). Treatment of incest families with the father temporarily removed: A structural approach. *Journal of Strategic and Systemic Therapy, 8,* 53–65.

Fisher, G., & Howell, L. (1970). Psychological needs of homosexual pedophiliacs. *Diseases of the Nervous System, 3,* 623–625.

Fitch, J.H. (1962). Men convicted of sexual offenses against children: A descriptive follow-up study. *British Journal of Criminology, 3,* 18–37.

Flavell, J.H. (1985). *Cognitive development* (2nd ed.). Englewood Cliffs, NJ: Prentice-Hall.

Flavell, J.H., Green, F.G., & Flavell, E.R. (1983). Development of knowledge about the appearance–reality distinction. *Cognitive Psychology, 15,* 95-120.

Fontes, L.A. (1993). Disclosures of sexual abuse by Puerto Rican children: Oppression and cultural barriers. *Journal of Child Sexual Abuse, 2,* 21–35.

Forward, S., & Buck, C. (1978). *Betrayal of innocence: Incest and its devastation.* Los Angeles: J. P. Tarcher.

Freeman, K.R., & Estrada-Mullaney, T. (1988). Using dolls to interview child victims: Legal concerns and interview procedures. *NIJ Reports, 2–6.*

Freeman-Longo, R.E. (1986). The impact of sexual victimization on males. *Child Abuse & Neglect, 10,* 411–414.

Freud, A. (1965). *Normality and pathology in childhood.* New York: International Universities Press.

Freud, S. (1933). *New introductory lectures in psychoanalysis.* New York: W. W. Norton.

Freud, S. (1948). *Three contributions to the theory of sex* (4th ed.). New York: Nervous and Mental Disease Monographs.

Freud, S. (1963). *Three essays on the theory of sexuality.* (J. Strachey, Trans. & Ed.). New York: Basic Books. (Original work published 1905)

Freund, K. (1967). Erotic preference in pedophilia. *Behavior Research and Therapy, 5,* 339–348.

Freund, K., & Blanchard, R. (1989). Phallometric diagnosis of pedophilia. *Journal of Consulting and Clinical Psychology, 57,* 100–105.

Freund, K., & Langevin, R. (1976). Bisexuality in homosexual pedophilia. *Archives of Sexual Behavior, 5,* 415–423.

Freund, K., Langevin, R., & Cibiri, S. (1973). Heterosexual aversion in homosexual males. *British Journal of Psychiatry, 122,* 163–169.

Freund, K., McKnight, C.K., Langevin, R., & Cibiri, S. (1972). The female child as surrogate object. *Archives of Sexual Behavior, 2,* 119–133.

Freund, K., & Watson, R. (1990). Mapping the boundaries of courtship disorder. *The Journal of Sex Research, 27,* 589-606.

Freund, K., Watson, R., & Dickey, R. (1990). Is there support for the notion that sexual abuse in childhood causes pedophilia: An exploratory study. *Archives of Sexual Behavior, 19,* 557–568.

Freund, K., Watson, R., & Dickey, R. (1991). Sex offenses against female children perpetrated by men who are not pedophiles. *Journal of Sex Research, 28*(4), 409–423.

Freund, K., Watson, K.R., Dickey, R., & Rienzo, D. (1991). Erotic gender differentiation in pedophilia. *Archives of Sexual Behavior 20*(6), 555–566.

Friedemann, V.M. & Morgan, M.K. (1985). *Interviewing sexual abuse victims using anatomical dolls: The professionals guidebook.* Eugene, OR: Shamrock.

Friedrich, W.N. (1987). The sexual abuse of children: Current research reviewed. *Psychiatric Annals, 17,* 233–241.

Friedrich, W.N. (1989, June). *The child sexual behavior inventory: A comparison of normal and clinical populations.* Paper presented at the meeting of the International Academy of Sex Research, Princeton, New Jersey.

Friedrich, W.N. (1990). *The child sexual behavior inventory* (rev. ed.). Rochester, MN: Mayo Clinic.

Friedrich, W.N. (1993). Sexual victimization and sexual behavior in children: A review of the recent literature. *Child Abuse & Neglect, 17,* 59–66.

Friedrich, W.N., Beilke, R., & Urquiza, A. (1987). Children from sexually abusive families: A behavioral comparison. *Journal of Interpersonal Violence, 9*(4), 391–402.

Friedrich, W.N., & Friedrich, W. (1981). The role of the child in abuse: A review of the literature. *American Journal of Orthopsychiatry, 46,* 580–590.

Friedrich, W.N., Grambsch, P., Broughton, D., & Beilke, R.L. (1988, August). *Child sexual behavior inventory: A normative study.* Paper presented at the meeting of the International Academy of Sex Research, Minneapolis, MN.

Friedrich, W.N., Grambsch, P., Broughton, D., Kuiper, J., & Beilke, R.L. (1991). Normative sexual behavior in children. *Pediatrics, 88,* 456–463.

Friedrich, W.N., Grambsch, P., Damon, L., Hewitt, S.K., Koverola, C., Lang, R., & Wolfe, V. (1992). The child sexual behavior inventory: Normative and clinical comparisons. *Psychological Assessment: A Journal of Consulting and Clinical Psychology, 4,* 303-314.

Friedrich, W.N., & Luecke, W.J. (1988). Young school-age sexually aggressive children. *Professional Psychology, Research and Practice, 19,* 155–164.

Friedrich, W.N., & Reams, R. (1987). Course of psychological symptoms in sexually abused young children. *Psychotherapy, 240,* 160–170.

Friedrich, W.N., Urquiza, A.J., & Beilke, R.L. (1986). Behavior problems in sexually abused young children. *Journal of Pediatric Psychology, 11,* 47–57.

Frisch, L.E., & Rhoads, F.A. (1982). Child abuse and neglect in children referred for learning evaluation. *Journal of Learning Disabilities, 15*(10), 583–586.

Fromuth, M.E. (1986). The relationship of childhood sexual abuse with later psychological and sexual adjustment in a sample of college women. *Child Abuse & Neglect, 10,* 5–15.

Fryer, G.E., Kraizer, S.K., & Miyoshi, T. (1987a). Measuring actual reduction of risk to child abuse: A new approach. *Child Abuse & Neglect, 11,* 173–179.

Fryer, G.E., Kraizer, S.K., & Miyoshi, T. (1987b). Measuring children's retention skills to resist stranger abduction: Use of simulation technique. *Child Abuse & Neglect, 11,* 181–185.

Gaffney, G.R., & Berlin, F.S. (1984). Is there hypothalamic pituitary gonadal dysfunction in pedophilia: A pilot study. *British Journal of Psychiatry, 145,* 657–660.

Gaffney, G.R., Shelly, F.L., & Berlin, F.S. (1984). Is there a familial transmission of pedophilia? *Journal of Nervous & Mental Disease, 172,* 546.

Gagnon, J. (1965a). Female child victims of sex offenses. *Social Problems, 13,* 176–192.

Gagnon, J.H. (1965b). Sexuality and sexual learning in the child. *Psychiatry, 28,* 212–228.

Gainer, K. (1989). *Monster as metaphor: Symbolic expressions in early child-hood abuse victims* [Summary]. Proceedings of the Sixth International Conference on Multiple Personality/Dissociative States.

Gaines, A. (1982). Cultural definitions, behavior, and the person in American psychiatry. In A.J. Marsella and A. White (Eds.), *Cultural conceptions of mental health and therapy* (p. 182). London: Reidel.

Gale, J., Thompson, R.J., Moran, T., & Sack, W.H. (1988). Sexual abuse in young children: Its clinical presentation and characteristic patterns. *Child Abuse & Neglect, 12,* 163–170.

Garbarino, J. (1987a). The abuse and neglect of special children: An introduction to the issues. In J. Garbarino, P.E. Brookhouser, & K.J. Authier (Eds.), *Special children–special risks: The maltreatment of children with disabilities* (pp. 3–14). New York: deGruyter.

Garbarino, J. (1987b). Children's response to a sexual abuse prevention program: A study of the Spiderman comic. *Child Abuse & Neglect, 11,* 143–148.

Garbarino, J., Dubrow, N., Kostelny, K., & Pardo, C. (1992). *Children in danger: Coping with the consequences of community violence.* San Francisco: Jossey-Bass.

Garbarino, J., & Gillian, G. (1980). *Understanding abusive families.* Lexington, MA: Lexington Books.

Garbarino, J., Stott, F.M., and the faculty of the Erickson Institute. (1989). *What children can tell us: Eliciting, interpreting, and evaluating information from children.* San Francisco: Jossey-Bass.

Gardner, M., & Jones, J.G. (1984). Genital herpes acquired by sexual abuse of children. *Journal of Pediatrics, 104,* 243–244.

Gardner, R. (1971). *Therapeutic communication with children: The mutual story-telling technique.* New York: Science House.

Garland, R.J., & Dougher, M.J. (1990). The abused/abuser hypothesis of child sexual abuse: A critical review of theory and research. In J.R. Frierman (Ed.), *Pedophilia: Biosocial dimensions* (pp. 488–509). New York: Springer-Verlag.

Gath, A. (1985). Sibling reactions to mental handicap: A comparison of the brothers and sisters of mongol children. *Jounal of Child Psychology and Psychiatry, 15,* 187-198.

Gebhard, P.H., & Gagnon, J.H. (1964). Male sex offenders against very young children. *American Journal of Psychiatry, 121,* 576–579.

Gebhard, P.H., Gagnon, J.H., Pomeroy, W.B., & Christenson, C. (1965). *Sex offenders.* New York: Bantam Books.

Geiser, R.L. (1979). *Hidden victims: The sexual abuse of children.* Boston: Beacon Press.

Gelinas, D.J. (1983). The persisting negative effects of incest. *Psychiatry, 46,* 313–332.

Gelles, R.J. (1973). Child abuse as psychopathology: A sociological critique and reformulation. *American Journal of Orthopsychiatry, 43,* 611–621.

Gibson, G., & Bogat, G.A. (1993). Pretesting effects in the evaluation of a sexual abuse education program for preschool children. *Journal of Child Sexual Abuse, 2*(3), 15–31.

Gil, E. (1988). *Treatment of adult survivors of childhood abuse.* Walnut Creek, CA: Launch Press.

Gill, D. (1970). *Violence against children: Physical child abuse.* Cambridge, MA: Harvard University.

Gilbert, N., Berrick, J. D., LeProhn, N., & Nyman, N. (1990). *Protecting young children from sexual abuse: Does preschool training work.* Lexington, MA: Lexington Books.

Gilbert, N., Daro, D., Duerr, J., LeProhn, N., & Nyman, N. (1988). *Child sexual abuse prevention: Evaluation of educational materials for preschool programs.* Berkeley, CA: University of California Family Research Group, School of Social Welfare.

Gilgun, J., & Connor, T. (1989). How perpetrators view child sexual abuse. *Social Work, 34*(3), 249–251.

Gilligan, C. (1982). *In a different voice.* Cambridge, MA: Harvard University Press.

Gilligan, C., Ward, J.V., & Taylor, J. (Eds.). (1988). *Mapping the moral domain.* Cambridge, MA: Harvard University Press.

Giobbe, E. (1993). Women hurt in systems of prostitution. *Trouble and Strife, 26,* 22–27.

Glaser, D., & Collins, C. (1989). The response of young, nonsexually abused children to anatomically correct dolls. *Journal of Child Psychology and Psychiatry, 30,* 547–560.

Glueck, B.C., Jr. (1965). Pedophilia. In R. Slovenko (Ed.), *Sexual behavior and the law* (pp. 89-110). Springfield, IL: Charles C. Thomas.

Goldstein, J., Freud, A., & Solnit, A. (1973). *Beyond the best interests of the child.* New York: Free Press.

Goldstein, M.J., Kant, H.S., & Hartman, J.J. (1973). *Pornography and sexual deviance.* Los Angeles: University of California Press.

Goldstein, S. (1984). Investigating child sexual exploitation: Law enforcement's role. *Federal Bureau of Investigation Law Enforcement Bulletin, 53,* 23–31.

Goldston, D.B., Turnquist, D.C. ,& Knuston, J.F. (1989). Presenting problems of sexually abused girls receiving psychiatric services. *Journal of Abnormal Psychology, 98,* 314–317.

Golston, J.C. (1992). Ritual abuse: Raising hell in psychotherapy. *Treating Abuse Today, 2,* 4–12.

Gomes-Schwartz, B., Horowitz, J., Cardarelli, A. (1990). *Child sexual abuse: The initial effects.* Newbury Park, CA: Sage.

Gomes-Schwartz, B., Horowitz, J., Cardarelli, A., & Sauzier, M. (1990). The aftermath of child sexual abuse: 18 months later. In B. Gomes-Schwartz, J. Horowitz, & A.P. Cardarelli (Eds.), *Child sexual abuse: The initial effects* (pp. 132–152). Newbury Park, CA: Sage.

Gomes-Schwartz, B., Horowitz, J.M., & Sauzier, M. (1985). Severity of emotional distress among sexually abused preschool, school-age, and adolescent children. *Hospital and Community Psychiatry, 36,* 503–508.

Gomez, M.V. (1992). Some suggestions for change regarding culturally appropriate interventions in child sexual abuse: A reaction to Heras. *Journal of Child Sexual Abuse, 1*(3), 125–127.

Goodwin, J. (1982). *Sexual abuse, incest victims and their families.* Bristol: John Wright.

Goodwin, J., & Di Vasto, P. (1979). Mother–daughter incest. *Child Abuse & Neglect, 3,* 953–957.

Gorcey, M., Santiago, J.M., & McCall-Perez, F. (1986). Psychological consequences for women sexually abused in childhood. *Social Psychiatry, 21,* 129–133.

Gould, C. (1988). *Signs and symptoms of ritualistic abuse in children.* Available from author at 16055 Ventura Blvd, Suite 714, Encino, CA 91436.

Gould, C. (1992). Diagnosis and treatment of ritually abused children. In D.K. Sakheim & S.E. Devine (Eds.), *Out of darkness: Exploring satanism and ritual abuse* (pp. 207–248). New York: Lexington Books.

Greaves, G.B. (1992). Alternative hypotheses regarding claims of satanic cult activity: A critical analysis. In M. Katchen & D. Sakheim (Eds.), *Out of darkness: Exploring satanism and ritual abuse* (pp. 44–78). New York: Lexington Books.

Grevious, C. (1985). The role of the family therapist with low-income black families. *Family Therapy, 12,* 115–122.

Grossman, T. (1987). *Recognition of dissociative states in the evaluation and treatment of severe child sexual abuse.* Paper presented at the 4th Annual Conference on MPD and Dissociation, Chicago, October, 1987.

Groth, A.N. (1979a). *Men who rape: The psychology of the offender.* New York: Plenum.

Groth, A.N. (1979b). Sexual trauma in the life histories of rapists and child molesters. *Victimology, 4,* 10–16.

Groth, A.N. (1982). The incest offender. In S.M. Sgroi (Ed.), *Handbook of clinical intervention in child sexual abuse* (pp. 215–239). Lexington, MA: Lexington Books.

Groth, A.N., & Birnbaum, H.J. (1978). Adult sexual orientation and attraction to underage persons. *Archives of Sexual Behavior, 7,* 175-178.

Groth, A.N., Hobson, W.F., & Gary, T.S. (1982). The child molester: Clinical observations. In J. Conte & D.A. Shore (Eds.), *Social work and child sexual abuse* (pp. 129–144). New York: Haworth.

Groth, A.N., & Burgess, A.W. (1977). Rape: A sexual deviation. *American Journal of Orthopsychiatry, 27,* 400–406.

Groth, A.N., & Loredo, C.M. (1981). Juvenile sex offenders: Guidelines for assessment. *International Journal of Offender Therapy and Comparative Criminology, 25,* 31–39.

Gruber, K.J., & Jones, R.J. (1983). Identifying determinants of risk of sexual victimization of youth: A multivariate approach. *Child Abuse & Neglect, 7,* 17–24.

Gutheil, T.G., & Avery, N.C. (1977). Multiple overt incest as a defense against loss. *Family Process, 16,* 105–116.

Hall, G.C. (1989). WAIS-R and MMPI profiles of men who have sexually assaulted children: Evidence of unlimited utility. *Journal of Personality Assessment, 53,* 404–412.

Hall, G.C., Maiuro, R.D., Vitaliano, P.P., & Proctor, W.C. (1986). The utility of the MMPI with men who have sexually assaulted children. *Journal of Consulting and Clinical Psychology, 54,* 493–496.

Halleck, S.L. (1965). Emotional effects of victimizations. In R. Slovenko (Ed.), *Sexual behavior and the law* (pp. 673–686). Springfield, IL: Charles C. Thomas.

Hames, A. (1990). To be on the safe side. *Community Care, 799,* 22–23.

Hamilton, G.V. (1929). *A research in marriage.* New York: Albert & Charles Boni.

Hammer, R.F., & Glueck, B.C., Jr. (1957). Psychodynamic patterns in sex offenders: A four-factor theory. *Psychiatric Quarterly, 31,* 325–345.

Hammerschlag, M.R., Doraiswamy, B., Alexander, E., Cox, P., Price, W., & Gleyzer, A. (1984). Are rectogenital chlamydial infections a marker of sexual abuse in children? *Pediatrics Infectious Disease, 3,* 100–104.

Hart-Rossi, J. (1984). *Protect your child from sexual abuse: A parent's guide.* Seattle, WA: Parenting Press.

Hartup, W. (1983). Peer relations. In E. M. Hetherington (Ed.), *Handbook of child psychology: Socialization, personality, and development* (4th ed.) (pp. 103–196). New York: Wiley.

Harvey, P., Forehand, R., Brown, C., & Holmes, T. (1988). The prevention of sexual abuse: Examination of a program with kindergarten-age children. *Behavior Therapy, 19*, 429–435.

Haugaard, J.J., & Emery, R.E. (1989). Methodological issues in child sexual abuse research. *Child Abuse & Neglect, 13*, 89–100.

Haugaard, J.J., & Reppucci, N.D. (1988). *The sexual abuse of children: A comprehensive guide to current knowledge and intervention strategies.* San Francisco: Jossey-Bass.

Hayes, S., Brownell, K., & Barlow, D. (1983). Heterosocial skills training and covert sensitization effects on social skills and sexual arousal in sexual deviants. *Behavior Research and Therapy, 21*, 383–392.

Hazzard, A. (1984). Training teachers to identify and intervene with abused children. *Journal of Clinical Child Psychology, 13*, 288–293.

Hazzard, A., Webb, C., & Kleemeier, C.P. (1988). *Child sexual assault prevention programs: Helpful or harmful?* Unpublished manuscript, Emory University School of Medicine, Atlanta, GA.

Heiman, M.L. (1992). Putting the puzzle together: Validating allegations of child sexual abuse. *Journal of Child Psychology and Psychiatry, 33*, 311–329.

Helms, J.E. (1984). Toward a theatrical explanation of the effects of race on counseling: A black and white model. *The Counseling Psychologist, 12*, 153–165.

Henn, F.A., Herjanic, M., & Vanderpearl, R.H. (1976). Forensic psychiatry—profiles of two types of sex offenders. *American Journal of Psychiatry, 133*, 696.

Henson, D.E., & Rubin, H.B. (1971). Voluntary control of eroticism. *Journal of Applied Behavioral Analysis, 4*, 37–44.

Heras, P. (1992). Cultural considerations in the assessment and treatment of child sexual abuse. *Journal of Child Sexual Abuse, 1,* 119–124.

Herman, J. (1981). *Father–daughter incest.* Cambridge, MA: Harvard University Press.

Herman, J. (1990). Sex offenders: A feminist perspective. In W.L. Marshall, D.R. Laws, & H.E. Barbaree (Eds.), *Handbook of sexual assault* (pp. 177–193). New York: Plenum Press.

Herman, J., & Hirschman, L. (1977). Father–daughter incest. *Signs: Journal of Women in Culture and Society, 2,* 735–756.

Herman, J., Russell, D., & Trocki, K. (1986). Long term effects of incestuous abuse in childhood. *American Journal of Psychiatry, 143,* 1293–1296.

Herman, J., & Schatzow, E. (1987). Recovery and verification of memories of childhood sexual trauma. *Psychoanalytic Psychology, 4,* 1–14.

Hibbard, R.A. & Hartman, G.L. (1990). Emotional indicators in human figure drawings of sexually victimized and nonabused children. *Journal of Clinical Psychology, 46,* 211–219.

Hibbard, R.A., Roghmann, K., & Hoekelman, R.A. (1987). Genitalia in children's drawings: An association with sexual abuse. *Pediatrics, 79,* 129–137.

Hill, S., & Goodwin, J. (1989). Satanism: Similarities between patient accounts and pre-Inquisition historical sources. *Dissociation, 2*(1), 39–44.

Hillman, D., & Solek-Tefft, J. (1988). *Spiders and flies.* Lexington, MA: Lexington Books.

Hines, A., & Pedersen, P. (1980). The cultural grid: Matching social system values and cultural perspectives. *Asian Pacific Training Development Journal, 1*(1), 5–12.
Hirschfeld, M. (1948) *Sexual anomalies: The origin, nature, and treatment of sexual disorders.* New York: Emerson Books.

Hite, S. (1981). *The Hite report on male sexuality.* New York: Alfred Knopf.

Hollin, C.R., & Howells, K. (Eds). (1991). *Clinical approaches to sex offenders and their victims.* New York: John Wiley & Sons.

Horevitz, R.P., & Braun, B.G. (1984). Are multiple personalities borderline? An analysis of 33 cases. *Psychiatric Clinics of North America, 7,* 69–78.

Howells, K. (1981). Adult sexual interest in children: Considerations relevant to theories of aetiology. In M. Cook & K. Howells (Eds.), *Adult sexual interest in children* (pp. 77–93). New York: Academic Press.

Hudson, P.S. (1990). Ritual child abuse: A survey of symptoms and allegations. *Journal of Child and Youth Care, Special Issue,* 27–54.

Hudson, P.S. (1991). *Ritual child abuse: Discovery, diagnosis, and treatment.* Saratoga, CA: R & E Publishers.

Hughes, H.M., & Barad, S.J. (1983). Psychological functioning of children in a battered women's shelter: A preliminary investigation. *American Journal of Orthopsychiatry 53,* 525–531.

Hunt, J. (1991). Ten reasons not to hit your kids. In A. Miller, *Breaking down the wall of silence* (pp. 168–171). New York: Dutton.

Hunt, P., & Baird, M. (1990). Children of sex rings. *Child Welfare, 69,* 195–207.

Hunter, M. (1990). *Sexually abused males, Volume 1: Prevalence, impact and treatment.* Lexington, MA: Free Press.

Illusion Theater Company and Media Ventures, Inc. (Coproducers). (1984). *Touch* [Film]. Deerfield, IL: MTI Teleprograms.

Ingersoll, S.L. & Patton, S.O. (1990). *Treating perpetrators of sexual abuse.* Lexington, MA: Lexington Books.

Ingram, D., White, S., Durfee, M., & Pearson, A. (1982). Sexual contact in children with gonorrhea. *American Journal of Diseases of Children, 136,* 994–996.
Ireland, K. (1993). *Sexual exploitation of children and the connection with tourism.* London: Save the Children Fund.

Jackson, J.F. (1984). *A preliminary survey of adolescent sex offenses in New York: Remedies and recommendations.* Orwell, VT: Safer Society Press.

Jaffe, P., Wolfe, D., Wilson, S., & Zak, L. (1986). Similarities in behavioral and social maladjustment among child victims and witnesses to family violence. *American Journal of Orthopsychiatry, 56,* 142–146.

Jampole, L., & Weber, M.K. (1987). An assessment of the behavior of sexually abused and nonsexually abused children with anatomically correct dolls. *Child Abuse & Neglect, 11,* 187–192.

Jason, J., Williams, S., Burton, A., & Rochat, R. (1982). Epidemiologic differences between sexual and physical abuse. *Journal of the American Medical Association, 247,* 3344–3358.

Jaudes, P.K., & Diamond, J. (1985). The handicapped child and child abuse. *Child Abuse & Neglect, 9,* 341–347.

Johnson, B., & Morse, A. (1968). Injured children and their parents. *Children, 15,* 147–152.

Johnson, R.L., & Shrier, D.K. (1985). Sexual victimization of boys: Experiences at an adolescent medicine clinic. *Journal of Adolescent Health Care, 6,* 372–376.

Johnson, T.C. (1988). Child perpetrators—children who molest other children: Preliminary findings. *Child Abuse & Neglect, 12,* 219–229.

Johnson, T.C., & Berry, B. (1989). Children who molest: A treatment program. *Journal of Interpersonal Violence, 4,* 185–203.

Jones, D., & Garfinkel, L. (1993). Defining the unknown: Therapy for children with disabilities who have been sexually abused. *Journal of Child Sexual Abuse, 2,* 127–129.

Jones, D.P.H. (1991). Ritualism and child sexual abuse. *Child Abuse & Neglect, 15,* 163–170.

Jones, D.P.H., & McQuiston, M. (1986). *Interviewing the sexually abused child* (2nd ed.). Denver, CO: The C. Henry Kempe National Center for the Prevention and Treatment of Child Abuse and Neglect.

Jones, G.P. (1982). The social study of pederasty. In search of a literature base: An annotated bibliography of sources in English. *Journal of Homosexuality, 8*(1), 61–85.

Jones, G.P. (1991). The study of intergenerational intimacy in North America: Beyond politics and pedophilia. *Journal of Homosexuality, 3,* 275–295.

Juda, D.P. (1986). The usefulness of self-psychology in understanding and treating a case of homosexual pedophilia. *Dynamic Psychotherapy, 9*, 99–123.

Justice, B., & Justice, R. (1979). *The broken taboo: Sex in the family.* New York: Human Sciences Press.

Kagan, J. (1984). *The nature of the child.* New York: Basic Books.

Kahr, B. (1991). The sexual molestation of children: Historical perspective. *The Journal of Psychohistory, 19*(2), 191–214.

Kail, R. (1984). *The development of memory in children.* New York: W. H. Freeman.

Karpman, B. (1954). *The sexual offender and his offenses: Aetiology, pathology, psychodynamics and treatment.* New York: Julian Press.

Kaschak, E. (1992). *Engendered lives: A new psychology of women's experience.* New York: Basic Books.

Katchen, M.H., & Sakheim, D.K. (1992). Satanic beliefs and practices. In D.K. Sakheim & S.E. Devine (Eds.), *Out of darkness: Exploring satanism and ritual abuse* (pp. 21–43). New York: Lexington Books.

Katz, R.C. (1990). Psychosocial adjustment in adolescent child molesters. *Child Abuse & Neglect, 14*, 567–575.

Kazak, A., & Clark, M. (1986). Stress in families of children with myelomeniogocele. *Developmental Medicine and Child Neurology, 28*, 220–228.

Keckley Market Research. (1983). *Sexual abuse in Nashville: A report on incidence and long term effects.* Nashville, TN: Keckley Market Research.

Kehoe, P. (1988). *Helping abused children.* Seattle, WA: Parenting Press.

Kelley, S.J. (1989). Stress responses of children to sexual abuse and ritualistic abuse in day-care centers. *Journal of Interpersonal Violence, 4*, 502–513.

Kelly, L. (1992). The connection between disability and child abuse: A review of the research evidence. *Child Abuse Review, 1*, 157–167.

Kelly, R. J., & Scott, M. M. (1986). Sociocultural considerations in child sexual abuse. In K. MacFarlane & J. Waterman (Eds.), *Sexually abused young children: Evaluation and treatment* (pp. 15–31). New York: Guilford.

Kempe, C.H. (1978). Sexual abuse, another hidden pediatric problem: The 1977 C. Anderson Aldrich Lecture. *Pediatrics, 62,* 382–389.

Kempe, R.S., & Kempe, H. (1984). *The common secret: Sexual abuse of children and adolescents.* New York: Freeman.

Kendall-Tackett, K.A., & Simon, A.F. (1987). Perpetrators and their acts: Data from 365 adults molested as children. *Child Abuse & Neglect, 11*(2), 237–245.

Kendall-Tackett, K.A., & Simon, A.F. (1992). A comparison of the abuse experiences of male and female adults molested as children. *Journal of Family Violence, 77*(1), 57–62.

Kendall-Tackett, K.A., Williams, L.M., & Finkelhor, D. (1993). Impact of sexual abuse on children: A review and synthesis of recent empirical studies. *Psychological Bulletin, 113,* 164–180.

Kennedy, M. (1989). The abuse of deaf children. *Child Abuse Review, 3*(1), 3–7.

Kennedy, M. (1990). The deaf child who is sexually abused. *Child Abuse Review, 4*(2), 3–6.

Kennedy, M. (1992). Not the only way to communicate: A challenge to voice in child protection work. *Child Abuse Review, 1,* 169–177.

Kenning, M., Gallmeier, T., Jackson, T.L., & Plemons, S. (1987). *Evaluation of child sexual abuse prevention programs: A summary of two studies.* Paper presented at the National Conference on Violence, Durham, NH.

Kercher, G., & McShane, M. (1984). Characterizing child sexual abuse on the basis of a multi-agency sample. *Victimology, 9,* 364–382.

Kilpatrick, D.B., Saunders, B.E., Veronen, L.J., Best, C.L., & Von, J.M. (1987). Criminal victimization: Lifetime prevalence, reporting to police, and psychological impact. *Crime and Delinquency, 13,* 479–489.

Kincannon, J.C. (1968). Prediction of the standard MMPI scale scores from 71 items: The Mini-Mult. *Journal of Consulting and Clinical Psychology, 32,* 321–325.

Kinsey, A.C., Pomeroy, W.B., Martin, C.E., & Gebhard, P.H. (1953). *Sexual behavior in the human female.* Philadelphia: Saunders.

Klepsch, M., & Logle, L. (1985). *Children draw and tell.* New York: Brunner/Mazel.

Kluft, R.P. (1984). Multiple personality in childhood. *Psychiatric Clinics of North America, 7,* 121–134.

Kluft, R.P. (1985). The natural history of multiple personality disorder. In R. P. Kluft (Ed.), *Childhood antecedents of multiple personality* (pp. 197–238). Washington, DC: American Psychiatric Press.

Kluft, R.P. (1988). On giving consultations to therapists treating MPD. *Dissociation, 1*(3), 23–29.

Knight, R.A., & Prentky, R.A. (1990). Classifying sexual offenders. In W.L. Marshall, D.R. Laws, & H.E. Barbaree (Eds.), *Handbook of sexual assault: Issues, theories, and treatment of the offender* (pp. 32–57). New York: Plenum Press.

Kogutt, M.S., Swischuk, L.E., & Fagan, C.J. (1974). Patterns of injury and significance of uncommon fractures in the battered child syndrome. *American Journal of Roentgenology in Radium Therapy and Nuclear Medicine, 121,* 143.

Kohlberg, L. (1969). Stage end sequence: The cognitive-developmental approach to socialization. In D. Goslin (Ed.), *Handbook of socialization theory and research* (pp. 347–480). Chicago: Rand McNally.

Kohlberg, L. (1978). The cognitive development approach to behavior disorders: A study of the development of moral reasoning in dilinquents. In G.S. Erban (Ed.), *Cognitive defects in the development of mental illness* (pp. 101–133). New York: Brunner/Mazel.

Kohut, H. (1977). *The restoration of the self.* New York: International Universities Press.

Kolko, D., Moser, J., Litz, J., & Hughes, J. (1987). Promoting awareness and prevention of child sexual victimization using the Red Flag/Green Flag Program: An evaluation with follow-up. *Journal of Family Violence, 2,* 11–35.

Kolko, D.J. (1988). Educational programs to promote the awareness and prevention of sexual victimization: A methodological critique. *Clinical Psychology Review, 8,* 195–209.

Kopp, C. (1982). Antecedents of self-regulation. A developmental perspective. *Developmental Psychology, 18,* 199–214.

Korbin, J. (1980). The cultural context of child abuse and neglect. *Child Abuse & Neglect, 4,* 3–13.

Kournay, R.F.C., Martin, J.E., & Armstrong, S.H. (1979). Sexual experimentation by adolescents while babysitting. *Adolesence, 14,* 283–288.

Krafft-Ebing, R.V. (1886/1965). *Psychopathia sexualis.* New York: Putnam. (Original work published 1886)

Kraizer, S.K. (1985). *The safe child book.* New York: Dell.

Kraizer, S.K. (1986). Rethinking prevention. *Child Abuse & Neglect, 10,* 259–261.

Kraizer, S.K. (1990). *The safe child program.* Morris Plains, NJ: Lucerne Media.

Kraizer, S.K., Witte, S.S., & Fryer, G.E., Jr. (1989). Child sexual abuse prevention programs: What makes them effective in protecting children? *Children Today, 18,* 23–27.

Krents, E., Schulman, V., & Brenner, S. (1987). Child abuse and the disabled child: Prospectives for parents. *Volta Review, 89,* 78–95.

Krivacska, J.J. (1990). *Designing child sexual abuse prevention programs: Current approaches and a proposal for the prevention, reduction, and identification of sexual misuse.* Springfield, IL: Charles C. Thomas.

Krug, R.S. (1989). Adult male report of childhood sexual abuse by mothers: Case descriptions, motivations and long-term consequences. *Child Abuse & Neglect, 13,* 111–119.

Krugman, R. (1986). Recognition of sexual abuse in children. *Pediatrics in Review, 8*(1), 25–39.

Lahti, J. (1982). A follow-up study of foster children in permanent placements. *Social Services Review, 9,* 556-571.

Lamb, M., Thompson, R.A., Gardner, W.P., Charnov, E.L., & Estes, D. (1984). Security of infantile attachment as assessed in the "Strange Situation": Its study and biological implications. *Behavioral and Brain Sciences, 7,* 127–147.

Landis, C., Landis, A. T., & Bolles, T. (1940). *Sex in development.* New York: Hoeber.

Landis, J.T. (1956). Experience of 500 children with adult sexual deviants. *Psychiatric Quarterly Supplement, 30,* 91–109.

Landrine, H. (1992). Clinical implication of cultural differences: The referential versus the indexical self. *Clinical Psychology Review, 12,* 401–415.

Lane, S. (1991). The sexual abuse cycle. In G. Ryan & S. Lane (Eds.), *Juvenile sexual offending: Cause, consequences and corrections* (pp. 103–141). Lexington, MA: Lexington Books.

Lane, S., & Zamora, P. (1984). A method for treating the adolescent sex offender. In R. Mathias, P. Demuro, & R. Allinson (Eds.), *Violent juvenile offenders* (pp. 347–363). San Francisco, CA: National Council on Crime and Delinquency.

Lang, A. (Ed.). (1900). *The Grey fairy book.* New York: Longmans, Green.

Langevin, R. (1983). *Sexual strands.* Hillsdale, NJ: Lawrence Erlbaum Associates.

Langevin, R., Hucker, S.J., Ben-Avon, M.H., Purins, J.E., & Hook, H.J. (1985). Why are pedophiles attracted to children? In R. Langevin (Ed.), *Erotic preference, gender identity, and aggression in men: New research studies* (pp. 181–209). Hillsdale, NJ: Lawrence Erlbaum Associates.

Lanktree, C., & Briere, J., (1991, January). *Early data on the Trauma Symptom Checklist for Children (TSC-C).* Paper presented at the meeting of the American Professional Society on the Abuse of Children, San Diego, CA.

Lanktree, C., & Briere, J. (1992, January). *Further data on the Trauma Symptom Checklist for Children (TSC-C): Reliability, validity, and sensitivity to treatment.* Paper presented at the San Diego Conference on Responding to Child Maltreatment, San Diego, CA.

Lanning, K. (1984). Collectors. In A. Burgess & M. Clark (Eds.), *Child pornography and sex rings* (pp. 83–92). Lexington, MA: Lexington Books.

Lanning, K. (1991). Commentary. Ritual abuse: Another view. *Child Abuse & Neglect, 15,* 171–173.

Lanyon, R. (1985). Theory and treatment in child molestation. *Journal of Consulting and Clinical Psychology, 54*(2), 176–182.

Lanyon, R. (1986). Psychological assessment procedure in court-related settings. *Professional Psychology, 17,* 260–268.

LaVey, A. (1969). *The Satanic bible.* New York: Avon.

LaVey, A. (1972). *The Satanic rituals.* New York: Avon.

Laviola, M. (1992). Effects of older brother–younger sister incest: A study of the dynamics of 17 cases. *Child Abuse & Neglect, 16,* 409–421.

Laws, D.R. (1988). *Use of pornography by pedophiles.* Unpublished raw data.

Laws, D.R., & Osborn, C.A. (1983). How to build and operate a behavioral laboratory to evaluate and treat sexual deviance. In J.G. Greer & I.R. Stuart (Eds.), *The sexual aggressor: Current perspectives on treatment* (pp. 292–335). New York: Van Nostrand Reinhold.

Laws, D.R., & Rubin, H.B. (1969). Instructional control of an automatic sexual response. *Journal of Applied Behavioral Analysis, 2,* 93–99.

Lawson, C. (1991). Clinical assessment of mother–son sexual abuse. *Clinical Social Work Journal, 19*(4), 391–403.

Lee-Wright, C. (1990). *Child slaves.* London: Earthscan.

Lester, J.C., & Wilson, D.L. (1972). *Ku Klux Klan: It's origin, growth, and disbandment.* St. Clair Shores, MI: Scholarly Press.

LeVay, S. (1991). A difference in hypothalamic structure between heterosexual and homosexual men. *Science, 253,* 1034–1037.

Leventhal, J.M. (1987). Programs to prevent sexual abuse: What outcomes should be measured? *Child Abuse & Neglect, 11,* 169–171.

Leventhal, J.M., Hamilton, J., Rekedal, S., Tebano-Micci, A., & Eyster, C. (1989). Anatomically correct dolls used in interviews of young children suspected of having been sexually abused. *Pediatrics, 84,* 900–906.

Levin, S., & Stava, L. (1987). Personality characteristics of sex offenders: a review. *Archives of Sexual Behavior, 16,* 57–59.

Levy, B. (1988). Taking care of me: Preventing child sexual abuse in the Hispanic community. In L. Auerbach-Walker (Ed.), *Handbook on sexual abuse of children: Assessment and treatment issues* (pp. 387–401). New York: Springer.

Lewis, D.O., Shanok, S., & Pincus, J. (1981). Juvenile male sexual assaulters: Psychiatric, neurological, psychoeducational and abuse factors. In D.O. Lewis (Ed.), *Vulnerability to delinquency* (pp. 89–105). Jamaica, NY: Spectrum Publications.

Liddell, T., Young, B., & Yamagishi, M. (1988). *Implementation and evaluation of a preschool sexual abuse prevention resource.* Seattle, WA: Department of Human Resources.

Lilly, R., Cummings, J.L., Benson, D.F., & Frankel, M. (1983). The human Kluver-Bucy syndrome. *Neurology, 33,* 1141.

Lindberg, F.H., & Distad, L.J. (1985a). Post-traumatic distress disorder in women who experienced childhood incest. *Child Abuse & Neglect, 9,* 329-334.

Lindberg, F.H., & Distad, L.J. (1985b). Survival responses to incest: Adolescents in crisis. *Child Abuse & Neglect, 9,* 521-526.

Livingston, R. (1987). Sexually and physically abused children. *Journal of the American Academy of Child and Adolescent Psychiatry 26,* 413–415.

Lloyd, R. (1976). *For money or love: Boy prostitution in America.* New York: Vanguard.

Loftus, E.F., & Davies, G.M.T. (1984). Distortions in the memory of children. *Journal of Social issues, 40(2)*, 51–67.

Longo, R.E. (1982). Sexual learning and experience among adolescent sexual offenders. *International Journal of Offender Therapy and Comparative Criminology, 26*, 235–241.

Longo, R.E., & Groth, A.N. (1983). Juvenile sexual offenses in the histories of adult rapists and child molesters. *International Journal of Offender Therapy and Comparative Criminology, 27*, 150–155.

Loredo, C. (1982). Sibling incest. In S. M. Sgroi (Ed.), *Handbook of clinical intervention in child sexual abuse* (pp. 177–188). Lexington, MA: Heath & Co.

Los Angeles Count Commission for Women (1989). Report of ritual abuse task force. *Ritual abuse: Definitions, glossary, and the use of mind control.* 383 Hall of Administration, 500 W. Temple Street, Los Angeles, CA 90012.

Los Angeles Unified School District Elementary Curriculum. (1988). *Child abuse recognize and eliminate curriculum.* Los Angeles, CA: Author.

Losel, F., & Bliesener, T. (1990). Resilience in adolescence: A study on the generalizability of protective factors. In K. Hurrelmann & F. Losel (Eds.), *Health hazards in adolesence* (p. 233). New York: Gruyter.

Lukianowicz, N. (1972). Incest. *British Journal of Psychiatry, 120*, 301–313.

Lum, D. (1986). *Social work practice and people of color.* Monterey, CA: Brooks/ Cole.

Lustig, N., Dresser, J., Spellman, S., & Murray, T. (1966). Incest: A family group survival pattern. *Archives of General Psychiatry, 14,* 13–40.

MacFarlane, K.M., & Korbin, J. (1983). Confronting the incest secret long after the fact: A family study of multiple victimization with strategies for intervention. *Child Abuse & Neglect, 7,* 225–237.

Machotka, P., Pittman, F., & Flomenhaft, F. (1967). Incest as a family affair. *Family Process, 6*(1), 98–116.

MacHovec, F. (1992). Standardizing classification of sex offenders: A 10 factor continua and treatment factor system. *Treating Abuse Today, 2*(6), 17–21.

MacHovec, F.J., & Wieckowski, E. (1992). The 10-FC: Ten-factor continua of classification and treatment criteria for male and female sex offenders. *Medical Psychotherapy, 5*, 53–63.

Mackey, G. (1983). *Bubbylonian encounter*. Kansas Committee for Prevention of Child Abuse, 435 S. Kansas, 2nd floor, Topeka, KS 66603.

Mahler, M.S., Pine, F., & Bergman, A. (1975). T*he psychological birth of the human infant*. New York: Basic Books.

Malenbaum, R., & Russell, A.T. (1987). Multiple personality disorder in an eleven-year-old boy and his mother. *Journal of the American Academy of Child and Adolescent Psychiatry, 26*, 436–439.

Mankoff, A. (1973). *Mankoff's lusty Europe*. New York: Viking Press.

Mannarino, A.P., & Cohen, J.A. (1986). A clinical-demographic study of sexually abused children. *Child Abuse & Neglect, 10*, 17–23.

Mannarino, A.P., Cohen, J.A., Gregor, M. (1989). Emotional and behavioral difficulties in sexually abused girls. *Journal of Interpersonal Violence, 4*, 437–451.

Marchant, R., & Page, M. (1992). Bridging the gap: Investigating the abuse of children with multiple disabilities. *Child Abuse Review, 1*, 179–183.

Margolin, L. (1987). The effects of mother-son incest. *Lifestyles, 8*(2), 104-114.

Margolin, L. (1991). Child sexual abuse by nonrelated caregivers. *Child Abuse & Neglect, 15*, 213–221.

Margolin, L. (1992). Sexual abuse by grandparents. *Child Abuse & Neglect, 16*, 735–741.

Margolin, L., & Craft, J.L. (1989). Sexual abuse by caretakers. *Family Relations, 38*, 450–455.

Margolin, L., & Craft, J.L. (1990). Child abuse by adolescent caregivers. *Child Abuse & Neglect, 14*, 365–373.

Marissakalian, M., Blanchard, E.B., Abel, G.G., & Barlow, D.K. (1975). Responses to complex erotic stimuli in homosexual and heterosexual males. *British Journal of Psychiatry, 126*, 252–257.

Marsell, A.J., Devos, G., & Hsu, F.L.K. (1985). *Culture and self: Asian and Western perspective.* New York: Tavistok.

Marsella, S., & White, G. (1982). *Cultural conceptions of mental health and therapy.* London: Reidel.

Marshall, W.L. (1988). The use of explicit stimuli by rapists, child molesters, and nonoffender males. *Journal of Sex Research, 25,* 267–288.

Marshall, W.L., & Barbaree, H.E. (1990). An integrated theory of the etiology of sexual offending. In W.L. Marshall, D.R. Laws, & H.E. Barbaree (Eds.), *Handbook of sexual assault* (pp. 257–275). New York: Plenum.

Marshall, W.L., Barbaree, H.E., & Butt, J. (1988). Sexual offenders against male children: Sexual preferences. *Behavior Research Therapy, 26*(5), 383–391.

Martin, H.P., Beezley, P., Conway, E.F., & Kempe, C.H. (1974). The development of abused children: A review of the literature and physical, neurologic, and intellectual findings. *Advances in Pediatrics, 21,* 25-73.

Martin, N., & Martin, B. (1990). Sexual abuse: Special considerations when teaching children who have severe learning difficulties. *Mental Handicap, 18,* 69–74.

Martinez, J.L., Jr. (1977). *Chicano psychology.* New York: Academic Press.

Masson, J.M. (1984). *The assault on truth: Freud's suppression of the seduction theory.* New York: Farrar, Straus, & Giroux.

Mathews, J., Matthews, R.K., & Speltz, K. (1989). *Female sexual offenders: An exploratory study.* Orwell, VT: Safer Society Press.

Mathis, J.L. (1972). *Clear thinking about sexual deviations: A new look at an old problem.* Chicago: Nelson-Holt.

Matsuda, B., & Rasmussen, L.A. (1990, November). *Comprehensive plan for juvenile sex offenders: Preliminary report.* Salt Lake City, UT: The Utah Govenor's Council on Juvenile Sex Offenders.

Mayer, A. (1983). *Incest: A treatment manual for therapy with victims, spouses, and offenders.* Holmes Beach, FL: Learning Publications.

Mayer, P. (1988). *Sexual abuse of children with disabilities: A vulnerable population in need of protection.* Paper presented at the National Symposium on Child Abuse, San Diego, CA.

McCaghy, C.H. (1971). Child molesting. *Sexual Behavior, 1,* 16–24.

McCaghy, C.H. (1979, November). *The moral crusade against child pornography.* Paper presented at the meeting of the American Society of Criminology, Philadelphia, PA.

McCarthy, L. (1986). Mother–child incest: Characteristics of the offender. *Child Welfare, 65*(5), 447–458.

McGoldrick, M., Pearce, J., & Giordano, J. (1982). *Ethnicity and family therapy.* New York: Guilford Press.

McGuire, R.J., Carlisle, J.M., & Young, B.G. (1965). Sexual deviations as conditioned behavior: A hypothesis. *Behavior Research and Therapy, 2,* 185–190.

McLeer, S.V., Deblinger, E., Atkins, M.S., Foa, E.B., & Ralphe, D.L. (1988). Post-traumatic stress disorder in sexually abused children. *Journal of the American Academy of Child and Adolescent Psychiatry, 27,* 650–654.

Meiselman, K. (1978). *Incest: A psychological study of cause and effects with treatment recommendations.* San Francisco: Jossey-Bass.

Melton, G. (1988). The improbability of the prevention of sexual abuse. In D. Willis, E.W. Holden, & M. Rosenberg (Eds.), *Prevention of child maltreatment. Developmental and ecological perspectives* (pp. 168–189). New York: John Wiley & Sons.

Messer, A.A. (1969). The "Phaedra complex." *Archives of General Psychiatry, 21,* 213–218.

Mian, M., Wehrspan, W., Klajner-Diamond, H., LeBaron, D., & Winder, C. (1986). Review of 125 children 6 years of age and under who were sexually abused. *Child Abuse & Neglect, 10,* 223–229.

Middleton, B.J. (1989). WHO—We Help Ourselves: A project in anti-victimization. In R.E. Hess & J. DeLeon (Eds.), *The National Mental Health Association: Eight years of involvement in the field of prevention* (pp. 71–79). New York: Haworth Press.

Miller, A. (1981). *Prisoners of childhood.* New York: Basic Books.

Miller, A. (1984). *Thou shalt not be aware: Society's betrayal of the child.* New York: Farrar, Straus, Giroux.

Miller, A. (1990). *Banished knowledge.* New York: Doubleday.

Miller, A. (1991). *Breaking down the walls of silence.* New York: Dutton.

Miller, B.L., Cummings, J.L., McIntryre, H., Ebers, G., & Grode, M. (1986). Hypersexuality or altered sexual preference following brain injury. *Journal of Neurology, Neurosurgery, & Psychiatry, 49*, 867.

Miller, L.C. (1981). *Louisville behavior checklist.* Palo Alto, CA: Western Psychological Services.

Miltenberger, R.G., & Thiesse-Duffy, E. (1988). Evaluation of home-based programs for teaching personal safety skills to children. *Journal of Applied Behavioral Analysis, 21*, 81–87.

Mitchell, J.W. (1992). *Adult female survivors of child sexual abuse by female perpetrators.* Unpublished raw data.

Mohr, J.W., Turner, R.E., & Jerry, M.B. (1964). *Pedophilia and exhibitionism.* Toronto: University of Toronto Press.

Money, J. (1984). Paraphilias: Phenomenology and classifications. *American Journal of Psychotherapy, 38*, 164–179.

Money, J. (1986). *Love maps.* New York: Irvington Publishers.

Moorehead, C. (1989). *Betrayal: Child exploitation in today's world.* London: Barrie and Jenkins.

Morgan, P. (1972). Alcohol and family violence: A review of the literature. *Alcohol and Health Monograph, (1).* Washington, DC: DHHS.

Morgan, S.R. (1987). *Abuse and neglect of handicapped children.* Boston: College-Hill Press.

Morrow, K.B., & Sorrell, G. (1989). Factors affecting self-esteem, depression, and negative behaviors in sexually abused female adolescents. *Journal of Marriage and the Family, 51*, 677–686.

Morse, C.W., Sahler, O.Z., & Friedman, S.B. (1970). A three-year follow-up study of abused and neglected children. *American Journal of Diseases of Children, 120,* 439–446.

Mullen, P.E., Romans-Clarkson, S.E., Walton, V.A., & Herbison, G.P. (1988). Impact of sexual and physical abuse on women's mental health. *Lancet, 1,* 841–845.

Murphy, M. (1982). The family with a handicapped child: A review of the literature. *Development of Behavioral Pediatrics, 3,* 73–81.

Murphy, W.D., Haynes, M.R., Stalgaitis, S.J., & Flanagan, B. (1986). Differential sexual responding among four groups of sexual offenders against children. *Journal of Psychopathic Behavior Assessment, 8,* 339–353.

Murrin, M.R., & Laws, D.R. (1990). The influence of pornography on sexual crimes. In W.L. Marshall, D.R. Laws, & H.E. Barbaree (Eds.), *Handbook of sexual assault: Issues, theories, and treatment of the offender* (pp. 73–91). New York: Plenum Press.

Nash, D. (1981). Legal issues related to child pornography: Legal response. *Child Advocacy and Protection, 2,* 8–9.

Nasjleti, M. (1980). Suffering in silence: The male incest victim. *Child Welfare, 49*(5), 269–275.

National Committee for the Prevention of Child Abuse. (1984). *Summary report: Spiderman and power pack comic on the prevention of sexual abuse.* Chicago: National Committee for the Prevention of Sexual Abuse.

National Committee for the Prevention of Child Abuse. (1988). *Basic facts about child sexual abuse.* Chicago, IL: Author.

National Legal Resource Center for Child Advocacy and Protection (1984). *Child sexual exploitation: Background and legal analysis.* Washington, DC: Young Lawyers Division, American Bar Association.

Neinstein, L.S., Goldenring, J., & Carpenter, S. (1984). Nonsexual transmission of sexually transmitted diseases: An infrequent occurrence. *Pediatrics, 74,* 67–76.

Nelson, D. (1981). *An evaluation of the student outcomes and instructional characteristics of the "You're In Charge" program.* Unpublished manuscript, Utah State Office of Education, Salt Lake City, Utah.

New Larousse encyclopedia of mythology (13th ed.) (1977). (R. Aldington & D. Ames, Trans.). London: Hyman.

Newberger, E. & Newberger, C. (1984, April 26). *Sex with children: Toward a moral policy.* Presented at the Third National Conference on the Sexual Victimization of Children, Washington, D.C.

Nibert, D., Cooper, S., & Ford, J. (1989). Parent's observations of the effects of a sexual abuse prevention program on preschool children. *Child Welfare, 68*(5), 539–546.

Nichols, H.R., & Molinder, I. (1984). *Multiphasic sex inventory manual.* Tacoma, WA: Authors.

Nishio, K., & Blimes, M. (1987). Psychotherapy with Southeast Asian clients. *Professional Psychology, Research and Practice, 18*(4), 342–346.

Noble, P. (1976). Introduction. In E. Kramer (Ed.), *The normal and abnormal love of children* (pp. 5–15). Kansas City, MO: Sheed, Andrews, & McMeel.

Nobles, W.W. (1976). Extended self: Rethinking the so-called "Negro" self-concept. *Journal of Black Psychology, 2*, 2–8.

O'Brien, M.J. (1991). Taking sibling incest seriously. In M. Patton (Ed.), *Family sexual abuse patterns* (pp. 75–92). Newbury Park, CA: Sage.

O'Brien, M.J., & Bera, W.H. (1986). Adolescent sexual offenders: A descriptive typology, *Preventing Sexual Abuse, 1,* 1–4.

O'Brien, S. (1983). *Child pornography.* Dubuque, IA: Kendall-Hunt.

O'Day, B. (1983). *Preventing sexual abuse of persons with disabilities: A curriculum for hearing impaired, physically disabled, blind, and mentally retarded students.* Santa Cruz, CA: Network Publications.

O'Neil, J.A., Meacham, W.F., & Griffin, R.P. (1973). Patterns of injury in the battered child syndrome. *Journal of Trauma, 13,* 332.

Oates, R.K. (Ed.). (1990). *Understanding and managing child sexual abuse.* Philadelphia: Harcourt, Brace, Jovanovich.

Ogata, S.N , Silk, K.R., Goodrich, S., Lohr, N.E., Westen, D., & Hill, E.M. (1990). Childhood sexual and physical abuse in adult patients with borderline personality disorder. *American Journal of Psychiatry, 147,* 1008–1013.

Orr, D.P. (1980). Management of childhood sexual abuse. *Journal of Family Practice, 11,* 1057–1064.

Orr, D.P., & Prietto, S.V. (1979). Emergency management of sexually abused children. *American Journal of Diseases of Children, 133,* 628–631.

Ounce of Prevention Fund (1987). *Child sexual abuse: A hidden factor in adolescent sexual behavior.* Chicago, IL: Ounce of Prevention Fund.

Overholser, J.C., & Beck, S. (1986). Multimethod assessment of rapists, child molesters, and three control groups on behavioral and psychological measures. *Journal of Consulting and Clinical Psychology, 54*(5), 682–687.

Pacht, A.R., & Cowden, J.E. (1974). An exploratory study of five hundred sex offenders. *Criminal Justice Behavior, 1,* 13–20.

Padilla, A.M., Ruiz, R.A., & Alvarez, R. (1975). Community mental health services for the Spanish-speaking surnames population. *American Psychologist, 30,* 892–905.

Paley, V. (1988). *Bad guys don't have birthdays: Fantasy play at four.* Chicago, IL: University of Chicago Press.

Paley, V. (1990). *The boy who would be a helicopter.* Boston, MA: Harvard University Press.

Paley, V.G. (1984). *Boys and girls: Superheroes in the doll corner.* Chicago: University of Chicago Press.

Panton, J. (1978). Personality differences appearing between rapists of adults, rapists of children, and non-violent sexual molesters of children. *Research Communications in Psychological Psychiatry and Behavior, 3,* 385–393.

Paradise, J.E. (1990). The medical evaluation of the sexually abused child. *Pediatric Clinics of North America, 37,* 839–862.

Patterson, S. (1986). *Preschool curriculum.* Marin, CA: Touch Safety Program.

Pawlak, A., Boulet, J., & Bradford, J. (1991). Discriminant analysis of a sexual-functioning inventory with intrafamilial and extrafamilial child molesters. *Archives of Sexual Behavior, 20,* 27–34.

Peake, A. (1989). Issue of under-reporting: The sexual abuse of boys. *Educational and Child Psychology, 6,* 42–50.

Pedersen, P. (1988). *A handbook for developing multicultural awareness.* Alexandria, VA: American Association of Counseling and Development.

Pelto, V. (1981). *Male incest offenders and non-offenders: A comparison of early sexual history* (dissertation). Ann Arbor, MI: United States International University, University Microfilms.

Perry, G.P., & Orchard, J. (1992). *Assessment and treatment of adolescent sex offenders.* Sarasota, FL: Professional Resource Press.

Perry, G.P., & Orchard, J.M. (1989). Assessment and treatment of adolescent sex offenders. In P.A. Keller & S.R. Heyman (Eds.), *Innovations in clinical practice: A sourcebook (Volume 8)* (pp.187–211). Sarasota, FL: Professional Resource Exchange.

Pescosolido, F.J. (1992). Sexual abuse of boys by males: Theoretical and treatment implications. *Treating Abuse Today, 2*(2), 10–13.

Peterfreund, E. (1978). Some critical comments on psychoanalytic conceptualizations of childhood. *International Journal of Psychoanalysis, 59,* 427–441.

Peters, J.J. (1976). Children who are victims of sexual assault and the psychology of the offenders. *American Journal of Psychotherapy, 30,* 398–421.

Peters, S.D. (1988). Child sexual abuse and later psychological problems. In G.E. Wyatt & G.J. Powells (Eds.), *Lasting effects of child sexual abuse* (pp. 101-117). Newbury Park, CA: Sage.

Peters, S.D., Wyatt, G.E., & Finkelhor, D. (1986). Prevalence. In D. Finkelhor (Ed.), *A sourcebook on child sexual abuse* (pp. 15–59). Beverly Hills, CA: Sage.

Peterson, G. (1991). Children coping with trauma: Diagnosis of "dissociation identity disorders." *Dissociation, 4*(3), 152–164.

Piaget, J. (1952). *The origins of intelligence in children.* New York: International Universities Press.

Piaget, J. (1962). *The moral judgement of the child.* New York: Collier. (Original work published 1932)

Pierce, R., & Pierce, L.H. (1985). The sexually abused child: A comparison of male and female victims. *Child Abuse & Neglect, 9,* 191–199.

Pierce, R.L. (1984). Child pornography: A hidden dimension of child abuse. *Child Abuse & Neglect, 8,* 483–493.

Plummer, C. (1984a). *Preventing sexual abuse: Activities and strategies for working with children and adolescents.* Holmes Beach, FL: Learning Publications.

Plummer, C. (1984b). *Preventing sexual abuse: What in-school programs teach children.* Unpublished manuscript.

Plummer, K. (1981). Pedophilia: Constructing a sociological baseline. In M. Cook & K. Howells (Eds.), *Adult sexual interest in children* (pp. 221–250). New York: New York Academic Press.

Poche, C., Brouwer, R., & Swearingen, M. (1981). Teaching self-protection to young children. *Journal of Applied Behavior Analysis, 14,* 169–176.

Porch, T.L., & Petretic-Jackson, P.A. (1986, August). *Child sexual assault prevention: Evaluating parent education workshops.* Paper presented at the 94th annual convention of the American Psychological Association, Washington, DC.

Porter, B., & O'Leary, D. (1989). Marital discord and childhood behavior problems. *Journal of Abnormal Psychology, 8,* 287-295.

Putnam, F.W. (1984). The psychophysiological investigation of multiple personality disorder. *Psychiatric Clinics of America, 7,* 31–41.

Putnam, F.W. (1985). Dissociation as a response to extreme trauma. In R. P. Kluft (Ed.), *Childhood antecedents of multiple personality* (pp. 66–97). Washington, DC: American Psychiatric Press.

Putnam, F.W. (1989). *Diagnosis and treatment of multiple personality disorder.* New York: Guilford.

Putnam, F.W. (1991). The satanic ritual abuse controversy. *Child Abuse & Neglect, 15*, 175–179.

Quinsey, V.L. (1977). The assessment and treatment of child molesters. *Canadian Psychological Review, 18*, 204–220.

Quinsey, V.L., & Laws, D.R. (1990). Validity of physiological measures of pedophilic sexual arousal in a sex offender population: A critique of Hall, Proctor, and Nelson. *Journal of Consulting and Clinical Psychology, 58*, 886–888.

Quintano, J.H. (1992). Case profiles of early childhood enema abuse. *Treating Abuse Today, 2*, 11–13.

Rada, R.T. (1976). Alcoholism and the child molester. *Annals of the New York Academy of Science, 272*, 492–496.

Rada, R.T. (Ed.). (1978). *Clinical aspects of the rapist.* New York: Grune & Stratton.

Raglan, L. (1933). *Jocasta's crime: An anthropological study.* London: Methuen.

Raschke, C.A. (1990). *Painted black.* New York: Harper Collins.

Rasmussen, L.A., Burton, J.E., & Christopherson, B.J. (1992). Precursors to offending and the trauma outcome process in sexually reactive children. *Journal of Child Sexual Abuse, 1*(1), 33–48.

Ray, J. (1984). *Evaluation of the child sexual abuse prevention program.* Available from the Rape Crisis Network, N. 1226 Howard, Spokane, WA 99201.

Ray, J., & Dietzel, M. (1985). Teaching child sexual abuse prevention. *School of Social Work Journal, 1*, 100–108.

Ray, J., & Dietzel, M. (1984). *Teaching child sexual abuse prevention.* Unpublished manuscript.

Ray-Keil, A. (1989). *Intersect: Of social theory and management practice in preventing children's exploitation.* Seattle, WA: Committee for Children.

Realmuto, G.M., & Wescoe, S. (1992). Agreement among professionals about a child's sexual abuse status: Interviews with sexually anatomically correct dolls as indicators of abuse. *Child Abuse & Neglect, 16*, 719–725.

Reiker, P., & Carmen, E. (1986). The victim-to-patient process: The disconfirmation and transformation of abuse. *American Journal of Orthopsychiatry, 56,* 360–370.

Renfro, N. (1984). *Puppetry, language and the special child.* Austin, TX: Nancy Renfro Studio.

Report of the Ritual Abuse Task Force, Los Angeles County Commission for Women (p. 1). (1989, September 15). Copies available from Los Angeles County Commission for Women, 383 Hall of Administration, 500 West Temple Street, Los Angeles, CA 90012.

Reppucci, N., & Haugaard, J. (1989). Prevention'of child sexual abuse: Myth or reality. *American Psychologist, 44,* 1266–1275.

Rew, L., & Esparza, D. (1990). Barriers to disclosure among sexually abused male children. *Journal of Child and Adolescent Psychiatric and Mental Health Nursing, 3,* 120–127.

Rich, J.M., & DeVitis, J.L. (1985). *Theories of moral development.* Springfield, IL: Charles C. Thomas.

Richardson, J., Loss, P., & Ross, J.E. (1988). *Psychoeducational curriculum for the adolescent sex offender.* Order by contacting: Ross, Loss, & Associates, P. O. Box 666, Mystic, CT 06355-0666.

Ridgeway, S.M. (1993). Abuse and deaf children: Some factors to consider. *Child Abuse Review, 2,* 166–173.

Riley, R.I., & Mead, J. (1988). The development of symptoms of multiple personality disorder in a child of three. *Dissociation, 1*(4), 43–46.

Rogers, C.M., & Terry, T. (1984). Clinical intervention with boy victims of sexual abuse. In I.R. Stuart & J.G. Greer (Eds.), *Victims of sexual aggression: Treatment of children, women, and men* (pp. 91–104). New York: Van Nostrand Reinhold.

Root, M.P.P. (1985). Guidelines for facilitating therapy with Asian-American clients. *Psychotherapy, 22,* 349–356.

Root, M.P.P., & Fallon, P. (1988). The incidence of victimization experiences in a bulimic sample. *Journal of Interpersonal Violence, 3,* 161–173.

Rosenfeld, A.A. (1979). The clinical management of incest and sexual abuse of children. *Journal of the American Medical Association, 242,* 1761–1764.

Rosenthal, T.L., & Zimmerman, B.J. (1978). *Social learning and cognition.* New York: Academic Press.

Ross, C.A. (1989). *Multiple personality disorder: Diagnosis, clinical features, treatment.* New York: John Wiley & Sons.

Roth, N. (1993). *Integrating the shattered self: Psychotherapy with adult incest survivors.* Northvale, NJ: Jason Aronson.

Rothblum, E.D., Solomon, L.J., Albee, G.W. (1986). A sociopolitical perspective of DSM-III. In T. Millon & G. L. Klerman (Eds.), *Contemporary directions in psychopathology: Toward the DSM-IV* (pp. 167–189). New York: Guilford Press.

Rouleau, J.L., Abel, G.G., Mittleman, M.S., Becker, J.V., & Cunningham-Rathner, J. (1986, February). *Effectiveness of each component of a treatment program for non-incarcerated pedophiles.* Paper presented at the NIMH sponsored conference on sex offenders, Tampa, FL.

Runtz, M., & Briere, J. (1986). Adolescent "acting out" and childhood history of sexual abuse. *Journal of Interpersonal Violence, 1,* 326–334.

Runtz, M.G. (1987). *The sexual victimization of women: The link between child abuse and victimization.* Paper presented at the annual meeting of the Canadian Psychological Association, Vancouver, BC.

Rush, F. (1980). *The best kept secret: Sexual abuse of children.* Englewood Cliffs: Prentice-Hall.

Russell, D.E.H. (1975). *The politics of rape.* New York: Stein & Day.

Russell, D.E.H. (1983). The incidence and prevalence of intrafamilial and extrafamilial sexual abuse of female children. *Child Abuse & Neglect, 1,* 133–146.

Russell, D.E.H. (1984a). The prevalence and seriousness of incestuous abuse: Stepfathers vs. biological fathers. *Child Abuse & Neglect, 8,* 15–22.

Russell, D.E.H. (1984b). *Sexual exploitation: Rape, child sexual abuse, and workplace harassment.* Beverly Hills, CA: Sage.

Russell, D.E.H. (1986). *The secret trauma: Incest in the lives of girls and women.* New York: Basic Books.

Ryan, G.D., Metzner, J.L., & Krugman, R.D. (1990). When the abuser is a child. In R. K. Oates (Ed.), *Understanding and managing child sexual abuse* (pp. 258–273). Philadelphia: W. B. Saunders.

Ryan, M.G., Davis, A.A. & Oates, R.K. (1977). One hundred and eighty-seven cases of child abuse and neglect. *Medical Journal of Australia, 2,* 623.

Ryan, M.T. (1984). Identifying the sexually abused child. *Pediatric Nursing, 10,* 419–421.

Ryder, D. (1992). *Breaking the cycle of satanic ritual abuse: Recognizing and recovering from the hidden trauma.* Minneapolis, MN: Compcare Publishers.

Sanday, P.R. (1981). The socio-cultural context of rape: A cross-cultural study. *Journal of Social Issues, 37,* 5–27.

Sanford, L. (1980). *The silent children: A parent's guide to the prevention of child sexual abuse.* New York: Doubleday.

Sanford, L. (1982). *Come tell me right away.* Fayetteville, NY: Ed-U-Press.

Sangrund, H., Gaines, R., & Green, A. (1974). Child abuse and mental retardation: A problem of cause and effect. *American Journal of Mental Deficiency, 79,* 327–330.

Sansonnet-Hayden, H., Haley, G., Marriage, K., & Fine, S. (1987). Sexual abuse and psychopathology in hospitalized adolescents. *Journal of the American Academy of Child and Adolescent Psychiatry, 26,* 753–757.

Sarles, R. (1975). Incest. *Pediatric Clinics of North America. 22*(3), 637.

Sarrel, P., & Masters, W. (1982). Sexual molestations of men by women. *Archives of Sexual Behavior, 11*(2), 117–131.

Saslawsky, D., & Wurtele, S. (1986). Educating children about sexual abuse. Implication for pediatric intervention and possible intervention. *Journal of Pediatric Psychology, 11*(2), 235–243.

Sattem. L., Savells, J., & Murray, E. (1984). Sex-role stereotypes and commitment of rape. *Sex Roles, 11*, 849–860.

Saywitz, K. (1987). Children's testimony: Age-related patterns of memory errors. In S.J. Ceci, M.P. Toglia, & D.F. Ross (Eds.), *Children's eyewitness memory* (pp. 142–154). New York: Springer-Verlag.

Schindehett, S. (1990, February 5). After the verdict, solace for none. *People Weekly, 33*(5), 75.

Schneider, J.W. (1987). *Suggestibility in children: What role does memory play? Unpublished paper.* Erikson Institute for Advanced Study in Child Development, Chicago, IL.

Schor, E.L. (1982). The foster care system and health status of foster children. *Pediatrics, 69*, 521–528.

Schultz, L.G. (1982). Child sexual abuse in historical perspective. *Journal of Social Work and Human Sexuality, 1*, 21–35.

Schwartz, M.F., & Masters, W.H. (1983). Conceptual factors in the treatment of paraphilias: A preliminary report. *Journal of Sex and Marital Therapy, 9*, 3–18.

Scott, R.L., & Stone, P.A. (1986). MMPI profile constellations in incest families. *Journal of Consulting and Clinical Psychology, 54*, 364–368.

Sedney, M.A., & Brooks, B. (1984). Factors associated with a history of childhood sexual experience in a nonclinical female population. *Journal of the American Academy of Child Psychiatry, 23*, 215–218.

Segal, Z.V., & Marshall, W.L. (1985). Heterosexual social skills in a population of rapists and child molesters. *Journal of Consulting and Clinical Psychology, 53*, 55–63.

Segal, Z.V., & Marshall, W.L. (1986). Discrepancies between self-efficacy predictors and actual performance in a population of rapists and child molesters. *Cognitive Therapy and Research, 10*(3), 363–376.

Seghorn, T., Prentky, R.A., & Boucher, R.J. (1987). Childhood sexual abuse in the lives of sexually aggressive offenders. *Journal of the American Academy of Child and Adolescent Psychiatry, 26*, 262–267.

Seghorn, T.K. (1981, August). *The decision tree: Factors in the clinical subtyping of sexually dangerous persons.* Presented at the American Psychological Association annual meeting in Los Angeles.

Sgroi, S., Blick, L.C., & Porter, F.S. (1982). A conceptual framework for child sexual abuse. In S. Sgroi (Ed.), *Handbook of clinical intervention in child sexual abuse* (pp. 9–37). Lexington, MA: Lexington Books.

Sgroi, S.M., & Bunk, B.S. (1988). A clinical approach to adult survivors of child sexual abuse. In S.M. Sgroi (Ed.), *Vulnerable populations: Evaluation and treatment of sexually abused children (Volume 1)* (pp. 137–186). Lexington, MA: Lexington Books.

Sgroi, S.M., Carey, J.A., & Wheaton, A.B. (1989). Sexual abuse avoidance training for adults with mental retardation. In S.M. Sgroi (Ed.), *Vulnerable populations: Volume 2* (pp. 203–244). Lexington, MA: Lexington Books.

Shapiro, J. (1983). Family reactions and coping strategies in response to the physically ill or handicapped child: A review. *Social Science Medicine, 17,* 919–920.

Shearer, S.L., Peters, C.P., Quaytman, M.S., & Ogden, R.L. (1990). Frequency and correlates of childhood sexual and physical abuse histories with adult female borderline inpatients. *American Journal of Psychiatry, 147,* 214–216.

Showers, J., Farber, E., Joseph, J., Oshins, L., & Johnson, C. (1983). The sexual victimizations of boys: A three year survey. *Health Values, 7,* 15–18.

Showers, J., & Johnson, C.F. (1988). *Diagnosis and management of sexual abuse of children: A self-instructional program.* Columbus, OH: Children's Hospital.

Sigel, J., Sorenson, S., Golding, J., Burnam, M., & Stein, J. (1987). The prevalence of childhood sexual assault: The Los Angeles epidemiologic catchment area project. *American Journal of Epidemiology, 126,* 1141–1153.

Sigurdson, E., Strang, M., & Doig, T. (1987). What do children know about preventing sexual assault? How can their awareness be increased? *Canadian Journal of Psychiatry, 32,* 551–557.

Silbert, M.H., & Pines, A.M. (1981). Sexual child abuse as an antecedent to prostitution. *Child Abuse & Neglect, 5,* 407–411.

Silbert, M.H., & Pines, A.M. (1984). Pornography and sexual abuse of women. *Sex Roles, 10,* 857–868.

Silverman, F.N. (1954). Roentgen manifestations of unrecognized skeletal trauma in infants. *American Journal of Roentgenology, 69,* 413–427.

Singer, M.I., Hussey, D., & Strom, K.J. (1992). Grooming the victim: An analysis of a perpetrator's seduction letter. *Child Abuse & Neglect, 16,* 877–886.

Sirles, E.A., Smith, J.A., & Kusama, H. (1989). Psychiatric status of intrafamilial child sexual abuse victims. *Journal of the American Academy of Child & Adolescent Psychiatry, 28,* 225–229.

Sivan, A.B., Schor, D.P., Koeppl, G.K., & Noble, L.D. (1988). Interaction of normal children with anatomical dolls. *Child Abuse & Neglect, 12,* 295–304.

Sloane, P., & Karpinski, E. (1942). Effects of incest on participants. *American Journal of Orthopsychiatry, 12,* 666–673.

Smetana, J.G. (1984). Toddlers' social interactions regarding moral and social rules. *Child Development, 52,* 1333–1336.

Smith, E.M.J. (1989). Black racial identity development. *The Counseling Psychologist, 17*(2), 277–288.

Smith, H., & Israel, E. (1987). Sibling incest: A study of the dynamics of 25 cases. *Child Abuse & Neglect, 11,* 101–108.

Snowden, C. (1988). *Where are all the childhood multiples? Identifying incipient multiple personality in children* [Summary]. Proceedings of the Fifth International Conference on Multiple Personality/Dissociative States.

Sobsey, D. (1993). Responding to the needs of sexually abused children with disabilities: Program criteria. *Journal of Child Sexual Abuse, 2,* 131–133.

Sobsey, D., & Doe, T. (1991). Patterns of sexual abuse and assault. *Journal of Sexuality and Disability, 9,* 243–259.

Sobsey, D., & Varnhagen, C. (1988). *Sexual abuse and exploitation of people with disabilities: A study of the victims.* Unpublished manuscript. Department of Educational Psychology, University of Alberta, Edmonton.

Solnit, A.J., & Stark, M.H. (1961). Mourning the birth of a defective child. *Psychoanalytic Study of the Child, 16,* 523.

Solomon, R. (1983). The use of MMPI with multiple personality patients. *Psychological Reports, 53,* 1004–1006.

Solomon, R.L. (1949). An extention of the control group design. *Psychological Bulletin, 46,* 137-150.

Spiegel, D. (1986). Dissociation, double binds, and posttraumatic stress in multiple personality disorder. In B.G. Braun (Ed.), *Treatment of multiple personality disorder* (pp. 72). Washington, DC: American Psychiatric Press, Inc.

Sprinthall, N.A., & Sprinthall, R.C. (1987). *Educational psychology: A developmental approach* (4th ed.). Reading, MA: Addison Wesley.

Sroufe, A. (1977). Wariness of strangers and the study of infant development. *Child Development, 48,* 731–746.

Steele, B.R., & Pollock, C.B. (1968). A psychiatric study of parents who abuse infants and small children. In R.E. Helfer & C.H. Kempe (Eds.), *The battered child* (pp. 103–147). Chicago: University of Chicago Press.

Steele, K., & Colrain, J. (1990). Abreaction work with sexual abuse survivors: Concepts and techniques. In M. Hinter (Ed.), *The sexually abused male: Application of treatment strategies Volume 2* (pp. 1–55). Lexington, MA: Lexington Books.

Stenson, P., & Anderson, C. (1987). Treating juvenile offenders and preventing the cycle of abuse. *Journal of Child Care, 3,* 91–101.

Stermac, L., & Segal, Z. (1987, November). *Cognitive assessment of child molesters.* Paper presented at the 21st annual convention of the Association for the Advancement of Behavior Therapy, Boston, MA.

Stern, C.R. (1984). The etiology of multiple personality. *Psychiatric Clinics of North America, 7,* 149–160.

Stern, D. (1977). *The first relationship.* Cambridge, MA: Harvard University Press.

Stern, D. (1985). Human intelligence: The model is the message. *Science, 230,* 1111–1117.

Stickrod, A. (1989, October). *New concepts in sexual abuse recovery: Healing the effects of trauma.* Proceedings of the Fourth Annual Training Conference on the Treatment of Juvenile Sex Offenders, Salt Lake City, UT.

Stillwell, S.L., Lutzker, J.R., & Greene, B.F. (1988). Evaluation of a sexual abuse prevention program for preschoolers. *Journal of Family Violence, 13* (4), 269–281.

Stokes, R.E. (1964). A research approach to sexual offenses involving children. *Canadian Journal of Corrections, 6,* 87–94.

Stoller, R.J. (1975). *Perversion: The erotic form of hatred.* New York: Pantheon.

Stoller, R.J. (1979). *Sexual excitement: Dynamics of erotic life.* New York: Pantheon.

Stoller, R.J. (1985). *Observing the erotic imagination.* New Haven: Yale University Press.

Storr, A. (1964). *Sexual deviation.* Baltimore, MD: Penguin Books.

Stowell, J., & Dietzel, M. (1982). *My very own book about me.* Spokane, WA: Lutheran Social Services.

Strauss, A.S. (1977). Northern Cheyenne ethnopsychology. *Ethos, 5,* 326–357.

Stricker, G. (1967). Stimulus properties of the Blacky to a sample of pedophiles. *Journal of General Psychology, 77,* 35–39.

Sue, D.W., Arredondo, P., & McDavis, R.J. (1992). Multicultural counseling competencies and standards: A call to the profession. *Journal of Counseling and Development, 70,* 477–486.

Sue, D.W., Bernier, J.E., Durran, A., Feinberg, L., Pedersen, P., Smith, C.J., & Vasquez-Nuttall, G. (1982). Cross-cultural counseling competencies. *The Counseling Psychologist, 19*(2), 45–52.

Sue, D.W., & Sue, S. (1972). Counseling Chinese Americans. *Personnel and Guidance Journal, 50,* 637–645.

Sue, D.W., & Sue, D. (1990). *Counseling the culturally different: Theory and practice.* New York: Wiley.

Sullivan, P.M. (1993). Sexual abuse therapy for special children. *Journal of Child Sexual Abuse, 2,* 117–125.

Sullivan, P.M., Brookhouser, P.E., Scanlan, J.M., Knutson, J.F., & Schulte, L.E. (1991). Patterns of physical and sexual abuse of communicatively handicapped children. *Annals of Otology, Rhinology, & Laryngology, 100*(3), 188–194.

Sullivan, P.M., & Scanlan, J.M. (1987). Therapeutic issues. In J. Garbarino, P.E. Brookhouser, & K.J. Authier (Eds.), *Special children–special risks: The maltreatment of children with disabilities* (pp. 127–159). New York: deGruyter.

Sullivan, P.M., & Scanlan, J.M. (1988). *Abuse issues with handicapped children.* Paper presented at the National Symposium on Child Abuse, San Diego, CA.

Sullivan, P.M., Scanlan, J.M., Brookhouser, P.E., Schulte, L.E., & Knutson, J.F. (1992). The effects of psychotherapy on behavior problems of sexually abused deaf children. *Child Abuse & Neglect, 16,* 297–307.

Sullivan, P.M., Vernon, M., & Scanlan, J.M. (1987). Sexual abuse of deaf youth. *American Annals of the Deaf, 3,* 256–262.

Summit, R. (1983). The child sexual abuse accommodation syndrome. *Child Abuse & Neglect, 1,* 177–193.

Summit, R.C. (1990). A specific vulnerability of children. In R.K. Oates (Ed.), *Understanding and managing child sexual abuse* (pp. 59–74). Philadelphia: Harcourt Brace Jovanovich Publishers.

Summit, R.C., & Kryso, J. (1978). Sexual abuse of children: A clinical spectrum. *American Journal of Orthopsychiatry, 48,* 237–251.

Swan, H.L., Press, A.N., & Briggs, S.L. (1985). Child sexual abuse prevention: Does it work? *Child Welfare, 64,* 395–405.

Swanson, D.W. (1971). Who violates children sexually? *Medical Aspects of Human Sexuality, 5,* 184–197.

Symonds, M. (1980). *The "second injury" to victims.* [Special issue]. *Evaluation and Change, 1,* 36–38.

Talking about touching: A personal safety curriculum. Seattle, WA: Seattle Institute for Child Advocacy, Committee for Children, 172 20th Avenue, Seattle, WA 98122.

Tate, T. (1990). *Child pornography: An investigation.* London: Methuen.

Tew, B., & Laurence, K. (1975). Some sources of stress found in mothers of spina bifida children. *British Journal of Preventive Social Medicine, 29,* 27–30.

Tharinger, D., Horton, C.B., & Millea, S. (1990). Sexual abuse and exploitation of children and adults with mental retardation and other handicaps. *Child Abuse & Neglect, 14,* 301–312.

Tharinger, D.J., Krivacka, J.J., Laye-McDonough, M., Jamison, L., Vincent, G.G., & Hedlund, A.D. (1988). Prevention of child sexual abuse: An analysis of issues, educational programs, and research findings. *School Psychology Review, 17*(4), 614–634.

Thomas, J. (1981). Child sexual abuse victim assistance project. Research Foundation of Children's Hospital, Washington, DC. Personal communication cited in A.N. Groth & C. Loredo (Eds.), Juvenile sex offenders: Guidelines for assessment. *International Journal of Offender Therapy and Comparative Criminology, 25,* 31–39.

Thompson, V.L.S., & Smith, S. (1993). Attitudes of African-American adults toward treatment in cases of child sexual abuse. *Journal of Child Sexual Abuse, 2,* 5–19.

Tobin, P., Levinson, S., Russell, T., & Valdez, M. (1983). *Children's self-help project.* Elementary School Curriculum, 3368 22nd St., San Francisco, CA 94110.

Tollison, C.D., & Adams, H.E. (1979). *Sexual disorders: Treatment, theory, and research.* New York: Gardner Press.

Tong, B. (1971). The ghetto of the mind: Notes on the historical psychology of Chinese Americans. *Amerasia Journal, 1,* 28.

Tong, L., Oates, K., & McDowell, M. (1987). Personality development following sexual abuse. *Child Abuse & Neglect, 11,* 371–383.

The touch program. (1987). Brochure available from The Touch Program, P. O. Box 52, San Luis Obispo, CA 93406.

Trepper, T., & Barrett, M.J. (1989). *Systematic treatment of incest: A therapeutic handbook.* New York: Brunner/Mazel.

Trevelyan, J. (1988). When it's difficult to say no. *Nursing Times, 84,* 16–17.

Trout, M. (1983). Birth of a sick or handicapped infant: Impact on the family. *Child Welfare, 63,* 337–348.

Trumbach, R. (1977). London's sodomites: Homosexual behavior and Western culture in eighteenth century. *Journal of Social History, 11,* 1–33.

Truong, T. (1990). *Sex, money, and morality: Prostitution and tourism in Southeast Asia.* London: Zed Books.

Tsai, M., Feldman-Summers, S., & Edgar, M. (1979). Childhood molestation: Variables related to differential impacts of psychosexual functioning in adult women. *Journal of Abnormal Psychology, 88,* 407–417.

Tufts New England Medical Center, Division of Child Psychiatry. (1984). *Sexually exploited children: Service and research project.* (Final report for the Office of Juvenile Justice and Delinquency Prevention.) Washington, DC: U.S. Department of Justice.

Tutty, L.M. (1990). Preventing child sexual abuse: A review of current research and theory. In M. Rothery & G. Cameron (Eds.), *Child maltreatment: Expanding our concept of helping* (pp. 259–275). Hillsdale, NJ: Lawrence Erlbaum Associates.

Tutty, L.M. (1991, Fall). Child sexual abuse prevention programs: A range of options. *Journal of Child and Youth Care,* 23–41.

Tutty, L.M. (1992). The ability of elementary school children to learn child sexual abuse prevention concepts. *Child Abuse & Neglect, 16,* 369–384.

Tutty, L.M. (1993). Parent's perceptions of their child's knowledge of sexual abuse prevention concepts. *Journal of Child Sexual Abuse, 2,* 83–103.

Tyler, R.P., & Stone, L.E. (1985). Child pornography: Perpetuating the sexual victimization of children. *Child Abuse & Neglect, 9,* 313–318.

United Nations (1992). UN Commission on Human Rights. *Program of action for the prevention of the sale of children, child prostitution and child pornog-*

raphy and for the elimination of child labor (Resolution 1992/74). New York: Author.

United States Department of Health and Human Services. (1988a). *Study findings: Study of the national incidence and prevalence of child abuse and neglect.* Washington, DC: Author.

United States Department of Health and Human Services. (1988b). *Study of national incidence and prevalence of child abuse and neglect.* Washington, DC: Author.

van der Kolk, B., & Kadish, W. (1987). Amnesia, dissociation, and the return of the repressed. In B. van der Kolk (Ed.), *Psychological trauma* (p. 186). Washington, DC: American Psychiatric Press.

VanNess, S.R. (1984). Rape as instrumental violence: A study of youth offenders. *Journal of Offender Counseling Services and Rehabilitation, 9,* 161–170.

Vermont Department of Health (1985). Adolescent sex offenders—Vermont, 1984. Morbidity and mortality weekly report. *Journal of the American Medical Association, 255* (2), 181.

Violato, C., & Mark Genuis, M. (1993). Problems of research in male child sexual abuse: A review. *Journal of Child Sexual Abuse, 2,* 33–54.

Virkkunen, M. (1976). The pedophilic offender with antisocial character. *Acta Psychiatria Scandinavia, 53,* 401–405.

Voigt, D.R. (1984). *Male and female role attitudes and perceived quality of life among Hmong refugees.* Unpublished master's thesis, University of Nebraska, Lincoln.

Volpe, R. (1984). A psychoeducational program dealing with child abuse for elementary school children. *Child Abuse & Neglect, 8,* 511–517.

Vontress, C.E. (1981). Racial and ethnic barriers in counseling. In P. Pedersen, J. Draguns, W. Lonner, & J. Trimble (Eds.), *Counseling across cultures: Revised and expanded edition* (pp. 87–107). Honolulu: University of Hawaii Press.

Wahl, C. (1960). The psychodynamics of consummated maternal incest. *Archives of General Psychiatry, 3,* 188–193.

Wald, M.S., & Cohen, S. (1986). Preventing child abuse: What will it take? *Family Law Quarterly, 20*, 281–302.

Walker, C., Bonner, B., & Kaufman, K. (1988). *The physically and sexually abused child.* New York: Pergamon Press.

Wallerstein, J.S., & Kelly, J.B. (1980). *Surviving the break-up: How children and parents cope with divorce.* New York: Basic Books.

Walters, D. (1975). *Physical and sexual abuse of children.* Bloomington: Indiana University Press.

Ward, E. (1985). *Father–daughter rape.* New York: Grove Press.

Warnke, L. (1986). *The philosophy and practice of Satanism.* Danville, KY: Warnke Industries.

Wasserman, J., Kappel, S., Coffin, R., Aronson, R., & Walton, A.J. (1986). Adolescent sex offenders—Vermont, 1984. *Journal of the American Medical Association, 255,* 181–182.

Waterman, J., Kelly, R.J., Oliveri, M.K., & McCord, J. (1993). *Behind the playground walls: Sexual abuse in preschools.* New York: Guilford.

Waters, F.S. (1989). *Non-hypnotic therapeutic techniques of multiple personality disorder in children* [Summary]. Proceedings of the Sixth International Conference on Multiple Personality/Dissociative States.

Weiner, I. (1964). On incest: A survey. *Excerpta Criminologica, 4,* 37.

Weiss, J., Rogers, E., Darwin, M.R., & Dutton, C.E. (1955). A study of girl sex victims. *Psychiatric Quarterly, 29,* 1–27.

Weiss, M., Sutton, P., & Utecht, A.J. (1985). Multiple personality in a ten-year-old girl. *Journal of the American Academy of Child and Adolescent Psychiatry, 24,* 495–501.

Weissman, H.N. (1991). Forensic psychological examination of the child witness in cases of alleged sexual abuse. *American Journal of Orthopsychiatry, 6,* 48–58.

Welldon, E.V. (1988). *Mother, madonna, whore: The idealization and denigration of motherhood.* New York: Guilford Press.

West, D.J. (!977). *Homosexuality re-examined.* London: Duckworth.

Westcott, H. (1991). The abuse of disabled children: A review of the literature. *Child: Care, Health, and Development, 17,* 243–258.

Westermeyer, J. (1986). Migration and psychopathology. In C.L. Williams & J. Westermeyer (Eds.), *Refugee mental health in resettlement countries* (pp. 39–60). Washington, DC: Hemisphere.

Westermeyer, J., & Williams, C.L. (1986). Planning mental health services for refugees. In C.L. Williams & J. Westermeyer (Eds.), *Refugee mental health in resettlement countries* (pp. 235–245). Washington, DC: Hemisphere.

Wheeler, C. (1989). Faulty fathering: Working ideas on the treatment of male incest perpetrators. *Journal of Feminist Family Therapy, 1,* 27–48.

White, J.L., & Parham, T.A. (1990). *The psychology of Blacks.* Englewood Cliffs, NJ: Prentice-Hall.

White, R.B., Benedict, M.I., Wulff, L.M., & Kelley, M. (1987). Physical disabilities as risk factors for child maltreatment: A selected review. *American Journal of Orthopsychiatry, 57*(1), 93–101.

White, S., & Santilli, G. (1988). A review of clinical practices and research data on anatomical dolls. *Journal of Interpersonal Violence, 3,* 430–442.

White, S., Strom, G.A., Santilli, G., & Halpin, B.M. (1986). Interviewing young sexual abuse victims with anatomically correct dolls. *Child Abuse & Neglect, 10,* 519–529.

Wiehe, V.R. (1990). *Sibling abuse: Hidden physical, emotional, and sexual trauma.* New York: Lexington Books.

Will, D. (1983). Approaching the incestuous and sexually abusive family. *Journal of Adolescence, 6,* 229–246.

Williams, J. (1980). *Red flag/green flag people coloring book.* Available from Rape and Abuse Crisis Center, Fargo, ND.

Williams, L., & Finkelhor, D. (1990). The characteristics of incestuous fathers: A review of recent studies. In W. Marshall, D. Laws, & H. Barbaree (Eds.),

The handbook of sexual assault: Issues, theories, and treatment of offenders (pp. 231–255). New York: Plenum.

Willner, S.K., & Crane, R. (1979). A parental dilemma: The child with a marginal handicap. *Social Casework, 40,* 30–35.

Wilson, P. (1981). *The man they called a monster.* Victoria, Australia: Cassell.

Winnicott, D.W. (1971). *Therapeutic consultations in child psychiatry.* New York: Basic Books.

Wolfe, D., MacPherson, T., Blount, R., & Wolfe, V. (1986). Evaluation of a brief intervention for educating school children in awareness of physical and sexual abuse. *Child Abuse & Neglect, 10,* 85–92.

Wolfe, S.C. (1984, November). *A multi-factor model of deviant sexuality.* Paper presented at the Third National Conference on Victimology, Lisbon, Portugal.

Woods, S.C., & Dean, K.S. (1984). *Final report: Sexual abuse of males* [Research project (NCCAN Report No. 90-CA-812)]. Washington, DC: National Center on Child Abuse and Neglect.

Wozencraft, T., Wagner, W., & Pellegrin, A. (1991). Depression and suicidal ideation in sexually abused children. *Child Abuse & Neglect, 15,* 505–511.

Wurtele, S.K. (1986). *Teaching young children personal body safety: The behavioral skills training program.* Colorado Springs, CO: Author.

Wurtele, S.K. (1987). School-based sexual abuse prevention programs: A review. *Child Abuse & Neglect, 11,* 483–495.

Wurtele, S.K. (1990). Teaching personal safety skills to four-year-old children. A behavioral approach. *Behavior Therapy, 22,* 25–32.

Wurtele, S.K. (1993). The role of maintaining telephone contact with parents during the teaching of a personal safety program. *Journal of Child Sexual Abuse, 2,* 65–82.

Wurtele, S.K., & Miller-Perrin, C.L. (1987). An evaluation of side effects associated with participation in a child sexual abuse prevention program. *Journal of School Health, 57,* 228–231.

Wurtele, S.K., & Miller-Perrin, C.L. (1992). *Preventing child sexual abuse: Sharing the responsibility*. Lincoln: University of Nebraska Press.

Wurtele, S.K., Gillispie, E.I., Currier, L.L., & Franklin, C.F. (1992). A comparison of teachers vs. parents as instructors of a personal safety program for preschoolers. *Child Abuse & Neglect, 16,* 127–137.

Wurtele, S.K., Kast, L.C., Miller-Perrin, C.L., & Kondrick, P.A. (1989). Comparison of programs for teaching personal safety skills to preschoolers. *Journal of Consulting and Clinical Psychology, 57,* 505–511.

Wurtele, S.K., Marrs, S.R., & Miller-Perrin, C.L. (1987). Practice makes perfect? The role of participant modeling in sexual abuse prevention programs. *Journal of Consulting and Clinical Psychology, 55,* 599–602.

Wurtele, S.K., Saslawsky, D., Miller, C., Marrs, S., & Britcher, J. (1986). *Teaching personal safety skills for potential prevention of sexual abuse: A comparison of treatments*. Pullman: Department of Psychology, Washington State University.

Wyatt, G.E. (1985). The sexual abuse of Afro-American and White American women in childhood. *Child Abuse & Neglect, 9.* 507–519.

Wyatt, G.E. (1990). Sexual abuse of ethnic minority children: Identifying dimensions of victimization. *Professional Psychology: Research and Practice, 5,* 338–343.

Wyatt, G.E., Strayer, R., & Lobitz, W.C. (1976). Issues in treatment of sexually dysfunctioning couples of Afro-American descent. *Psychotherapy, Theory, Research and Practice, 13*(1), 44–50.

Yates, A. (1982). Children eroticized by incest. *American Journal of Psychiatry, 139,* 482–485.

Yates, A., & Terr, L. (1988). Anatomically correct dolls: Should they be used as the basis for expert testimony? [Debate Forum]. *Journal of the American Academy of Child and Adolescent Psychiatry, 27,* 254–257.

Young, W.C., Sachs, R.G., Braun, B.G., & Watkins, R.J. (1991). Patients reporting ritual abuse in childhood: A clinical syndrome report of 37 cases. *Child Abuse & Neglect, 15,* 181–189.

Zanarini, M.C., Gunderson, J.G., Marino, M.F., Schwartz, R.O., & Frankenburg, F.R. (1989). Childhood experiences of borderline patients. *Comprehensive Psychiatry, 30*, 18–25.

Zigler, E. (1961). Social deprivation and rigidity in the performance of feeble-minded children. *Journal of Abnormal and Social Psychology, 62*, 413–421.

Zigler, E., & Hodapp, R.M. (1986). *Understanding mental retardation.* New York: Cambridge University Press.

Zigler, E., Balla, D., & Butterfield, E.C. (1968). A longitudinal investigation between preinstitutional social deprivation and social motivation in institutionalized retardates. *Journal of Personality and Social Psychology, 10*, 437–445.

Zirpoli, T.J. (1986). Child abuse and children with handicaps. *Remedial and Special Education, 1*, 39–48.

BIBLIOGRAPHY

Adams, C.M. (1990). Women as perpetrators of child sexual abuse: Recognition barriers. In A. L. Horton, B.L. Johnson, L.M. Roundy, & D. Williams (Eds.), *The incest perpetrator: A family member no one wants to treat* (pp.108–125). Newbury Park, CA: Sage.

Bancroft, J.H., Jones, H.G., & Pullen, B.R. (1966). A simple transducer for measuring penile erection, with comments on its use in the treatment of sexual disorders. *Behavior Research Therapy, 4,* 239–241.

Barbaree, H.E., & Marshall, W.L. (1989). Erectile responses among heterosexual child molesters, father-daughter incest offenders and matched non-offenders: Five distinct age-preference profiles. *Canadian Journal of Behavioral Science, 21,* 70–82.

Bauman, R.C., Kaspar, C.J., & Alford, J.M. (1983). The child sex abusers. *Journal of Social and Correctional Psychiatry, 3,* 76–80.

Beahrs, J.O. (1982). *Unity and multiplicity: Multilevel consciousness of self in hypnosis, psychiatric disorder and mental health.* New York: Brunner/Mazel.

Becker, J.V. (1988). *Treatment for sexual offenders and victims.* Paper presented at the bicentennial conference of the Australian Behavior Modification Association, Adelaide, Australia.

Becker, J.V., & Quinsey, V.L. (1993). Assessing suspected child molesters. *Child Abuse & Neglect, 17,* 169–174.

Beitchman, J.H., Zucker, K.J., Hood, J.E., da Costa, G.A., & Akman, D. (1991). A review of the short-term effects of childhood sexual abuse. *Child Abuse & Neglect, 15,* 537–556.

Blume, E.S. (1986). The walking wounded: Post-incest syndrome. *SIECUS Report, 15,* 1–3.

Braun, B.G. (1989). *Comments. Ritual child abuse: A professional overview* [video]. Ukia, CA: Cavalcade Productions.

Briere, J., Evans, D., Runtz, M., & Wall, B. (1988). Symptomatology in men who were molested as children: A comparison study. *American Journal of Orthopsychiatry,* 457–461.

Brooks, B. (1985). Sexually abused children and adolescent identity development. *American Journal of Psychology, 39,* 401–410.

Burgess, A.W., Groth, A.N., & McCausland, M.P. (1987). Child sex initiation rings. *American Journal of Orthopsychiatry, 1,* 110–119.

Burt, M. (1980). Cultural myths and supports for rape. *Journal of Personality and Social Psychology, 36,* 217–230.

Chilcott, J. (1987). Where are you coming from and where are you going? *American Educational Research Journal, 24*(2), 199–218.

Conte, J.R., Briere, J., & Schuerman, J. (1989). *Mediators of long term symptomatology in women molested as children.* Unpublished manuscript. Available from the first author at School of Social Work, University of Washington.

Cramer, P. (1991). *The development of defense mechanisms: Theory, research, and assessment.* New York: Springer-Verlag.

DeFrancis, V. (1969). *Protecting the child victim of sex crimes committed by adults.* Denver: American Humane Association.

deMause, L. (1974). The evolution of childhood. In L. deMause (Ed.), *The history of childhood* (pp 1–73). New York: Psychohistory Press.

DeMott, R. (1980, March). The pro-incest lobby. *Psychology Today, 3,* 11–16.

deYoung, M. (1984). Ethics and the "lunatic fringe": The case of pedophile organizations. *Human Organization, 43,* 72–74.

Dunn, J. (1988). *The beginnings of social understanding.* London: Basil Blackwell.

Eaton, A.P., & Vastbinder, E. (1969). The sexually molested child: A plan of management. *Clinical Pediatrics, 8,* 438–441.

Fabrega, H. (1974). *Disease and social behavior.* Cambridge, MA: MIT Press.

Farar, J., & Farar, S. (1984a). *A witches bible compleat.* New York: Magick Childe Press.

Foseth, L., & Brown, A. (1981). A survey of intrafamilial sexual abuse treatment centers: Implications for intervention. *Child Abuse & Neglect, 5,* 177–186.

Fraser, M. (1976). *The death of Narcissus.* New York: Paul Hoeber.

Freud, S. (1966). *The complete introductory lectures of psychoanalysis.* New York: W. W. Norton.

Furby, L., Weinrott, M.R., & Blackshaw, L. (1989). Sex offender recidivism: A review. *Psychological Bulletin, 105,* 3–30.

Ganaway, G. (1989). Historical truth versus narrative truth: Clarifying the role of exogenous trauma in the etiology of multiple personality and its variants. *Dissociation, 2*(4), 205–220.

Ganaway, G. (1990, November). *A psychodynamic look at alternative explanations for satanic ritual abuse in MPD patients.* Paper delivered at Seventh International Conference on Multiple Personality/Dissociative States in Chicago, IL.

Gardner, R. (1975). *Psychotherapeutic approaches to the resistant child.* New York: J. Aronson.

Gayle, J., Thompson, R.J., Moran, T., & Sack, W.H. (1988). Sexual abuse in young children: Its clinical presentation and characteristic patterns. *Child Abuse & Neglect, 12,* 163–170.

Gelman, J. (1989, November, 13). The sex-abuse puzzle. *Newsweek, 114,* 99–100.

Gershenson, H.P., Musick, J.S., Ruch-Ross, H.S., Magee, V., Rubino, K.K., & Rosenberg, D. (1989). The prevalence of coercive sexual experiences among teenage mothers. *Journal of Interpersonal Violence, 4,* 204–219.

Gilbert, N. (1988). Teaching children to prevent sexual abuse. *The Public Interest, 93,* 3–15.

Gladston, R. (1979). Disorders of early parenthood: Neglect, deprivation, exploitation, and abuse of little children. In J.D. Nospitz (Ed.), *Basic handbook of child psychiatry* (p. 581). New York: Basic Books.

Glaser, D., & Bentovim, A. (1979). Abuse and risk to handicapped and chronically ill children. *Child Abuse & Neglect, 3,* 565–575.

Goodwin, J. (1990, November). *Sadistic sexual abuse: Illustration from the Marquis de Sade.* Paper delivered at the Seventh International Conference on Multiple Personality/Dissociative States, Chicago, IL.

Goodwin, J., Simm , M., & Bergman R. (1979). Hysterical seizures: A sequel to incest. *American Journal of Orthopsychiatry, 40,* 698–703.

Gordon, S.G. (1971). Missing in special education: Sex. *The Journal of Special Education, 5,* 351–354.

Gould, C. (1989). *Comments. Ritual child abuse: A professional overview.* Ukia, CA: Cavalcade Productions [video].

Grant, L.J. (1984). Assessment of child sexual abuse: Eighteen months experience at the Child Protection Center. *American Journal of Obstetrics and Gynecology, 148,* 617–620.

Groth , A.N. (1978). Patterns of sexual assault against children and adolescents. In A.W. Burgess, A.N. Groth, L.L. Holstrom, & S.M. Sgroi (Eds.), *Sexual assault of children and adolescents* (pp. 3–24). Lexington, MA: Lexington Books.

Groth, A.N., Longo, R., & McFaden, J. (1982). Undetected recidivism among rapists and child molesters. *Crime and Delinquency, 128,* 450–458.

Guttmacher, M., & Weihofen, H. (1951). *Sex offenses: The problem, causes and prevention.* New York: W. W. Norton.

Hall, E. (1983). *The dance of life.* New York: Anchor/Doubleday.

Hanson, R.K., & Slater, S. (1988). Sexual victimization in the history of sexual abuses: A review. *Annals of Sex Research, 1,* 485–499.

Herman, J., & Hirschman, L. (1981). Families at risk for father–daughter incest. *American Journal of Psychiatry, 138,* 967–970.

Hicks, R. (1990a). Police pursuit of satanic crime: I. *Skeptical Inquirer, 14*(2), 276–286.

Hicks, R. (1990b). Police pursuit of satanic crime: II. *Skeptical Inquirer, 14*(2), 378–389.

Hindman, J. (1988). Research disputes and assumptions about child molesters. *NDAA Bulletin, 7,* 1–3.

Hollingsworth, J. (1986). *Unspeakable acts.* New York: Congdon & Weed.

Hunter, M. (1989). *Abused boys: The neglected victims of sexual abuse.* Lexington, MA: Lexington Books.

James, B. (1989). *Treating traumatized children: New insights and creative interventions.* Lexington, MA: Lexington Books.

Janus, M.D., Burgess, A.W., & McCormack, A. (1987). Histories of sexual abuse in adolescent male runaways. *Adolescence, 22,* 405–417.

Jehu, D., Klassen, C., & Gazan, R. (1985/1986). Cognitive restructuring of distorted beliefs associated with childhood sexual abuse. *Journal of Social Work and Human Sexuality, 4,* 1–35.

Jleemeier, C., & Webb, C. (1986, August). *Evaluation of a school based prevention program.* Paper presented at the 94th annual meeting of the American Psychological Association, Washington, DC.

Johnston, M.S.K. (1979). The sexually mistreated child. Diagnostic evaluation. *Child Abuse & Neglect, 3,* 943–951.

Jones, E.D., & McCurdy, K. (1992). The links between types of maltreatment and demographic characteristics of children. *Child Abuse & Neglect, 16,* 201–215.

Jonker, F., & Jonker-Bakker, P. (1991). Experiences with ritualistic child sexual abuse: A case study from the Netherlands. *Child Abuse & Neglect, 15,* 191–196.

Keller, E.F. (1985). *Reflections on gender and science.* New Haven, CT: Yale University Press.

Kelley, S.J. (1981, April). *Responses of children to sexual abuse and satanic ritualistic abuse in day care centers.* Paper presented at the National Symposium on Child Victimization, Anaheim, CA.

Kempe, H., Silverman, F.N., Steele, B.F., Droegmueller, W., & Silver, H.K. (1962). The battered child syndrome. *Journal of the American Medical Association, 181,* 17–24.

Kendall-Tackett, K.A., & Watson, M.W. (1992). Use of anatomical dolls by Boston-area professionals. *Child Abuse & Neglect, 16,* 423–428.

Kent, C.A. (1981). *Curriculum for prevention of child's sexual abuse.* Tacoma, WA: Personal Safety Curriculum, Tacoma Public Schools.

Knight, R.A., Carter, D.L., & Prentky, R.A. (1989). A system for the classification of child molesters: Reliability and application. *Journal of Interpersonal Violence, 4,* 3–23.

Knopp, F.H. & Lackey, L.B. (1987). *Female sexual abusers: A summary of data from 44 treatment providers.* Orwell, VT: Safer Society Press.

Kolko, D.J., Moser, J.T., & Weldy, S.R. (1988). Behavioral/emotional indicators of sexual abuse in child psychiatric patients: A controlled comparison with physical abuse. *Child Abuse & Neglect, 10,* 529–541.

Koss, M.P., & Dinero, T.E. (1987, January). *Predictors of sexual aggressions among a national sample of male college students.* Paper presented at the New York Academy of Sciences Conference of Human Sexual Aggression: Current Perspectives, New York.

Kraemer, W. (Ed). (1976). *The forbidden love: The normal and abnormal love of children.* London: Sheldon.

Krugman, S. (1987). Trauma in the family: Perspectives on the intergenerational transmissions of violence. In B. van der Kolk (Ed.), *Psychological trauma,* (p. 128). Washington, DC: American Psychiatric Press.

Langevin, R., Wright, P., & Hardy, L. (1989). Characteristics of sex offenders who were sexually victimized as children. *Annals of Sex Research, 2,* 227–253.

Lanning, K. (1989, October). Satanic, occult, ritualistic crime: A law enforcement perspective. *The Police Chief,* 88–107.

Ledray, L.E. (1986). *Recovery from rape.* New York: Holt.

Levi, E. (1969). *The history of magick: Including an actual and precise exposition of procedures, rites, and mystery.* London: Ryder.

Lew, M. (1988). *Victims no longer.* New York: Nerraumont Publishing.

Lyons, A. (1988). *Satan wants you: The cult of devil worship in America.* New York: Mysterious Press.

MacFarlane, K., & Krebs, S. (1986). Techniques for interviewing and gathering evidence. In K. MacFarlane, J. Waterman, S. Conerly, L. Damon, M. Durfee, & S. Long (Eds.), *Sexual abuse of young children: Evaluation and treatment* (pp. 67–100). New York: Guildford.

Mackey, G. (1980). *Bubbylonian encounter.* Available from Theater for Young America, 7204 W. 80th Street, Overland Park, KS 66204.

Malmuth, N.M. (1986). Predictors of naturalistic sexual aggression. *Journal of Personality and Social Psychology, 50,* 953–962.

Maltz, W. (1988). Identifying and treating the sexual repercussions of incest: A couples therapy approach. *Journal of Sex and Marital Therapy, 14,* 145–163.

Marshall, W., Ward, T., Jones, R., Johnson, P., & Barbaree, H. (1991, March). An optimistic evaluation of treatment outcome with sex offenders. *Violence Update, 1,* 1.

Masters, R.E.L. (1963). *Patterns of incest.* New York: Julian Press.

Mohr, J.W. (1962). The pedophilias: Their clinical, social and legal implications. *Canadian Psychiatric Association Journal, 7,* 225–260.

Money, J. (1988). *Gay, straight, and in-between.* New York: Oxford.

Murphy, S.M., Kilpatrick, D.G., Auick-McMullan, A., Veronen, L.J., Paduhovich, J., Best, C.L., Villeponteauz, L.A., & Saunders, B.E. (1988). Current psychological functioning of child sexual assault survivors. *Journal of Interpersonal Violence, 3,* 55–79.

Murphy, W.D., Coleman, E.M., & Haynes, M.R. (1986). Factors related to co-ercive sexual behavior in a nonclinical sample of males. *Violence and Victims, 1,* 255–278.

National Center for Child Abuse and Neglect. (1988). *Study findings: National study of incidence and severity of child abuse and neglect.* Washington, DC: DHEW.

Noll, R. (1990). *Bizarre diseases of the mind.* New York: Berkeley.

Nurcombe, B. (1986). The child as witness: Competency and credibility. *Journal of the American Academy of Child Psychiatry, 25,* 473–480.

Olafson, E., Corwin, D.L., & Summit, R.C. (1993). Modern history of child sexual abuse awareness: Cycles of discovery and suppression. *Child Abuse & Neglect, 17,* 7–24.

Orne, M.T. (1979). The use and misuse of hypnosis in court. International *Journal of Clinical and Experimental Hypnosis, 27,* 311–341.

Peller, L.E. (1978). *On development and education of young children.* New York: Philosophical Library.

Pendersen, P.B. (1988). *A handbook for development of multicultural aware-ness.* Alexandria, VA: American Association for Counseling and Development.

Peters, S.D. (1981). Child sexual abuse and later psychological problems. In G.E. Wyatt & G.J. Powell (Eds.), *Lasting effects of child sexual abuse* (pp 101–117). Newbury Park, CA: Sage.

Pettinati, H.M. (Ed.). (1988). *Hypnosis and memory.* New York: Guilford.

Piaget, J. (1936). *The origins of intelligence in children.* New York: Interna-tional Universities Press.

Prentky, R.A., Knight, R.A., Rosenberg, R., & Lee, A. (1989). A path analytic approach to the validation of a taxonomic system for classifying child molest-ers. *Journal of Quantitative Criminology, 5,* 231–257.

Putnam, F.W., Guroff, J.J., Silverman, E.K., Barban, L., & Post, R.M. (1986). The clinical phenomenology of multiple personality disorder: A review of 100 recent cases. *Journal of Clinical Psychiatry, 47,* 285–293.

Quinsey, V.L., Steinman, C.M., & Bergensen, S.G. (1975). Penile circumference, skin conduction, and ranking responses of child molesters and "normals" to sexual and nonsexual visual stimuli. *Behavior Therapy, 6,* 214–219.

Rapaport, K., & Burkhart, B.R. (1984). Personality and attitudinal characteristics of sexually coercive college males. *Journal of Abnormal Psychology, 93,* 216–221.

Risin, L. & Koss, M. (1987). The sexual abuse of boys. *Journal of Interpersonal Violence, 2*(3), 309–323.

Rist, K. (1979). Incest: Theoretical and clinical views. *American Journal of Orthopsychiatry, 49,* 680–691.

Ross, C.A., Norton, G.R., & Wozney, K. (1989). Multiple personality disorder: An analysis of 236 cases. *Canadian Journal of Psychiatry, 34,* 413–418.

Sassoon, D. (1988). The sexual trafficking of children: Silence and taboo trigger. *Action for Children, 3*(1), 1–10.

Saunders, E.J. (1988). A comparative study of attitudes toward child sexual abuse among social work and judicial system professionals. *Child Abuse & Neglect, 12,* 83–90.

Schaef, A.W. (1981). Women's reality: An emerging female system in the white male society. Minneapolis, MN: Winston Press.

Schweder, R., & Bourne, E. J. (1982). Does the concept of the person vary cross-culturally? In A.J. Marsella and G.M. White (Eds.), *Cultural conceptions of mental health and therapy* (pp. 97–137). London: Reidel.

Schweder, R. & Miller, J. (1985). The social construction of the person: How is it possible? In K. Gergen and K. Davis (Eds.), *The social construction of the person* (pp. 41–69). New York: Springer-Verlag.

Sedlak, A.J., & Alldredge, E.E. (1987). *Study of the national incidence and prevalence of child abuse and neglect: Report on data collection.* Washington, DC: National Center on Child Abuse and Neglect.

Seidner, A., & Calhoun, K.S. (1984). *Childhood sexual abuse: Factors related to differential adult adjustment.* Paper presented at the Second National Conference for Family Violence Researchers, Durham, NH.

Seidner, A., Calhoun, K.S., & Kilpatrick, D.G. (1985). *Childhood and/or adolescent sexual experiences: Predicting variability in subsequent adjustment.* Paper presented at the meeting of the American Psychological Association, Los Angeles.

Sgroi, S.M. (1977). Kids with clap: Gonorrhea as an indicator of chid sexual assault. *Victimology, 2,* 255–267.

Sgroi, S.M. (1982). *Handbook of clinical intervention in child sexual abuse.* Lexington, MA: Lexington Books.

Shaul, S. (1981, June). Deafness and human sexuality: A developmental review. *American Annals of the Deaf, 6,* 432–439.

Silber, T., & Controi, G. (1983). Clinical spectrum of pharyngeal gonorrhea in children and adolescents: A report of 16 patients. *Journal of Adolescent Health Care, 4,* 51–54.

Simari, C.G., & Baskin, D. (1982). Incestuous experiences within homosexual populations: A preliminary study. *Archives of Sexual Behavior, 11,* 329–344.

Slaughter, J.B. (1989, October 7). Bigotry is back in fashion. *Los Angeles Times,* p. 8.

Summit, R. (1989). *Comments. Ritual child abuse: A professional overview.* Ukia, CA: Cavalcade Productions [video].

Terry, M. (1987). *The ultimate evil: An investigation of America's most dangerous satanic cult.* Garden City, NY: Doubleday Co.

Trad, P.V. (1989). *The preschool child.* New York: Wiley.

Ungaretti, J. (1978). Pederasty, heroism, and the family in classical Greece. *Journal of Homosexuality, 2,* 291–300.

VanderMey, B.J. (1988). The sexual victimization of male children: A review of previous literature. *Child Abuse & Neglect, 12,* 61–72.

Vanggaard, T. (1972). *Phallos: A symbol of its history in the male world.* London: Cape.

Weisz, J.R., Rothbaum, F.M., & Blackburn, T.C. (1984). Standing out and standing in: The psychology of control in America and Japan. *American Psychologist, 39,* 955–969.

Westermeyer, J. (1987). Prevention of mental disorder among Hmong refugees in the U.S.: Lessons from the period 1976–1986. *Social Science and Medicine, 25*(8), 941–947.

White, J.L. (1984). *The psychology of Blacks: An Afro-American perspective.* Englewood Cliffs, NJ: Prentice-Hall.

White, S., Strom, G.A., & Santilli, G. (1985). *Clinical protocol for interviewing preschoolers with sexually anatomically correct dolls.* Unpublished manuscript, Case Western Reserve University, School of Medicine, Cleveland, OH.

Wild, N.J. (1989). Prevalence of sex-rings. *Pediatrics, 83,* 553–558.

Wyatt, G.E. (1988). The relationship between child sexual abuse and adolescent sexual functioning in Afro-American and White American women. *The Annals of the New York Academy of Science, 528,* 111–122.

RESOURCES
(All resources have not been screened. Use your own judgment.
This is not a complete list of all groups and newsletters available.)

Meetings—USA, National

Incest Survivors Anonymous
P. O. Box 5613
Long Beach, CA 90805
Provides twelve-step meetings.

Survivors of Incest Anonymous, Inc.
P. O. Box 21817
Baltimore, MD 21222-6817
Send SASE; use two 32-cent stamps for listings of local meetings.

Journals Specific to Sexual Abuse

Child Abuse & Neglect The International Journal
Pergamon Press, Inc.
660 White Plains Road
Tarrytown, NY 10591-5154

Child Abuse Review
British Association for the Study and Prevention of Child Abuse
    and Neglect
10 Priory Street
York, YO1 1EZ
Great Britain

Journal of Child Sexual Abuse
The Haworth Press, Inc.
10 Alice Street
Binghamton, NY 13904-1580

Treating Abuse Today
Clinical Training Publications
2722 Eastlake Avenue East, Suite 300
Seattle, WA 98102

Publishers Specific to Abuse and Treatment

Safer Society Press
P. O. Box 340
Brandon, VT 05733-0340

Organizations

American Professional Society on the Abuse of Children
323 South Michigan Avenue, Suite 1600
Chicago, IL 60604

Family Violence & Sexual Assault Institute
1310 Cinic Drive
Tyler, TX 75701

National Child Rights Alliance
P.O. Box 422
Ellenville, NY 12428

National Resource Center on Child Sexual Abuse
107 Lincoln Street
Huntsville, AL 35801

Voices in Action, Inc.
P.O. Box 148309
Chicago, IL 60614
Publishes newsletter and resource lists, and organizes conferences.

Newsletters

Body Memories: Radical Perspectives on Childhood Sexual Abuse
P. O. Box 14941
Berkeley, CA 94701
Addresses sexual abuse of children in a radical way.

Cutting Edge
P. O. Box 20819
Cleveland, OH 44120
For women who experience self-inflicted violence.

Healing Hearts
P. O. Box 807
Mendocino, CA 95400
For survivors.

The Healing Woman
P. O. Box 3038
Moss Beach, CA 94038
For survivors.

Incest Survivor Information Exchange
P.O. Box 3399
New Haven, CT 06516
For incest survivors.

Moving Forward: A Newsletter for Survivors of Sexual Abuse
and Those Who Care for Them
P.O. Box 4426
Arlington, VA 22204

P. L. E. A.
356 W. Zia Rd.
Santa Fe, NM 78505
For nonoffending male survivors.

S. O. F. I. E.—Survivors of Female Incest Emerge
P. O. Box 2794
Renton, WA 98056
For survivors of female perpetrators.

Speaking Out: Incest Awareness Project Newsletter
Box 8122
Fargo, ND 58109-8122
For survivors.

Stand Fast
P. O. Box 9107
Warwick, RI 02889
For nonperpetrating partners/supporters of survivors of abuse.

Survivor Connections
52 Lyndon Road
Cranston, RI 02905-1121
For survivors.

Vermont—Incest Survivors Enlightened and Empowered (VT—ISEE)
P. O. Box 82
Milton, VT 05468-3525
For survivors.

Multiple Personality Newsletters

B. E. A.M.—Being Energetic About Multiplicity
P. O. Box 20428
Louisville, KY 40250-0428

Just Us
P. O. Box 1121
Parker, CO 80134

Many Voices
P. O. Box 2639
Cincinnati, OH 45201

The MAZE
P. O. Box 88722
Tukwila, WA 98138-2722

Multiple Personality Dignity/Loved Ones of Multiples
P. O. Box 4367
Boulder, CO 80306-4367

Ritual Abuse Survivors

Believe The Children
P.O. Box 268462
Chicago, IL 60626

CARAC—Committee Against Ritual Abuse of Children
P. O. Box 74
Saskatoon Sask.37K-3K1
Canada

Cult Awareness Network
2412 W. Pratt Blvd., Suite 1173
Chicago, IL 60645

Families of Crimes of Silence
P. O. Box 2338
Canoga Park, CA 93106

Los Angeles County Commission for Women
383 Hall of Administration
500 W. Temple Street
Los Angeles, CA 90012

SurvivorShip
3181 Mission #139
San Francisco, CA 94110

Survivors of Clergy Abuse

Adults Abused By Clergy
The Special Project
175 North Main Street
Branford, CT 06405

Anonymous Victims of Clergy Sexual Abuse
Box 115, Zeckendoff Towers
111 East 14th Street
New York, NY 10003

Clergy Abuse Survivors Alliance
5490 Judith Street #3
San Jose, CA 95123

Services and Resources for Survivors and ProSurvivors

Childhelp USA
(800) 422-4453
Hotline.

Clearinghouse on Child Abuse & Neglect Information
P. O. Box 1182
Washington, DC 20013-1182
(800) 394-3366

Family Violence & Sexual Assault Institute Bulletin
Robert Geffner, Ph.D., President
1310 Clinic Drive
Tyler, TX 75701

Incest Survivors Resource Network International
P. O. Box 7375
Las Cruces, NM 88006-7375

Juvenile Justice Clearinghouse
P. O. Box 6000
Rockville, MD 20850

Kempe Children's Foundation
3607 Martin Luther King Blvd.
Denver, CO 80205

National Center for Missing and Exploited Children
2101 Wilson Blvd., Suite 550
Arlington, VA 22201-2617
(800) 843-5678 or (800) 826-7653 (TDD)

National Clearinghouse on Runaway and Homeless Youth
P.O. Box 13505
Silver Spring, MD 20911-3505

National Coalition Against Domestic Violence
National Office
P.O. Box 18749
Denver, CO 80218-1749

National Coalition Against Domestic Violence
P.O. Box 34103
Washington, DC 20043-4103

National Coalition Against Sexual Assault
Self Help Center
341 East E Street, Suite 135A
Casper, WY 82601

National Information Clearinghouse For Infants
with Disabilities and Life-Threatening Conditions
Center for Developmental Disabilities
University of South Carolina
Benson Building, First Floor
Columbia, SC 29208
(800) 922-9234, ext. 201

National Organization for Victim Assistance
1757 Park Road, NW
Washington, DC 20010

National Resource Center on Child Sexual Abuse
107 Lincoln Street
Huntsville, AL 35801

National Self-Help Clearinghouse
25 West 43rd Street
New York, NY 10036

National Victim Center
309 West Seventh Street , Suite 705
Fort Worth, TX 76102

National Victim Center InfoLink
P. O. Box 17150
Ft. Worth, TX   76102

Catalogs

Childs Work/Childs Play
Center for Applied Psychology
P. O. Box 1586
King of Prussia, PA 19406
(800) 962-1141

National Committee to Prevent Child Abuse
Fulfillment Center
200 State Road
South Deerfield, MA 01373-0200
(800) 835-2671

Resources for Professionals

National Resource Center on Child Sexual Abuse
(800) 543-7006
Information line, bibliographies, information papers and think tank.

National Training Program On Effective Treatment
   Approaches in Child Sexual Abuse
107 Lincoln Street
Huntsville, AL 35801
(800) 239-9939

AUTHOR INDEX

Ellison, P.H., 231
Elwell, M.E., 29
Emery, R.E., 24
Ennew, J., 208
Ephross, P.H., 29
Erickson, M.T., 146
Erickson, W.D., 53
Erikson, E., 146–150, 152, 160
Esparza, D., 57
Estes, D., 150
Estrada-Mullaney, T., 160
Everson, M.D., 23, 32, 160
Eyster, C., 160

Fagan, C.J., 231
Fagan, J., 121
Fagot, B.I., 31
Faller, K.C., 4, 62–63, 68, 73, 123, 125, 199–200, 202, 205, 244–247
Fallon, P., 34
Farber, E.D., 57
Fay, J., 135, 178, 182, 184
Faynik, C., 49
Fehrenbach, P.A., 87, 88
Feinauer, L.L., 29
Feinberg, L., 214
Feldman-Summers, S., 19
Feldman, E., 7
Feldman, W., 7
Fenichel, D., 243
Fine, S., 25, 30, 32
Finkel, M.A., 21
Finkelhor, D., 1, 11, 13–22, 24–25, 28–32, 34, 48, 50–52, 57–61, 66, 68, 75, 78, 87, 97, 104, 111, 122–125, 173, 182–184, 191, 194, 197, 205, 227, 242, 245–247, 249–251
Fischer, K.W., 169
Fish, V., 49

Fisher, G., 47
Fitch, J.H., 37, 40
Flanagan, B., 55, 64
Flanagan, T., 87
Flavell, E.R., 168
Flavell, J.H., 168–169
Flomenhaft, F., 6
Foa, E.B., 22, 25, 29
Fogarty, L., 22, 196
Fontes, L.A., 219–220
Ford, J., 182
Forehand, R., 166, 187, 192
Forward, S., 6
Fosen, R.H., 210
Frank, L., 166, 186, 189
Frankel, M., 42
Frankenburg, F.R., 34
Franklin, C.F., 166, 180
Freeman-Longo, R.E., 44
Freeman, K.R., 160
Freidrich, W.N., 22
Freud, A., 4, 150, 248
Freud, S., 5, 42–43, 165, 242–248, 250–251
Freund, K., 55
Friedemann, V.M., 160
Friedman, S.B., 232
Friedrich, W.N., 22–23, 25, 29–31, 89, 92, 235
Frisch, L.E., 232
Fromuth, M.E., 34
Fryer, G.E., Jr., 179, 181, 185–186, 193
Fuller, A.K., 88

Gaffney, G.R., 42
Gagnon, J.H., 37, 40, 47, 50, 75, 97, 245, 248
Gainer, K., 121
Gaines, A., 218
Gaines, R., 227

SUBJECT INDEX

ABOUT THE AUTHOR

Dr. Juliann Whetsell-Mitchell, Ph.D., is a licensed psychologist and a nationally certified counselor. Dr. Whetsell-Mitchell works in a private practice setting where she provides psychotherapy to individuals and families. Additionally, she designs and implements workshops for businesses and professional groups. She is president of her own educational cassette company, which markets and sells audio tapes that focus on stress management, relaxation, creative visualization and improving relationships, conflict resolution, and communication skills. Dr. Whetsell-Mitchell has worked in the mental health field for over 15 years and has presented over 200 workshops on local, national, and international levels for both professionals, paraprofessionals (e.g., funeral directors, mental health professionals, nurses, Head Start workers, office staffs of professionals, social workers, etc.), and the general public. Dr. Whetshell-Mitchell has been interviewed on talk radio shows. She writes a bi-monthly column for a women's magazine on the issues women face in the workplace and how to improve communication among coworkers. She is available on both a national and local level as a speaker, workshop presenter, and consultant.